The Shadow of War

The Blackwell History of Russia

General Editor: Simon M. Dixon

This series provides a provocative reinterpretation of fundamental questions in Russian history. Integrating the wave of new scholarship that followed the collapse of the Soviet Union, it focuses on Russia's development from the mid-seventeenth century to the present day, exploring the interplay of continuity and change. Volumes in the series demonstrate how new sources of information have reshaped traditional debates and present clear, stimulating overviews for students, scholars and general readers.

Published

Russia's Age of Serfdom: Russia and the USSR, 1649–1861
Elise Kimerling Wirtschafter

Across the Revolutionary Divide: Russia and the USSR, 1861–1945
Theodore R. Weeks

The Shadow of War: Russia and the USSR, 1941 to the Present
Stephen Lovell

The Shadow of War
Russia and the USSR, 1941 to the Present

Stephen Lovell

A John Wiley & Sons, Ltd., Publication

This edition first published 2010
© 2010 Stephen Lovell

Blackwell Publishing was acquired by John Wiley & Sons in February 2007. Blackwell's publishing program has been merged with Wiley's global Scientific, Technical, and Medical business to form Wiley-Blackwell.

Registered Office
John Wiley & Sons Ltd, The Atrium, Southern Gate, Chichester, West Sussex, PO19 8SQ, United Kingdom

Editorial Offices
350 Main Street, Malden, MA 02148-5020, USA
9600 Garsington Road, Oxford, OX4 2DQ, UK

The Atrium, Southern Gate, Chichester, West Sussex, PO19 8SQ, UK
For details of our global editorial offices, for customer services, and for information about how to apply for permission to reuse the copyright material in this book please see our website at www.wiley.com/wiley-blackwell.

Library of Congress Cataloging-in-Publication Data

Lovell, Stephen, 1972-
 The shadow of war : the Soviet Union and Russia, 1941 to the present / Stephen Lovell.
   p. cm. – (The Blackwell history of Russia)
 Includes bibliographical references and index.
 ISBN 978-1-4051-6959-2 (hardcover : alk. paper) – ISBN 978-1-4051-6958-5 (pbk. : alk. paper) 1. Soviet Union–History–1939–1945. 2. World War, 1939–1945–Influence.
3. Soviet Union–History–1925–1953. 4. Soviet Union–History–1953–1985. 5. Soviet Union–History–1985–1991. 6. Russia (Federation)–History–1991- I. Title.
 DK266.3.L68 2010
 947.085–dc22

                                                        2010010020

A catalogue record for this book is available from the British Library.

Set in 10/12.5pt Minion by Toppan Best-set Premedia Limited

1 2010

Contents

Illustrations

Series Editor's Preface

In this final volume in the Blackwell History of Russia, Stephen Lovell brilliantly exemplifies the aims of the series as a whole. By integrating well-known information with new approaches stimulated by discoveries in previously inaccessible archives, he presents a fresh synthesis, studded with original insight. By opening his analysis in 1941 and taking it beyond the collapse of the USSR 50 years later, he adopts an unconventional chronological framework that allows familiar material to be interpreted in unfamiliar ways. And by telling the story of the emergent Russian Federation from the point of view of a contemporary historian, rather than from the perspective of the political scientists who have hitherto dominated the subject, he crosses not only a significant chronological divide, but also a disciplinary one.

As Lovell explains, one reason why historians have been slow to make the leap into recent decades has lain in a lack of the sorts of evidence on which they customarily rely. It is a striking contribution of his book to reveal how much such evidence is nevertheless now available to the researcher. Another deterrent to contemporary history has been the longstanding obsession with the inter-war years shared by many undergraduate students of "twentieth-century" Europe. It is true that the history of European integration can sometimes seem insipid by comparison with that of the Europe of the dictators. But in Russia there is no reason to think the latter part of the twentieth century uneventful. And the extraordinary developments of 1989–91 and beyond are scarcely comprehensible without an understanding of the Khrushchev and Brezhnev years (the latter, it transpires, being far from the "era of stagnation" of popular myth). A further virtue of this attractively written book, therefore, is to bring to a wider readership the fruits of the growing body of scholarship – in Russian and other languages – devoted to the period between 1953 and 1991.

The Utopian fervor with which the party leadership tried to revivify the revolutionary tradition after Stalin's death was matched only by romantic hopes for the regeneration of communism in the late 1980s under Gorbachev – Khrushchev *redivivus* in the eyes of many. However, this is not a book concerned only with ideology and high politics, and Lovell is properly skeptical of the temptation to divide Soviet and post-Soviet history into periods bounded by the tenures of successive political leaders. Stalinist coercion is a crucial part of his account, but he is just as interested in the destabilizing effects of its sudden relaxation. Moreover, now that historians no longer instinctively conceive social activity in Russia solely in terms of resistance to a repressive, centralized state, there is room not only to investigate the more "normal" contours of everyday life – housing, shopping, work, and leisure – but also to consider its kaleidoscopic variety in the thousands of provincial villages and towns that make up the multinational Russian polity. Quite what has defined the boundaries of the "normal" in Russia and the Soviet Union is one of Lovell's major concerns. He has particularly revealing things to say about the formation, by the 1960s, of a distinctive "personal sphere," whose boundaries were significantly extended after the collapse of the USSR. Religion, gender, and culture (in its widest sense) are all more prominent in the writings of the current generation of scholars than they were in the work of their more materialist predecessors. So they are here. The author's deep immersion in twentieth-century films and print culture gives him an especially acute sense of what makes Russians tick, what makes them laugh, and how far they have come into contact (and conflict) with Western values. This new cultural emphasis is not to say that hard economics can be ignored in an era in which energy resources have been increasingly crucial to the state's balance of trade. However, the key contribution of Lovell's book is not so much to isolate themes for discussion as to explore the connections between them. Economic questions are shown to be inseparable from domestic politics, and both are inextricably linked to the international order shaped by the outcome of the Second World War.

It is that war and its multiple legacies that give Stephen Lovell's book its distinctive interpretative thrust. On the one hand, victory over fascism was crucial to "the re-launch of the Soviet project" in the 1950s and to the maintenance of both "inner" and "outer empires" until the end of the 1980s. On the other hand, the sacrifices made by the Soviet population in the Great Patriotic War cast a shadow over almost every aspect of the USSR for the remainder of its existence, from its command siege-economy to the best-selling war novels of Iurii Bondarev. A sense of geopolitical vulnerability haunts the Kremlin still. The uneasy balance between menace and opportunity bequeathed by the Second World War is set out in the Introduction and developed in a series of thematic chapters that combine the author's nose for telling detail with his aptitude for aphoristic generalization. The result is a book like no other. Unique in its combination of accessibility and sophistication, it helps us to see 70 years of Russian and Soviet history with a completely fresh eye. There could be no better way to end the series.

Simon Dixon
UCL SSEES

Acknowledgments

In preparing this book I have had to rely even more than usual on the expertise of various sympathetic colleagues. A *nizkii poklon* (low doffing of cap) to the people who read sprawling chapter drafts and helped me to fix at least some of their shortcomings: Nick Baron, Donald Filtzer, Yoram Gorlizki, Anne Gorsuch, Catriona Kelly, Kristin Roth-Ey and Kristina Spohr Readman. I also thank warmly the two anonymous readers of the full manuscript.

The most sympathetic colleague of all has proved to be Simon Dixon, the mastermind of this Blackwell series, who has been an unfailing source of good sense and encouragement (and, latterly, of close reading). He has been matched every step of the way by the excellent Tessa Harvey and Gillian Kane at Wiley-Blackwell.

I once more acknowledge the invaluable support of the Leverhulme Trust, whose award of a Philip Leverhulme Prize enabled me to spend half a year making headway with the reading for this book.

Finally, I thank King's College London, and in particular its Department of History, for providing such a congenial home over the past eight years. My colleagues will be skeptical, but I suspect a few conversations in the Strand building – whether in the prison cells of the third floor or the sun-drenched utopia on the eighth that we now inhabit – have found their way into this book.

MAP 1 Europe after World War II.

MAP 2   The German assault on the USSR.

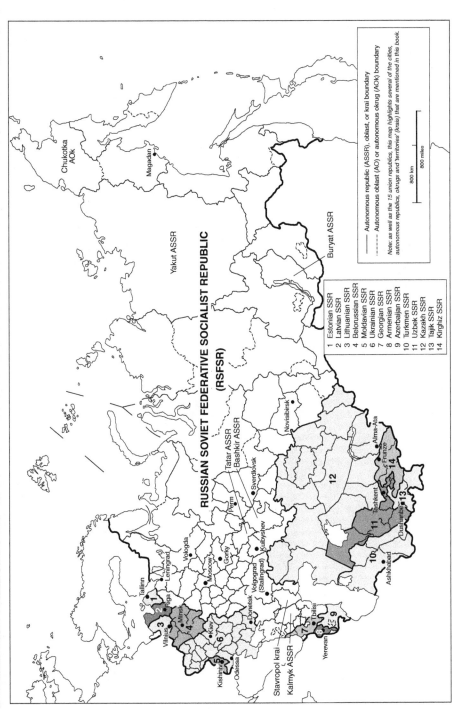

MAP 3   Administrative divisions in the USSR, 1989. As well as the 15 union republics, this map highlights several of the cities, autonomous republics, okrugs and "territories" (krais) that are mentioned in this book.

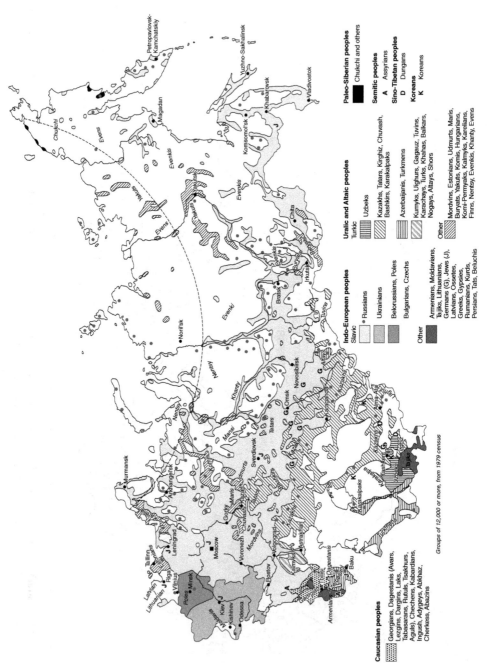

Caucasian peoples

▦ Georgians, Dagestanis (Avars, Lezgins, Dargins, Laks, Tabasarans, Rutuls, Tsakhurs, Aguls), Chechens, Kabardians, Ingush, Adygeys, Abkhaz, Cherkess, Abazins

Indo-European peoples

Slavic

· Russians

Ukrainians

Belorussians, Poles

Bulgarians, Czechs

Other

Armenians, Moldavians, Tajiks, Lithuanians, Germans (G), Jews (J), Latvians, Ossetes, Greeks, Gypsies, Rumanians, Kurds, Persians, Tats, Beluchis

Uralic and Altaic peoples

Turkic

▥ Uzbeks

▨ Kazakhs, Tatars, Kirghiz, Chuvash, Bashkirs, Karakalpaks

▤ Azerbaijanis, Turkmens

▧ Kumyks, Uighurs, Gagauz, Tuvins, Karachays, Turks, Khakas, Balkars, Nogays, Altays, Shors

Other

▨ Mordvins, Estonians, Udmurts, Maris, Buryats, Yakuts, Komis, Hungarians, Komi-Permyaks, Kalmyks, Karelians, Finns, Nentsy, Evenks, Khanty, Evens

Paleo-Siberian peoples

■ Chukchi and others

Semitic peoples

A Assyrians

Sino-Tibetan peoples

D Dungans

Koreans

K Koreans

Groups of 12,000 or more, from 1979 census

MAP 4   Ethnic groups in the USSR, 1982.

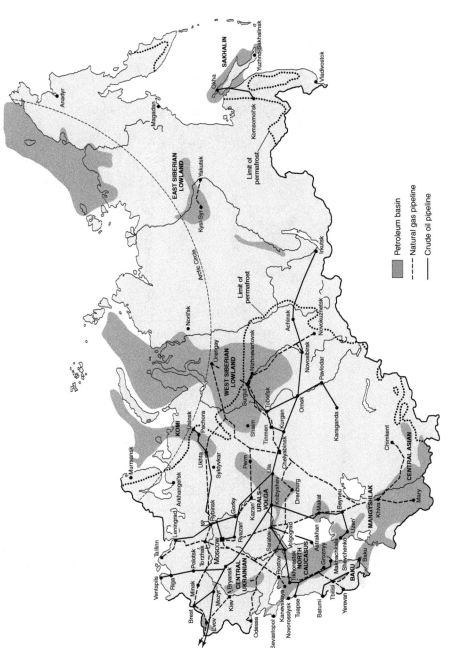

MAP 5   Oil and gas pipelines in the USSR, 1982.

Petroleum basin
Natural gas pipeline
Crude oil pipeline

EAST SIBERIAN LOWLAND
WEST SIBERIAN LOWLAND
CENTRAL ASIAN
MANGYSHLAK
URALS
VOLGA
NORTH CAUCASUS
CENTRAL UKRAINIAN
KOMI
BAKU
SAKHALIN
MOSCOW

Limit of permafrost
Arctic Circle

Anadyr
Magadan
Yakutsk
Kysyl-Syr
Vladivostok
Yuzhno-Sakhalinsk
Okha
Komsomol'sk
Irkutsk
Achinsk
Novokuznetsk
Novosibirsk
Karaganda
Pavlodar
Omsk
Kurgan
Chelyabinsk
Tobolsk
Tiumen
Shaim
Surgut
Nizhnevartovsk
Urengoy
Noril'sk
Murmansk
Pechora
Ukhta
Usinsk
Syktyvkar
Perm
Ufa
Arkhangel'sk
Leningrad
Tallinn
Ventspils
Riga
Minsk
Brest
Polotsk
Torzhak
Mozyr'
Kiev
L'vov
Odessa
Sevastopol
Novorossiysk
Kanevskaia
Tuapse
Batumi
Tbilisi
Yerevan
Baku
Shevchenko
Makhachkala
Grozny
Astrakhan
Volgograd
Rostov
Tikhoretsk
Saratov
Kazan'
Gorky
Rybinsk
Ryazan'
Bryansk
Kuibyshev
Orenburg
Uzen'
Beyneu
Makat
Khiva
Mary
Chimkent
Chimkent

Limit of permafrost

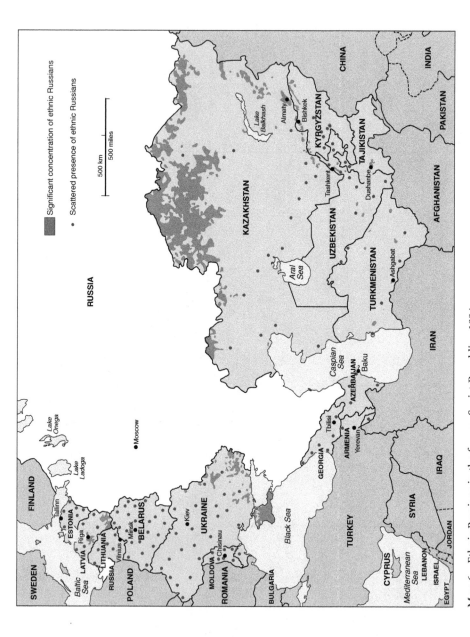

Map 6   Ethnic Russians in the former Soviet Republics, 1994.

1

Introduction

World War II and the Remaking of the Soviet Union

No foreigner needs to spend too much time in Russia to discover how central the war remains to how Russians see themselves even in the early twenty-first century. Most long-term visitors to Russia (whether Soviet or post-Soviet) will have been lectured at some stage on the failure of the Western allies to open a second front before 1944. Hedrick Smith, the highly informative *New York Times* correspondent in Moscow in the mid-1970s, caught the enormous outpouring of war commemoration on the thirtieth anniversary of victory: in his acclaimed *The Russians* he subtitled one of the chapters "World War II was only yesterday." At the same time there were some war-related topics on which Russians were less eager to hold forth: the volte-face in Soviet foreign policy that made Stalin an ally of Hitler between August 1939 and June 1941, the actions of the Soviet political police in Poland and the Baltic states, the extent of wartime cooperation between the USSR and the West (and the extent of Western aid through Lend-Lease).

Opinion polls of the post-Soviet era have consistently placed the Great Patriotic War at the top of Russians' list of defining historical moments. The October Revolution, by contrast, is now almost an irrelevance. This is not because Russians have abnormally short memories. Rather, it is because the prewar era is too complex and divisive to serve the purpose of historical myth. It is now fast becoming a cliché of Russian textbooks and public discourse to refer to the 1930s as a "complex and tragic era," as if it is futile even to attempt to establish human agency in the deaths of millions of people. Russia has never had a true moral reckoning with the catastrophes of collectivization and terror, and by now there are reasons to doubt that it ever will.

Another reason why the war scores so highly in the popular consciousness is that its other main rival as a historical milestone, the collapse of the Soviet Union, is not – to put it mildly – seen as an unmixed blessing. Even Russians with no

Figure 1.1 Stalingrad, summer 1945.
Source: © Mark Redkin / PhotoSoyuz.

great love of one-party socialism are likely to abhor the way in which the removal of Communist dictatorship led directly to the neglect of Russia's national interests and the florescence of crony capitalism.

But the prominence of the war in contemporary Russia is not due primarily to the lack of suitable alternative historical markers. It matters in absolute, not relative, terms. It cost the Soviet Union almost 30 million people: somewhere between 24 and 27 million premature deaths and the best part of 3 million other Soviet citizens who were displaced by the war and never returned to the USSR. If further account is taken of the wartime birth deficit, losses may run as high as 35 million. The Soviet population figure at the start of the war – 200 million – was not reached again until 1956.[1]

Many of the previously most developed parts of the country lay in ruins. Capital losses amounted to about 30 percent of national wealth. War damage had destroyed or disabled close to 32,000 industrial enterprises, 65,000 kilometers of railway, and housing for 25 million people. Infrastructure had all but collapsed. At the end of war, 90 percent of Moscow's central heating and around half of water and sewage systems were out of action, while 80 percent of roofs required urgent repairs. Despite the Soviet victory, much of the population endured unimaginable hardship. Household consumption fell from 74 percent of national income in 1940 to 66 percent of a significantly reduced national income in 1945. In 1945, the average peasant on a collective farm received 190 grams of grain and 70 grams of potatoes for a day's work. In 1946–7, acute postwar scarcity, compounded by harvest failure and the government's commitment to industrial reconstruction, brought what turned out to be the last Soviet famine, whose death toll was at least 1 million and possibly a good deal higher.[2]

The war brought not only death, devastation and hunger but mass displacement and upheaval. During the war, the enemy occupied territory with a prewar population of 85 million (or 45 percent of the total Soviet population). Millions of people were displaced by the German advance. Around 15 million more were moved to the rear in 1941–2; by the end of 1942, more than half of workers and employees in Kazakhstan, one of the principal destinations, were evacuees. An industrial evacuation effort of unprecedented scale and speed was launched within days of the German invasion. In the critical early months of the war hundreds of large factories were relocated – the greatest proportion to the Urals, others to the Volga region, Western Siberia, Eastern Siberia, and Central Asia. Without the evacuated facilities, which included some of the crown jewels of the Soviet defense sector, the war effort would have been all but doomed. Two-thirds of prewar ammunition production, for example, had taken place on territory that would be occupied or wrecked by the enemy. The evacuation of Leningrad's all-important Kirov tank factory had to be completed in late 1941 by air after the city had been isolated by German forces.[3]

At the end of the war 11.4 million men in the armed forces had to find their way home somehow. Demobilization was a gradual process, but the vast numbers placed immense strain on Soviet society and infrastructure: about 3.5 million men had returned to civilian life by September 1945, 8.5 million by 1948. And then there were the captured enemy combatants. According to the Soviet General Staff, the Soviet Army took 4,377,300 prisoners between 22 June 1941 and 8 May 1945; at the end of June 1945, the Ministry of Internal Affairs gave a figure of 2 million prisoners taken in 1945 alone. Nearly 700,000 Germans from the combat zone were sent home immediately at the end of the war, as were 65,000 Japanese. Thereafter, repatriation would be a slow process that ended only in spring 1950. German prisoners convicted of specific crimes were allowed home only in 1956.[4]

There is, then, no shortage of ways in which the war may be seen to have cast a "shadow" over the later Soviet era. This makes it all the more surprising how little use existing histories of the Soviet Union have for it. The foundational decades of Soviet history are usually seen as the 1920s and (especially) the 1930s. Over the last half-century, and especially since the opening of the archives in the late 1980s, scholars have produced a vast quantity of interesting dissertations, books, and articles on the Soviet "system" as it came to be in the first ten or fifteen years of Stalin's rule. The war is usually recognized as traumatic and important, but ultimately is granted the status of a cataclysmic interlude between two phases of Stalinism: the turbulent and bloody era of the 1930s and the deep freeze of the late 1940s (which would soon, under Stalin's successors, turn to thaw).

Nonmilitary historians do not quite know what to do with the war.[5] It can – indeed must – be mentioned, but its impact on the paradigms and agendas of Soviet history has so far been vastly more limited than its human and material cost might seem to warrant. Russian historians – and Western specialists – have produced an enormous amount of writing on military aspects of the conflict of 1941–5, but this impressive body of work has mostly failed to connect with the preoccupations of those who study Soviet history over a longer range.

The design of this three-volume Blackwell history of Russia forces us to take the war seriously. Periodization is not an empty formality but rather an intel-lectual choice with far-reaching consequences. The chronological boundaries of this volume invite consideration of the war as a conditioning factor for later Soviet and Russian history – all the way to the early twenty-first century present. To my knowledge, there is no other book that examines exactly the period from 1941 to the end of the century and beyond. Most authors zero their clock in 1917, 1945 or 1953, while 1991 has tended up to now to mark the watershed between history and political science. To start an account with the Nazi invasion rather than the Soviet triumph makes it possible to see the war not just as a catastrophe that had to be withstood and overcome but rather as a starting point for much that followed.

The legacy of the war was not only destructive. It also brought the Soviet regime new opportunities. Internally, its hand was strengthened by the growth of Soviet patriotism and the consolidation of a loyal new elite. Internationally, it now had a large part of Europe (and in due course of the entire world) directly in its sights. The war also had ideological value: it could also be interpreted by the regime and its committed servants as the delayed culmination of the revolu-tion, a "Bolshevik Armageddon." It was a self-destructive conflict among the main parties to world capitalism that picked up where 1918 had left off. It was the moment that the home of world Communism had to fight off the renewed threat to its existence of which the Soviet leadership had been warning its population since the late 1920s. The war finally sorted out the enemies from the friends of Soviet power, the truly committed from the impostors and opportunists. In this life-or-death struggle, "enemies of the people" (who had needed violent unmask-ing in the 1930s) were exposed as such: as traitors, cowards, collaborators. The Soviet body politic was now fully purged and could look to the future with confidence.[6]

The war was quite literally an ordeal by fire for the new generation of com-mitted Stalinists who had got their career breaks in the 1930s. The Soviet political system and its armed forces had to learn quickly on the job. The Red Army in particular had started from a low base. In the late 1930s Stalin had launched a bloody purge of his military elite. The first major action seen by the army since then had been a disaster: in the Winter War of 1939–40, the Finns had successfully defended their independence in the face of a Soviet assault, inflicting heavy casualties on their enormous adversary. Over the three and a half months of the conflict, nearly 127,000 Soviet soldiers were killed or lost in action, which was more than 90 percent of all the combat losses sustained by the Soviet armed forces since 1922. The early months of the conflict with Nazi Germany were more disastrous still. By the start of the rearguard defense of Moscow in early December 1941, the Soviet armed forces had lost almost 3 million men killed or captured and over a million more sick and wounded.[7] Catastrophic failures of command and preparation were compounded by collapsing morale: it is hard otherwise to explain how 2 million or more Soviet soldiers were taken prisoner in the late summer and autumn of 1941. Discipline was instilled at gunpoint: in the first three months of the war alone, the political police (NKVD) shot 10,000 Soviet soldiers for desertion, a third of them in front of their units.[8]

Disaster, however, brought a form of rebirth. The Red Army of 1941 perished in the first months of the war not just physically but also operationally. From mid-1942 onwards, the Party authorities ceded more authority and autonomy to frontline officers. The men brought in to replace their dead comrades managed to learn fast, and the poorly led army of 1941 became a more effective fighting force. Human endeavor and know-how was backed up by technology. The Soviet mode of war became faster moving as production of tanks and mobile artillery increased. Transport and communications also helped to boost military coordination: more than half a million American jeeps and trucks were combined with vastly improved radio communications.[9]

In the spring of 1943, with victory at Stalingrad, the momentum of the conflict swung to the Soviet side, and by the end of that year the Soviet leadership could begin to reflect on the likely shape of the postwar European order. In 1945, as the Red Army rushed toward Berlin, it might be thought that the Great Patriotic War had succeeded where the civil war had failed: it had delivered on Lenin's promise that socialism would spread west. It also, in due course, appeared to have spread revolution east: from mid-1946 onward China was convulsed by a civil war between nationalists and Communists.

But this apparently favorable geographical conjuncture did not make the Soviet leadership rest easy. Stalin might have gained a more comfortable buffer zone in eastern and central Europe, but he soon found himself drawn into competition with a capitalist adversary, the United States of America, that had not previously been one of the Bolsheviks' principal hate figures. The victory of 1945 had not fully assuaged Soviet feelings of weakness, vulnerability and encirclement by hostile powers. Stalin and his comrades had hardly forgotten how poorly the Soviet Union – a thoroughly militarized society by 1941 – had been prepared for the German assault.

Besides failing to remove external sources of unease, the war had also created or exacerbated internal divisions in Soviet society. The USSR now contained tens of millions of people who had experienced German occupation. About 1 million Soviet soldiers ended up fighting against the USSR, whether voluntarily or under duress.[10] The Soviet regime was expert at making enemies of its own people. During the war, POWs were classified as traitors by Soviet officialdom; their families might face reprisals. After the war, more than 5 million Soviet citizens (POWs or forced laborers) were repatriated to the USSR, where they immediately came under suspicion; hundreds of thousands of them spent time in the camps.

The problem of potentially disloyal elements in the Soviet population had a large ethnic dimension. In Ukraine and Belorussia, around 300,000 people had served in the local police of the occupation forces by 1943.[11] Levels of collaboration would surely have been much greater if the Germans had not done so much to antagonize the population of the occupied territories. Although the experience of Nazi overlordship in the western regions had for many people not been much preferable to Stalinist rule, these parts of the Soviet Union had strong reasons – national, ethnic, religious, political – to resent the reimposition of Stalinist controls. Soviet measures against the populations perceived to have committed collective treason – mass deportation – hardly provided a long-term solution.

The war represented the apotheosis of the social mobilization for which Soviet ideology was striving, yet this too had disturbing implications for Stalin's rule. Besides the possibility of a Bonapartist threat from the military High Command, the postwar regime faced the challenge of bringing a vast army – close to 12 million men at the moment of victory in Europe – under control. Loyal servants of the Soviet cause during the war might not prove so loyal or committed when returning to civilian life, or when government austerity could no longer be justified by the fact of a life-and-death struggle. The problem was compounded by the rapid wartime growth in Party membership. Frontline soldiers had been admitted to the Party in their hundreds of thousands. While this mass constituency was in principle a good thing, it also carried the danger that the purpose and ideological purity of the Party would be compromised. Had the Party taken over Soviet society, or vice versa?

Even government and administrative elites were a source of concern for an ageing dictator. After the disastrous early months, the Soviet political system had functioned remarkably effectively in wartime. Its successes, however, had been bought at the cost of blurring the boundaries between the military, the political system, and economic administration. The war had forced the regime to give administrators and managers more leeway, and to punish them less arbitrarily, than in the preceding era of Great Terror. How was Stalin to make sure that they did not feel too comfortable in their positions and that the administrative system did not end up subverting his political will?

Even at the moment of victory, then, there were reasons for Stalin to feel "embattled."[12] Later sections of this book – especially Chapter 2 – will explain how he set about maintaining his kind of order: by extending the military discipline and austerity of the war years into the late 1940s, and by periodically striking fear into his loyal servants. But Stalin's rule also asserted itself in less tangible ways – notably by controlling the memory of the war itself.

The War Remembered

The process began even before the war ended. Especially after victory at Stalingrad, the personality cult fostered by Stalin entered a new, more intense, phase. From the beginning, the war had caused Stalin to take on a more public role. In the summer of 1941 he quickly outgrew his notional Party post, becoming Supreme Commander almost immediately after the Nazi invasion. With an engaging radio address two weeks after the start of the war, and then with his last-minute decision in October 1941 not to join much of his government in evacuation, he allied himself with popular patriotism to an extent inconceivable in the 1930s. Even if Stalin's military command was largely a disaster until he started paying attention to his generals in 1942, his symbolic authority took on a new martial coloring.[13]

After 1945 Stalin remained at the core of accounts of the war, but patriotic memory abandoned any populist concessions to become entirely Party-centered. In a famous Kremlin speech two weeks after the victory over Germany, Stalin raised a glass to the powers of endurance of the Russian people (*narod*); a month later, on a similar occasion, he spoke warmly of the "simple, ordinary, modest people" who formed the "cogs" of the mighty state mechanism that was the Soviet Union.[14] These, however, were toasts at banquets rather than statements of intent: very soon the much-cited *narod* would be handed back its normal Stalinist role as a bit-player in the narrative of Communist triumph. Naturally, this required writing out of the story the many ambiguities and contradictions of Russia's war. Nothing was heard of the NKVD atrocities in Poland and the Baltics before the *Wehrmacht*'s arrival, or of the war crimes of the Soviet Army on its westward march in 1944–5. The mass panic of Moscow's population in October 1941, at a moment when the government itself appeared to be turning tail, was taboo. Nor, of course, could it be mentioned that not all Soviet people had thrown themselves

FIGURE 1.2   Stalin and Zhukov on the Lenin Mausoleum, 1945. The Party and the military in uneasy equilibrium.
Source: © Eugeny Khaldei / PhotoSoyuz.

into the cause with patriotic aplomb: hundreds of thousands had been worked to death in the Gulag, others had been conscripted into labor battalions, while frontline soldiers had been kept fighting by "blocking units" (*zagradotriady*) instructed to mow down any troops who appeared to be retreating. Any Soviet people who did not have an exemplary record – notably those conscripted or captured by the Germans – were automatically under suspicion after the war; many of them could never shake off the stigma.

   Even the men and women who unquestionably had done their patriotic duty – the frontline soldiers, or *frontoviki* – were denied adequate recognition by the postwar Soviet state. Soviet provisions for returning soldiers always lagged far behind the American G. I. Bill, with its extensive package of welfare benefits, educational opportunities and home loans. By 1948 veterans in the USSR had ceased to exist as a coherent category of welfare recipient. They were even denied symbolic recognition: Victory Day was celebrated in 1946 and 1947 but then discontinued as a public holiday.[15]

Veterans gained a louder public voice almost by accident in the mid-1950s, when the Soviet authorities permitted – as an international propaganda move – the creation of a Soviet Committee of War Veterans, which quickly outgrew its brief to take on welfare and lobbying functions. At the same time, a less state-centered version of the war made a comeback for reasons that were less accidental. One important factor was Nikita Khrushchev's pride in his own war record and his indignation at Stalin's monopoly on heroic wartime leadership. Khrushchev could argue that, unlike Stalin, he had spent most of his war not in the Kremlin but in several of the most intense theaters: Kiev, Kharkov, Stalingrad, Kursk. In his Secret Speech of February 1956, besides exposing some of the crimes of the Great Terror, he set about tarnishing Stalin's war record. Even on the printed page, Khrushchev's tone and delivery are noticeably more vivid and heartfelt when his four-hour oration moves on from the 1930s to the Great Patriotic War.[16] De-Stalinization was at least in part driven by the need of the Soviet elite to reclaim the memory of the war from its deceased progenitor. Like Stalin, moreover, Khrushchev felt it necessary in due course to remove and disgrace the war's most famous Soviet general, Georgii Zhukov. Yet, while this Kremlin revisionism may have been self-interested, in combination with a slight liberalization of public discourse it made war memory a more honest and democratic affair. The 1950s and 1960s saw an outpouring of fiction and film that gave the war a more nuanced human dimension and brought to light some of its moral ambiguities.

The Brezhnev era confirmed the centrality of the war to Soviet self-understanding. Brezhnev, like Khrushchev, was concerned to burnish his own image as war hero, most notoriously by awarding himself medals and having his ghostwritten memoirs win a state prize. But he was prepared to share at least some of the credit with Soviet society. Victory Day was re-instituted as a public holiday in 1965, while veterans were given more generous state provision. The edginess and contentiousness of Khrushchev-era war culture faded into stable bombast at the level of public ritual, even if film directors of the 1970s continued to produce a few morally complex accounts of the war.[17]

Mikhail Gorbachev was not only young for a General Secretary, he was also the Soviet Union's first properly postwar leader. He had been ten years old at the time of the Nazi invasion. Not only had he not served in the armed forces at any point in his life, he had spent several months, from August 1942 to January 1943, under German occupation in his home village in southern Russia. If he had been just a few years older, his war record would have been considered compromised and suspicious; at the very least, it was not heroic. War was not central to

Figure 1.3 A veteran in the schoolroom, 1970s.
Source: © Victor Akhlomov / PhotoSoyuz.

Gorbachev's self-understanding as it had been for his predecessors. The Germans he encountered were relatively well behaved, and he did not witness any atrocities. He had, however, observed at close quarters Soviet-style atrocity: one grandfather had been arrested in the Terror of 1937, while the other had seen three children die in the famine of 1933 before himself being arrested for "sabotage" and doing two years of forced labor in Siberia.[18] When the time came for another reckoning with the Soviet past, in the era of Gorbachev's glasnost, what came under scrutiny above all was the prewar Stalin era, from collectivization through Great Terror to the last great crime Stalin had time for before the Nazi invasion: mass murder in the Soviet-occupied western borderlands in 1940. For Gorbachev, the Secret Speech meant 1937 rather than 1941.

The result was an intense phase of recovering a gruesome and long-suppressed past. Yet, while relatively few outright apologists for Stalinist terror could be found in the early 1990s, the momentum of this re-de-Stalinization soon petered out. One reason for this was the simple fact that Russian society had a great deal else to preoccupy it in the first years after the Soviet collapse. Another was that prewar Terror was receding into a distant past, and its victims, participants and eye-witnesses were dying out. Given the length of time that had elapsed, it became increasingly possible to see the crimes of the Soviet regime against its own population as the collateral damage of history rather than a matter of present-day moral and political import.

But perhaps the most important reason that the Terror faded from Russian consciousness was that it interfered too much with patriotic memory of the war. Was not victory over the Nazis proof that, whatever the "excesses" of the 1930s, Stalin's rule was ultimately justified? Did not the Soviet Union save Europe, and sacrifice itself, in 1941–5? This historiographical reflex is very strong in Russia even in places where one might not expect to find it. It is hard for an American or British audience to appreciate the extent to which Russians believe in the Soviet "liberation" of eastern Europe. In November 1969, a year after the Soviet crackdown in Prague and more than 20 years after the forced imposition of Communist rule, the up-and-coming Mikhail Gorbachev was part of a delegation to Czechoslovakia. He was taken aback by the hostility of the reaction he encountered from ordinary people. Prague he found to be in a state of "semiparalysis." His hosts did not dare to take their visitors to workplaces for that ritual socialist encounter between government and people. On a visit to a factory in Brno, the Soviet delegation was cold-shouldered by the workers. In Bratislava too there were some awkward moments. Then the delegation spent the night in a Slovak village where they finally received a warm-hearted reception with food, wine, music, and open conversation. The peasants, it turned out, had been less impressed than the urban population by the mantra of "socialism with a human face" that had been adopted by the previous year's reformist leadership: their concern was what it would mean in real terms for their lives. Seizing on evidence that Soviet-backed Communism in Czechoslovakia was in some sense popular, Gorbachev could not help recalling that his own father had been seriously wounded not far away, near Košice, when fighting to claim the region from the Germans.[19]

Patriotic pride born of wartime sacrifice went rapidly from psychological reflex to state-sponsored orthodoxy when the political and economic chaos of the 1990s was replaced by a more secure order under Vladimir Putin. The early twenty-first century saw a resurgent Russian cult of World War II. It was accompanied by acute hostility to any depiction of the war's less glorious sides. In 2009, the defense of the cult went so far as the creation of a "Commission for Countering Attempts to Falsify History to the Detriment of the Interests of Russia": the membership of this body was a lineup of state functionaries, including representatives of the military and security agencies, that would not have been out of place in the Moscow of c. 1975.[20] Once upon a time, it was Western scholars foraging for documents on the 1920s and 1930s who were likely to be rebuffed when they arrived in Russia to do their research. Now, the war was the research topic most likely to elicit the vigilance of archive officials. The reason for the change is presumably that, whereas revelations on the Terror are already too numerous to be

FIGURE 1.4   War memorial, Zvenigorod, west of Moscow, August 2007. The memory of
the war is manifestly alive in this small town, which saw terrible bloodshed in 1941. In
September 2009, the local authorities announced the imminent construction of an
improved granite memorial engraved with the names of the 149 local inhabitants who died
in the fighting.
Source: Author's photograph.

repressed entirely, very little light has ever been shone in Russia on the dark side
of the war. Although World War II has been taken up by patriotic rhetoric as a
more straightforward alternative to the 1930s, the silences and evasions in its
treatment are just as great as they once were for prewar Stalinism. Little is heard
or known about wartime Soviet atrocities, or about the extent of wartime repression of the Soviet population. In the current patriotic memory of World War II,
we are witnessing an unedifying competition for victimhood by a generation of
people who were not themselves victims. In mainstream Russian accounts of
World War II, it is hard to discern the fact that half of the Soviet Union's 5 million
Jewish population perished, or that Poles and Lithuanians, following the experience of 1939–41, had few reasons to consider the Red Army preferable to the
Wehrmacht. It is little consolation that omissions and evasions are found on
practically all sides of public historical debates in eastern Europe.[21]

——— After the War: Interpreting Later Soviet History ———

The place of the war in Russian patriotic discourse is clear enough. What, though, can historians contribute by way of interpreting the six decades that have elapsed since 1945? The answer is surely that they can contribute a good deal more than ten or fifteen years ago. The postwar and post-Stalin eras have only recently started to generate detailed original research by social and political historians with access to all the tools of their trade (archives, memoirs, oral history, nonideologized publications by Russian historians). In the historiography of the post-1941 era, every half-decade that passes makes a difference in a way that is no longer the case for the 1920s and 1930s, where a critical mass of empirical material and historiographical reflection was achieved by the end of the 1990s. Thanks to recent books, articles and Ph.D. dissertations, it is now possible to write with greater certainty on a wide range of topics from the history of the Gulag to the development of Soviet television. The material at the disposal of a would-be synthesizer is immeasurably richer even than seven or eight years ago, and it will only get richer.

The question the synthesizer must ask, however, is what it all means. How does the stream of new information affect our notion of what took place in the Soviet Union and its successor states between the war and the present? For all the recent outpouring of new research on the 1940s, 1950s and 1960s, we still have to confront fundamental discontinuities in the ways that Soviet history is conceived and narrated. There is a break between the period 1945–70, increasingly well served by historical research, and a historians' "black box" period of 1970–85, for which archival holdings are mostly still unavailable and which has been the preserve of area studies specialists writing close to the time of the events they investigated. In effect, this book has to cross at least three historiographical divides: between the war and everything else; between history and political/social science (otherwise known as the "Sovietology" of the 1970s and 1980s); and between Sovietology – which was obliged to study Soviet affairs from some distance, relying above all on published sources – and the revitalized area studies of the 1990s that could take the end of the Soviet Union as a given and gather firsthand information to an extent beyond the wildest dreams of the previous generation of specialists. To try to tell the story of the second half of the twentieth century in Russia is to make a bumpy journey along a twisted and uneven road.

But can we at least agree on the direction of the journey? By all appearances, the answer is only too simple: the later history of the Soviet Union tells us the story of that state's unviability, the profound flaws in its economic system, the inevitability of its collapse. Yet, while it would be perverse to argue that the Soviet planned economy of the early 1980s was set fair for prosperity, the inevitability argument is not quite satisfactory. It does not do justice to the elements of contingency in the way the Soviet system actually collapsed; nor does it allow us to determine which of the many potential causes were fundamental to that outcome and which less so. It also does not help us to make sense of developments beyond 1991: yes, Russia is no longer part of the Soviet Union, but that by itself is not much of an analytical breakthrough. The notion of the inevitability of the Soviet collapse also invites teleological reasoning: all aspects of Soviet society, culture, economics, or politics become interesting *ex post facto* for what they reveal of the incipient disintegration of the Soviet order. The guiding presumption of this book is that there are other, often more interesting, things to say about them.

The narrative of inexorable Soviet decline has its subdivisions, many of them drawn from Soviet political discourse. The postwar era begins with the unloved period of "late Stalinism" (1945–53), a prolonged coda to the era of terroristic one-party dictatorship. With the old dictator's death in 1953, Stalinism makes way for thaw and de-Stalinization. "Thaw" is a term first dreamt up by a talented novelist and former war journalist, Ilya Ehrenburg, while de-Stalinization is a Western gloss on Nikita Khrushchev's campaign against "the cult of personality and its consequences," as manifested most famously in his Secret Speech. Following Khrushchev's removal in 1964, de-Stalinization peters out into a prolonged era of economic and social "stagnation" under Leonid Brezhnev. Brezhnev's immediate successors, Iurii Andropov and Konstantin Chernenko, were too sickly to make much impact, but the next man in the Kremlin, Mikhail Gorbachev, was young, energetic, and full of programmatic statements. His best-known reform slogan, perestroika (literally "reconstruction"), has given the era its name. Soon, however, this reconstruction came to seem the work of a jerry-builder: in 1991 it brought the collapse of a superpower state in what has been called the "second Russian revolution." Following that, Russia embarked on a phase of "transition" that would take it away from the legacy of state socialism.

The periodization I have sketched out informs most accounts of postwar Soviet history – whether scholarly or otherwise – and has much to recommend it. Leaders mattered a great deal in the Soviet Union, and it is clear that epoch-defining changes came about very soon after the death of Stalin (to take only the most important example). It is also clear, however, that many of the labels we attach to these periods were dreamt up by contemporary participants or observers: they come with a political agenda or at the very least a degree of historiographical "spin." They practically define in advance the ways we might interpret the periods to which they refer. If the years 1945–53 are called "late Stalinism," the war becomes an interruption to the "general line" of Soviet history: normal service is resumed in 1945 with the hegemony of the secret police, the extension of the personality cult to ever more baroque dimensions, and ruthless exploitation of the population to boost the industrial economy. Yet, as this book will suggest, a great many things in the postwar Soviet Union were novel, not normal – most obviously, the Soviet domination of central and eastern Europe. "Thaw" is an attractive notion, but it does not do justice to the many ways in which the Soviet Union in the 1950s remained a profoundly illiberal, even "Stalinist" place. De-Stalinization, on closer inspection of the Secret Speech and its preparation, was as much to do with bolstering the authority of Khrushchev's leadership and reclaiming the memory of the war from Stalin as it was about "rehabilitating" Stalin's victims and righting historical wrongs.

The political baggage attached to periodization does not lighten when we enter the ostensibly least eventful phase of Soviet history. The tag of "stagnation" was applied to the tenure of Brezhnev by the Gorbachev regime, and for that reason alone deserves to be treated with suspicion. All newly installed politicians like to bolster their authority by casting aspersions on their predecessors. It is certainly true that the Soviet economy was in a sorry state by the early 1980s, but it is unclear to what extent that failure should be laid at Brezhnev's door rather than ascribed to the inherent logic of Soviet industrial development. On the international front, the period 1964–82 was far from uneventful and not without Soviet successes – at least until the invasion of Afghanistan in December 1979. The label Gorbachev applied to his own enterprise – perestroika – is no less open to questioning. Quickly taken up in the Western press as a sign of liberalization, the term is conventional in Soviet political discourse as a vague signal of reforming intent. What it might mean in practice is unclear – and was made no clearer by Gorbachev's opaque policy statements. Even when we reach the Soviet collapse, events are not easy to interpret. "Revolution" is plausible enough as a one-word description, but it does not by itself sort out the causes of events: was popular pressure the critical factor, or a failure of nerve by the ruling elite, or a self-interested decision by members of that elite that they would be better off abandoning the system that had reared them? Finally, the notion of "transition" – widely adopted by economists and political scientists in the 1990s – implies a direction of change that was rarely borne out by developments in Russia's fin de siècle.

It is relatively easy to ask questions of existing periodization, rather less so to propose meaningful alternatives. As this introduction has already elaborated, the significance of the war will provide a large part of this book's analytical thrust. Beyond that, I will be asking a simple question: if we take the period from 1941 to the present as a whole, and without necessarily taking our lead from the periods in office of General Secretaries, what fundamental changes can we perceive in Soviet/Russian history?

A useful starting point is to ask when, if ever, the Soviet Union reached any kind of steady state. Soviet history in the interwar period had been characterized by massive social upheaval, state-sponsored violence on a vast scale and chronic geopolitical insecurity. At the very end of the 1930s, following the worst ever outbreak of terror in 1937–8, there were signs that the political system might be reaching a kind of equilibrium. However, the Soviet leadership's way of alleviating its fear of major European war was to strike a deal with Adolf Hitler, which brought Soviet takeover of Eastern Poland, Bessarabia and the Baltic states but almost certainly made the USSR less well prepared for the Nazi assault when it duly came less than two years later. During the war – the most destructive such conflict in history, and one in which the Soviet Union bore a heavier cost than any other combatant – equilibrium was the last thing that could be achieved. It was also inconceivable in the war's immediate aftermath, with much of the more developed western part of the country laid waste and millions of people on the move.

Within a few years, however, signs of "normalization" – not that life in the Soviet Union had ever previously been "normal" – began to appear. Around 1950 the prospect of life-threatening hunger began to lift for the Soviet population. The economy entered a phase of steady growth. Unlike the 1930s, moreover, increases in industrial output were not accompanied by terror. Although the regime still relied heavily on its state security agencies, it eschewed mass violence as a primary technique of governance. By the late 1950s, the Soviet leadership could put forward a plausible account of historical progress toward socialism: this narrative seems to have been sufficient to generate a robust Soviet patriotism among much of the general population.

The Soviets could also feel that history was on their side because the postwar world was in a phase of decolonization. Throughout the first two decades of Soviet power, the Bolshevik leadership had railed at the forces of world imperialism. In their analysis, Western imperialists provoked World War I, engineered the postwar settlement in their favor, and thereafter kept a predatory eye on states – notably the USSR – that did not fit their ideas of how markets and territories should be controlled. The British were the main culprits, but the Bolsheviks also anticipated a resurgence of German militarism. In the East, a militaristic Japan posed a more immediate, and extremely serious, threat to Soviet security.

The situation was transformed in the postwar era. Germany and Japan had wrought terrible havoc on the world, but they were now devastated and militarily disabled. The Germans had created an empire in Europe itself, but that had now gone. Although Stalin anticipated a further German threat sometime in the future, it was not imminent. No less important, the British empire – which reached its greatest territorial extent between the wars – began to shrivel rapidly in the late 1940s. By the 1950s decolonization was sweeping the globe, and the Soviet Union – as an impeccably anti-imperialist state – could feel that it belonged at the head of the movement.

But things were not so simple. The actions of the Soviet state in the 1930s and 1940s had seemed to prove that the USSR belonged in the camp of the colonizers as a modern and far more brutal version of the Russian empire. Millions of non-Russians had perished in the Bolshevik assault on their way of life, mainly during the collectivization campaign of the early 1930s. Hundreds of thousands more had been deported, on the grounds of their real or potential disloyalty, between the late 1930s and the late 1940s. Worse still – from a postcolonial perspective – the USSR had acquired political domination of half a dozen nations in eastern Europe. Here, one might say, was a Soviet empire that filled the vacuum left by the eastern half of the Nazi empire.

We can in fact push the idea of the USSR as imperial power even further to argue that, in the Stalin era, the Soviet Union subjected its own population – Russian as well as non-Russian – to a form of internal colonization. Tens of millions of rural people were ruthlessly subjugated to the demands of crash industrialization: in the collectivized villages they entered what has justly been called a "second serfdom." The industrial workforce – largely, of course, made up of peasants – was not much better off as it slaved in factories and on construction sites. And then there was the Gulag, a vast network of prison camps and settlements whose primary rationale was economic exploitation.

When Stalinist rule came to an end, the Soviet Union entered a period of internal decolonization. This did not mean, of course, any granting of sovereignty to the non-Russian nationalities. Rather, it implied that tens of millions of Soviet people – Russian and non-Russian – would be raised from the status of colonial subject to that of modern citizen. Naturally, Stalinist discourse – exemplified by the Constitution of 1936 – pronounced that Soviet power had already brought the gift of nondiscriminatory citizenship to its population, but such claims were so at variance with the reality of state–society relations in the Stalin era that they barely deserve comment. From the 1930s onward, a growing section of the population – party-state functionaries, army officers, educated specialists, skilled workers – could feel themselves to be fully empowered members of Soviet society, but such people remained a minority, and citizenship for them was a privilege attached to their position rather than a civic right.

Decolonization is always a fraught and difficult business. If it is ever unproblematic for imperial powers, that is because they can turn their back on distant colonial territories and leave others to sort out the mess. The Soviet Union did not have that option. Nevertheless, it set about the task of internal decolonization with determination and to much demonstrable effect. The Gulag – the worst example of Stalinist exploitation – was scaled back by a series of mass releases of prisoners in the mid-1950s. The post-Stalin leadership showed that it took the discourse of citizenship rather more seriously than its predecessor. The landmark social policies of the Khrushchev era – a mass housing campaign, the introduction of a comprehensive pensions system – made popular wellbeing a regime priority to an unprecedented extent. Civic participation was encouraged, whether that meant writing letters to the authorities, voting in elections to the soviets, or participating in the Komsomol, the Party, or other "voluntary" organizations. Collective farmers were given greater opportunities to turn themselves into something else, and in the mid-1970s those who remained on the *kolkhoz* were finally granted that key attribute of Soviet citizenship: the internal passport.

But the changes at work in the post-Stalin USSR were a matter not only of direct government action. They also came as broad, often unintended, consequences of the social and economic transformation the Bolsheviks had brought about. The Soviet Union was not just a self-colonizing backwater; it was also the twentieth century's quintessential fast modernizer. New cities were built, old ones swelled to bursting, millions of people were given tertiary education and took their place in a new urban civilization. That civilization was not just about pig iron and ball bearings: it came with many of the attributes of modernity that were found in more developed parts of the world. Soviet urbanites were not just producers, they were also consumers, and their notion of consumption expanded over the later Soviet period to include color television sets and automatic washing machines as well as vodka and pork fat. Once people became educated and ambitious, they were less ready for the self-sacrifice of earlier generations (which had often been driven by the absence of less sacrificial alternatives). Much as the Soviet state might tell people to reproduce, its citizens drew the same conclusions as everyone else from declining infant mortality: they had fewer children. The decline in the birth rate was only hastened by the public insistence that women work and by the chronic shortage of urban housing.

In short, the postwar Soviet Union experienced a demographic and cultural revolution that was the logical corollary of the Soviet project of urbanization and modernization but was not straightforwardly compatible with other core Soviet goals: collectivism, equality, social unity, transparency of political control. The discordance between society and politics was exacerbated by the fact that many attributes of late industrial consumerist modernity were now truly global and able to cross even the least permeable national boundaries. The most striking example was audio-visual mass culture. For the Soviet regime, it was a source of patriotic pride that production of wireless radios had been vastly increased in the late 1940s and 1950s, while TV sets had become routine household items by the 1970s. But this also meant that millions of Soviet people had the opportunity to listen in to Western radio at just the moment that the Americans and British wished to get through to the Soviet audience, while the investment in radio and TV implied a more interactive and more public form of politics. For all that Soviet media were often deadening in their content, would Leonid Brezhnev's poor health in the late 1970s have mattered so much if he had been able to control his public image in the same way as Stalin, who was seen by the population mostly in touched-up press photographs?[22]

All this caused Soviet elites from Khrushchev onward a degree of discomfort. The archives of Agitprop in the 1950s are peppered with minuted discussions of what to do about Voice of America and the BBC, while the KGB at various moments expended vast resources on tracking down and punishing forms of behavior that in a liberal country would have been considered apolitical. Another source of disorientation for the Soviet Union was that the new bugbear of the anti-imperialist USSR, the United States, was not an empire in the sense that had been known hitherto. From time to time, in locations from the Bay of Pigs to Vietnam, it certainly behaved like one; in its treatment of its own black population, moreover, it had its own, very nasty, version of internal colonialism. There was no question that the USA was a global power with the capacity to intervene almost anywhere in the world it pleased. But it did not dominate other states' political systems in the direct way that the Soviet Union did in eastern Europe, and a large part of America's enormous power around the world was exercised not militarily but economically and culturally. As well as a superpower, it was an amazingly successful world brand.

The postwar Soviet Union, then, had to negotiate the global transition from an era of decolonization (which started in World War I and was completed after World War II) to one of American hegemony – while at the same time maintaining its own, newly acquired superpower status. The challenge was so formidable that it is almost possible to feel sorry for the Soviet leadership. The chapters that follow will describe, from a number of different perspectives, how they went about the task, what response they met from their population, and to what extent their efforts have left a mark on the society, politics, and economy of the former Soviet Union as it has moved into the twenty-first century. The rest of the book's contents may usefully be seen as four linked pairs of chapters. The first pair examines the fundamentals of Soviet/Russian life: its mode of government (Chapter 2) and the economic system that has mostly been inseparable from politics (Chapter 3). Chapters 4 and 5 put Soviet/Russian society under scrutiny, exploring both broad sociological trends and patterns of everyday life. The next pair of chapters is concerned with the social and political issues arising from the Soviet Union's immense size and diversity: Chapter 6 investigates how the Soviet system governed such a huge territory and managed its population, while Chapter 7 looks into what might be considered the main distinguishing attribute of the Soviet Union – the fact that this country contained dozens of different ethnic groups, gave many of them the attributes of nationhood, yet maintained a strong central state. Chapters 8 and 9 go beyond the borders of the Soviet Union to consider Russia's relationship with the wider world, whether geopolitical or cultural. A brief conclusion attempts to make sense of it all.

2

Reform, Reaction, Revolution

This chapter will consider the technicalities of power in the Soviet Union. Everyone knows that politics was inescapable in the USSR, but that does not mean that it was straightforward or uninteresting. How was it that this hybrid of party and state exercised its dictatorship for so long? What mutations and adaptations did it undergo along the way? What exactly were its mechanisms of domination?

The usual answers to these questions stress the rigidity and permanence of political structures: the Communist Party, the Red Army, the state security services (known from 1954 as the KGB), the strict hierarchy of state and Party institutions at all levels of the administrative structure – from the Kremlin down to the village – that constituted "the Soviet system."

These institutions clearly go a significant part of the way to explaining the durability of Soviet power. But we must not assume we know how they operated in practice. If we consider the USSR as it developed over the seven decades of its existence, we cannot fail to be struck by some meaningful changes that came about in this enormous authoritarian polity. The period covered by this book starts with the final years of one of the most violent regimes known in history, continues with a remarkable challenge to that regime's legitimacy from within the system (known as "de-Stalinization"), and ends with a decade when the Russian state was commonly believed to be disintegrating. The phrase "party-state," often used to characterize the Soviet system of rule, conceals as much as it reveals: the relationship between party and state was subject to significant fluctuation, especially in the first two-thirds of the Soviet period.

As the title of this chapter suggests, the Soviet system alternated – often unpredictably – between three basic modes of operation: radical upheaval and conflict (the revolutions that brought the Bolshevik state into being and launched it on the path of crash industrialization), retrenchment and conservatism ("reaction"), and supposedly planned and structured change ("reform"). At times these three principles can be observed in action simultaneously. Nikita Khrushchev had more than a little of the revolutionary in him, given his penchant for dramatic gestures and swingeing policy initiatives, but he was also constrained by the structures of the party-state and by his own fierce commitment to the ideological tenets of Soviet socialism; and of course he has gone down in history as a "reformer." In this light it might well be asked, not why the Soviet state collapsed, but how it retained so much power for so long.

The Soviet state, even in its most murderous phase, was far from being the all-seeing, all-controlling Minotaur that the label of "totalitarianism" has tended to imply. No regime that relies on violence to the extent that the Bolsheviks did between 1917 and 1953 can be totally in control of itself or its subjects. Up to Stalin's death, this was a political system effectively at war with large sections of its own people for extended periods. When examined at close quarters, many institutions of Soviet power – especially, but by no means only, those at the lower administrative levels – were chaotically run, inadequately staffed, and directionless.

In these conditions, fear and coercion were important ways of getting things done, but coercion could be delegated or disseminated. As well as exercising close supervision over a few prominent individuals, the Stalinist regime let Soviet people loose on each other, making it possible for everyone to call on the coercive powers of the state (by informing on their neighbor, speaking up at a meeting, or joining the Party or the police) while also leaving everyone vulnerable to the exercise of those powers. This was not conventional authoritarianism, according to which people have to accommodate themselves passively to the status quo, and where failure to do so will be punished. In Soviet Russia people had manifold opportunities to engage the state as well as accepting its diktats: by writing petitions and complaints, denouncing each other, volunteering for public duties. For those that took up these opportunities, rewards were possible: wrongs might be righted, benefits granted, careers made. Conversely, staying still and keeping a low profile did not protect Soviet people against punishment, since punishment – at least until the 1950s – was very often inflicted for such accidental crimes as having an undesirable family background or associating with the wrong kind of people.

Thus, while insisting on obeisance to a number of key symbols of authority (Marxism–Leninism, Stalin, socialism – whatever those terms might be held to mean at particular times), the Soviet Union was also a mobilizational political system: it required people not only to refrain from "anti-Soviet" activity but also to participate in "building socialism," to deliver conclusive evidence that they were not "anti-Soviet." In the 1930s especially, the burden of proof in this matter lay with the individual citizen. And this reckoning was taking place in a colossal melting pot of a society, with millions of people thrown together in unfamiliar and squalid surroundings, against the backdrop of rising internal and international tensions, and under the suspicious (if not always observant) eye of a violent, conspiratorial and fanatical one-party dictatorship. Unsurprisingly, the results – culminating in the Great Terror of 1937–8 – were horrific.

But violence was by no means the only way in which power was exercised in the Soviet Union. This chapter will draw attention to the ways that, for all the apparent fixity of Soviet political structures, the techniques of power and the sources of legitimation for Soviet rulers varied over time. The most obvious innovation of Soviet life in the postwar decades was relative internal peace. The Soviet state suppressed specific cases of resistance and opposition – notably in the newly incorporated territories of the Baltic republics and Western Ukraine – and it continued to send hundreds of thousands of people to labor camps and exile, but it did not revert to the mass killing of the late 1930s. This, if nothing else, implied that politics was a rather different matter under "late" Stalinism and its less draconian successor regimes.

Soviet Government and Total War

By 1941 the Soviet regime had amply shown its capacity for unleashing violence. The question for the future was whether that violence could be brought under control and directed at the governing elite's core goals. Collectivization and industrialization had forced through the economic agenda of the Stalinist regime. The Terror of 1937–8 had decapitated the Party, removing any remaining obstacles to Stalin's supremacy. A purge of the upper echelons of the military in the late 1930s had eliminated any chance, however remote, of a political challenge from within the armed forces. But, while these measures might have served a purpose in securing Stalin's rule from internal threat, they did not necessarily prepare the Soviet system well for war with an equally ruthless external enemy. The early signs, from the Winter War with Finland in 1939–40, were dismal. The Red Army sustained casualties – dead, missing and wounded – of nearly 400,000 in its struggle with an adversary it was expected to overwhelm. It was poorly led: in the wake of the purges, officers were inexperienced and inadequately trained. They were also much too few: a week before the German invasion, the army was almost 70,000 officers short of its manning needs, and the shortage became far more acute when it lost more than 200,000 officers in the second half of 1941. The Red Army on the eve of World War II has with justice been called "institutionally incompetent."[1]

In this light, it might seem close to miraculous that the Soviet system was able to withstand the life-and-death struggle with Nazi Germany and the total social and economic mobilization that it required. On closer inspection, however, the

Soviet victory becomes less baffling. The war might have come at a bad moment for the Soviet leadership and the armed forces, which suffered appalling losses in the first six months of combat, but in a more general sense it arrived at the right time to make sense of Stalinist rule. The USSR had developed in the 1930s into a militarized society espousing a kind of barracks socialism. It had a colossal capacity for violence, partly because it was full of hungry, deprived and brutalized people, but mainly because power was concentrated in the hands of a dictator with extensive mechanisms of coercion at his disposal. The 1930s had brought the effective fusion of party and state and the monopolization of both ruling institutions by Stalin and his inner circle. In a symbolic culmination of this process, Stalin became head of the Soviet government in May 1941, replacing Molotov. Leadership of the Party and of the state was now concentrated in one man de jure as well as de facto.[2]

The German invasion only increased the existing Soviet tendency to centralization and dictatorial rule. The regime was able to adapt rapidly by concentrating power in a new executive institution. On 30 June, the Politburo was superseded by the State Defense Committee (GKO), the supreme political body for the wartime emergency, which continued the domination of the ruling circle that had been established after the Terror. The initial membership comprised a mere five men: Stalin, Commissar of Foreign Affairs Viacheslav Molotov, Central Committee Secretary Georgii Malenkov, the Head of the NKVD Lavrentii Beria, and Marshal Kliment Voroshilov.[3] The members of the GKO held vast executive powers in several different areas. Stalin, of course, was closely involved in all manner of issues; he personally signed 2,256 of the 9,971 GKO decrees over the course of its existence.[4] Beria too was a workhorse during the war years: besides his control of the security apparatus, he took upon himself wide-ranging responsibilities in the defense industries.[5] This extreme concentration of central decision-making was combined with greater delegation of power to plenipotentiaries in different regions and sectors of the wartime economy. General commands were issued in the Kremlin, while detailed planning and implementation was often left to people on the ground (with the proviso that failure would not be tolerated). It was this rapid shift to extraordinary forms of administration and control that permitted the Soviet state to remain viable despite the chaos and disruption of the first months of the war. The crucial decision to evacuate heavy industry was quickly taken and implemented: more than 1,500 enterprises, most of them large, were moved out of harm's way between July and November 1941.[6]

The GKO still needed an elaborate apparatus of rule to implement its decisions. Although the Central Committee and even the Politburo were sidelined during the war, party and state bureaucracies remained crucial. In the 1930s Stalin had destroyed the Party as an autonomous political force, but this organization retained a vast membership and a strict hierarchical structure, which made it an effective transmission belt for wartime commands. The comparison with the Nazi empire, where state and party agencies accumulated chaotically and decision-making became accordingly fragmented, is favorable to the Stalinist model. The Soviet system showed itself better able than the German to withstand the enormous strain of war – not in the sense that it had microscopic control over all aspects of life but because "it was able to maintain economic integration under intense stress."[7] All precedents indicated that a country with a per capita GDP as low as that of the Soviet Union should fall apart under the pressure of total war. Yet, in 1942, the Soviet economy not only failed to collapse but heavily outperformed Nazi Germany in all areas of weapons production. The living standards of the civilian population plummeted, but the machine guns, mortars, and tanks kept coming.[8]

The economic performance of the Soviet system was fundamental to the war's outcome, but military leadership was also required. Shortly after the Nazi invasion the decision was taken to establish a High Command (known as the Stavka), and within three weeks Stalin had made himself Supreme Commander. Against the backdrop of the traditional Bolshevik ambivalence – or downright antipathy – toward military professionals, this was a remarkable step. The dominant representative of the Party was allying himself with the armed forces. The ground was prepared for a closer and – by Stalinist standards – more even-handed relationship between the generals and their political master. In July 1941, a handful of unfortunate commanders were held responsible for the collapse of the Western front, tried by military tribunal, and shot. After the disastrous early months of the war, however, Stalin showed a greater willingness to listen to military advice and refrained from using terror against his generals. A telling example came in February 1942, when Marshall Grigorii Kulik, until then the deputy commissar of defense, was accused at a closed trial of conceding the Crimean city of Kerch in November 1941 against the express instructions of the High Command. The charge was compounded by accusations of drunkenness and theft of state property. He lost his Party membership, his post of deputy commissar, his titles of Marshal and Hero of the Soviet Union, and his medals. But he retained his life and partially redeemed himself through further service (though eventually, in 1950, he was tried on political grounds and shot). After the first year of war, state policy granted the army greater latitude. Although Stalin's habitual mistrust of the military resurfaced in July 1941, with the reintroduction of political supervision in the army (it had been abolished in August 1940 following the fiasco of the Finnish campaign), the notorious and much resented commissars were once again removed in October 1942.[9]

Ensuring the political loyalty of the armed forces was a rather easier job at a time of national struggle for survival than in the Stalinist version of peacetime. In the light of the preceding Great Terror, it is not altogether absurd to say that the war simplified Soviet life. Instead of fighting a constant war against poorly defined internal adversaries, the Soviet Union now had a genuine enemy. Instead of slaughtering or starving hundreds of thousands of its own people, it could wage righteous war on outsiders. The Party was now mobilizing people not for social combat ("class war") but for military combat. The barracks socialism and war economy of the 1930s now had a real war to fight. From now on, if Soviet people were to be shot, they would be killed as traitors and deserters rather than Trotskyites or agents of capital.

Some historians and memoirists have gone so far as to write of the war as a time of liberation for Soviet people from the all-pervading fear of "ordinary" Stalinism. It is almost certainly true that men and women at the front or under bombardment might now be less cowed by the authorities because their life was likely to be ended by German bombs or bullets, or by starvation and disease in a German POW camp. The war seems also to have brought a convergence between the popular mood – a compound of rage, fear, solidarity and national pride – and state militarism. There is abundant evidence of Soviet people forming bonds of trust – within an army unit or a tank crew – that formed the emotional base for a superstructure of patriotism. Yet, if this was liberation, it was of a highly attenuated kind. This was a time of extraordinary violence and coercion even if we avert our gaze from the killing fields of the Nazi–Soviet conflict and examine internal Soviet affairs. Whole populations were deported in acts of ethnic cleansing in the Caucasus and the Crimea (see Chapter 7). Although the Gulag population fell in absolute terms from almost 2.3 million at the start of the war to under 1.5 million at the start of 1945, this did not mean that the NKVD had stopped arresting people. The turnover of the camp population remained high, while the Soviet system of incarceration and forced labor was at its deadliest in 1942–3. A million or so prisoners were released into the armed forces during the war, but at least that number died in the Gulag. Mortality in the camps rose from about 3 percent in the first half of 1941 to a staggering 25 percent in the first half of 1943.[10]

Nor was the notionally free population let off lightly. Even as far into the war as 1943 the security organs arrested 582,515 soldiers. In total, over the course of the war, 158,000 soldiers were shot by sentence of military tribunals. Commanders routinely resorted to threats of violence. The notorious Order no. 270 of 16 August 1941, which made surrender synonymous with treason, was a codification and only slight extension of an existing draconian political culture. "Blocking units" took aim at Soviet soldiers who attempted to take flight, or redeployed them in the "penal battalions" sent on the most dangerous missions.[11]

Summary justice was handed out not only to soldiers who were believed to have retreated but also to civilians. In one notorious case, during the mass panic in Moscow triggered by news of the imminent government evacuation, the NKVD were given powers to restore order that extended to shooting looters and

БУДЬ НА ЧЕКУ,
В ТАКИЕ ДНИ
ПОДСЛУШИВАЮТ СТЕНЫ.
НЕДАЛЕКО ОТ БОЛТОВНИ
И СПЛЕТНИ
ДО ИЗМЕНЫ.

НЕ БОЛТАЙ!

FIGURE 2.1   Poster "Do Not Babble!" (1941). Prewar paranoia becomes wartime vigilance. *Source*: akg-images / ullstein bild.

panic-mongers on the spot. In October and November 1941, 6,678 people were arrested, of whom 357 were shot after trial and 15 were summarily executed.[12]

All this leads us to an obvious conclusion. The main – though not the only – reason the Soviet system was able to function so relatively well in wartime was its extensive use of coercion. And coercion was so successful because Soviet people were accustomed to it, whether as perpetrators or as victims (or both): the Soviet Union under Stalin was an extraordinarily violent political culture where "politics became an extension of war, not the other way around."[13] Responsibility for the escalation of violence on the Eastern Front lies overwhelmingly on the German side, but the Soviet political system and the Soviet people were prepared by their own recent history for a war of annihilation. In some cases, moreover, they preempted it: by ethnic cleansing in the Soviet-occupied territories of 1939–41 and by a string of NKVD atrocities in the desperate retreat of summer 1941. For all its operational failures and periodic military disasters, the Soviet state between 1941 and 1945 was hypercentralized, coercive, and brutally effective. For at least a decade, the Soviet economy had been a war economy; Soviet ideology and propaganda had dictated that war was inevitable and that Soviet people should be ready for it; and the agents of Soviet power at its many levels were habituated to violence to a greater degree than their counterparts in Nazi Germany (let alone those in the liberal democracies of the Alliance). If the Soviet system could not fight a war, then what could it do?

Nevertheless, the war experience had side effects that raised interesting questions for the future of Soviet political mobilization. In the late 1930s, the state had briefly threatened to swallow the Party as a ruling institution: the prewar purges had shown the terrifying power of the political police and the inability of even elite Party members to resist it. Yet, during the war, the Party had once again shown its indispensability as a source of loyal and reliable cadres and an interface between the ruling class and the society it dominated. Perhaps here we find the reverse of the 1930s' "statization" of the Party: something approaching a "partification" of the state. As Soviet fortunes in the war stabilized in 1942–3, Party structures made a comeback in the Soviet heartland, while in the newly occupied territories they were created from scratch.[14]

The war, moreover, gave a huge boost to the Communist Party as the mass institution of Soviet power. Between 1941 and 1945, 8.4 million new members and candidate members were recruited; almost four in every five of these came from the armed forces. By contrast, only a little more than 3 million new members and candidates had been admitted to the Party between 1936 and 1940. By the end of hostilities, two-thirds of the Party membership had joined during the war. The open-doors policy to admissions that was pursued until October 1944 meant that the Party membership became notably more "democratic." Almost a third of wartime admissions were classified as workers, and a quarter as peasants. The remaining 42 percent were the white-collar workers and intelligentsia that had been the focus of Party recruitment in the period 1937–41.[15]

The war established a connection between Party membership, patriotism, and self-sacrifice that had largely eroded in the twenty years since the civil war. Around 1.1 million Party members were called up for service in the early months of the war, and almost half of these became casualties in this same period. This shocking rate of attrition meant that, despite sharp increases in recruitment, Party membership fell from 4 million to just over 3 million at the end of 1941. By the start of 1946, membership had risen to 6 million, but these were raw recruits to Communism: only one-third had been in the Party before the German invasion.[16]

In the late 1940s measures were taken to bring procedural order to the chaotic recruitment patterns of the war years. Careful scrutiny of individual applications was resumed, with the result that Party membership saw net falls in 1948 and 1949, and only a modest rise of 500,000 over the period 1950–3. The tendency toward a more educated and white-collar membership was resumed after the hiatus of the war. At the same time, however, Party penetration of rural areas was far greater than hitherto, as the demobilized Party recruits of 1941–5 were redistributed around the USSR. Just before the war, Party organizations were to be found in only one collective farm in eight; by 1953 that proportion had risen to five out of six.[17]

Oscillations in Party membership policy were a constant feature of Soviet history. The Communist Party was required to be a mass party truly representative of Soviet society by virtue of including a healthy proportion of workers and peasants. But it was also a vanguard party, a custodian of Marxist-Leninist truth, and could not make itself too accessible if that was likely to bring the danger of ideological contamination or dilution. The postwar period accordingly saw a drive for what has been dubbed "Party revivalism": an effort to reclaim the Party from the armed forces into which it had come close to being subsumed during the war. Political commissars attached to army units had been synonymous with Party supervision of the military, but they were removed in the second year of the war; Party control had decreased even as the mass Party membership had risen steeply.

This was a trend that the postwar leadership was determined to reverse. Just over a year after the end of the war, in August 1946, the Central Committee decreed that Party secretaries in the armed forces operate independently of the military authorities, thus effectively reinstating the system of political commissars. The promotion of the party-state official Nikolai Bulganin to Minister of the Armed Forces in 1947, followed by his raising to the rank of Marshal of the Soviet Union later in the same year, was a further reassertion of Party influence at the expense of the military. Marshal Zhukov was unceremoniously demoted as Stalin crushed even the vaguest prospect of a Bonapartist challenge to his authority. Grass-roots Party organizations swelled with the return from the front of millions of members. Great efforts were made to rebuild spheres of activity specific to the Party, to undermine excessively cosy relationships that might exist between Party and state functionaries, and to restore the Party's watchdog function. The clearest public evidence of this "revivalism" came in the surge of propaganda and "ideological work" of all kinds. In Sverdlovsk oblast, for example, close to 15,000 people in 1946 were recorded as taking part regularly in agitation work. In the year from March 1946, the Sverdlovsk Party organization oversaw more than 100,000 lectures and speeches just on the subject of the new five-year plan.[18]

Yet the Party was by no means the only powerful institution in the postwar USSR; some of the others, moreover, did not need to be "revived," as they emerged from the war extremely robust. Foremost among them was the police, which had a vast repressive apparatus and an economic empire of its own. At the start of 1941, Stalin carried out one of several reshuffles that the police force underwent during the Soviet period: he reduced its unitary power by splitting it into the People's Commissariat for Internal Affairs (NKVD), which took care of the economic functions of the police (notably the administration of the system of labor camps), and the People's Commissariat for State Security, which would carry out the deportations of national groups in 1943–4 and the later repression of nationalist guerrillas in Lithuania and Western Ukraine. All told, the NKVD probably controlled between 600,000 and 700,000 troops during the war.[19]

The multiple functions of the police were embodied by its main overseer in the second half of the Stalin period, Lavrentii Beria. Back in the 1930s, Beria had carried out a purge of the Georgian Party apparatus that was brutal even by Stalinist standards, and he had been summoned to Moscow to head the entire NKVD in 1938. He is second only to Stalin as a notorious symbol of Soviet political violence. But Beria was also put in charge of a number of complex technical and administrative tasks: the evacuation of industrial enterprises to the east in the early stages of the war, the atomic bomb project in the second half of the 1940s, and the management of the vast economic empire that the Gulag had become by the time he took it over. During the war the police gained very broad economic functions, and Beria had an exceptionally wide brief that included, besides general oversight of domestic policing, armaments and munitions production. During the war, the NKVD provided tens of thousands of laborers for key sectors such as weapons, ammunition, aviation, and tank production.[20]

Beria's operational involvement in the security agencies was weakened by yet another reshuffle in 1946: the Ministry of State Security (MGB), which had responsibility for especially sensitive political matters, came under the control of his rival, Viktor Abakumov. But Beria retained oversight over the NKVD (known from March 1946 as the MVD), still by far the larger and more powerful of the two state security organizations. Combined with his roles as full Politburo member and deputy chairman of the Council of Ministers, this made him one of the three or four most powerful men in the Soviet Union.[21] The postwar Soviet police continued to have broad powers and a heavy workload. The reconstruction effort required hundreds of thousands of forced laborers, and there was plenty of real or imagined dissent to repress, especially in the newly incorporated western borderlands. Documents from the archive of the political police reveal just how invasive state supervision was in the late 1940s. At the very end of 1946, Beria reported to Stalin that the organs of state security had registered 4,616 letters in Voronezh region, and 3,275 in Stalingrad region, that mentioned the famine in southern Russia. The following month Abakumov, the new Minister for State Security, delivered a report on complaints of hunger contained in letters from Leningrad students.[22] Throughout the postwar period, the authorities were alert to any hint of "anti-Communist" attitudes among young people. In the postwar Stalin years, the political police identified more than two dozen illegal youth organizations. The ringleaders could expect 25 years in the camps or worse.[23]

Beria's most important political ally by the late 1940s was Georgii Malenkov, the epitome of the Party functionary grown powerful through wartime service. Born in 1902, Malenkov received an education at the Higher Technical School in Moscow, where he ran that institution's Party organization. Later on he entered the apparatus of the Central Committee and spent the prewar years in increasingly responsible posts in the Moscow regional Party organization and the Central Committee secretariat. His real launch to prominence, however, came during the war. Besides retaining control of the crucial secretariat, he was made one of the original five members of the GKO and took a wide range of responsibilities in the wartime economy. As an economic fixer, he headed the Party equivalent of Beria's police empire.

But this empire needed its viceroys and lord lieutenants. The ambitious targets of the GKO were not achievable without the energy and know-how of the men running the factories. Industrial managers were a powerful lobbying group at the end of the war, and they could not be straightforwardly beaten down by Stalin: they were too important and too numerous. Branch ministries, too, had some power to obstruct or to reshape the directives of the leadership. Even where effective mechanisms of central control did exist, the command economy was so large, complex, and untransparent that ministers and their bureaucracies had real opportunities to follow their own course.

Industrial ministries were an exceptionally well-resourced set of interest groups. But the trend to greater institutional stability and robustness was found even in one of the more beleaguered professions of the late Stalin era: the justice system. Judges and procuracy officials came under enormous pressure in the late 1940s to mete out harsher sentences – especially for the crime of "theft of socialist property" – but they acted with more circumspection than might have been expected under the circumstances. Procuracy officials had strong incentives not to put forward to trial cases that would be thrown out by judges as this would reflect badly on their performance. Although the campaign against theft achieved its goals of rounding up more culprits and giving them longer sentences, it is notable that it did not bring a slide to the summary justice characteristic of the Great Terror, and it did not seriously compromise the rest of the legal system.[24]

All in all, the postwar period continued a trend whose origins can be traced back to the interlude of 1939–41 between Terror and world war. Political and administrative life became less unruly for those in office. The nomenklatura of the Central Committee – the list of posts vetted by the top Party elite – grew to more than 45,000 by March 1953.[25] Moreover, this nomenklatura was not subject to panoptic control from the top; Stalin was not able to micromanage personnel policy in the way that is sometimes attributed to him. The nomenklatura had numerous points of entry, and was closely bound up with the network of patron–client relations among the military-bureaucratic ruling class that formed during the war. This was less a monolith than a living organism.[26]

This is not to say that the incumbents of the nomenklatura were anything other than loyal Stalinists. The postwar regional representatives of Soviet power – the first secretaries of the regional Party committees (obkoms) – were slightly younger and better educated than their prewar predecessors.[27] They owed their education, training, and promotion to the Stalinist system; the ideological controversies of the 1920s and 1930s were for them abstractions. Most importantly, they had their common war experience to bind them. If their war record passed muster – though that was no foregone conclusion, especially in borderland territories that had undergone or come close to occupation – they had a source of authority and legitimacy that none of the desperately beleaguered managers and administrators of the 1930s could match.[28]

It is, then, inaccurate to speak of the late (postwar) Stalin period as one of unremitting repression, as a slightly less indiscriminate follow-up to the Terror of 1937–8. Rather, this was a time when power relations in the Soviet Union, after close to three decades of bloody turmoil, were beginning to stabilize. For those on the wrong end of these power relations – inmates of the Gulag, deported Chechens or Volga Germans, collective farmers, conscripted workers stranded in factories hundreds of kilometers from their homes – life in the Soviet Union continued to be bleak. But the small but growing group of people on the right end of them had much to look forward to. Violence was on the retreat, but so was unruly mass participation. A local Party boss was now less likely to be brought down by an anonymous denunciation than in the 1930s. The political police remained a major force, but it relied increasingly on regular informants, who were carefully recruited and vetted. By September 1951, the branch of the police that combated economic crime ("theft of socialist property") had more than 380,000 informants on its books, which represented a ninefold increase over 1942.[29] The target was now not "counterrevolution" in general but rather much more specific criminal and subversive threats.[30]

The center employed various methods of control over the regions: the Central Committee had its own inspection apparatus, Party and state organs had control commissions, the procuracy could investigate alleged criminal activity, the political police retained its menacing presence, and first Party secretaries from the regions were regularly called upon to account for themselves at meetings of the secretariat and orgburo of the Central Committee. Checks on their activities could be provoked by the anonymous letters that were always streaming into Moscow. Local Party bosses were regularly held to account for departing from planned campaigns and for a range of other abuses of their position. All the same, this was no return to the 1930s. The bloodletting was on a far smaller scale, and cadre changes most often did not end the careers (let alone the lives) of the objects of the reshuffle. Officials moved from region to region, or from region to Moscow and back. They might also interrupt their careers for periods of study in higher Party institutions. Here was a new generation of Party administrators, unquestionably loyal to Stalin, but with enough physical security to spin a dense web of horizontal and vertical ties.[31]

The Patrimonial Principle of Governance: The Last Years of Stalin

The main exceptions to this trend of greater physical security and autonomy for the elite came in Stalin's inner circle. In the postwar years, the loyal Stalinist henchmen in and around the Kremlin – Molotov, Kaganovich, Mikoian, Malenkov, Beria, Zhdanov – would have needed much convincing that power relations were stabilizing. They spent much of their working lives with an elderly and irascible dictator, who combined some of the mental symptoms of arterio-sclerosis with an undiminished capacity for intrigue. Foreign minister Viacheslav Molotov was the first to incur Stalin's displeasure, ostensibly for relaxing controls over the Western press in Moscow; at the end of the decade he was savaged for his supposed responsibility for the diplomatic failures of 1949 (the Berlin block-ade, the creation of NATO, the establishment of the Federal Republic of Germany) and was forced to join in the denunciation of his own wife that would lead to her arrest and dispatch to the Gulag. Malenkov was kept on tenterhooks for a few months in 1946 after his perceived failures in managing aircraft production; a decade earlier he would almost certainly have been arrested. Andrei Zhdanov was forced to issue a public reprimand to his own son, Iurii, who had dared to question the scientific conclusions of the Soviet Union's premier quack agronomist, Trofim Lysenko. Stalin most likely never had any intention of purging his closest associates. He did, however, mean to keep them on their toes and make them suspicious of each other. The inner circle of the late 1940s was divided according to institutional affiliation. The "Party revivalist" Zhdanov competed for influence with the statists Beria and Malenkov, whose power base lay in the security forces and the economic agencies. All the while, Stalin retained his mastery of the secret police.[32]

His continued control of the apparatus of violence was demonstrated one more time in the postwar era. In addition to humiliating the members of his inner circle, Stalin unleashed terror on the upper Party elite in the notorious Leningrad Affair of 1949. This case demonstrated how dangerous it could still be to arouse the dictator's suspicions. Quite by chance, at the start of 1949, reports reached Stalin of a trade fair in Leningrad that had not undergone the due process of authorization. Nikolai Voznesensky, a prominent wartime administrator, now the Chairman of Gosplan, and a man with a Leningrad background, came to be suspected of unduly favoring his native city. Shortly after, a relatively minor failure to amend upward planning targets for the first quarter of 1949 brought Voznesensky under further hostile scrutiny. Fresh allegations duly appeared, and Voznesensky was found to be guilty of the cardinal sin of concealing important information from the top leadership. Stalin's suspicion of any hint of independent activity in the USSR's second city, his hatred of administrative insubordination and his susceptibility to conspiracy theories came together with dire consequences. Voznesensky and a number of his Leningrad associates were arrested and eventually executed, while Gosplan was subjected to a less lethal purge of personnel.

The Leningrad and Gosplan Affairs were a shocking echo of the Great Terror, but no less remarkable is the fact that they were the only case of high-level bloodletting in the late Stalin era. For all that the dictator had not ceased to be paranoid, he retained a streak of pragmatism, and had little interest in unleashing a frenzy of mutual incrimination within the Party; conversely, members of the leading group were not bent on each other's destruction as they had been in the 1930s and would again be for a short period in 1953. Whatever the hardening of his arteries, Stalin understood that did not have to fear outright revolt from an elite that he had formed. But that still left him with the problem of retaining adequate control over a vast country with economic structures of ever increasing complexity at a time when his powers were starting to fail. Stalin was a long-distance dictator in the last years of his life. Between 1945 and 1951, he averaged three months per year in the south.

In these changed circumstances, Stalin once again showed himself to be an extraordinarily able political operator. His day-to-day intervention in technicalities became less frequent. Important reorganizations of the economic system in February 1947 left decision-making in the hands of specialized committees in the Council of Ministers. Branches of the bureaucracy were left to develop their own forms of administration. But these trends toward rationalization in the state apparatus were juxtaposed by the extreme informality of elite politics. Although Politburo meetings became more regular from the end of 1945, real power still resided in an inner circle that met separately from the full Politburo – and very often in the informal setting of Stalin's dacha, where policy discussions were followed by late-night binges and film viewings. Stalin kept his associates in their place by humiliating them from time to time, and also retained for himself the right to intervene with decisive effect on any issue. Thus, for all the modern administrative trappings of the Soviet Union in the late 1940s, the exercise of power was thoroughly patrimonial: it lay at the discretion of a ruler who could ignore formal rules and institutions if he chose, thereby demonstrating his de facto ownership of the state. When Stalin sent out certain signals, even complex bureaucracies were bound to respond accordingly.

The patrimonialism, however, rested on one man, which rather begged the question of what would replace it when he departed the scene. It was clear that no one would be able to take on Stalin's precise role in the future. All his potential successors shared their position of humiliating dependence at the dictator's court. This common experience actually made them the least fractious ruling elite in Soviet history: there was every prospect of collective leadership, at least for a while. But, in Stalin's absence, there would be no procedures to resolve conflicts or succession within the leadership.

The other point was that whoever did end up as Stalin's successor would have the opportunity to reinvigorate political structures that had been largely bypassed under the dictator. The main deliberative forum of the Party elite, the Central Committee, had been emptied of meaning in the late Stalin period, but now it was available again for political service. Likewise the Politburo, which in Stalin's last reshuffle of 1952 was turned into a "Presidium" with an expanded and younger membership. Beyond the Kremlin walls, too, there were signs of political awakening in the early 1950s. The unexpected convocation of the Nineteenth Party Congress in 1952 – thirteen years after the Eighteenth – broadened political participation in the elite and gave aspiring leaders a new kind of platform. If this degree of de-Stalinization was possible even in Stalin's lifetime, what might the future hold without him?[33]

— The Succession Problem: Legitimacy without Dictatorship —

The new leadership wasted little time. On the morning of 1 March, Stalin was discovered, lying paralyzed by a stroke, on the floor of his dacha. Over the next four days, as he drifted toward death, his inner circle hatched plans for the future. On 5 March, with Stalin in the last hours of his life, the members of this group assembled a joint meeting of the top political institutions of the Soviet Union: the Central Committee, the Council of Ministers, and the Presidium of the Supreme Soviet. Malenkov and Beria stage-managed proceedings and nominated each other for what were ostensibly the two top jobs in the Soviet Union: Beria was made head of a newly consolidated Ministry of Internal Affairs, which combined regular policing with jurisdiction over matters of state security, while Malenkov became Chairman of the Council of Ministers (in other words, head of the Soviet government). Viacheslav Molotov, Stalin's longest associate and the senior member of the leadership in career terms, was given the Ministry of Foreign Affairs. Nikita Khrushchev was evidently a notch lower in the pecking order: his power base was the Party, which lacked the obvious executive clout of the government apparatus and the police. In mid-March he took the position of senior Central Committee secretary (which had just been relinquished by Malenkov, who seems to have been forced by colleagues to restrict himself to his government job).

Stalin's successors paid attention to institutions as well as personnel. They immediately trimmed the Presidium back down to the size of the former Politburo, thereby creating for themselves a strong executive body. This was to be a tiny oligarchy rather than a bloated committee designed to rubber-stamp dictatorial rule. The restoration of the Presidium as a meaningful political body was accompanied, over the following months and years, by a return to a more routine use of broader Party gatherings. Central Committee plenums were held regularly (for the most part twice a year) and were an occasion for the leaders to set out their policies, mobilize support, claim credit, apportion blame, and settle scores with each other.

Given that formal institutions had until recently been overridden by Stalin's personal authority, the field was open for aspiring leaders to build up new power bases and use political structures to their advantage. At Stalin's death, Malenkov appeared to have secure control over the state bureaucracy and the economic administration, while Beria had at his fingertips the terrifying Soviet apparatus of violence. Khrushchev's institutional home, the Party, while hardly insignificant, seemed to give him rather less political leverage. But the collection of ageing Stalinists who made up the post-Stalin leadership must have known from bitter experience that the real clout of institutions in the Soviet system depended less on their formal powers but on the way they were controlled and manipulated by the men at the top. The NKVD, for example, might be the handmaid of the Party or its executioner: which was it to be?

Khrushchev won the inevitable power struggle because he proved himself the most able political operator in the post-Stalin leadership. As the leadership contender with a power base in the Party, he was able to draw on a vast political organization and on its unique ideological cachet. Appeals to the spirit of "Leninism" were much more plausible coming from the First Secretary than from the head of the Council of Ministers or (still less) the NKVD. Khrushchev was in a position to benefit from – having helped to bring about – the growth of "reciprocal accountability" between the ruling circle and the wider Party elite of the Central Committee.[34]

Khrushchev also had more than his fair share of the low cunning essential for success at the highest levels of Soviet politics. He picked off his rivals in time-honored fashion. The first victim was Lavrentii Beria, the notorious secret police chief, who in the second quarter of 1953 came out with an extraordinary series of enlightened policy initiatives. First he set in motion a wave of amnesties that freed more than a million people from the Gulag and began to reveal the extent of Stalinist repression. Then he stated his intention to reduce Russian chauvinism in the troublesome western borderlands of the Soviet Union: the Baltic republics and Western Ukraine. No less astonishing, he led the way in softening Soviet policy on the thorny German question. When the government of the GDR announced a series of increases in the output demanded from industry and construction, its leaders were summoned to Moscow and ordered by Beria to adopt milder policies.[35]

The immediate effects were dramatic. The mixed signals from the East German leadership caused unrest in Berlin, which quickly spread to the provinces. Before long, several hundred thousand Germans were engaged in strikes and antigovernment demonstrations. The inevitable suppression of this opposition brought more than 50 deaths among the demonstrators, a few dozen more among Party functionaries, 10,000 arrests, and about 20 death sentences.[36] For Beria the consequences were dire. His comrades in the Soviet leadership had never imagined that his intentions were honorable, and his failed foreign policy initiatives gave them an excuse to act. After an elaborate conspiracy instigated by Khrushchev, Beria was arrested in the Kremlin at the end of June 1953. The plotters recruited army men to seize their colleague at a Presidium meeting: such was Beria's control of the police and security forces that no one else who knew how to handle weapons was reliable. Beria was subjected to a secret trial in December, sentenced to death, and dispatched by a general.[37]

Khrushchev's power struggle with Malenkov was more protracted. After Stalin's death, Malenkov was widely perceived to be first among equals. He was confident enough to take the initiative in major policy areas such as agriculture and international affairs. But he was slightly weakened by the removal of Beria, with whom he had been closely associated, and in September 1953 saw Khrushchev confirmed as First Secretary of the Central Committee. In the Soviet system, the Party apparatus was, despite the depredations of the Stalin era, the best power base available, and Khrushchev was now in a position to take it firmly under his control. He wasted little time in purging regional first secretaries and appointing his own men in their stead. Annoyed that Malenkov had stolen a march on him by putting forward an agricultural reform package in August 1953, he seized back the initiative with further-reaching counterproposals at the

FIGURE 2.2   A man of the people: Khrushchev in Kuibyshev region, 1958.
Source: © Alexandre Ustinov / PhotoSoyuz.

September 1953 Central Committee plenum, while the following year he launched the eye-catching Virgin Lands scheme in order to boost Soviet agriculture in traditional mobilizational fashion (see Chapter 4). Khrushchev gained further political advantage by pouncing on heterodox statements by Malenkov on international relations, the role of the Party, and the balance between heavy and light industry. All the while, the awkward legacy of the Stalin era checked Malenkov's political momentum: Khrushchev managed revelations of Stalinist crimes in a way that cast shadows on his rival. In January 1955, Malenkov was hauled over the coals at a Party plenum, accused of spreading dark thoughts about a nuclear third world war and of excessively friendly relations with Beria. With his back to the wall, he relinquished his post as head of government, though he remained in the Presidium until he and other disgruntled colleagues made a bid for power in June 1957 that brought his final disgrace.[38]

As is often the case in politics – not just in the Soviet Union – the differences between Khrushchev and Malenkov were as much a matter of presentation as of substance. Khrushchev outmaneuvered his rival, who was less careful in tailoring his message to key political constituencies, even if Malenkov's actual policies were little different from those of Khrushchev, and certainly no worse. Khrushchev's reputation as a hands-on manager and as a safe custodian of Party ideology was key to his success. He was able to pledge his commitment to the mainstays of the Soviet system – heavy industry, the military, the Party – while making credible initiatives in neglected policy areas like agriculture and light industry.[39]

All this was practically indistinguishable in form from earlier Soviet practice – with the crucial difference that, once Beria had been executed, Soviet leaders were no longer killed for disagreeing with the top dog. But the astonishing thing about this latest power struggle in the Kremlin was that it was conducted against the backdrop of fundamental ideological revisions. The Soviet Union, that ideological state par excellence, began to undermine what had been central to its ideological vision: the infallibility of Stalin's interpretation of Marxism–Leninism. This modern theocracy was ripping up a substantial part of its own scripture.

— The Soviet Union as Theocracy: De-Stalinization and After —

In the early spring of 1953, even the least attentive Kremlinologist would have noticed the dead dictator's sudden loss of prominence. Stalin disappeared from the Soviet press toward the end of March 1953, and the publication of his collected works stopped at volume 13. It was already clear that he would not usurp Lenin as a focus for Communist commemoration and adoration. It was also clear that Stalin's successors needed to define a historical course independent of their predecessor. But it was still an open question how exactly they would handle their ideological legacy.

The ensuing change of ideological orientation was a tentative and fraught process. The key terms of the era served notice of the improvised and politicized nature of what would soon be known outside the Soviet Union as "de-Stalinization." This was branded a campaign not against "Stalinism" or "Stalin" but rather against "the cult of personality." The latter phrase had a pedigree in Bolshevik circles as a rhetorical weapon against socialist opponents, who earlier in the twentieth century were accused of an unhealthy "anarchist" enthusiasm for the values of the individual "personality" at the expense of those of the "collective." The term was adopted by Malenkov at a Central Committee plenum as early as April 1953. But it was used in circumlocutory fashion. To make direct criticism of Stalin so soon after his death was unthinkable. Indeed, Malenkov even cited Stalin's authority in support of the values of "collective leadership" over those of the individual "personality": "Many of those present know that Comrade Stalin several time made comments in this vein and strongly condemned the un-Marxist, socialist revolutionary understanding of the role of the personality in history." By June 1953, however, the phrase "cult of personality" began to be publicly construed in opposition to Stalin; two-and-a-half years later it would provide the key phrase in the title of Khrushchev's famous "secret" speech of denunciation to the Twentieth Party Congress.[40]

A more tangible sign of ideological revision was the series of amnesties that took place in the spring of 1953. In the first instance, on Beria's initiative, the more prominent Party victims of the later Stalin period were released or exonerated. Victims of the anti-Semitic campaigns of the early 1950s were rehabilitated. Molotov's wife Polina Zhemchuzhina was reinstated in the Party within three weeks of the dictator's death. As yet nothing was said of the crimes of the 1930s. Then, at the July 1953 plenum, Malenkov spoke publicly of Stalin's "cult of personality." The process of re-evaluating the Stalin period gained new impetus in early 1954 as Khrushchev tightened his political grip. The victims of the Leningrad Affair were a high priority for rehabilitation, not least because this was a way of undermining Malenkov. In May 1954, a centrally organized committee started reassessing the cases of those convicted of "counterrevolutionary crimes." A further commission, under the chairmanship of Voroshilov, considered relaxing measures against the "special settlers" (groups of people exiled under Stalin); a resolution followed on 5 July 1954.

"Rehabilitation" was another curious term of the post-Stalin era. It had no legal status in 1953 but was quickly taken up in post-Stalin public discourse and gained official status after the Twentieth Party Congress. It enabled the de-Stalinizing leadership – in the first instance Khrushchev – to make discretionary judgments about who should be considered legitimate victims of the Stalin era but also to give these judgments a legal basis.[41] Progress was slow and cautious; all important decisions were referred to the Presidium. The top leadership could agree that rehabilitation must have certain limits. Trotskyites, Socialist Revolutionaries, Mensheviks, and other socialist deviants could expect no pardon; as far as possible, there was to be no return of confiscated property to special settlers; and Ukrainian and Baltic nationalists were to stay in places of exile. It was increasingly acknowledged that terrible things had happened in the Stalin era, and the question of personal responsibility hung uncomfortably in the air, given that Malenkov, Molotov, Khrushchev, and others had been politically prominent at precisely the time these "crimes" were taking place. Beria was a convenient scapegoat, but even he could not have borne all of the responsibility.

In March 1954, the leadership received a memorandum on the activities of the Special Board of the Ministry of Internal Affairs. Between November 1934 and September 1953, this body had sentenced 442,531 people, of whom 10,101 had been shot, 360,921 imprisoned and 67,539 exiled. It was revealed to have perpetrated numerous abuses, such as the re-arrest in 1948 of people who had already served their sentences. In the six months from August 1953 to March 1954, the authorities had received almost 80,000 complaints from or on behalf of those convicted for "counterrevolutionary" crimes. There were currently close to half a million such people behind barbed wire.[42]

Besides taking aim at Beria and his men, Khrushchev could also cast sly aspersions on his current comrades and rivals for power. But he also found himself inching toward open criticism of Stalin himself. At a meeting of Leningrad Party activists in May 1954, Khrushchev acknowledged that Stalin was a "great man, a Marxist genius," but observed that "even people like that should not be given the rights that he enjoyed." Khrushchev also mentioned Stalin's erratic and irritable behavior in his later years of deteriorating health.[43]

The categories of victims eligible for rehabilitation broadened in the middle of 1954. Memos of May 1954 pointed out the plight of those exiled and imprisoned for various political crimes. Many of these people had now been in exile for more than ten years, and opinion was building in favor of their release. The immediate result was a government decree of 5 July 1954 that removed certain residence restrictions on special settlers. But political rehabilitation remained limited. When Anna Akhmatova wrote a petition on behalf of her son, it was turned down on 6 July 1954 on the grounds that he was correctly convicted for anti-Soviet utterances.[44]

As the months went by, the Soviet leaders edged toward a more robust public position on Stalin's legacy. A Presidium meeting of 5 November 1955 considered the question of how to mark the anniversary of Stalin's birth, 21 December, which until then had been a significant date in the calendar. The Central Committee had declared itself against the idea of holding public meetings, but Kaganovich and Voroshilov were not so sure. As Voroshilov noted, "The people won't like it if we don't hold meetings." Bulganin and Mikoian took the opposite view, and by the end of the discussion Kaganovich was on the defensive.[45]

Even thornier issues came up as the Twentieth Party Congress approached. At a meeting of 1 February 1956, Molotov insisted that in his forthcoming speech Khrushchev must acknowledge that Stalin was a "Lenin's great successor." Others, however, were shocked by revelations that it was now impossible to pass over in silence. As one comrade in the Presidium observed: "If these facts are true, what kind of Communism is this? You can't forgive this." The elder statesmen argued for a more qualified response. Voroshilov agreed that "the Party must know the truth," but argued that this truth should "be offered up as life dictates." In other words, times had been hard under Stalin, and much of the cruelty of the era could be justified in terms of historical circumstances. Khrushchev summed up in emotional style: "Stalin was devoted to the cause of socialism, but by barbaric means. He destroyed the Party. He was no Marxist. He wiped out everything sacred in people. Subjected everything to his caprices. We won't talk about terror at the congress. We need to take the line of putting Stalin in his rightful place (by purging posters and books)."[46]

The impetus for denunciation grew a few days later when a commission appointed to investigate the causes of mass repression in the 1930s delivered its results. The report gave a figure of 353,074 shot in 1937, and 328,618 in 1938.[47] Unlike the Red Terror of 1918–19, this violence could not be justified. The leadership had to think fast how they would present this news to the wider Party. Presidium members responded emotionally, both justifying themselves and conveying their sense that something had to be done to account for these crimes. Although Molotov continued to sound a note of caution and admiration for Stalin, the general view was that "if we don't say anything, we'll show dishonesty toward the congress."[48]

The key question of what exactly to say was resolved by Khrushchev and his speech-writers over the following two weeks. After receiving a draft of his speech on 18 February, Khrushchev dictated additions on 19 February that included much more personal criticisms of Stalin. After yet more revisions, on 23 February a near-final draft was sent round to Presidium members, but Khrushchev still had time to dictate further additions before he gave his performance on 25 February. The speech was delivered in a highly charged style, and Khrushchev did not hold back from the unscripted asides that were his specialty. He delivered a stomach-churning indictment of Stalin's assault on the Party in the Terror of the 1930s, but also took aim at Stalin's record as war leader and gave vent to his very personal fury at Stalin's self-aggrandizing style of rule.

The fact of this semipublic denunciation is so remarkable that it is all the more important to realize how haphazard, emotional, and opportunistic a business it was. Stalin's successors did not distance themselves from Stalin because they wished to right historical wrongs or admit their own or their party's responsibility. Although any account of Khrushchev's motivations is somewhat speculative, his decision to give the Secret Speech can plausibly be seen as being driven more by tactical considerations and by personal resentment than by a drive for ideological renewal. He seems to have been genuinely shocked by the mounting firsthand evidence of the sufferings of people he had known: it is one thing to know about "repressions" in general terms, quite another to read and hear firsthand testimony. But Khrushchev was also burning with indignation at the humiliations Stalin had inflicted on him personally. And he was confident, as ever, that he would be able to manage the awkward issue of his own complicity in Stalinist violence while implicating his colleagues as necessary.

However, the speech was much more significant than a mere tactical coup: it had profound implications for Soviet politics and society that were not foreseen by Khrushchev and his entourage. For a regime unusually well versed in the black arts of propaganda, the Soviet leadership made a peculiarly bad job of managing the public impact of the Secret Speech. No foreigners were present at the session where Khrushchev spoke, but on 27 February the Central Committee apparatus made available the text to the leaders of various "fraternal" parties who were in Moscow for the congress (a total of 13 people); the copies were to be returned before these individuals' departure. Lesser foreign leaders received merely a summary of the speech. On 28 March, a Presidium resolution permitted further representatives of foreign Communist parties to acquaint themselves with the speech (a total of 16 people mainly from Asia and America). How socialist parties abroad managed the revelations was left very much up to them; most responded hesitantly in the absence of strong signals from Moscow, seeking guidance as to how widely the speech should be disseminated. They increasingly felt betrayed as they were left in an information vacuum while the Western press got started on the story. The lack of coordination was demonstrated visually by the portrait policy adopted by different Communist regimes for the May Day festivities. Moscow silently withdrew Stalin from its pageantry, Beijing kept him, while Warsaw reinstated Communist leaders who had been repressed in the 1930s and rehabilitated just before the Twentieth Party Congress.[49]

The public response was similarly rudderless in the Soviet Union itself. Nothing was said in the Soviet press until, finally, on 28 March, *Pravda* carried an item entitled "Why Is the Cult of Personality Alien to the Spirit of Marxism–Leninism?" Then, on 30 June 1956, a Central Committee decree entitled "On Overcoming the Cult of Personality and Its Consequences" restated the basic propositions of the Secret Speech while also setting limits to historical critique. But the regime also took steps to check the momentum of de-Stalinization. On New Year's Eve 1956 Khrushchev proposed a toast to Stalin, and by 1957 the phrase "cult of personality" was nowhere to be found in the eastern European Communist press. Poland even eschewed the phrase "Stalinist period," preferring the coy "former period."[50]

Such evasiveness fooled no one, not least because Khrushchev's oration had never been particularly secret in the first place. A Central Committee decree of 5 March 1956 provided for a brochure with Khrushchev's speech to be sent round to republic and district Party committees. In due course its contents were made known to tens of thousands of people around the country at local Party meetings, and Party organizations were clamoring to receive more copies.[51] All in all, 7 million Party members and 18 million Komsomol members would hear the speech.[52]

The oral dissemination of the Secret Speech led to impassioned discussions at the grass roots. Ideological plenipotentiaries were dispatched to manage public opinion among ordinary Party members. One such messenger was the Komsomol functionary Mikhail Gorbachev, who was sent to gloss the Secret Speech to Komsomol and Party members in one Stavropol district. His colleagues – in particular the local Party secretary – regarded this as a thankless task. Gorbachev

recalled encountering a wide variety of responses. The younger and more educated, and those whose families had personal experience of Stalinist violence, were
receptive to Khrushchev's condemnation of the "Cult." Others refused to believe
the revelations, or were simply baffled why Khrushchev had chosen to make
them.[53] A metropolitan ambassador for the Secret Speech was Anna Pankratova,
the main editor of the major journal *Issues in History*, who gave a series of nine
lectures in Leningrad between 20 and 23 March 1956 to audiences consisting of
ideological workers and historians. These events were well attended (the combined
audience was almost 6,000), and a total of 825 questions were submitted in writing
to the speaker. What emerged was that already, less than a month after the Secret
Speech, even the loyal Soviet intelligentsia was willing to go much further than the
Party in reassessing the ideological foundations of Soviet socialism. One reason
was that the Party had made such a poor job of imposing a single interpretation
of the Secret Speech. Party meetings around the Soviet Union were stormy affairs
where vigorous criticism of the Stalinist past was sometimes seen by the central
authorities to cross the line into hyperbole and anti-Sovietism. Never, in Soviet
practice, had the famous distinction between criticism and self-criticism been so
blurred. And this was taking place in disciplined Party circles; less circumspect
members of Soviet society were tearing down Stalin portraits in public places.[54]

The prevailing confusion was picked up by students in elite institutions such
as Moscow State University, where 1956 was a year of vigorous political discussion. The Twentieth Party Congress was taken as a sign that independent thought
and debate were now their prerogative. If student debate had been loyal to the
post-Stalin Party line until 1956, it turned more tempestuous in the second half
of that year.[55]

Over the months and years to come, the Party leadership would make efforts
to rein in the criticism of the Soviet order that it had itself unleashed. Little more
than a month after the Party congress, stern measures were taken against "hostile
sallies" in one outspoken Party organization.[56] People who defaced pictures or
statues of Stalin could be branded hooligans or criminals.[57] Another tactic was
diversion: the Party made efforts to deflect the thrust of de-Stalinization from a
critique of authority to the quest for measures to improve the economy.[58] At the
same time, rehabilitation continued to be highly selective. In the autumn of 1956,
the Presidium set up a commission to "prevent hostile activity by recently rehabilitated persons." Victims of Stalinism needed relatives to appeal on their behalf;
Trotskyites, Socialist Revolutionaries and the most prominent victims of the show
trials of the 1930s were still beyond the pale. On the international front, the crises
of 1956 in Hungary and Poland gave the leadership cause for second thoughts
about the whole enterprise of de-Stalinization: a domestic crackdown duly followed at the end of the year.

All the while, de-Stalinization continued to serve as a tactic of post-Stalin political struggle. At the June 1957 plenum where Khrushchev beat off an attempted coup by his rivals in the leadership, he was able to ask Molotov Kaganovich, Malenkov and Voroshilov pointed questions about their involvement in Stalinist terror while ignoring similar – and equally pertinent – questions that were asked of him. After the plenum, the pace of rehabilitation would slow – perhaps because Khrushchev no longer needed it for his political cause. Over the next few years, de-Stalinization would wax and wane. It reached a new peak with the removal at the end of October 1961 of Stalin's body from the mausoleum on Red Square. But the Twenty-Second Party Congress, which generated the momentum for this symbolic gesture, presented a more stable script for narrating the crimes of the Stalin era. Awkward questions – notably regarding the complicity of other members of the leadership – were put firmly in the shadows, where they would remain until the late 1980s.[59]

Nonetheless, the turbulent de-Stalinizing phase under Khrushchev had brought an astonishing and irreversible change in the relationship between the ruling party and its subjects, and it had catapulted back into public discourse a term with a substantial Soviet pedigree: *demokratizatsiia*.

The Soviet Union as a Democracy

"Democracy" is a politicized notion, and perhaps nowhere more so than in the history of the USSR. It was usually invoked by Soviet leaders not because of any yearning for popular involvement in government but as a means of achieving specific political ends. Campaigns for "democracy" signaled not a breakthrough to popular mobilization but a redistribution of power among political agencies. A good example was the "democratization" campaign that preceded the Nineteenth Party Congress in 1952, which came quite unexpectedly, a full 13 years after the Eighteenth Congress. "Party revivalist" rhetoric, which had surged just after the war but abated in the late 1940s, had a resurgence, while the ageing dictator was a curiously remote figure; one scholar has seen here signs of "de-Stalinization under Stalin." The leading contenders for the succession, Khrushchev and Malenkov, could use this platform to build their own legitimacy and their bureaucratic power base. Khrushchev, as a man with deep roots in the Party apparatus, was rather better placed to do this than the more technocratic Malenkov.[60]

The early post-Stalin years indicated that, for all the rising power of the state economic agencies in the late Stalin period, the Communist Party remained the key power base for an aspiring Soviet leader. When forced to choose between state and Party jobs, Malenkov chose the former, perhaps underestimating the leverage enjoyed by the Party. The First Secretary of the Communist Party might not have had direct control over the "commanding heights" of the economy, but he was in a position to control key personnel areas and to direct the terms and the drift of political discourse at crucial moments.

"Party democracy" was Khrushchev's salvation at the moment when he faced his greatest political threat. By the middle of 1957, a majority of Presidium members had turned against Khrushchev because of his erratic behavior and his humiliation and demotion of them personally. Taking advantage of Khrushchev's absence for a week at the start of June, they confronted him at a meeting of the Presidium later in the month. Stalling for time, Khrushchev insisted that the decision of the Presidium be ratified by a plenum of the Central Committee. Facing a struggle for political survival, Khrushchev was able to mobilize enough support from regional Party bosses at the plenum to prevail over his opponents from what was soon dubbed the "Anti-Party Group." Its leading figures – Molotov, Malenkov, and Kaganovich – were disgraced and removed to undesirable minor posts.

This was an unprecedented moment in Soviet politics: a time when regional leaders had the opportunity to settle a power struggle at the top. Never mind that this was a measure taken by Khrushchev in extremis, or that he was not averse to the palace coup as a political tactic when it was to his advantage (as had been the case with Beria). The fact remained that appeals to a constituency wider than the top leadership were characteristic of Khrushchev's style. In this sense, Khrushchev could lay claim to a political inheritance of "Leninist" democracy. The final confirmation of his success at changing the political culture of the Soviet elite came in 1964 when he was removed from power in much the same way.

Democracy, of course, is a difficult notion – especially in a political system with no genuinely contested elections. But for the Soviet Union to call its political life "democratic" was slightly more than a propaganda exercise. Such claims rested on numerous forms of assembly, discussion, and representation. In the Soviet Union, single-candidate elections were treated with remarkable earnestness. Since the Supreme Soviet elections of 1937, voting had been widely promoted as a civic ritual; election statistics claimed near-universal turnout.[61] By 1959, the Soviet Union had 57,000 representative state institutions with a total of 1.8 million deputies. According to data presented at a Party plenum, 14 million people (every tenth adult) were elected to the soviets between 1939 and 1964. At election times there were about 2 million electoral commissions staffed by about 8 million people. Their efforts were supplemented by those of hundreds of thousands of "agitators," whose role was to knock on people's doors, explain to them the salient political issues of the day, and bring them out to vote. Soviet elections could also claim to be democratic in their outcomes: of the almost 1 million people elected to local soviets in the RSFSR in March 1961, more than 40 percent were women and 60 percent were (at least on paper) workers and collective farm workers. The various "mass organizations" of the USSR boasted impressive membership figures. The proportion of young people belonging to the Komsomol rose steadily from 34 percent in 1959 to 43 percent in 1965, and would exceed 50 percent by 1970. Trade union membership was practically universal (exceptions included the army and the KGB) and, even if the unions did not have the right to undertake strike action, they played a significant part in housing allocation, distribution of social benefits, and workplace relations.[62]

While the forms of Soviet democracy predated Khrushchev, the new leader sought to reinvigorate them. One of the main themes of the open sessions of the Twentieth Party Congress was "democratization" at the workplace – in other words, greater opportunities for employees to express their views on their managers and on the work process.[63] Khrushchev also revisited the perennial question of Party admissions. After a period of headlong expansion during the war, when hundreds of thousands of men had been accepted into the Party straight from their army units, membership policy had entered a phase of retrenchment in the later Stalin period. Party membership fell in absolute terms in 1953, but thereafter it entered a phase of steady growth. The number of new candidate members in the epoch-making year of 1956 reached 381,000, and the figure grew to 879,000 in 1964. By mid-1965 the Communist Party had more than 12 million members (a rise of more than 70 percent since Stalin's death). Only after Khrushchev's departure did admissions procedures become stricter again. Not only that, the Khrushchev era saw a new emphasis on recruiting workers and collective farmers. Between the Twentieth and the Twenty-Second Party Congresses, two in five new members were classified as workers, while just over one in five was a *kolkhoznik*. The white-collar and intelligentsia share of the membership sank to under half in 1955 and then declined further (though it started to recover in the early 1960s).[64]

The Khrushchev leadership also moved to make the system more responsive to voices "from below." The prerogatives of district soviets were increased so that administrators at the local level could be more responsive to the problems and complaints of constituents.[65] The welfare reforms of the era – housing, pensions – bore witness to an unprecedented concern by the Soviet leadership for popular well-being. There was in Khrushchev's period of ascendancy a strain of unabashed populism that represented a break with the past. The populism came to the fore especially after 1960, as Khrushchev strove to keep up his political momentum and legitimacy.

Naturally, this expansion of socialist democracy was not born of liberal intentions. To elicit mass political participation was a means of ensuring conformity and mutual supervision even if it also increasingly implied a welfare contract between people and state. Even in an authoritarian one-party state, however, popular mobilization might lead in troubling directions: witness the grass-roots agitation provoked by de-Stalinization or the mass unrest of the early 1960s, when aggrieved workers protested against price rises on the grounds that the promised Soviet welfare state had fallen short of expectations.[66]

In the following decades, Soviet-style democracy would continue to deliver on its performance indicators. Party and Komsomol membership kept on rising, and popular opinion continued to pour into Party and state agencies in the form of letters to the authorities: the Central Committee received 2 million of them just between 1971 and 1976.[67] But firm limits were placed on how far public discussion could go, and decision-making remained in the hands of an unaccountable and increasingly static elite. Khrushchev's experiments in popular mobilization never led to serious institutional reform; that would have to wait until the 1980s and the next leader with a reformist platform.

Technocracy and its Limits

The refusal of the Soviet Union to go the way of unruly liberal democracy could be justified by the notion that the Party continued to know best. The country's leading organization could base its claim to superior knowledge not only on its mastery of the esoteric doctrine of Marxism–Leninism but also on its scientific and technological expertise. A commitment to rationalist modernity had always been an element in Soviet thinking. The 1920s, for example, had seen a Soviet craze for "scientific" American management techniques. World War II, with its ensuing nuclear age, had only boosted the prestige of science, and the incipient Cold War made it imperative for the Soviet Union not only to imitate and match the West but to outstrip it. In the late Stalin era, physicists could aspire to real political influence in their role as expert advisers to the State Committee for Defense and various commissariats. Highly educated experts could also expect to be well rewarded. In the late Stalin era, a fully qualified and tenured academic earned about four times as much as a qualified worker, and a professor earned seven times as much.[68] In the late 1940s, Stalin's grip on everyday politics weakened, but he found the time and energy to make decisive interventions in several academic and scientific fields: philosophy, agronomy, economics, physics, linguistics, psychology.[69] Even if it was ultimately subservient to ideology, science was taken very seriously by the leadership.

The postwar Party membership became significantly better educated. Between the late 1940s and the late 1960s, more and more Party members were to be found in the fields of industry, science, education, health, and culture, and relatively fewer in the party-state bureaucracy.[70] Both the industrial and the Party elites were becoming more technically competent. The proportion of the Moscow Party elite with a higher education rose from just under two-thirds in the Khrushchev era to more than 80 percent over the period 1964–85.[71] The trend over the postwar decades was toward a more technocratic style of government.

The Central Committee – the Communist Party's mini-parliament – was populated increasingly by men pursuing specialized careers in a particular sphere of government or the economy. This was a general occupational trend. The "Party generalist" – the kind of troubleshooter who might at a moment's notice move from a ministry to a territorial Party organization – was a far less common phenomenon than in the prewar era. Even in the postwar Stalin era, there were only three cases of territorial Party bosses taking ministerial jobs. When the Central Committee expanded in 1952 from 71 to 125 full members and from 68 to 111 candidate members, this was almost certainly a reflection of the greater specialization of the Soviet elite. As the apparatus of government and economic administration became more elaborate, there were simply more leading functionaries who deserved Central Committee membership on the "job-slot" principle.[72] Not only that, Party bosses tended to have an impressive level of technical competence in areas for which they were responsible. In 1966, for example, 19 of 25 first Party secretaries in the industrialized regions of the Russian and Ukrainian republics were trained engineers; in the 25 most agricultural regions, there was a similar bias toward agronomy.[73]

For all his rambunctious anti-intellectualism, Nikita Khrushchev was himself in thrall to science and technical expertise. Although often happy to play up his peasant and proletarian origins, and to berate intellectuals, he was also enamored of ambitious technological solutions to economic and political problems. In 1955 he was bowled over by the earthy Iowa farmer Roswell Garst, seeing in cornfields and cutting-edge agronomy a solution to many of the Soviet Union's economic woes. Six years later he was beside himself with glee when Iurii Gagarin completed the first manned expedition into space.

The Soviet system of the 1950s inherited from the Stalin era an absolute faith in the power of large-scale technological development to shape human society, but the nature of the technology changed. The prestige projects of the 1930s had been canals and hydroelectric complexes, but under Khrushchev physicists took over from engineers as the main scientific heroes of the age. Their main cause was nuclear energy, which in the mid-1950s gained a position of prestige in Soviet culture that it would only relinquish with the Chernobyl disaster of 1986. If in the late 1940s scientists still had to fight off the ideological attentions of late Stalinism – physicists, for example, had to defend themselves against the charge of "idealism" – by the mid-Khrushchev era, they were in a position to lobby effectively for their favorite projects. In 1954, with the completion of the first nuclear reactor generating power for a national grid, the USSR could claim a vanguard position. By the time the Soviet Union collapsed, the nuclear power sector employed 1.5 million people, and there were 47 cities dedicated to research or production in this area.[74]

Scientists were able to communicate to policymakers their belief in the potential of science to lighten the burden of heavy labor, boost productive forces, and demonstrate the superiority of Soviet civilization over that of the West. The field of application of atomic energy was extensive – it went so far as the irradiation of foodstuffs to extend their shelf life. "Peaceful nuclear explosions" became a means of geological engineering: more than 100 such operations were carried out. It appears that the enthusiasm of policymakers was shared by significant parts of the general public: radio and TV programs on scientific topics were popular, and the circulation of the journal *Science and Life* reached 3.5 million. Admittedly, the alliance between politicians, scientists, and Soviet patriotism had its dark side. Safety and ecological issues were often neglected, with components standardized without due testing, inadequate containment of reactors, and construction of nuclear sites too close to population centers.[75]

Post-Stalin technocracy was a matter not only of physics and engineering but also of purportedly scientific and rational techniques of government. The central institutions of Soviet power were now claiming to be not only essential for maintaining the Soviet order but also good at their jobs. A striking example was the political police, which launched nothing short of a public relations offensive in the mid-50s. This period saw the publication of many popular histories of the KGB's predecessor organizations, which depicted the police as heroic figures, as custodians of Soviet security and morality. Although Khrushchev in his denunciation of Stalin had just exposed the past abuses committed by the secret police, he still sought to persuade the Soviet population that the KGB could be trusted. Aleksandr Shelepin, a former partisan and Komsomol leader rather than a police professional, was made KGB chairman in December 1958 with the idea that his clean image would give the KGB's reputation a boost. In May 1955, the Soviet government established new controls over the investigative agencies of the KGB: it created a new department within the USSR procuracy for this purpose. Between 1958 and 1962, new laws and rules on criminal procedure defined state crimes in a more precise way and – in principle at least – required the security organs to operate according to the same rules as the ordinary police (by, for example, obtaining permission to detain a suspect further within 48 hours of the initial arrest). A new law on state crimes of December 1958 made definitions less vague, and the 1960 RSFSR Criminal Code stipulated that a person had to have committed a crime before facing criminal prosecution (under the 1926 code, a person could be prosecuted just for constituting a "social danger").[76]

At the same time, however, countertendencies could be observed. The range of crimes over which the KGB had jurisdiction increased from 1961 onward. The security forces, moreover, would soon once more assert themselves politically by supporting Khrushchev's ouster in 1964: the General Secretary had done too much to undermine their prerogatives. The relatively mild Shelepin was soon replaced by the more hard-line Vladimir Semichastnyi. A decree of December 1965 once again extended the KGB's investigative powers. In 1966, the RSFSR Criminal Code gained two significant new articles targeted against political dissent: one on "circulating false statements which defame the Soviet state," the other on "the organization or active participation in group activities which violate public order." The campaign to extol the moral qualities of the *chekist* went into overdrive: the fiftieth anniversary of the founding of the Cheka in December 1967 gave rise to a frenzy of public celebration. Political arrests rose sharply from 1966, averaging 185 per annum for the period to 1973. A fall in the mid-1970s was followed by a further rise due to the war in Afghanistan and the crisis of détente. The security services also had extrajudicial means of struggling against dissent. Between 1962 and 1977, more than 200 people were placed in Soviet psychiatric hospitals on political grounds, and the KGB almost certainly carried out the killings of some religious and cultural activists in the late 1970s and early 1980s.[77]

All the same, Iurii Andropov, the head of the KGB from 1967 until he became General Secretary in 1982, was reckoned to be a singularly enlightened chief of secret police. He earned a reputation for consulting widely among bright young things from academia and journalism, a habit he had developed when employed in the apparatus of the Central Committee in the mid-1960s and continued as Head of the KGB.[78]

The KGB workforce grew substantially under Andropov – to nearly half a million salaried employees by the start of 1991. The number of political convictions in the USSR fell from 4,676 in the period 1956–60 to only 347 in 1976–80 (although ways were also found of prosecuting dissidents under the provisions of the Criminal Code). The KGB developed more intensive and sophisticated ways of disabling opposition: it was reputed to have assembled more than 500 volumes of documents on Andrei Sakharov by the time these records were burned in 1989–90.[79]

An alternative, less flattering conclusion might be drawn from the Sakharov investigation and many other less high-profile cases: this police state was prepared to waste colossal amounts of expertise and resources on manifestations of opposition that were a long way from being system-threatening. As Christopher Andrew and Vasili Mitrokhin note, the resources expended by the KGB on tracking down the anonymous author of anti-Soviet material "frequently exceeded those devoted in the West to a major murder enquiry."[80] Andropov's first annual report as KGB Chairman informed Brezhnev that 11,856 leaflets and other anti-Soviet documents had been recorded as disseminated in 1967; a total of 1,198 anonymous authors had been uncovered, and 114 of them had faced criminal prosecution. In addition, 456 attempts to spread manuscripts, foreign periodicals, and other anti-Soviet material in the armed forced had been averted.[81]

The problem with a Soviet-style system of centralized bureaucratic government was that the center took upon itself too much: it suffered from an information glut without possessing the means to sort information effectively and distinguish effectively between short- and long-term priorities. For all its talk of plans and rationality, Soviet decision-making was affected by the same short-termism as elsewhere, but without the market to drive things on.

The failings were concealed by the oil crises of the 1970s, which gave the Soviet economy a huge windfall. In the longer term, however, Soviet failures in research and development would prove crucial. As new oil and gas locations became more remote, exploratory drilling dipped in the 1970s, with the result that Soviet planners exploited existing fields for ever diminishing returns. In defense of Leonid Brezhnev and his planners, it should be said that policy on energy resources is notoriously complex and risky. The risks involved are hard to assess at the best of times, but the Soviet leadership faced particular difficulties. Committed to centralized decision-making, it was unable to spread risk among multiple independent operators; but at the same time it was at the mercy of often skewed information it was receiving from lobbying groups in the oil- and gas-producing regions and from technical experts with links to particular state agencies.[82]

Another powerful and immovable lobby in Soviet politics was the military. For the first ten years or so, the Brezhnev regime enjoyed very good relations with the armed forces. But it discovered that generals could become a political irritant when they pressed for resources and tried to meddle in foreign policy. The military, although it remained a loyal bastion of Soviet power, was in a more robust state than it had been for much of the Stalin period. Although Khrushchev did much to antagonize the officer corps during his decade in power, after his removal in 1964 the Party leadership and the army reached a stable and harmonious modus vivendi. There was much common ground on a personal level. In 1966, near the start of the Brezhnev era, almost a third of Politburo members had spent seven years or more in the military or related occupations. The consensual Brezhnev Politburo was prepared to give senior officers considerable freedom in formulating military policy. In 1967, Marshal Grechko, a military man rather than a civilian, was appointed minister of defense, and in 1973 he was made a member of the Politburo (the only previous military representation on this body had been Zhukov in 1956–7).[83]

From the mid-1970s onward, however, civilian and military priorities increasingly came into tension. Brezhnev's shift to détente and peaceful coexistence found little favor with the generals. Dmitrii Ustinov, a Brezhnev loyalist, was appointed the first civilian minister of defense since 1955. Brezhnev's much-parodied love of military decorations and readiness to write up his wartime exploits did little to endear him to his comrades in the armed forces. More substantively, the Party leadership made a striking statement at the start of 1977 by formally renouncing the long-standing Soviet goal of achieving strategic superiority; the corollary of this was an effort to slow the increase in weapons procurement.[84]

But the military remained an enormous and unavoidable economic commitment for any General Secretary. By 1985, the Soviet armed forces numbered almost 6 million, which made them the largest in the world. Although the Khrushchev era had seen a partial demobilization, troop levels had risen steadily from a figure of 3.6 million in 1960. The Soviet military was also top-heavy, containing proportionately 2.5 times as many generals as the US Army. The educational level of the officer corps had also risen greatly since the 1950s, which only made the military better able to articulate its interests.[85]

Corruption and Governability

The Soviet Union's claims to be a problem-solving technocracy in the Brezhnev era were often subverted by its cumbersome market-averse centralization; its inability to prioritize, to innovate, and to assess risk; and its heavy reliance on major institutions (notably the KGB and the army) that were increasingly in a position to assert their own interests. But there was an even more fundamental problem: Soviet institutions, in the Brezhnev period as earlier, did not work as they were declared to do. As one sociologist has observed: "Anyone who grew up under socialism understands that he lived not at all under a totalitarian regime but in a country where you could do just about anything, but in particular conditions."[86] Politics, economics, and law were completely entangled in the Soviet Union. Jurisdictions overlapped, and the workings of power were by no means as transparent as the hierarchical Soviet system would imply. As the *New York Times* journalist Hedrick Smith observed, Russians were scornful of foreigners' attempts to make distinctions between "liberal" and "conservative" Soviet political figures. For them, patron–client relations, cliques, even family ties were far more important than purported ideological convictions for understanding the drift of Soviet policy.[87]

In the Stalin era, the tendencies of institutional atrophy and lower-level protectionism were kept in check by periodic "purges": moments when the operations of party-state agencies at various levels were held up to unforgiving scrutiny. But the effects of each purge wore off in due course, and in any case they were not a cost-free and rational means of improving the system's performance.

In the post-Stalin era, when purges of the Stalinist variety ceased to be used as routine disciplining measures, bureaucracies were able to grow relatively unhindered and develop a stable modus operandi. They were able to lobby for resources and to form relationships with each other that cut out the "center." Over the years, power had a tendency to diffuse downward. Officials proved adept at holding their immediate superiors at bay, lobbying hard for resources from "above" while delivering as little as possible in return. Technical expertise was not used as a means of pursuing ideally rational solutions but rather as a lobbying instrument for particular agencies. The Soviet Union had a class of "policy entrepreneurs."[88]

The vast military complex was a case in point. The armed forces had acquired their own bureaucracy in 1935 with the creation of a Soviet General Staff. In the Cold War era, the organizational structure of the military, and its relationship with heavy industry and R&D, became so complex that its affairs increasingly escaped direct political control from the center. Lower bureaucratic agencies had to take more of the burden, and political leaders were more reliant on expert advice on issues such as weapons procurement.

Transparency was not in itself a goal of the system. The relationship between Party and state agencies, or between different branches of the economy, was governed by convention and personal authority as much as by formal rules. In the Soviet Union the telephone could be a primary instrument of power. One estimate of the size of the elite at the end of the Soviet period simply takes the number of people listed in the top category of the government telephone directory: at 1 June 1991, this accounted for more than 600 people. Regional bosses, who had automatic intercity telephone links, were on the next rung – they numbered about 2,800.[89]

The nomenklatura system of controlling appointments remained crucial to the operation of Soviet power. To take the important example of Moscow, about 37,000 positions in 1950 were filled on the explicit authorization of the Party organs. The number fell in the Khrushchev era, but was still in the range 23,000–24,000 in the early 1980s.[90] Leonid Brezhnev was known to start his working day with two hours on the phone to other members of the elite and to regional Party bosses. Although he cultivated an unassuming and consultative style of leadership, he was far from diffident on matters of appointments. As one scholar observed of the late Soviet period, "patronage has become a sort of functional equivalent to law."[91]

The loyalty of nomenklatura workers was bought by a generous package of benefits that was only slightly reflected in salaries. Members of the elite could buy groceries in specially supplied shops, they could take meals in specially catered canteens, they received high-quality medical treatment, use of a car and a dacha, and heavily subsidized holidays.

The content of the work was not always so glamorous. Igor' Sinitsin, an eager recruit who was committed to the model of rational-technical administration, within a few years found the experience of working in the Central Committee apparatus profoundly frustrating. Exasperated by the "pompous emptiness, verbosity and tedium of every document arriving from the Central Committee," he began to lose his faith in the Party and the symbols of Marxism–Leninism. Documents bore only an approximate relationship to reality. Sinitsin soon discovered that five-year plans were never properly fulfilled, and that people constantly lied "upwards."[92]

What this implied was that the Soviet system had a strong predisposition to corruption. Even in the late 1950s, Party plenums were presented with plenty of evidence of malfeasance in high places. For example, the Uzbek first secretary was revealed in September 1959 to have spent 7 million rubles on a new dacha. To prepare the design, Uzbek apparatchiks went to Moscow to copy the government villas on the Lenin Hills.[93] The new Uzbek first secretary was Sharaf Rashidov, who twenty years later would be implicated in the most notorious corruption case of the later Soviet period. The problem was by no means confined to the upper Party elite. In Azerbaijan, the head of a district police department earned 200–250 rubles per month, while a prosecutor received only 150–180. Such low salaries were practically an invitation to take bribes. It was alleged that every administrative position in Azerbaijan in the Brezhnev period could be bought: the post of police chief was worth 50,000 rubles in 1969, while the going rate for district prosecutor was 30,000.[94]

Corruption was especially rife in parts of the system where goods and resources were distributed. Trade workers had much to gain by trading their access to shortage items. An investigation of the mid-1980s revealed that an official in the Moscow food trade had received hundreds of thousands of rubles in bribes over the preceding decade or more. Worse still, the official himself handed out bribes to ensure that he had friends in high places who were prepared to turn a blind eye to his schemes. The testimony of the accused implicated a large part of the Moscow Party elite, which left the investigative agencies with a tremendous problem of damage limitation.[95]

Before too long, Iurii Andropov's KGB was cracking down not only on dissent against the regime but also on corruption in the Soviet bureaucracy. By the early Gorbachev period, high-profile cases of economic crime were constantly finding their way into the press.[96] But anticorruption campaigns were short-term fixes for an endemic problem. In a hierarchical and highly secretive system where incentive structures did not always favor virtuous behavior, bending or breaking the rules was a way of life for many functionaries at various levels. Indeed, corruption in the Brezhnev era has plausibly been called a "substitute for reform."[97]

------ Reform to Revolution: Gorbachev and the Collapse ------

The next reformist leader in Soviet history drew much international attention as a representative of a dynamic new generation in the Soviet elite: as a man who could break with the gerontocracy and cronyism of the Brezhnev era. In his background, however, Mikhail Gorbachev could hardly have been a more classic representative of the Communist apparat. He came to power as a virtuoso operator in Soviet Party structures. He joined the Party at the unusually young age of twenty-one and, after a very brief stint in the Stavropol procuracy, he had never had a job outside the CPSU and its feeder institution for young people, the Komsomol. For most of the 1970s he had headed the Party organization in Stavropol province, a significant agricultural region in southern Russia. In 1978 he was summoned to Moscow to become Central Committee secretary for agriculture. A protégé of KGB chief Iurii Andropov (who would become Soviet leader in 1982), Gorbachev was an adept participant in the patron–client networks essential for self-advancement in Soviet politics. Under Konstantin Chernenko, Andropov's sickly successor who ruled from February 1984 to March 1985, Gorbachev took the most influential job in the Soviet Union apart from General Secretary: he was the Politburo member with direct oversight over personnel questions. This had been Stalin's route to power in the 1920s, and all subsequent Soviet leaders had asserted themselves through control of appointments. Chernenko himself had taken this role in the later Brezhnev period. Gorbachev and his lieutenants spared no efforts in ensuring the support of Central Committee members for the leadership contest that seemed imminent as Chernenko's health weakened in early 1985. The succession was secured at high speed on 10–11 March, just hours after Chernenko died. The young and vigorous new General Secretary – a mere 54 years old in March 1985 – was then in a position to advance his cause further. Within a year, he removed three Politburo members – an unprecedented rate of turnover in the Party inner circle.[98] At lower levels of the Party hierarchy, change – partly brought about by controlled elections – was even more dramatic. Between 1986 and 1989 more than 80 percent of district and city Party secretaries, and more than 90 percent of regional and republican Party secretaries, were replaced.[99]

Gorbachev, then, was a man of the Party system to an extent greater even than Leonid Brezhnev, who at least had the war as a formative career experience. When he came to power, Gorbachev enjoyed the strong backing of the Central Committee elite of republican and regional Party bosses, economic administrators and representatives of the military and security organs. All this makes all the more curious the fact that within a few years Gorbachev destroyed the political monopoly of the CPSU and brought about the collapse of the entire Soviet system.

FIGURE 2.3   *Demokratiya* in action: Gorbachev, Yeltsin and the Kyrgyz president Askar Akaev at the 3rd Congress of People's Deputies, December 1990.
Source: © Vladimir Bogdanov / PhotoSoyuz.

Gorbachev's early mentions of "democratization" would not have turned too many Central Committee hairs. The Soviet system, as we have seen, had always claimed to be democratic and had periodically sought to reaffirm this through elections and various other public rituals. Gorbachev's use of the term "democracy" in the first two years of his rule was opaque but not inconsistent with Soviet traditions of (attempted) mass mobilization. By the start of 1987, like previous Soviet reformers, he was finding his initiatives slowed down by their passage through the structures of the party-state. At this point, as a means of outflanking bureaucratic resistance, he embarked on the democratization of the Party itself. In March 1987, it was announced that elections would have multiple candidates in a restricted number of constituencies.[100] From 1988 onward, Gorbachevite "democracy" became an altogether messier affair. Although Gorbachev's belief in the one-party state remained undimmed, he wanted that party to earn its right to lead. The Nineteenth Party Conference of June–July 1988 – which in a striking departure was fully televised – adopted institutional reforms and took the decision to elect a new body, the Congress of People's Deputies, which would in turn elect a working parliament (the Supreme Soviet). In the spring of 1989 came partially contested elections to the Congress. Independent candidates were carefully screened by electoral commissions, and a third of the 2,250 seats were reserved for members of public organizations (notably including the CPSU itself). Gorbachev himself took the role of Chairman of the Congress as his political center of gravity drifted away from the traditional institutions of power. The following year, he created for himself an office with greater executive clout than Chairman of Congress: he became the first President of the USSR. In a deviation from the democratizing trend of the time, he obtained this office by a vote of the deputies rather than by a popular vote (which he would surely have won).

By this time, however, the key political innovations were occurring not at the all-union level but in the RSFSR. From late 1989 onward, individual republics began to create their own democratized legislatures. Elections to the RSFSR Congress of People's Deputies – considerably freer than those to the USSR Congress – took place in the spring of 1990. A new electoral bloc, Democratic Russia, was set up in January 1990 with a program that was vague on all points but one: it stood in opposition to one-party Soviet Communism. Ranged against the self-styled "democrats" stood representatives of the Communist Party, while assorted centrists made up the balance. The election results were a success for the democrats, who gained a third of the seats in the Congress and denied the Communists a majority. In May 1990, by a whisker, Gorbachev's rival Boris Yeltsin was elected Chairman by the deputies, thus becoming Gorbachev's RSFSR counterpart. With the backing of Democratic Russia, he took up the language of democracy, market reform, and Russian sovereignty. It remained unclear what precise policy commitments lay behind these slogans. What was not in doubt was that Yeltsin's election initiated an acrimonious struggle for legitimacy, jurisdiction, and ownership between Soviet and Russian institutions. When an attempt was finally made, in the notorious coup of August 1991, to avert the disintegration of the USSR, it was poorly implemented and only enhanced Yeltsin's charisma and legitimacy. In seeking to save the Soviet Union, the ringleaders of the coup – prominent representatives of the military, security and industrial sectors – had buried it.

Here we must return to the key question: what was Gorbachev thinking when he embarked on the path of radical democratization, and why did he not put up a more effective defense of the state in which he so fervently believed? The answer may well lie in a paradoxical combination of naive idealism and ingenuity. On the one hand, Gorbachev seems genuinely to have believed that democracy would provide an expeditious remedy for the social and economic malaise of the USSR. He had rather little sense of what truly contested democracy would mean. In the words of Jerry Hough, he "seemed to think of democracy in terms of the old village commune or Marx's utopian vision of the socialist future: a system in which people reason together and come to a consensus, not one in which leaders push through and legitimate their policies with close votes."[101] By his own account in his memoirs, he was taken aback by the unruliness and sheer unpleasantness of debate in the lead-up to the 1989 elections. He saw the purpose of his political reforms as a return to the true meaning of the revolutionary slogan "All Power to the Soviets!" It is symptomatic that Gorbachev initially disregarded the advice of some of members of his team and took the post of Chairman (more a coordinator or master of ceremonies than a strong executive figure) rather than creating a strong executive presidency; although he soon recognized this as a mistake, he believed that the institution of a presidency was incompatible with the grass-roots democratic system of the soviets.[102] Equally, he had very little sense of what the wider effects would be of televising live debates from the floor of the Congress. There was a huge amount of latent politicization in the Soviet Union. By the start of 1990, the membership of the Communist Party was close to 19 million, and the educational level of Party members was continually rising. The Soviet Union had 433,192 grass-roots Party organizations, of which nearly 40 percent had fewer than 15 members and a further 40 percent from 15 to 45 members.[103] By all appearances, Soviet society was entirely saturated by the key political institution. But the problem was that the Party leadership was itself divided by this stage, and the mass membership was about to fracture into many different political constituencies – along professional, class and national lines. By 1990, the Party had splintered into several new proto-parties. Its liberal wing had mutated into various forms of "democrat." Those Communists who retained their commitment to the existing system were drifting into alliance with Soviet/Russian "patriots." In an important sense, the Soviet Communist Party had ceased to exist as a coherent entity even before it was abolished on Russian soil in 1991.

Where, then, did Gorbachev's ingenuity lie? As a consummate Soviet political operator, he was confident that he could use the new institutional arrangements to strengthen his position. Indeed, one of the top priorities for a Soviet leader in the post-Stalin era was to cultivate more than one constituency, to show flexibility, not to put all his political eggs in one institutional basket. As late as 1989, Gorbachev might have reflected that the Congress of People's Deputies had served rather well as a political innovation designed to energize Soviet society without compromising Soviet power. Gorbachev was an arch-coordinator, a man adept at balancing different constituencies, a politician whose natural habitat was the middle ground. But at the same time he had set a course for radical change, more irrevocably in the field of foreign policy but also in domestic politics. When Soviet people were given the freedom to express their views on the direction such change should take, a huge number of contentious issues emerged, and hard decisions had to be made. Gorbachev – by virtue of his temperament and his political background – proved unable to make them. Having styled himself as a liberal reformer in the late 1980s, he took a more conservative direction in 1990–1. Not the least of his problems was that the transformation he had unleashed was not just about democratization and economic reform but also about the conversion of an empire to a more liberal polity. The consequence was that several of the non-Russian republics soon presented a challenge to the integrity of the union – which was precisely where Gorbachev's power and legitimacy lay. As the preservation of the union became his priority, he needed to take friends where he could find them: notably, in the military and security elites. But his liberal instincts prevented him from taking the authoritarian measures that were the logical corollary; this was left to the coup leaders of August 1991.

It is hard not to see Gorbachev in oxymoronic terms: as a radical centrist, a one-party pluralist. Such inherent contradictions meant that his reform program never crystallized, and by the middle of 1990 the country was in economic and political turmoil. In Gorbachev's defense, it might be said that he was hardly the only politician to have difficulty in finding his bearings in these circumstances.

Revolution to Reaction: Yeltsin to Putin

What, then, made Gorbachev's rival Boris Yeltsin stand out? In the first instance, he had democratic legitimacy. Yeltsin had gambled and broken with Soviet Party structures in the late 1980s (in the process undergoing a number of bruising confrontations with Gorbachev). He then staked everything on the brand-new institutions of the RSFSR. The 1990 Russian election was more genuinely contested than the USSR equivalent of the previous year – an average of 6.3 candidates per ballot compared to a mere 1.9 in 1989. In 1989, just under half of electoral districts were contested; in 1990, almost all were.[104] In June 1991, moreover, Yeltsin was elected by popular vote as Russian president.

Yeltsin had a surer touch than Gorbachev in the new political conditions. To be sure, like his rival, he had risen through Party structures to membership of the Politburo. But his career had been slightly less meteoric. Born a month before Gorbachev at the start of 1931, Yeltsin had become a Party member ten years later than him and had only become a full-time Party employee in his forties. Before that he had gained many years' experience as a manager in the construction industry and had earned a reputation as a hands-on and effective Party boss in the important industrial region of Sverdlovsk. He was an energetic fixer with a populist touch and acute political instincts. He could readily set himself in opposition to Gorbachev, whom he clearly regarded as a windbag, a conformist, and an apparatchik. Gorbachev, with no less justification, saw Yeltsin as a demagogue, an opportunist, and (even by the standards of high politics) an egotist.

More than anything else, Yeltsin in 1990–1 had a cause: the independence of Russia (or, conversely, the undermining of the Soviet Union). When independence was achieved, however, the question was whether he would be any more successful than Gorbachev at designing and implementing a reform program and

FIGURE 2.4 Russian politics at the barricades: Boris Yeltsin speaking in defiance of the coup of August 1991.
Source: © Oleg Lastochkin / PhotoSoyuz.

whether he would be able to find any more stable basis for political life. In the short term, for a period of one year from November 1991, he was granted powers of decree by the Russian Supreme Soviet. But how was the president to achieve a working relationship with the parliament in the longer term?

The answer was that he did not. The defeat of the August coup had given Yeltsin enormous political momentum but had done nothing to resolve the question of what the institutional arrangements of the new Russia should be. Fundamental political reform was not Yeltsin's priority in 1991–2, for reasons that were regrettable if understandable: he had temporary powers of decree, a drastic economic reform program to implement, and no guarantees that a newly elected parliament would be any more malleable. In the short term, the transfer of power was relatively straightforward. The Soviet Communist Party had gone, its property had been confiscated (or embezzled), and Soviet institutions and personnel had been transferred to Russian jurisdiction. Yeltsin did not feel the need to organize a presidential party. In July 1992 he created a Soviet-style executive body, the Security Council, which was effectively a new Politburo.

Yet, by the time Yeltsin turned his attention to fundamental political reform – the drafting of a new constitution – he had comprehensively lost favor among his parliamentarians. The radical economic reforms launched at the start of 1992 raised the temperature of political debate: the middle ground rapidly melted away. At the end of the year the Congress of People's Deputies declined to extend the president's powers of decree. The Communist Party made a strong comeback in a Russian guise, becoming the largest political party in Russia by 1993. The loose electoral bloc Democratic Russia, which had played such a vocal role in 1990–1, fractured into various forms of liberalism and social democracy. It offered no unity of purpose to match that of the Communists and nationalists who articulated the population's resentment at the collapse of the Soviet Union and the pain of economic reforms. Personal animosity also played its part in the political stalemate: the working life of the Supreme Soviet was increasingly dominated by its chairman Ruslan Khasbulatov, an erstwhile ally of the president, whose political ambitions knew few bounds. The relationship between president and Supreme Soviet broke down completely in 1992–3 as Russian institutions waged the same war for authority that they had unleashed on the USSR in 1990–1. Yeltsin found himself in an intractable standoff with his own political establishment. The conflict escalated over the issue of institutional reform: the president set up his own Constitutional Conference, while the Congress pressed ahead with plans to ratify its own constitution at the Tenth Congress in October 1993. Presidential Decree no. 1400 of 21 September dissolved Congress and called for popular ratification of a new constitution. Barricades went up around the parliament building. When, on 3 October, a hard core of parliamentarians went as far as ordering armed resistance to the president, Yeltsin authorized the use of force. He was then in a position to dictate his own constitution – which, unsurprisingly, established strong presidential power.

For the heroic defender of the White House in August 1991 to set tanks on the Russian parliament building only two years later was a very tragic irony. It was only too easy to see Yeltsin as the usurper of Russian democracy. Nor was this the end of the political problems (some of them of his own creation) that he faced. He held power at a time of collapsing living standards and national humiliation. He faced intransigent opposition in the newly created Duma from the Russian Communist Party and from extreme nationalists. Between December 1994 and August 1996 Russia was mired in a disastrous war against the breakaway republic of Chechnya. In the later 1990s, the president's alcoholism and poor health were serious impediments to his performance in office.

But Yeltsin won a presidential election, held on to power and transferred it at a time of his choosing, a sequence of events that requires explanation. After 1993, relations between the president and the parliament (now a 450-member Duma) remained antagonistic, but viable working relations were established. A few years into the postcommunist era, the basic legitimacy of economic liberalization and privatization were no longer explosive issues, while the idea of attempting to restore the Soviet Union could be left to marginalized extremists. After the turmoil of the early 1990s, elections were held on time, and their results were accepted by the main parties.

The new presidential system made it imperative to win the presidential election. The crucial ballot came in the summer of 1996, a year when Yeltsin's approval ratings had started in single digits. Part of his success was no doubt due to biased media, the financial backing of the "oligarchs," and flawed elections.[105] Another important factor was that Yeltsin's charisma did not fade completely until the later 1990s: his brand of uncouth charm played much better in Russia than it would have done in an America wooed by Bill Clinton. But the main reason for Yeltsin's re-election was that the alternatives were even more unpalatable. The Russian population might have been appalled by the war in Chechnya and by the conduct of economic reform, but by 1996 a majority accepted that the move from Communism to a form of market economy was irrevocable. The other main presidential candidate, the Communist Gennadii Ziuganov, was too much of a throwback. Still less appealing were nationalist and neo-imperialist alternatives. The flamboyant fascist Vladimir Zhirinovsky received protest votes in the parliamentary elections of the 1990s, but Russians were not willing to countenance the hard political implications of such an ideology: the necessity of further strife and geopolitical aggression. Chechnya was quite bad enough.

All this might explain how Yeltsin was able to rule for the best part of a decade, but it does not explain how he ruled. Did post-Soviet politics represent a clean break with Soviet practice? It was certainly more lively and contested. Elections were held and drew turnouts higher than in the West in the same period. But political contestation was chaotic and unstructured. Parties formed, disbanded and reformed at a bewildering rate. Distinctions between "communists" and "democrats," or "hard-liners" and "moderates," which had seemed so meaningful in 1990–1, were a poor guide to the political realities of the 1990s.

This political kaleidoscope effect was only to be expected at such an early stage of establishing a democratic system. More significant was the fact that President Yeltsin never found it necessary or desirable to cultivate a party allegiance. For the most part, he stood above contested politics rather than participating in it. While he adapted with some gusto to modern televisual electioneering, in other ways his style of rule followed established Soviet traditions. As he was to some extent obliged to do, he relied on Soviet-era personnel and old patron–client networks. He also came increasingly to resemble a Russian patrimonial ruler: an authoritarian figure who lacks the physical or technological capacity to keep close control over the political system, but reserves for himself the right to intervene arbitrarily at any moment to assert his authority. For a patrimonial ruler, institutional opacity and overlapping jurisdictions are positively desirable, as they undermine the capacity of any single subordinate to act independently of the patriarch. The presidential administration soon became a bureaucratic Goliath – larger, in fact, than the elaborate Central Committee apparatus in Soviet times.[106]

This might have been a good means for Yeltsin to safeguard his own power, but it was one of many factors in a weakening of the state's administrative capacity. In 1989–91, state structures had failed to act as an effective restraint as members of the nomenklatura rushed to cash in assets such as energy and metals. The Russian state remained massively corrupt and inefficient through the 1990s.[107] In Yeltsin's second term, the mental and physical enfeeblement of the patriarch further hampered its effectiveness. The question of the succession was, however, awkward. By definition, under a patrimonial leader the choice of a successor is arbitrary and personalistic. In his period of office, Yeltsin had appointed and discarded prime ministers at a dismaying rate. How was anyone to establish a firm foundation for rule?

In the event, the succession issue was resolved in a hurry at the end of 1999. Yeltsin abruptly stood aside, and the incumbent prime minister, Vladimir Putin, took over until the next presidential election (of 2000). Putin was at the time a relatively obscure figure, but his CV was impressive and varied. The bedrock of his career was a 15-year stint in the KGB that included a posting to the GDR in the second half of the 1980s. He then spent five years in a particularly lively arena of civilian politics, establishing himself as a key figure in the administration of St. Petersburg's first elected mayor, Anatolii Sobchak. Putin then got his break in Kremlin politics through an appointment in the presidential administration, where he began a steep political ascent. In July 1998 he re-entered the security services at the very top with an appointment as head of the FSB (the successor to the KGB), while in August 1999 he was elevated to be the latest of Yeltsin's prime ministers.[108]

Although Putin might have been expected to be as transient a political figure as some of his recent predecessors, it quickly turned out that the time was right for a leader of a new type. With a little help from his image-makers, Putin quickly established himself as the temperamental opposite of Yeltsin: cold, sober, efficient, rational – but also strong and energetic. As a cross between a technocrat and an army officer, he was just the kind of figure to appeal to an electorate craving an end to social disorder and basic competence from those in government. Putin also had the great good fortune to arrive in office at a moment when energy prices were about to soar. The improving economic conditions made it possible for him to reassert the prerogatives of the Russian state while at the same time presiding over a consumer boom. He was able to put forward liberal business-friendly credentials while at the same time launching crowd-pleasing and asset-grabbing campaigns against selected "oligarchs" (first Vladimir Gusinsky and Boris Berezovsky, then Mikhail Khodorkovsky and his enormous concern Yukos). Last but by no means least, he was able to prove himself a strong ruler by prosecuting a second war in Chechnya that was immeasurably more popular than the first.

Putin also benefited from a general change in the political climate that enabled him to bring the legislature into line with the presidential executive. It was now possible for a Russian president to ally himself firmly with a party – a step that Yeltsin always stopped short of taking. In the 2003 elections the pro-presidential party, United Russia, secured a dominating position in the Duma. All the while, Putin saw his own popularity rise and continued to profit from all the unfair advantages enjoyed by the incumbent in an unregulated strong presidential system. He achieved crushing victories in the presidential elections of 2000 and 2004. His administration brought the techniques of "managed democracy" to a new peak of effectiveness. And, despite much speculation that he would attempt to get round the constitutional limit of two successive terms, in 2008 he passed on presidential power to a polished and apparently pliable younger successor, Dmitrii Medvedev. Here, surely, was an indication of the normalization of Russian politics.

But Putin was not just a man of the new Russia. Also crucial to his success was his background in the old regime. This was a matter not so much of his mastery of the techniques of KGB skulduggery as of his ability to draw on powerful interest groups in the military and the security services. In time-honored Soviet fashion, he was placing trusted people from his own patron–client networks (located mainly in the military and security apparatuses) in positions of responsibility. One of his earliest measures to reassert state power was to create seven new federal administrative districts, which were headed and staffed largely by men from a military or security background.

Such developments led to much speculation that the arrival in power of Putin signaled a takeover by representatives of the "force" agencies (dubbed the *siloviki*). While this idea is not without foundation, it needs to be qualified.[109] The prominence of the police, FSB, and army in Russian life was hardly Putin's innovation. The "new" Russia had a larger political police presence than the authoritarian Soviet Union. According to one plausible estimate, the KGB could call on one agent for every 430 or so citizens, while its post-Soviet successor had one agent for around 300 citizens.[110] Following the collapse of the Soviet system, moreover, members of the armed forces took a more prominent role in politics than would be acceptable in a liberal polity where the distinction between government and military was more rigorously maintained. In the first half of the 1990s military officers freely put themselves forward as candidates in elections and openly encouraged their subordinates to do the same. After 1995, military participation in elections went into decline, though the army elite retained a healthy sense of its own importance. The late Yeltsin era saw gross examples of military insubordination to the government (notably General Anatolii Kvashnin's dash to Pristina in June 1999 in defiance of the NATO forces, which was done with Yeltsin's approval but without informing the Ministry of Defense).[111]

For the most part, however, the military and security forces knew their political limits. The Russian military showed itself incapable of enacting a Bonapartist takeover even when it had every incentive to do so – under a leader, Mikhail Gorbachev, who radically undermined the status of the armed forces. In the 1990s, a demoralized and divided military was even less likely to launch a bid for power. Instead, officers tolerated or actively participated in the spread of corruption that involved the use of military resources for personal gain. At the political level, the army lobbied for increased resources and against military reform that would reduce the troop numbers and the clout of the military sector. After reaching their nadir in 1998 (at a time of economic crisis), military budgets rose consistently. During Putin's first term they increased at an average rate of over 10 percent (even if it was still only a tenth of the last Soviet military budget in 1991, which itself was far smaller than the gigantic budgets of the Brezhnev era).[112]

Under Putin the public prestige of the armed forces rose enormously. While the apparently technocratic new regime brought military reform back on to the agenda, the resolve of the military lobby to safeguard its prerogatives was undiminished. In 2008–9, however, the new president Dmitrii Medvedev overrode opposition from parts of the military establishment and backed plans to modernize the armed forces by making them smaller, more professional, better equipped, and capable of instant reaction in future conflicts such as the successful five-day South Ossetian war of August 2008. But any shift to a more professional army, with consequent investment in cutting-edge technologies, was likely to be retarded by the financial crisis of 2008; and, given the lack of transparency and accountability in all of Russia's state institutions, the military and security elites retained their perennial capacity to frustrate rationalizing initiatives that threatened their prerogatives. There was little reason to suppose that the close but hierarchical relationship between state and armed forces, first established with the rapprochement between Party and Red Army in 1941–2, was about to change: the armed forces would continue to know their place and not pose a direct political threat, but in exchange they would remain a high investment priority and a central component in the government's sense of national purpose.[113]

Conclusion

The figure of Vladimir Putin poses like few others the basic question: how much has actually changed in the structure of power in Russian since the fall of Communism?

The basic lack of transparency and accountability in the political system, the enormous role of patron–client networks, and the cross-contamination of economic, political, security, and military elites: these attributes of the Soviet system have all been preserved in post-Soviet Russia.

Russia has thoroughly disproved the idea that postcommunist transition is necessarily a linear process from authoritarian state socialism to liberal democracy. It turns out that a capitalist authoritarianism with the appurtenances of democracy is entirely possible. But that should not lead us to ascribe everything to a Russian "political culture" that safely outlasted the Soviet collapse. Soviet politicians and their successors had a large range of political strategies at their disposal, and they switched freely between them: technocracy, theocracy, mobilizational democracy, patrimonialism. We should not underestimate the capacity for change of the Soviet/Russian system. Change, in fact, was not just a capacity, but an imperative.

This chapter has focused primarily on high politics: on the key central institutions, on rulers and other important political actors, and on their strategies for obtaining and maintaining power. A more rounded account of Russian politics will require two further chapters. One of them, Chapter 6, will examine the crucial question of how political leaders in Moscow secured the allegiance, or at least compliance, of smaller bosses in the far-flung corners of this enormous country. The other, which follows directly after this paragraph, will investigate what was perhaps the most important legacy of the Soviet "system": the total interpenetration of politics and economics. When the ideology of Soviet socialism collapsed, and when the unity of the ruling class disintegrated, Russia was left with a fight for control of resources. In this light, the Putin era should be seen less as a revanche of militarist power than as the conclusion of a decades-long struggle for effective ownership of resources.

3

From Plan to Market

In Soviet ideology, economics was an equal partner of politics. As Marxists, the Bolsheviks believed that economic relationships underlay all political outcomes. Capital accumulation in the "bourgeois" world intensified class conflict, making such societies unstable and belligerent. World War I had been caused by the quest of "imperialist" powers for new markets, while World War II was the result of the latest crisis in world capitalism (which could not contain the imperialist ambitions of Germany and Japan).

The same commitment to political economy guided the Bolsheviks' analysis of developments in their own country. The Communists were not just imposing their economic solutions on the former Russian empire; they were themselves subject to objective laws of economic development. As an authoritative textbook of the Brezhnev era observed: "Socialist society is not something rigid and immobile. It is continually developing. Its productive forces are growing and its production relations are becoming increasingly mature. On its way to Communism, socialist society passes through definite stages of development and the operation of the economic laws of socialism and the possibilities of applying them become modified."[1]

This did not make Bolshevik discussions of the economy calm and dispassionate; quite the reverse. The Soviet experiment was taking political economy in wholly new directions. This was the first ever large-scale experiment in state ownership and management of the economy; the nature and the tempo of the transition from the largely agrarian economy bequeathed to the Bolsheviks were a matter of acute controversy throughout the 1920s. At the close of the civil war, facing social unrest and economic implosion, the new regime was forced to curtail its immediate ambitions. With the introduction of the New Economic Policy in 1921, it tolerated a greater degree of market activity and lifted the crushing burden placed on the peasantry during the civil war. This policy was unpopular and controversial with many Party members, and from the mid-1920s debate raged on the question of how to take the next step toward a socialized economy.

The debate was resolved in abrupt and brutal fashion at the end of the 1920s, when the Party took Stalin's course for all-out industrialization and forced collectivization of agriculture. Here, it would seem, was the foundational moment of the Soviet economy. The Bolsheviks gave full vent to their hatred of liberal economic activity, of purely commercial relationships, of unearned income. They imposed an ambitious system of centralized planning that was supposed to provide rationality and long-term analysis in place of the boom-and-bust cycles of capitalism. Consciously opposing themselves to patterns of early industrial development in the capitalist West, they drove on heavy industry at the expense of consumer goods. Their aim was to ensure the Soviet Union would be in a condition to defend itself against capitalist encirclement without needing to take its chances on a world market dominated by those same capitalist powers. Austerity and autarchy were the essence of the Stalinist economy as it emerged in the early 1930s.

But the Soviet regime could not rest easy. Industrialization was certainly a radical break with the NEP, but it was far from the end of the road of economic development. It had been close to a truism of Bolshevik economic thought in the 1920s that socialism would do away with the money economy, but money remained as a facilitator of exchange. Commodity relations still obtained in Soviet society – in the bazaars and collective farm markets of the 1930s.

Soviet economic policy also had to confront a number of less doctrinal and more practical matters. The shift to planning was good ideology, but it placed a crushing burden on the central agencies. How could the Soviet party-state hope to manage an increasingly complex industrialized economy without letting impersonal forces (prices, markets) take some of the strain? The evidence of the 1930s was not reassuring on this score. The system of economic planning developed from a low base in the late 1920s. At the start of 1930, the Central Committee – the nerve center of the Soviet system – had a staff of only 375 people. The available personnel did not permit plans to be anything but general, and the Party's supervision of the economy was far from omniscient. The extraordinarily ambitious prewar five-year plans were no more than two-thirds fulfilled. Five-year plans appeared to be mobilizational tactics and rhetorical coups more than they were clear operational agendas. The Politburo in the 1930s was hugely overloaded with economic decision-making. In the mid-1930s it would commonly consider several hundred issues per meeting, and even this was a tiny fraction of the decisions needed to keep this enormous "command" economy running. Even when the planning apparatus of Gosplan (the state planning organization) developed, it was not capable of micromanaging the hundreds of substantial enterprises scattered around the USSR. The justifiable conclusion of one historian is that "the Soviet administrative-command system had many jockeys, not just one." The functioning of this system depended on a vast network of interlocking relationships – horizontal as well as vertical, informal as well as formal.[2]

This begged another question that was bound to preoccupy the centralized and overcontrolling Party: how to maintain the integrity of Bolshevik power when operational control was seeping down to economic institutions such as ministries and enterprises? How, in other words, to balance economics and sheer power? The answer thrown up by the 1930s was again far from reassuring: the Bolshevik leadership responded to the potential dispersal of its prerogatives across the ever-growing economic apparatus by unleashing mass terror on industrial managers. Leaving aside the human cost, this was hardly a viable long-term strategy for economic growth. How was the Soviet system to put management on a more stable footing? Who were going to be the socialist equivalents of capitalist "owners"?

——————— The Stalinist Economy from War to Peace ———————

Economics, in a Bolshevik understanding, could not stay still: it was a science based on analysis of empirical data. The next big expansion of the data set came with the war of 1941–5. By the late 1930s, the Soviet Union had a war economy without a war. Collectivization had been a disaster in economic as well as moral terms, but through draconian exploitation of an expanding labor force, and by funding industrial production at the expense of consumption, the USSR had achieved impressive growth rates. This "planned" economy had, however, been chaotic and violent. How would it stand up to the ultimate test: an assault by a major industrialized power whose commitment to rearmament in the second half of the 1930s had made it every bit the equal of Stalin's USSR?

In fact, even before the German invasion of June 1941, the Soviet economic order was showing signs of stabilization. In the late 1930s, the system of economic management through the people's commissariats (which would be renamed ministries in 1946) had begun to achieve consolidation. The role of the security organs in the running of the economy was reduced, even if the NKVD still ran a vast network of labor camps. By 1939, the number of industrial commissariats had risen to twenty from three in 1932, and the postwar period would see further rapid expansion.[3]

But these administrative arrangements did not change the fact that the USSR was soon in desperate straits after the German invasion. By the end of 1941, the country had lost one-third of its economic capacity. The government's response was to maintain the war effort through even more thorough exploitation of the civilian population. If in the 1930s the Soviet Union had been an austerity regime, in the first half of the 1940s it worked society to the bone. At their peak, in 1943, defense outlays accounted for 60 percent of government spending. The huge expenditure on the military was paid for by increases in direct taxes and by resources requisitioned from the population. A war tax was introduced at the start of 1942; it made up more than half of all taxes on personal income. Further taxes were levied on single people and on couples of reproductive age with no children. The wartime regime also forced people to work harder. Within days of the start of the war, the government permitted enterprise directors to lengthen the working day by up to three hours. A million or so women and schoolgirls were drafted into industry. A decree of 26 December 1941 made it illegal for workers to leave their jobs, and a further decree of 13 February 1942 imposed labor mobilization on all men aged from 16 to 55 and all women from 16 to 45. More than 730,000 people had been drafted in this way by the end of 1942, most of them into the war industries such as metals, chemicals, and fuel. All the same, there was no concealing the desperate labor shortage: the industrial workforce fell from 11 million to 7.2 million between 1940 and 1942.[4]

Even by Soviet standards, the war years were times of extreme scarcity. Resources were targeted at the pressing needs of the state. Some engineers and workers received decent wages and bonuses, while many white-collar employees and their dependents could expect very little; wage differentials increased during the war. The rubles circulating in the economy were chasing a decreasing number of goods – only a third as many in 1945 as there had been in 1940. The transition to rationing was automatic, initially, by a decree of July 1941, in Moscow, Leningrad, and numerous other towns and districts in the Moscow and Leningrad regions. Bread and sugar rationing was quickly extended until it became universal in November 1941. Large cities around the USSR also saw rationing of meat, fish, fat, groats, and macaroni. Rations were provided on a sliding scale down from workers to children and other dependents: they ranged from 4,418 calories per day to 780 calories.[5] In mid-1943, the basic ration for the top category of workers came to just over 2,000 calories per day (of which five-sixths were provided by bread and flour), while for those at the lower end of the scale it had fallen below 1,000 calories.[6]

Feeding of the population was to an increasing extent organized through the workplace via "departments of worker supply" (ORS), which rose in number from just under 2,000 at the end of 1942 to 7,720 at the start of August 1945. At the start of 1946, these organizations ran more than 17,000 canteens. In an expansion of 1930s' practice, local authorities were ordered to make land available to enterprises; between 1941 and 1943 the ORS gained control of more than 550 farms. As of October 1942, 10,000 farms existed under the auspices of enterprises and organizations. Workers and employees were also encouraged to feed themselves by cultivating allotments in and around cities. The number of such plots of land rose from 5.9 million in 1942 to 11.8 million in 1943 and 16.5 million in 1944, and by 1944 they met perhaps one-eighth of the food requirements of the urban population. In addition, the state was forced to acquiesce in the continued existence of collective farm markets, where prices by April 1943 were 16 times as high as in 1940. However, the resources demanded by the Soviet state ensured that conditions on the collective farm were bleak. The grain and money distributed to collective farm members fell to starvation levels. The only means of survival was the household plot, which state regulations had shrunk to an average 0.27 hectares in 1944. The state came down still harder on individual farming through the forced "purchase" of livestock owned by collective farm households; in a throwback to collectivization, some peasants resorted to slaughtering their animals.[7]

Whatever the costs of the war effort, the Soviet leadership could soon claim that the state socialist model of planning had shown its superiority to capitalism. The economy had been mobilized for war at high speed. Enterprises were converted to war production, raw materials were reallocated to war industry, industrial plants and workforce were evacuated east. Over a period of three months in 1941, according to the official who oversaw this project, more than 1,360 large factories were moved to the Urals, Western Siberia, Central Asia, and Kazakhstan. By 1943, the industrial production of these areas was three times that of 1940, and their share in total Soviet industrial output had likewise trebled. The Soviets could also boast wartime improvements in electrification, automatization, and overall efficiency. Under the circumstances, the quantity of armaments production was astonishing. Tank production nearly doubled over 1942 despite the loss of major facilities in Kharkov and Stalingrad, as did production of artillery shells.[8]

The command economy, then, had shown its fitness to tackle a postwar reconstruction effort that would be almost as demanding as the war itself. The task was enormous: more than 31,000 large enterprises were disabled, the country had lost the equivalent of six or seven years' economic growth, and the population deficit caused by the war probably ran as high as 35 million (taking into account death, displacement and the birth deficit).[9]

The solution to these problems was the prompt resumption of Stalinist economics. This meant a return to an autarchy that had been compromised during the war years. Western aid through wartime Lend-Lease was downplayed, and trade with the capitalist world shrank drastically in the early years of the Cold War. Imports from the United States plummeted from $236 million in 1946 to less than $10 million in 1950.[10] Most of all there was yet more austerity. Workers were coerced into construction projects. The Gulag continued to provide a large captive labor pool; in fact, the prison camp network grew to its maximum extent in the postwar period (see Chapter 4). Meanwhile, the peasantry continued to labor under its Stalinist corvée. The postwar era saw no lessening of the pressure on the collective farms. A new decree of September 1946 sought to crack down on the expansion of individual plots at the expense of collective land and the sale of "collective" produce. In the resulting wave of inspections, 177,000 hectares of individually held land was given back to collective farms. The draconian rural policies continued in the newly annexed territories in the west of the Soviet Union, which between 1948 and 1950 underwent forced collectivization. A currency reform of December 1947 then liquidated whatever was left of the money peasants had accumulated from market trading. Deposits held in the savings bank were converted to new rubles at the rate of one to one for deposits up to 3,000 rubles, of three to two for deposits in the range 3,000–10,000, and of two to one for deposits above 10,000 rubles. Bank deposits held by collective farms and cooperatives were revalued at the rate of five to four. Ready cash – the peasants' preferred means of storing money – was converted at the rate of ten to one. The prices paid by the state for compulsory deliveries of agricultural produce remained low, while retail prices were allowed to rise. The amount left over for the collective farmers after the state had claimed its share was derisory. In 1950, the average money income of an able-bodied farmer in the Moscow region from his labor in the collective was only 165 rubles at a time when the average for workers and employees was 7,668 rubles. For the country as a whole, the labor income of a collective farm worker was slightly higher, but still barely 5 percent of average wages across the whole economy.[11] The peasantry responded by seeking other earning opportunities, using all the "weapons of the weak" at their disposal: by taking paid work at slack moments of the agricultural year, by keeping to a minimum their labor on the collective farm, by manipulating the rules to expand their household plot, and by selling livestock and produce at the market. A survey in 1950 of the budgets of 12,600 collective farmers gave an average income – from all sources – of 1,133 rubles.[12]

The extraction of resources from the population, whether in agriculture or in industry, was managed by an ever more entrenched economic bureaucracy. The postwar period continued the immediate prewar and wartime trend of increasing ministerial power over industrial production. Whatever Stalin and the central planners might decree, ministerial bureaucrats had plenty of scope to do things their way: this industrial economy was already so large and complex that supervision could only be patchy. Knowing the ropes, and getting results, counted more than mere obedience. A ministerial official had to be a talented fixer who was in regular contact with various *glavki* responsible for his branch of industry in a particular territory, or with transport or supplies, as well as with other ministries and various other institutions under the auspices of the Council of Ministers. A decree of August 1946 expanded ministries' room for maneuver by releasing them from the obligation to submit quarterly plans to the government. Decentralization was occurring, but to the ministries rather than lower-level economic units such as enterprises or localities. Although central plans became more detailed over the immediate postwar period, industrial ministries could still devote a third or more of their output to "unfunded production" or simply deliver falsified reports on plan fulfillment to the government, a practice that was regularly bemoaned in the Soviet press but never effectively combated. In theory, the Party was supposed to act as a supervisory institution checking on the ministries, but in practice Party officials made little effort to apply disciplinary sanctions or even worked in tandem with their counterparts in the ministries. Gosplan, the state planning organization, also had checking responsibilities, but its opportunities for remedial action were very limited (not that this was recognized by the government, which conducted a bloody purge of Gosplan in the late 1940s).[13]

This system of economic management was soon able to claim successes. Even if it started from a very low base, the Soviet Union resumed its rapid prewar growth. It is possible to tell a reassuring story about the Soviet economic record until the late 1950s, when rapid postwar growth began to slow, and a moderately reassuring story about the entire postwar era up to the late 1980s. According to CIA figures, the only years over these four decades when Soviet output failed to rise were 1963 and 1979 (years of bad harvests).[14] This system not only survived Stalin but delivered stable growth for four decades.

More immediately, it brought an end to hunger. In the 25 years after Stalin's death, agricultural output increased by at least 3.5 percent per annum (over a period when population growth was only around 1.4 percent per annum). Soviet people were eating more, and were eating better: in ruble terms, food consumption doubled between the early 1950s and the 1980s.[15] This was an economy characterized by stable prices and minimal unemployment. It was not prey to the "boom and bust" cycles of capitalist economies, and it delivered to Soviet society modest but steady increases in material well-being.

Yet, curiously, even at its high-water mark in the late Stalin era, this was a system not at peace with itself. A nagging 1930s' question remained: how was the Soviet Union to continue its march toward full Communism? How was economic doctrine to move with the times? These were not easy questions even for a regime that was in a position to decree whatever dogma it pleased. Efforts to produce an authoritative new textbook on political economy dragged on from 1941 into the early 1950s. Practically all prominent economists and economic functionaries in the Soviet Union were drawn into the process at some stage, whether as authors, editors or critics. Stalin himself intervened on a number of occasions – most decisively in 1952, when he corrected the economists' mistaken belief in the state's primacy over economic laws along with various other errors. The book finally appeared only after Stalin's death, in 1954.[16]

It is hard to explain why, at a time when the international prestige of the USSR was at its highest and the victory over Nazi Germany seemed to have confirmed the rightness of the Soviet economic order, the authorities should find it so hard to produce a textbook on their pet discipline. This failure does not reflect any loss of will or of nerve on the dictator's part. Instead it suggests the enduring difficulty of certain core matters of economic doctrine. What *was* to be the future policy on money and commodity relations? Theoretically, these phenomena were to be abolished under socialism, but they were far too useful to be dispensed with in any envisageable future. How *was* this overcontrolling party-state to accommodate itself to the "laws" of economic life (which included the rising power of economic bureaucracies not directly subservient to the Politburo)? And finally, a conundrum that had faced many generations of pre-Bolshevik Russian rulers: what was to be done about the accursed "peasant question" (which, in Soviet terms, meant the gaping chasm between the collective farm and all other sections of the socialist economy)?

The Peasant Question

The agricultural sector was divided into collective farms (*kolkhozy*) and state farms (*sovkhozy*). State farms were classified as production units (enterprises) analogous to those in the cities and benefited from planned state investment. Peasants employed there drew money wages and other social benefits like workers in other sectors of the Soviet economy. *Sovkhozy* were on average three times as large as *kolkhozy* in the area they cultivated and more mechanized; their workforce was on average much smaller.[17] The collective farms were in a weak position when it came to machinery and investment. According to the administrative division established at the time of collectivization, farm machinery was owned by "machine-tractors stations" (MTS) and was leased out to collective farms. If collective farms needed investment, they were required to pay for it themselves out of earnings or to take out loans from the state bank. Surplus earnings were never large, since compulsory payments to the state and the MTS took out a substantial chunk of the *kolkhoz* budget.

Until the 1950s, the *sovkhozy* were far fewer than the *kolkhozy*, their poorer relation. Not only did the average collective farm cultivate less land than the *sovkhoz*, its labor force operated on very different terms. Its peasants took part in communal agriculture, and their income was a proportion of the collective output. First, however, the state took its cut in the form of taxes and deliveries of agricultural products at fixed prices (which were well below market values). Only then was the residue distributed among the *kolkhoz* workforce according to work performed during the year. The unit for judging work contribution was the "labor day" (*trudoden'*). Different forms of activity on the collective farm were assigned different values in this currency: one day of skilled work as, say, a tractor driver would have a higher value than a day digging potatoes.

The collective farm had been created in the cataclysmic early 1930s as a means for the state to extract resources from the rural population. During and just after the war, as we have seen, it amply served that purpose: taxes and compulsory deliveries to the state meant that income from *trudodni* was left at starvation level. The *kolkhozy* were under routine political control through the collective farm chairman, who acted as a transmission belt between Party and farm workers. They also had a clear ideological rationale: the underfed *kolkhozniki* could be seen as living the Soviet dream of collective endeavor and the moneyless economy.

That was the ideology. In reality, however, the peasant smallholder was alive, if not always well. The household plot (in Soviet parlance, "personal auxiliary landholding," or *lichnoe podsobnoe khoziaistvo*) was a way of life for generations of rural people. In the hungry years that lasted to the 1950s, it was quite literally a survival strategy. But it was also much more than that. One close analysis of a village in Tambov oblast in central Russia in the mid-1950s found that all 428 households had plots, many of them with cows, pigs, sheep, and fowl. Even people classified as workers and employees had their (slightly smaller) allotments and animals. A few households even produced tobacco, for which the state paid them 5 rubles per kilo. Work on the household plots was done mainly by women, as men were busy with collective farm obligations.[18]

The crucial factor in the economic well-being of a household, as in pre-Soviet times, was the ratio of able-bodied workers to dependents. Households without men of working age were likely to be worse off (with the partial exception of widows, who received special state support). In about two-thirds of cases, the ratio was favorable. A success story from the Tambov region was the household of the head of a work team, who lived with his wife, two preschool children and his old mother. Since taking up his position, his annual number of *trudodni* had jumped up to 540. The family also had 4 hectares of land, mainly for potatoes and vegetables, and livestock: a cow and calves, five sheep, about 20 chickens, and a pig. The household had built itself a two-room wooden house with an iron roof back in 1947. It was in a position to spend quite freely on clothing without being obliged to sell household produce. A contrasting scenario was found in the household of a war widow, who lost her husband in 1942 and was left with care of two young children. Her domestic responsibilities did not leave her free to earn more than 130–40 labor days per year, although this was supplemented by a 570-ruble pension for the children. Her daughter left for factory work in Moscow in 1951, while her son stayed behind. In 1953 the family managed 170 labor days (30 from the son). The household had a plot of 3.5 hectares along with two goats, sheep and chickens, but the food situation was difficult, and the widow was obliged to sell grain to pay taxes and meet current expenses. In 1954–5 the material situation of the family finally improved, as the son reached working age.[19]

Things had been far worse just after the war. A September 1946 decree took aim at "violations of the *kolkhoz* charter." The government picked up where it had left off just before the war with a campaign to restrict the size of private plots: almost 15 million acres of land were restored to the *kolkhozy*. Agricultural output had fallen with the devastation of wartime and the exodus of able-bodied males: the Soviet Union in 1945 produced less than half as much grain as it had in 1940. Over the same period, the number of tractors had fallen from 531,000 to less than 400,000, while combine harvesters had fallen from 182,000 to 148,000. The war had caused immense damage to the villages as well as the cities. Almost 100,000 collective farms were in need of repair, and almost 3,000 MTS. But urban reconstruction was the priority of the time.[20]

The post-Stalin leadership, with Nikita Khrushchev to the fore, made concerted efforts to drag the collectivized village out of its poverty and backwardness while at the same time making its activities more ideologically acceptable to a state with an aggressive modernizing vision. Even before he came to power, Khrushchev had rural issues close to his heart, and as Party boss in Ukraine he had seen the rural famine of 1946–7 at close quarters. In the late 1940s he appreciated better than his Politburo colleagues the desperate predicament of the Soviet village, which had been crippled by taxation and delivery quotas and by a continuing exodus of able-bodied workers to the cities. The first measure he proposed to alleviate the situation was a "consolidation" of collective farms whereby debilitated smaller *kolkhozy* would be joined to more robust larger farms. Initial results were impressive: a fall of two-thirds in the overall number of collective farms, as many smaller units were saved from collapse. In 1950–1, however, Khrushchev ran into trouble when he advocated creating "agrotowns" within the newly enlarged *kolkhozy*. He soon had to withdraw his proposal in the face of crushing opposition from the Stalinist elite, but within a couple of years he would return to the rural agenda with far greater political momentum.[21]

Stalin's successors soon set about lightening the burden on the collective farm peasantry. Agricultural taxes were lowered, and procurement prices raised. Restrictions on private plot cultivation, and on household livestock, were loosened. Wages for *trudodni* were raised in 1954–5. Compulsory deliveries of produce were abolished in January 1958, and all agricultural taxes were instead paid in money.[22]

These were sensible reforms that significantly improved the lot of rural people, but they could not on their own achieve the short-term boost in agricultural output that the Soviet Union badly needed in the mid-1950s. The dire social and economic legacy of Stalinism was compounded by continuing mass rural–urban

FIGURE 3.1 Peasant girls setting out for the fields, Tver region, 1954. A sympathetic image, but a far cry from the Khrushchev dream of modern agriculture.
Source: © Nikolai Bobrov / PhotoSoyuz.

migration: keeping the cities fed had never been so demanding. Khrushchev's solution to the crisis – and it was by no means a bad one – was to bring about a vast increase in the acreage under cultivation by launching the Virgin Lands scheme in Kazakhstan and Western Siberia. A mere two years later, in 1956, the harvest in the east was bountiful, and Khrushchev's initiative appeared to have been a master-stroke.

It was, however, no more than a temporary solution, and in the longer term Khrushchev's rural policy was blighted by its own excesses and contradictions. The *causes célèbres* of the time – the Virgin Lands project, the campaign to expand cultivation of Khrushchev's beloved crop of maize, and the drive to boost meat production – became articles of faith rather than rational responses to the crisis of Soviet agriculture: by the early 1960s they were bringing failed harvests and soil erosion rather than any agricultural miracle. Khrushchev's policy of "consolidation" of *kolkhozy* had brought some benefits to failing farms, but it later shaded into an ideological commitment to "industrialize" the village at all costs. *Kolkhozy* were to be forced to become production units like the *sovkhozy*. This was the rationale for the wrong-headed decision in 1958 to abolish the machine-tractor stations. The collective farms were suddenly placed under the crushing financial burden of having to buy the machinery that they had previously leased.

For all his village-friendly credentials, moreover, Khrushchev retained an ideological animus against private economic activity: in the village, that meant the household plots that were so crucial to the well-being of generations of Soviet people (both rural producers and urban consumers). The "agro-town" project that Khrushchev had backed in 1950–1 recommended reducing the size of household plots to a mere 0.15 hectares so that rural people's productive energies would be focused on mechanized collective agriculture. The cause was taken up once again in the mid-1950s. In 1956, strict new limits were placed on private ownership of cattle, pigs, geese, and chickens. Further restrictions were placed on personal orchards and vegetable plots, while the tax burden on these was raised. Between 1941 and 1966, the amount of livestock held by individual households slightly decreased, while state and collective livestock holdings almost tripled. The Khrushchev era has been described, with only mild hyperbole, as that of a "second collectivization."[23]

All the same, the methods of post-Stalin rural policy were not only coercive. Rather, they broke with the ruthless exploitation of the Stalin era and took aim at a number of more constructive goals. Rural people were to be modernized and urbanized not only in the sense that they adopted more productive and technologically advanced work methods but also by gaining the tools of modern civilization through education and training. New efforts were made to foster links between city and countryside. From the mid-1960s onward, various nonagricultural institutions (above all in the sectors of tertiary education and industry) were appointed "sponsors" of collective and state farms in a relationship called *shefstvo*. This meant that they would provide certain technical support but above all that they would deliver extra hands at harvest time. In the Moscow region in the 1980s, about 200,000 residents of the capital city would spend an average of ten days on the farm while officially remaining at their place of employment or study.[24]

The later Soviet era saw substantial investment in the village. By 1990, Russian agriculture used six times as much fertilizer as in 1965 and five times as much tractor power. Agriculture became a high-profile area of policy in the Brezhnev period. A study of regional Party bosses in the 1980s showed that a relatively high proportion had a background in agriculture. It is telling that Mikhail Gorbachev, first Party secretary in the agricultural province of Stavropol for most of the 1970s, was able to make a rapid ascent to the pinnacle of the Soviet system after his transfer to Moscow as Central Committee agriculture secretary. Even where state functionaries had no formal agricultural expertise, they very often had rural origins. Of the members of the Politburo and the Central Committee administrative elite who took up their posts in the 1970s, almost two-thirds were born in villages.[25]

Yet the results of agricultural investment were far from satisfactory. The gains of the 1950s soon appeared temporary. The Virgin Lands project brought under grain cultivation vast new territories, but the soil quality in these areas was not such as to sustain long-term productivity. Growth in agricultural output rose only 50 percent over the period 1965–90, which only slightly exceeded population growth (35 percent).[26] In a substantial blow to national self-esteem, the USSR lost its self-sufficiency in grain. The first time that grain was imported in substantial quantities came in 1963, when Khrushchev ordered the measure to alleviate the failed harvest of that year. In the 1970s the practice became almost routine, and the volume of imports grew through the 1970s–1980s.[27] The alternative to imports proved far from cost-effective. Between 1971 and 1985, 500 billion rubles of investment was pumped into Soviet agriculture; the return was a feeble increase in production of 2 billion rubles per annum to 1982 (at which point growth ceased).[28] When Gorbachev arrived in Moscow in 1978 as Central Committee agriculture secretary, he was dismayed by the evidence he found of low yields and by the inefficiency of the habitual campaigns to boost grain collection in every region, irrespective of its geography and economic profile.[29]

There was no hiding the basic fact of demographic decline in the Soviet village. The rural population of Russia fell by almost 30 percent between 1959 and 1989; depopulation was especially severe in the northwest and in central Russia. The number of Soviet people engaged in agriculture fell by 25 percent between 1959 and 1970. By 1989, more than one in five rural households consisted of only one person, and 20 percent of villages in Russia were inhabited by fewer than ten people.[30]

The campaigns of the Khrushchev era did little to shake the reliance of the rural population on household plots. In 1970, according to the official statistics, 34 million Soviet families were engaged in some form of "auxiliary" economic activity. The vast majority of these were rural people with landholdings: about half belonged to collective farms, while the others were employed by state farms or were rural people in other occupations. Rural people at this time spent on food only 41 percent as much as urbanites, which suggests that they were feeding themselves from household plots to a very large extent. Soviet economists reckoned that almost a third of the average *kolkhoznik*'s time was spent on auxiliary activity. In many cases this was the preserve of women: a rural version of the notorious "double burden," since women were also delivering their *trudodni* in the collective. In 1975, 59 percent of potatoes in the Soviet Union, 34 percent of vegetables and 31 percent of meat was produced on private plots; tens years later the proportions were not substantially different. Even in 1990, household plots were generating a quarter of Russia's agricultural output on 2 percent of the cultivated area.[31]

─────────── The Politics of Economic Management ───────────

The village was a source of frustration and disappointment to Soviet leaders when they tried to go beyond the Stalinist objective of merely subjugating the peasantry. But the Soviet order stood or fell not on its rural policy but on its handling of the modern industrial economy that was absolutely central to its sense of purpose. Over the first two decades of Bolshevik power an elaborate set of institutions was set up to that end, and the shifting relationships between them are crucial to any historical analysis of the Soviet economy.

Formally, the economic administration was headed by the Council of Ministers. This body was dominated by the heads of the ministries and state committees that made up the fundamental structural units of the Soviet economy. In the later Soviet period, for example, a total of 20 ministries represented the machine-building and metalworking industries, and nine of these were in the defense sector. The power and the proliferation of ministries were basic facts of Soviet economic life in the postwar era (despite various attempts to counteract them). Certain enterprises and branches of industry had hugely more clout than others. In 1983, Soviet industry had over 45,000 enterprises and production "associations." Less than 3 percent of these had at their disposal half of the capital stock and one-third of the industrial workforce.[32]

In addition, a number of "state committees" set the general rules for Soviet economic life. Goskomtsen set prices, or delegated this task to lower levels of the system. Goskomtrud was responsible for labor allocation. Gosplan set all Soviet enterprises detailed targets for economic performance. Gossnab – probably the most important and overworked committee of all – dealt with the hugely complex task of resource distribution.

This multitude of state institutions was itself overseen by a crucial coordinating bureaucracy: the Communist Party. The Party elite set general economic goals for the system, the Central Committee apparatus contained multiple departments specializing in particular sectors of the economy, and Party officials at all levels of the territorial hierarchy were entrusted with supervising economic activity on their patch. The Party also exercised control over appointments to significant management positions.

The task of the plan was to translate the Party's general goals into rational form. Each enterprise was given a detailed annual production plan with multiple targets (for output, labor productivity, capital construction, technological progress, and so on). When combined with subtargets within particular categories, the number of targets for each enterprise could easily run to several hundred.[33] The drawing up of the plan was an elaborate annual ritual that involved extensive communication between the state committees, the relevant ministries, and the enterprise in question. This exercise has been described as "bureaucratic guerrilla warfare": the enterprises, of course, had every interest in negotiating targets that were as low as possible, while Gosplan tried to eliminate any slack and to drive on economic growth.[34]

A perennial problem facing the Soviet planned economy was the information deficit of the agencies taking the major decisions. Enterprises had strong incentives to provide incomplete or misleading information to the higher authorities. In any case, there was far too much in this vast industrial economy that was impenetrable or unknowable for central planning agencies, whatever backing they enjoyed from the Party. In practice, Gosplan had to scale down its ambitions: by exercising control over only a few commodities, by basing its targets on projected growth from the previous year's figure, and by allowing revisions of plan targets that proved unrealistic. The danger was that central planning would become a hall of mirrors where targets were based on projections that were themselves based on projections. The *ex post facto* correction of targets for particular enterprises and ministries might lead, moreover, to a curious lack of coordination between the larger and smaller economic goals of the system.[35]

It would be wrong to say that the Soviet "command" economy in the post-terror era was entirely toothless. Gosplan, backed up by the Party authorities, could on occasion be an effective policeman of the Soviet economy. But the Party's role is best understood as that of "spotlight" rather than omniscient supervisor.[36] When quick results were needed on particular projects or in particular sectors (especially defense), the Soviet system could still be extremely effective even in the 1980s. But for more routine matters it was simply impossible for the Party to be so interventionist. At its local and regional levels, it was economic fixer at least as much as it was disciplinarian. The task of a Party secretary was not only to send economic information dutifully upwards but to ensure that life was viable in his region: that industrial enterprises were adequately supplied with materials, and that the workforce was adequately supplied with food and consumer goods. A prime exponent of this regional patriotism was Boris Yeltsin, first secretary in Sverdlovsk in the late 1970s and early 1980s, who lobbied energetically on behalf of his Urals stronghold. Across the Soviet Union as a whole, there was a gaping contrast between the long time horizons of the planning system and the short-termism of many economic actors.

Given the vagaries of the economic system, and the difficulty of ensuring regular supplies across sectors of the economy, particular enterprises and ministries had every incentive to make themselves as self-sufficient as possible. The ideal of autarchy existed not only in the Soviet Union as a whole but at every level of Soviet society, which may be seen as an archipelago rather than an island in the world economic system. For example, enterprises outside the machine-building sector owned 45 percent of all the metalworking equipment in the USSR,

FIGURE 3.2   Soviet management techniques in action. Front cover of satirical magazine *Krokodil*, no. 33, 1972.
Source: UCL School of Slavonic and East European Studies Library.

a capital stock greater than that of the entire machine-building sector in the USA.[37] This "vertical integration" was a pragmatic choice by enterprises and ministries, which were never adequately supplied by the engineering industry outside their sector, but it placed severe limits on the long-term growth potential of the Soviet economy. It led, in the first instance, to high transport costs, as ministries distributed supplies of everything from reinforced concrete to washing machines among "their" enterprises, whatever the distances involved.

Given the reality of autarchy within sectors, the Soviet economic bureaucracy was powerless to correct long-term structural imbalances. At least some of these dated back to the mobilized economy of the early 1940s. War losses may be viewed not only in absolute terms but also in terms of structural distortions. At a formative moment in its development, the Soviet industrial economy had been drastically skewed toward the defense sector, much of it in remote locations where coordination with the civilian economy was difficult. The culture of military secrecy and the isolationism fostered by a war of survival were also long-term legacies that undermined economic coordination.[38]

In capitalist economies information blockages are reduced by market pricing. In the Soviet Union, by contrast, prices were set by the economic authorities at various levels. The Soviet economy had more than 20 million products, all of which had to be assigned prices. Goskomtsen itself handled around 200,000 price proposals each year. The process of allocating prices had a tendency to become circular, as prices needed to be set at such a level that most enterprises could be profitable on paper. This effectively represented a cross-subsidy from good enterprises to weak ones and from certain sectors (notably consumer goods) to others (heavy industry). The lack of transparency was exacerbated by the fact that the Soviet economy had multiple price systems: one for wholesale trade, one for state retail, one for agricultural procurement, one for wages, and one for planning purposes – not to mention the far freer pricing that obtained at the collective farm market and in foreign trade with the capitalist world.[39]

The pricing system also gave enterprises incentives to introduce new products with a view to squeezing higher prices out of Goskomtsen; sales figures were not an important criterion. Producers in fact had disincentives to achieve rapid improvements in sales or efficiency, since past practice suggested that any such gains would simply be built into next year's planning norm. Instead of aiming for profits, Soviet enterprises tried to achieve growth by expanding their production capacity. With help from their ministries, they lobbied for state investment – which meant that new projects mushroomed and took longer to complete.[40]

It is hardly surprising that the Soviet economy was perennially incapable of guaranteeing quality. Enterprises had to fulfill plans whose indicators were overwhelmingly quantitative. Heavy-handed audit measures – such as the creation of a system of "quality certification" – did nothing to address structural flaws. Nor did the Soviet state have monetary levers by which to influence economic activity. It could not adjust credit through interest-rate policy, since credit was a political matter and interest rates remained symbolic. The State Bank (Gosbank) was overwhelmingly concerned with short-term finance as it tracked flows of money between enterprises. As one American economist observed, "it spends most of its time performing the duties of a very conservative commercial bank in the United States."[41] Microeconomics rather than macroeconomics were its preserve. The main day-to-day practical task of the 3,500 branches of Gosbank was making available the cash for Soviet enterprises to pay their workers. Beyond these immediate needs, enterprises were not allowed ready cash: transactions between enterprises were governed by offset procedures and conducted in "virtual" rubles.

What to do about these structural problems? Soviet leaders were not unaware of them: "reform" was a watchword of post-Stalin economic policy. The systemic problems of command economy were discussed as such from the 1960s onward.[42] The perennial bugbear of reforming efforts was the power of ministries, and the enterprises subordinated to them, to ignore or subvert instructions from the center.

Nikita Khrushchev was the first Soviet leader to attempt to make the economic apparatus more transparent, more responsive to the Party's directives, and more productive. An interesting snapshot of his early reforms was provided by Joseph Berliner towards the end of a pioneering 1957 study of Soviet industrial management. The Khrushchev regime had already carried out quite radical decentralizing measures. In certain key areas of heavy industry – for example the Ukrainian coal industry – control had shifted from central ministries to republic-level ministries. By the start of 1957, 55 percent of industrial production was controlled by republican councils of ministers; at Stalin's death, just four years earlier, the proportion had been less than a third. At the all-union level, two ambitious new committees had been set up under the auspices of the Council of Ministers: one was responsible for advancing the technological level of industry, the other for improving efficiency through labor and wage policy. There had also been measures to expand initiative-taking; the most striking was the removal of a 1941 law criminalizing the resale or exchange of commodities without formal permission.[43]

Khrushchev's most radical economic policy, which he embarked on shortly after defeating the leadership challenge of the "Anti-Party Group" in summer 1957, was the creation of Regional Economic Councils (*sovnarkhozy*). About 100 such bodies were created under the jurisdiction of republican Gosplan organizations. Almost all ministries in the sphere of production were disbanded. This was a decentralizing measure intended to tackle the problem of ministerial power head on, but it soon gave rise to the converse problem of localism. Where previously resources had been channeled by ministries to their own enterprises, they were now hoarded by the Regional Economic Councils; one kind of parochialism had given way to another. Growth rates and labor productivity soon tailed off, and the economy became no more transparent to the central authorities. In March 1963 came a major reversal, as the number of *sovnarkhozy* was reduced to 47.

The next major reform initiative in Soviet history came just after Khrushchev was ousted, and it tackled the question of incentives. From the early 1960s onward, debate had stirred among Soviet economists on this issue. In September 1965, prime minister Aleksei Kosygin came out and proposed a new package: as well as firmly reinstating the ministerial system that Khrushchev had tampered with, he proposed a reform of the enterprise incentive system and of pricing. Voluminous planning targets were to be reduced from as many as 40 targets to a mere eight, and output was to be measured not only in quantitative terms but also in terms of sales. Here was a gesture in the direction of market incentives. At long last, the enterprise manager was to be liberated from the central planning system and to become more responsive to a range of more purely economic stimuli. The price reform similarly was designed to take fuller consideration of the costs involved in production. But the subservience of pricing to planning objectives was still not in doubt. The pricing and incentive reforms did not begin in earnest until 1967, and in practice ministries and their subordinate committees had ample means of frustrating them: by stalling, by incorporating new procedures on their own terms, by ensuring that internal procedures were impenetrable to outsiders, and simply by ignoring the reforms. Within a few years, limits were placed on incentive funds, and the right to determine those limits shifted back to the central planners.[44]

With hindsight, the main effect of the Kosygin reform was that it reversed the Khrushchev reforms: ministries and the all-union economic institutions (Goskomtsen, Gossnab) were fully rehabilitated. Further reform initiatives followed in 1973 and 1979, but they were even more half-hearted than those of the mid-60s and did little to alleviate the curse of ministerial autarchy. From the late 1960s onward, various reform initiatives faced – and were defeated by – an essential conundrum: how to reform plan indicators to take into account quality rather than volume of production?[45]

The initiatives failed partly because they were half-hearted but also because no plan – however sophisticated – could on its own transform the deeply engrained institutional practices of the Soviet economy. Soviet managers had an inherent tendency to conservatism. In most cases, they had made their career in "their" sector by working successively as foreman, shop head and chief engineer before becoming enterprise director. For twenty years or more they had imbibed the ethos and the work practices of their enterprise.[46]

Moreover, the realities of the Soviet economy dictated a preoccupation not with quality of output but rather with supplies. A key part of the central planning apparatus was the massive supply organization named Gossnab. The task of allocating resources to the many branches of the Soviet economy was beyond the powers of a central bureaucracy, however elaborate, and in practice the task of securing supplies for production fell heavily on industrial managers themselves (who might find as much as half of their time taken up with supply issues), on the informal "fixers" (*tolkachi*) whose services they employed, and on local Party organs which were in a position to intervene across different sectors of the economy within a particular region. The role of Party organs was especially prominent in the years following 1957 when the Khrushchev economic reforms disrupted the centralized supply system, but it remained a constant of Soviet economic management even after Gossnab was restored to its functions after 1965.[47] The Party was constantly called on to resolve the problems of regional coordination thrown up by the vertically integrated system of ministerial control of enterprises in a particular economic sector. Its capacity to do so effectively was, however, limited by the fact that most enterprises were more inclined to take their orders from their branch ministry in Moscow. Unsurprisingly, ministerial officials in the 1970s spent rather little of their time (10 percent) on planning; the bulk of it went on short-term operational matters.[48]

So acute were the supply problems that enterprises were obliged to have permanent contingency arrangements. Spare parts were not produced centrally, so factories made them on their own. Around a third of the workforce in Soviet engineering plants were repair staff; the equivalent figure for the USA was 11 percent. Hoarding was an inevitable consequence of this system. To squeeze supplies out of other enterprises required energetic lobbying by industrial managers: dozens if not hundreds of telegrams and phone calls to the local Party authorities.[49]

The same principle extended to provisioning the workforce. Given the inadequacies of consumer goods production across the economy as a whole, particular branches of industry made it their business to keep their own people supplied. Every ministry had a department of "worker supplies" devoted to this task. Enterprises were especially active in producing consumer gadgets that lay outside their ostensible competence. In 1980, for example, about one-third of all the vacuum cleaners in the Soviet Union were produced under the auspices of the Ministry of the Aviation Industry. The defense sector had a near-monopoly on production of television sets, radios, and video recorders. Among its other achievements were potato-packaging machines and rotary lines for ice cream production.[50] By the late Brezhnev era, more than 50 different enterprises were making washing machines and 36 were making refrigerators. In most cases, moreover, the designs too were produced in-house, so many different models of fridges and TV sets were circulating in the Soviet economy.[51] While on the surface this might seem reminiscent of capitalist consumer choice, the reality could hardly have been more different: workers were obliged to "choose" the models made available in their branch of industry. This anarchic autarchy gave the lie to notions of the Soviet Union as a streamlined "planned" economy. It meant that consumer goods tended to be distributed within a particular branch of industry, not within a particular locality. This explains one notorious paradox of Soviet life: the fact that, for example, in a town with a lightbulb factory there might be no lamps in the shops. As in other cases, the local Party authorities were periodically called in

FIGURE 3.3 "The Komsomol is the Shock Team of the Five-Year Plan" (1969): An attempt to instill the spirit of 1930s labour heroism in the youth of the post-Stalin era.
Source: RIA Novosti.

as enforcers to make sure that such egregious cases did not recur, but their powers to change habits across the whole economy were limited by the leverage that the larger ministries continued to enjoy.

In the absence of market mechanisms, the Party had to resort to elaborate forms of intervention in order to improve quality and efficiency. One prominent initiative was a series of regional "Integrated Systems for Quality Management," whereby Party authorities in the 1970s urged enterprises to devote more resources to quality control departments. Another approach was to urge workers, through their trade unions, to crack down on waste. In the first half of the 1970s, the unions apparently elicited from the public 25 million specific proposals on how to improve conservation. There were also "control organs" beyond the Party. In 1965, a Committee of People's Control was set up as an antidote to bureaucratism. By 1984 it was reported to have drawn more than 10 million volunteers. A law of 1979 expanded the information-gathering and disciplinary powers of the Committee. On paper at least, the results were impressive: in the first half of 1984 the Committee carried out 152,000 "raids" on Soviet enterprises, helped to issue reprimands to 132,000 officials and workers, fined 27,400, and passed 3,000 cases on to the procurator.[52]

The system remained effective at mobilizing resources for particular projects – for example in the transport, energy, and defense sectors. The oil and gas fields of Western Siberia – absolutely crucial to the Soviet economy from the 1960s onward – were a case in point. When resources were needed to expand the extraction program, they could be found. This region was one of very few in the Soviet Union to benefit from an effective regional development plan.[53] The weapons industry likewise received consistently strong state backing. It was supported by at least 450 R&D organizations; all told, perhaps half of Soviet R&D spending went on the military. The defense sector had a stable administrative elite and did not suffer the same upheaval in the Khrushchev period as other branches of the economy. Those employed in the defense sector lived in "closed" cities that were well provisioned by Soviet standards.[54]

The Soviet economic system was untransparent and highly inefficient. It was delivering ever diminishing returns. By the mid-1970s, if not before, the evidence of declining economic performance was clear. By the 1980s, annual growth of GNP had fallen from 5 percent or more in the 1950s to around 2 percent.[55] So much evidence of Soviet economic failures can be adduced that it becomes hard to explain how this system kept going at any level and delivered any growth, however minimal, in the 1960s and 1970s.

A significant part of the explanation, no doubt, lies in the huge windfall that the USSR obtained as a result of escalating energy prices in the mid-1970s. But the system worked not in spite of but rather because of its lack of transparency. It was staffed by economic actors expert in maneuvering between the overlapping institutions of the Soviet party-state and who formed an impenetrable – but also functional – mesh of horizontal and vertical ties. These actors remained loyal executors of their formal and informal economic functions partly because of the esprit de corps in their enterprise or institution but also because their work position defined their place in the elaborate system of Soviet closed distribution. The Soviet system, unlike its capitalist counterparts, had made producers largely independent of consumers – which meant that the route to consumption for many Soviet people lay through their function as producer.

Another important reason, however, that the Soviet system remained viable was that the hard edges of its bureaucracy were smoothed by various forms of market activity. It is to these that we must now turn.

Socialist Markets

The title of this chapter is misleading: markets always existed in the Soviet Union, whether on the margins of the planned economy or (less frequently) under its wing. Urban markets, where city people could buy agricultural produce in short supply through the state distribution system, survived the introduction of the collective farm in the early 1930s. The extreme scarcity of wartime only confirmed their importance. During the war and just after, just about all pressing consumer needs could be met at the bazaars – at often astronomical prices. In 1943, for example, around 85 percent of outgoings on food in working-class households went into the private sector. While some market trade was illicit, much of it was tolerated by the authorities. Soviet society in these years was governed by a "survivalist consensus": the war had brought greater tolerance of make-do solutions to desperate material hardship. In conditions of social and economic breakdown, people simply had to find their own ways of getting things done – whether at the *kolkhoz* market, on the black market, through barter or even through bribery. In 1943, for example, it was possible to give blood, receive a loaf of bread, sell it at the market, and get bread ration cards for ten days with the money.[56]

In the aftermath of war, the authorities struggled with limited success to bring the situation under control. In the southern city of Rostov, which was recovering from German occupation and war damage, the authorities allowed the opening of "commercial" shops, thereby acknowledging that it was powerless to eradicate the market. Newspaper reports and internal Party documents alike provide abundant evidence of the extent of "speculation" in items ranging from ration cards to cigarettes to spare parts for tractors. Market activity was not the preserve of illegal traders: all kinds of people – veterans, women, young people, pensioners – were engaged in it as they scrambled to survive.[57]

In 1955, the recent law graduate Mikhail Gorbachev arrived in Stavropol to take up a post in the regional procuracy. Like any other person in his position, he had to confront the housing shortage. He spent several days wandering the city in a vain search for a room to rent. In due course his colleagues advised him to go through an agent, who gave him three addresses for a fee of 50 rubles. If the procuracy – an organization that was at that time fighting a campaign against forms of illegitimate economic activity – was using these informal methods, it was clear that antimarket campaigns were only moderately effective.[58]

FIGURE 3.4 Moscow, 1950s: People looking to exchange rooms at the unofficial housing market.
Source: © Yury Krivonosov / PhotoSoyuz.

Further up the social hierarchy, the formal and informal sectors of the economy were likewise interdependent. State functionaries were able to bend the rules with relative impunity in the interests of getting results quickly – or sometimes for entirely self-interested motives. One scholar has written of a "darker big deal" in the late Stalin period. Bribery, as far as we can judge, was rampant. The scale of illicit economic activity seems to have grown in line with the economy as a whole. The draconian antitheft law of 1947 probably did little to eradicate the illegal and informal economy: it mostly targeted people near the bottom of society rather than the office-holders and influence-wielders who made the economy possible.[59]

In the following three decades, the Soviet regime launched several campaigns against corruption and black-market "speculation." One of them dealt a blow to the flourishing black market in foreign currency in the late 1950s and early 1960s: it culminated in high-profile trials of "speculators" and even a few death sentences.[60] Another came in the mid-1980s and resulted in the purge of the Uzbek Party apparatus. But, while market activity might be harassed by the Soviet authorities, it could not be eradicated – not least because there were so many gray areas between licit, semilicit and illicit activity. One economist has gone so far as to color-code the various markets of the Soviet Union as red, pink, white, gray, black, and brown. In addition to the state-run "red" market of retail trade, there were "pink" commission shops where Soviet citizens could legally sell unwanted possessions at restricted markups. Next came "white" flea markets, bazaars, and collective farm markets, where pricing was generally unrestricted except for a few times of bad harvest in the late 1960s and 1970s when the state intervened. The semilegal "gray" market dealt primarily in services: rental of housing, private lessons, hairdressing, car repairs, and so on. Here a genuine market operated: the quality and location of a room, a flat or a dacha were reflected in its price. A Moscow bedsit with gas, electricity and modern bathroom, located within reach of the metro, would cost about 600 rubles per year, or a third of the average wage. A teacher giving private lessons could charge three rubles per session. Payments might be made "on the side" to doctors and nurses for good treatment. The "brown" market was above all the private sale of consumer goods and other items by the citizens who owned or had access to them (notably shop assistants), while the black market involved the larger-scale, professional sale of such goods at "speculative" prices.[61]

Another economist has written persuasively of a "Little Deal" in the Brezhnev era whereby the state tolerated "the expansion of a wide range of petty private economic activities, some legal, some in the penumbra of the legal, and some clearly and obviously illegal." The effect was "the reallocation by private means of a significant fraction of Soviet national income according to private preferences."[62] This arrangement was certainly an embarrassment to Soviet ideology and Communist morality, but it was an important means for this producer-dominated economy to muddle through and alleviate its failures on the consumer front. The Little Deal was system-maintaining, not system-threatening.

There were, however, two other kinds of market that provided a more serious challenge to the Soviet order. One was the international market of foreign trade. The leaders of the USSR were increasingly traducing the autarchic principles of Stalinism. On both sides of the Cold War divide, from the mid-1960s onward, opinion turned in favor of trade with the enemy. On both sides, the reasoning was at least as much pragmatic as ideological. American business was concerned that it might miss out on important commercial opportunities, while the Soviets had a pressing need of Western technology. Trade with the capitalist world rose from just under 20 percent of foreign trade in 1950 to one-third in 1988 (having peaked in the early 1980s). The Soviet national debt grew accordingly from $11.5 billion in 1975 to $38 billion in the mid-1980s. Soviet needs were not only hi-tech: the USSR also had to go on the world market in search of less sophisticated commodities. In 1972 it concluded an enormous deal for the import of grain from

North America on advantageous economic terms. Although Soviet trade negotiators found the world market operating according to very different rules than the internal Soviet economy, they showed they could be canny operators even when they were in a weak bargaining position.[63]

Why, then, did the international economy constitute a threat to the Soviet economic order? While Soviet negotiators might achieve short-term tactical successes, the Soviet system had been built for autarchy in the 1930s and 1940s. It was a self-contained world with its own formal and informal rules. When it came into contact with other economic systems – even the relatively tame ones to be found in eastern Europe – it had trouble.[64]

For much of the 1970s, it just so happened that the oil crisis and the American will to détente put the USSR in a strong position relative to Western business partners. In the longer term, however, the country was placing itself in thrall to Western economic cycles; the Soviet economy would be in poor shape to meet the downturn in world oil prices in 1986. The USSR was also engaging in ruinous economic competition with a richly endowed and technologically advanced superpower rival. As one economist estimated in the late Soviet period, at current rates of growth the USSR could expect to catch up the America of the 1970s in basic forms of consumer output not before the second half of the twenty-first century.[65] Yet the Soviet Union was spending vast sums on making sure its weapons systems were up to date.

The other market with which the Soviet system could find no effective long-term accommodation was the labor market. Ever since the abandonment of Stalinist coercion in the mid-1950s, the Soviet state had found itself in a weak position vis-à-vis the workforce. Much as the authorities might talk of discipline and mobilization, the economic reality was perennial labor shortage. Various carrot-and-stick methods were tried. In the 1950s, job-changing was decriminalized, but at the same time the state tried to squeeze greater productivity out of workers by reforming the wage system in industry. The previous arrangement based on production norms had been ably manipulated by managers, who had set norms deliberately low so as to give their workers bonuses. The reform brought a downturn in earnings for many workers, but they were in a position to vote with their feet. Labor turnover in some mines went as high as 50 percent or more, as workers sought better living conditions and higher earnings. Despite various disciplinary measures – press campaigns against "flitters," a new law on social "parasitism," a failed campaign in early 1964 to introduce a labor passport – labor in the Soviet Union was most of the time a "seller's market." In 1964, for example, Moscow alone was 100,000 operators short of its requirements in the machine-tool industry. In due course, managers proved just as adept at manipulating the new wage parameters (based on overall plan fulfillment, economizing on materials, and improvements in quality) as the old system of norms. Labor turnover in the later Soviet period was extremely high: around 20 percent per annum. Enterprises competed for skilled and reliable workers by offering them benefits in housing and provisions and by promoting them fast.[66]

In sum, the Soviet economy circa 1982 was a messy, inefficient but functioning system. It contained many gray areas and lacked clear-cut distinctions between "first" and "second" economies. Industrial managers had more discretion than Party officials were happy with. Workers were making less effort than either managers or apparatchiki would have liked. None of this was new – the Soviet system had been seeking fitfully to reform itself since the mid-1950s – but a few darker clouds were gathering. Growth had clearly slowed in the second half of the 1970s, and the global superpower mission was becoming economically unsustainable. It was one thing to identify these problems, quite another to do something about them. Within a few years, however, solutions would be in the air.

Towards Collapse

Mikhail Gorbachev's famous perestroika had its origins in yet another Soviet economic reform effort. In the early 1980s, a reformist body of opinion in the Communist Party leadership was reaching the conclusion that something had to be done about the economy, and that this time reform had to be less ineffectual than previous initiatives of the 1960s and 1970s. The leadership was well aware of the perennial Soviet problems: inefficiency, poor quality of production, falling labor productivity, structural imbalances, and supply failures. By a range of indexes, Soviet growth rate had fallen from the late 1960s onward. For most of its existence the USSR had achieved growth by expanding the resource base – above all, by drawing more people into the industrial economy through constant rural–urban migration. By the late 1970s, the labor pool in the villages was close to exhausted, and more qualitative improvements were required.

The regime was showing an unprecedented willingness to take advice. A meeting of representatives of the Central Committee, the Academy of Sciences and Gosplan heard in summer 1983 what came to be known as the "Novosibirsk Report." Written by an innovative group of Siberian sociologists headed by Tat'iana Zaslavskaia, this document noted that the Soviet system of centralized management was stuck in a 1930s rut. It might have been adequate for the tasks of early industrialization, but now the economy was vastly more complicated, its technology more advanced, and its workforce more diverse and better educated. It was time to abandon the exclusive reliance on top-down solutions and instead to allow both workers and management to take more initiative; in other words, to take the politics out of the economy and put society back in.[67]

The brief period in office of Iurii Andropov set new standards for frank discussion. In December 1982, the Soviet press began to carry selective summaries of topics discussed at Politburo meetings. Andropov himself called for greater discipline across all sectors of the economy. In 1983, the police conducted a campaign against absenteeism by hauling people off the streets during working hours. A decree of August 1983 increased the disciplinary powers of managers over their workers.[68] Andropov also sought more positive ways of stimulating the economy: he supported greater independence of units such as enterprises and farms. The perennial question of Soviet economic reform was how to weaken the interfering center. A decree of July 1983 announced the experimental adoption of a new incentive structure for five branches of industry (a total of 700 enterprises). In 1985, the experiments were extended to a further 1,600 enterprises.[69]

The Andropov reforms offered a more vigorous approach to familiar problems: how to motivate the workforce and weaken the grip of the ministries over effective economic policy. The short-term evidence was that increasing the pressure on management and workforce could bring some benefits, especially in the larger branches of the economy, but was this a medium-term solution? Conversely, how far could a Soviet leader tamper with the system without fundamentally destabilizing it?

Gorbachev started his period in power very much as Andropov's successor. His slogan of the "human factor" was of a piece with the motivational mantras of the previous three decades. Gorbachev too took unpopular disciplinary measures to improve efficiency, foremost among them an anti-alcoholism campaign that quickly brought him the nickname of "mineral-water Secretary" (*mineral'nyi sekretar'*).[70] But, as usual, economic reform was not taking place in a political vacuum, and political considerations would soon drive perestroika beyond the limits of any previous Soviet reform. Gorbachev started, in time-honored fashion, with a cull of personnel and a bureaucratic reshuffle to consolidate his power. His own field of policy expertise, agriculture, was subjected to constant reshuffles: at the end of 1985, a State Agro-Industrial Committee was created to replace the various ministries and the state committee that had previously been in charge of agriculture; this body was itself abolished in 1989, and the management of agriculture was transferred from the all-union authorities to the republics. The constant reorganizations had an adverse effect on agricultural management.[71]

The next stage was to stimulate small business activity, thereby creating responsible owners for property that had previously belonged to everyone and no one. A Law on Individual Labor Activity came into effect in May 1987. Although this expanded the range of legitimate economic activity, it still allowed local authorities considerable discretionary power over the registration of new businesses; hired labor, moreover, was still forbidden. A further law of May 1988 strengthened the position of cooperatives and reduced the discretion of local authorities.

The cooperative movement showed explosive growth: from 14,000 at the start of 1988 to 77,500 a year later. A further 150 percent growth came in 1989.[72] By the end of 1991, about 250,000 new small enterprises had been set up in the Russian Federation.[73] The more successful and better-connected of these had practically a license to print money by exploiting the manifold shortages in the collapsing state socialist economy.

At the same time, a new law (effective from 1 January 1988) gave state enterprises greater freedom to raise wages, avoid fixed pricing, and make their own production decisions. While this might have sounded like an enlightened incentive package, in the absence of more far-reaching reform of the economic system it led to price increases without greater availability of goods. Wages and benefits grew, while domestic production shrank by 12.8 percent in 1991.[74] Before long, in the absence of an effective financial system and of adequate political enforcement, enterprises were resorting to barter to overcome their supply problems. The latest in the succession of Soviet wage reforms was a time-wasting failure. All the while, the budget deficit rose to almost four times the figures of the early 1980s.[75] To make a bad situation worse, there was no oil boom to rescue Soviet finances. Quite the reverse: oil prices dipped in 1986.

Gorbachev neglected reform of the agricultural sector and held back from controlled price increases – a politically awkward but essential measure. The miners' strike of 1989 seems to have caused a comprehensive failure of nerve on this score. Most of all, however, Gorbachev neglected the political basis for carrying out any controlled economic reform. The undermining of the central Party's monopoly on power – through increasingly contested elections and the transfer of political functions from the center to the republics – transformed the basis for economic life. The Party had, to be sure, been an obstacle to far-reaching change, but it had also been a facilitator that ensured this complex and impenetrable system functioned. Party committees at various levels had upheld the rules of the system (both written and unwritten) and had helped enterprises to overcome supply bottlenecks. The capacity of the central Party and state agencies to monitor the activities of enterprises had in any case been falling over the previous two decades, but it now entered a phase of precipitous decline.

When the power of the CPSU started to disintegrate, the way was open for a bitter power struggle that was also a struggle for control (or, de facto, ownership) of major state assets. Economics would turn out to be a crucial element in the sovereignty war between Russia and the USSR. The essential struggle was not between "hardliners" and "reformers" but between different groups of claimants on state assets. In the acid assessment of Donald Filtzer, the conflict between Gorbachev and Yeltsin "was about which faction of the bureaucratic elite – the old All-Union bureaucracy or the emergent apparatus of the Russian Republic – would inherit the state property about to be privatized."[76] When that question

Figure 3.5   The impact of the shortage economy, Moscow 1991.
Source: © Dmitry Borko / PhotoSoyuz.

was answered in the last third of 1991, the struggle over ownership continued on a new footing in the 1990s.

Kapitalizm

The privatization campaign that followed within months of the Soviet collapse was designed to shake the hold of the ex-Soviet ministries over the tens of thousands of enterprises in the Russian Federation. The priority was to transfer ownership at high speed, and as far as possible to make ownership open to "outsiders" (that is, people other than the ex-Soviet management). According to the privatization program confirmed in August 1992, all Russian citizens were to be issued with vouchers which they could use to acquire shares in the joint-stock companies that were to replace Soviet-era enterprises. Ownership would be divided as follows: the first portion would go to the managers and workers of the company, a substantial minority stake would remain with the state, and the public would be able to bid for the rest. The scale of the program, which lasted until June 1994, was undeniably impressive: more than 20,000 enterprises were converted to joint-stock status, most of the Russian population received vouchers, and around 15,000 enterprises with a workforce of 17 million held voucher auctions. By the start of 1996, almost 18,000 industrial enterprises, accounting for 88 percent of industrial workers, had been privatized.[77]

But the notion of headlong privatization needs to be qualified on several counts. Most obviously, the state was a major shareholder in privatized enterprises and enjoyed corresponding scope to influence their operations. As of 1996, the state owned about 38 percent of Russia's 50 largest corporations, while many large enterprises had not been privatized at all. Furthermore, despite the ambitions of Yeltsin's privatization team, insiders were generally rather successful at keeping out outsiders. Many managers wasted little time in assuming de facto or de jure control of the shareholding of their workforce. One method of expropriating shares was to seize the holding of employees who resigned or were fired, or to ask or instruct the current workforce to transfer their voting rights to management. Takeover by outside investors was hindered by the absence in most cases of an open share market. Shareholder registers were closely kept secrets in 1993–4, and potential buyers had to go to enormous lengths to find people willing to sell shares. Almost no reliable financial information on the enterprise was available for potential investors; only insiders – and not all of those – had the basis for an informed decision. Outsiders were kept off boards of directors, which remained effectively management councils. Outsider shareholdings, moreover, were also "diluted" by generous interest-free share issues to insiders. The oil company Komineft – the 36th largest company in Russia with reserves of over 2 billion barrels – managed in this way to reduce the stake of outsiders by a third. Over the period 1994–6 there was a slight increase in ownership by outside investors, which rose to a third on average, while about a tenth of the stock remained with the state. In 1996, insider (employee) ownership accounted for 58 percent, outsider ownership for 32 percent, and the state for 9 percent. There was some evidence that such figures concealed the reality of continued managerial and nomenklatura hegemony: not all "outsiders" were as far outside as they seemed. The number of cases where outsiders formed the majority owners came to just under 20 percent.[78]

What was beyond doubt was that a majority of the larger corporations had no clear majority owner. In other words, the long-term relationship between insiders, outsiders, and the state had still to be established. This was all the more the case given that so much state property had not yet changed ownership. Many of the largest enterprises in the Russian economy remained beyond the scope of the privatization program of 1994–6: notably those in communications, metallurgy, and the energy sector. Conversely, a good deal of "privatization by exception" was taking place outside the privatization program proper. A notable example was Gazprom which was made a joint-stock company by presidential decree of 5 November 1992.[79]

A decree of July 1994 announced the procedures for the second great wave of privatization. Further state holdings were to be sold at auction, the rationale being to raise money for the cash-strapped Russian state but also to give better opportunities to outside investors and improve corporate governance. In January 1996, a new corporate law required every company with more than 50 employees to be openly traded, for the shareholder register to be regularly updated, for annual reports to be delivered to shareholders, and for auditor's reports to be compiled. Outsiders were gaining slightly greater representation on boards of directors, even if this still did not in many cases adequately reflect their ownership stake.[80]

But the slight tightening of corporate governance was much less significant than the frenzied property redistribution that continued to take place after the first wave of privatization in 1992–4. The most notorious example was the "loans-for-shares" scheme of 1995 whereby the state put up a number of major enterprises as collateral for loans from investors. The state duly defaulted on repayment, and ownership of the assets was taken over by the creditors. The investors in question (in due course dubbed "oligarchs") had acquired substantial capital, mostly by exploiting loopholes in the financial sector in the late 1980s and early 1990s. They were now ready to turn their cash into more tangible assets, and the president was willing to indulge them through a series of rigged auctions. The parties in the election agreed in advance not to bid against each other, and outsiders (notably including foreigners) were kept out. For example, a juicy 38 percent in Norilsk Nickel was secured by Oneksimbank for $170.1 million when the minimum bid was set at $170 billion. Not coincidentally, the auction was run by the very same Oneksimbank, which had excluded a rival bid of more than twice the minimum price.[81]

There was, however, much more to the struggle for property in the mid-1990s than loans-for-shares. After the conclusion of the initial voucher privatization, at least 40 percent of enterprises were still state-owned – not to mention the large stakes retained by the state in privatized enterprises. Between 1994 and 1997, thousands more Soviet-era enterprises passed from state into private ownership. Economic empires, many of them regional rather than Moscow-based, formed and re-formed as the struggle continued for control of privatized enterprises. The first wave of privatization left a legacy of multiple minority ownership, and there were now moves to clarify the lines of authority in the new Russian economy. Investors or managers might now look to form powerful "financial-industrial groups" or to develop close relations with the federal or regional government.[82]

Most of the struggles for property took place at the level of the individual enterprise. The various competing actors included managers, regional governments, and outsiders (whether Russian or foreign). Alliances between the various parties were sometimes fleeting. Both insiders and outsiders engaged in practices of dubious ethics. Given that an ex-Soviet regional economy was highly dependent on a number of key enterprises, politics and economics – or local government and enterprise management – were often tightly interwoven. As Jerry Hough has observed, "it made no sense to distinguish between politicians and managers in the Soviet system."[83] It made almost as little sense in the early post-Soviet economy.

In one reading of economic history, the privatization campaigns of the 1990s were not a radical and decisive break with the state-owned economy but rather the culmination of two or three decades when economic administrators had thrown off Party shackles and increasingly behaved like independent operators; they had become "not so much bureaucrats as a peculiarly Soviet type of economic actor operating in conditions where their simultaneous occupation of the posts of state and industry, and takeover of the powers of the state, reduced the latter to a husk." It is striking, for example, that only nine of the 69 new ministers appointed under Brezhnev had come up through the Party apparatus. Ministries socialized their officials as soldiers in an economic army, providing them with their own uniforms and insignia. Operational control of enterprises had given managers and ministerial officials effective ownership, which in the 1990s could finally be converted to legal ownership.[84]

But leaving aside the matter of ownership, there was the question of what the new owners would be able to do with their property: how was this economy going to work in conditions of desperate instability? The 1990s were a period of frantic making do. The reformers' goal of a transparent, dynamic, fully monetarized market economy was belied in any number of ways. Although pricing for many commodities was liberalized at the start of 1992, prices could not be properly "free" because of the political requirement to provide subsidized energy to Russia (and other parts of the former Soviet Union). In addition, the government was providing off-budget subsidies to some enterprises that would have failed in free market conditions – and to others that might have succeeded but enjoyed powerful protectors. In 1994, it is estimated that 3–4 percent of Russian GDP was eaten up by tax exemptions for enterprises.[85]

Enterprises themselves maneuvered creatively, and often desperately, to remain in business. As ready cash became the greatest shortage item in the liberalized

Russian economy, many economic actors resorted to barter (a practice that had begun as a response to shortages in the Gorbachev era but made a strong return in the 1990s). Almost half of industrial output in the Ekaterinburg and Novosibirsk regions in 1997 was sold through barter. The 1990s have been described as a period of economic "involution."[86] Very little capital was available to modernize enterprises, even if the will was there. The best means of survival was to reduce the scale of operations, seize whatever subsidies and loans were available, and delay as long as possible in paying taxes and creditors. Those creditors often included the workforce: the mid-1990s saw desperate delays in payment of salaries.

Trust and legal enforcement were in short supply. These were perfect conditions for the takeover of thousands of small businesses by organized crime – the notorious post-Soviet "mafia." According to police figures, cases of extortion grew at a rate of 15–30 percent per year from 1990 onward, reaching a peak of more than 17,000 in 1996 – and this was without doubt a serious underestimate, given the reluctance of victims to report such cases. The first half of the 1990s was, in one scholar's words, a phase of "ferocious competition between violence-managing agencies." As in other cases of mafia activity, wholesale and retail trade – which had mushroomed from 1987 onward – was an especially attractive field of activity: it required low technology but offered high turnover. In 1996, more than 40 percent of shop owners in Moscow, Smolensk, and Ulyanovsk admitted regular dealings with racketeers. Even more revealingly, they considered this less of a problem than state taxes and lack of capital. The state might in fact be seen as merely "one private protection company among others," and for much of the 1990s – with law enforcement ineffective and corrupt and tax demands escalating – it performed this function less adequately than the private sector proper. A private security company, by contrast, could provide a "roof" for business transactions: in other words, it had effective – sometimes violent – means of negotiating and enforcing contracts without recourse to the dysfunctional legal system. Symptomatically, the private security sector was staffed by a large number of defectors from the police: as of 1 July 1998, about one-third of the 156,169 private security employees in Russia came from the regular police (MVD) or the KGB/FSB.[87]

Even leaving aside criminal activity and violence, the key institutions of the post-Soviet economy tended to work in peculiar ways. The nonstate banking sector started existence in 1988 following the law on cooperatives and achieved impressive short-term expansion. By the launch of price liberalization, Russia had 1,360 banks. To call these institutions independent would, however, be a stretch. Most of them were "pocket banks" that existed to service ex-Soviet organizations (and whose existence was dependent on the patronage bequeathed by the Soviet period). One survey of the commercial banking sector in 1990 found that more than half had their origins in Soviet ministries, regional soviets, or organizations of the Communist Party. This was nomenklatura banking in a very real sense. The new Russian state and independent investors (especially foreign) were getting no piece of bank privatization.[88]

Against the backdrop of the unruly private sector, the Central Bank of Russia was unable and unwilling to impose financial discipline: to refrain from printing money and issuing credits. This was in large part a politically motivated decision, as the officials of the Central Bank took exception to Yeltsinite "shock therapy" and its likely impact on production. The Bank's scope for action was in any case limited, as it did not control the entire ruble zone of the CIS. It was not until 1993, when an IMF loan was made conditional on more restrictive monetary policies, that the CBR began to tighten its ship.[89]

All the while, the Russian finance industry was growing, but its operations were short-term. There were ample profits to be made by playing on inflation and few incentives to engage in risky long-term loans (which between 1992 and 1995 dropped below 5 percent of all loans). Nor were banks doing much to service the ordinary saver, who could choose between the derisory interest rates offered in the state savings book and any number of pyramid schemes. No deposit insurance system was in place to protect people who placed money with commercial banks. Russian banks were also protected from foreign competition by a presidential decree of November 1993, which was only repealed in April 1995. The only longer-term investment the banks committed to was the cash-starved Russian state: from 1993 onward they bought up state promissory notes (GKOs), judging with some reason that the state was as good a creditor as they were likely to find in the unstable 1990s. This decision, however, backfired badly in August 1998 with the ruble devaluation.[90]

Other financial institutions were characterized by the same short horizons. So-called "credit" cards were effectively debit cards, requiring of account holders substantial security deposits. Credit bureaus were not established in Russia until 2005 (and even then they had serious limitations, given the reluctance of commercial organizations to share information with each other), and information gathered from an applicant's employer or acquaintances was not considered reliable. Banks instead often relied on personal vetting of the applicant or on whatever contacts they could muster in other institutions (for example the police). Debit cards finally began to spread more widely through Russian society by means of "salary projects" whereby a bank made an agreement with a company to issue cards to the workforce. Companies had an onerous payroll task taken off their hands, and did not need to worry about raising cash to pay their employees, while banks gained new customers. The salary project method was especially successful in company towns like Cherepovets and Magnitogorsk, where it was possible to achieve high saturation of the population.[91]

In the banking sector, then, there was no immediate leap into economic liberalism. The survival of Soviet structures was all the more apparent in the Russian village of the 1990s. Although, in an unprecedented reversal of decades of urbanization, the rural population briefly swelled in 1992–4, this was a symptom of the economic crisis besetting the cities at that time and not a sign of rural renaissance. The demographic decline of the village soon resumed. According to the 2002 census, 22 percent of all villages now had fewer than ten inhabitants. This census was also the first to include the category of villages that had no population at all: these numbered 13,000.[92]

Boris Yeltsin and his team forced through, against parliamentary opposition, a program for commercialization of agriculture along the lines of privatization in industry. Decrees of December 1991 stipulated that collective farms should prepare for "reorganization" on a more commercial footing and that *kolkhozniki* should be issued with certificates for the amount of land they were due (thus in principle making possible the withdrawal of individual households from the collective). On paper the results were impressive. About two-thirds of farms had duly reorganized by the start of 1993, and almost all of them by the following year. Whether this meant more fundamental change was dubious. Farm directors were easily able to retain their control under the new legal arrangement of the joint-stock company. Many farm members leased the land they had received straight back to the collective; alternatively, farm managers and local authorities might stall in issuing their land certificates. Admittedly, the number of private farms jumped to an impressive 270,000 by the end of 1993, but their share of agricultural production was tiny. Given the difficulty of obtaining credit, the unfavorable terms of trade with industry, and the risks of independent agricultural enterprise at the best of times, it was small wonder that many rural people chose to remain within the collective while, as in Soviet times, devoting much of their time and energy to their private plots. In 1994, personal plots produced a healthy 67 percent of Russia's vegetables, but by 1997 that proportion had risen still further to 77 percent.[93]

In 1998, the output of Russian farming (in stable prices) was only just over half that of 1990. The agricultural economy began to grow again in 1999, but output in 2002 had still only reached two-thirds of the 1990 figure.[94] The development of the private sector in farming was puny, and agriculture was dominated by the successors to the collective farms (the joint-stock companies). The lack of change in institutional arrangements was due partly to the difficulty of making private farming viable, given that market rates now had to be paid for goods and transport, but also to the slowness of land reform in the 1990s. A new Land Code, which allowed the sale of agricultural land, was finally adopted in 2003 following a dozen years of fierce debates in the Russian legislature.

Individual farmers remained in the collectives largely because this connection gave them the best chance of obtaining what they needed – fertilizer, feed, equipment – for their household operations. As earlier in the twentieth century, the household plot was the center of agricultural energies. Large-scale specialized agriculture was a rarity. Proximity to the city, and the size of that city, was the surest indicator of the productivity of agricultural land: given the costs of transport over huge distances with still inadequate roads, this was only economic sense.

At the same time, some degree of consolidation took place with a view to ensuring local and regional autarchy. The more ambitious large farms built their own processors which took business away from the large processing plants. These plants produced two-thirds of Russia's meat and milk in 1990, but one-third or less in 1997. Agricultural assets were redistributed into regional economic groups, often with the clear intervention of regional governments. Here was a pragmatic return to the principle of "vertical integration" widely adopted by branches of industry in the Soviet period.[95]

It is all too easy, then, to find evidence of economic malaise in the 1990s; and, to the extent that cures were found, the continuities with Soviet practice were as evident as the breaks. The key question is perhaps not why Russia succumbed to a combination of involution and cut-throat primitive capital accumulation but rather how it was that an apparently stable new order was established so suddenly at the start of the twenty-first century.

Around the turn of the century came signs that key institutions were becoming more robust, and that a higher degree of trust was entering the economy on an everyday level. Ordinary bank depositors proved willing to leave a bit more of their salary in their accounts, and to make more transactions by card rather than in cash. Lending to households started rising steeply in the early twenty-first century: from $1 billion in 2000 to about $34 billion by the start of 2006. After the 1998 crash, banks needed new sources of profits and switched to a more proactive, consumer-driven model. The main location for handing out cards became not the workplace but the mall: Visa International reported that more than half of credit card holders in Russia acquired their cards through retail locations. By the end of 2006, there were more than 70 million plastic cards in Russia, even if credit cards still made up less than 2 percent of all cards issued.[96]

Signs of stabilization and consolidation could also be found in the most unruly areas of the post-Soviet economy. In the second half of the 1990s came a second wave of property redistribution which, whatever its iniquities, had the effect of consolidating and stabilizing ownership. Early privatization had taken place at the level of individual enterprises, which created difficulties in highly consolidated sectors such as oil and gas. In the late 1990s, a determined new group of oligarchs set about rounding out their corporate holdings and securing majority ownership of important companies. They used tried-and-tested dubious methods against minority shareholders and recalcitrant smaller companies, but the result was a far higher degree of consolidation in the oil and metals sectors by the end of the decade. It seemed that the oligarchs, whatever their vices, had turned from speculation to longer-term resource management.[97]

The state, moreover, appeared to be rediscovering its prerogative of setting and enforcing sensible ground rules for economic activity. The early Putin era quickly saw the introduction of a more enlightened fiscal policy: in July 2000 a flat rate of 13 percent was introduced for income tax. Efforts were made to tighten up corporate governance and the banking system, and to modernize the welfare system by making benefits less indiscriminate. Government finances started to look far healthier: 2000 was the first in a series of years when Russia managed a budget surplus. Energy revenues were surging, while there was no comparable increase in spending. Inflation was reduced to an acceptable level. Domestic capital investment grew in this more stable economic environment, as did foreign direct investment, which reached a total of $130 billion by the end of 2006. The state made partially successful efforts to crack down on capital flight. It used windfall revenues to slash Russia's foreign debt which reached a new low of 18 percent of GDP in 2006 – far below the figures in most western European countries. At the beginning, the government made a real and symbolic break with opportunism and short-termism by setting up a "stabilization fund."[98] The Russian state in the 1990s had turned from gamekeeper into poacher; now it was restored as a kind of gamekeeper.

Or was it? The early Putin era offered much evidence that the struggle for control of major assets, in which politics was thinly veiled economics (and vice versa), had not yet ended. After a new cohort of "oligarchs" came on the scene in the late 1990s, the Putinite state (dominated by military and security elites) undermined their property rights. It turned out that the oligarchs and conglomerates enriched by the privatization of the Yeltsin era could be challenged by a state that was thought to have been disastrously weak for most of the 1990s. The takeover of large assets between 1994 and 1997 had been not the end point of postcommunist property redistribution but just another stage. A serious source of weakness for privatized companies was the debt that they ran up to the state-dominated energy monopolies Gazprom and Unified Energy Systems. Under the terms of a new bankruptcy law of 1998, it was much easier for creditors to precipitate the collapse of private enterprises and thus to bring about a change of ownership. When the currency collapsed in August 1998, bankruptcy became all the more common: the figures rose from 4,300 in 1997 to 11,000 in 1999.[99] It turned out that the major economic groups in Russia were a good deal more precarious than they had appeared in the mid-1990s.

The surest means of achieving economic clout after 1998 was not to hold government bonds or to speculate on currency but to gain control over exports and the energy sector. Here it turned out that the state was in an excellent position to reassert itself, notably through its control of Gazprom. It could also call in debts, identify tax violations, and simply use force. These were the weapons employed against the oligarchs Vladimir Gusinsky and Boris Berezovsky, who were driven out of the country and forced to relinquish their media empires as well as sizable assets in other sectors. The state flexed its newfound muscles to even greater effect in the campaign against Mikhail Khodorkovsky and his oil company Yukos that began in the summer of 2003. Key executives were arrested, Yukos headquarters were raided, and astronomically high tax demands were made of the company. Then Yukos was denied the means even to begin paying as the legal system froze its shares and other assets. Then the government began selling off these assets, the main beneficiary being the *silovik* establishment. Finally, Khodorkovsky (who had been arrested in October 2003 for fraud and tax evasion) was put on trial, receiving a nine-year sentence in May 2005.[100]

The motivation for the campaign against Yukos was a matter of much speculation. The reasons lay partly in the personal antipathy between Putin and Khodorkovsky and in a general desire on the part of the president to put the oligarchs in their place. But it also served the hard-nosed purpose of boosting the tax-collecting capacity of the state. Other oligarchs quickly dropped tax minimization schemes. In 2004 the oil sector provided 22.8 percent of total tax revenues (as compared with a little over 14 percent in 1999–2001). Even if some of the increase was due to high oil prices, the shock administered to the oligarchs had played a substantial part: by the middle of 2005 tax revenues had risen 250 percent since the start of the Yukos affair.[101]

The longer-term question was whether this was a one-off shock administered to an energy sector that had been cheating the state budget for a decade or, rather, a sign that the state would continue to intervene arbitrarily in the economy. The Yukos affair certainly did not mean that the close relationship between government and big business was at an end. Certain other oligarchs did less to offend Putin and managed to hold their position. The state was merely the most powerful of many actors, and the tight connection between politics and economics remained. As Andrew Barnes observes, "regardless of how strong the central state became under Putin, it was not the only competitor for property." Russia's magnates continued to form a changing cast. Further privatization was occurring even as Yukos came under attack. One significant trend of the Putin years was a shift of economic power from the center to the regions. The oligarchs of the early twenty-first century were making good parallel careers in regional government.[102]

Future cycles of redistribution of property would depend to a great extent on the condition of the energy sector. An economic determinist might say that the apparent restoration of state power in the early twenty-first century was no more than the latest twist of the global economic cycle. Vladimir Putin was lucky enough to have the economic levers of political domination – state-dominated energy companies at a time of high world prices – at just the moment he needed them.

This brought an end to 15 dismal years in Russia's energy sector. Early post-communism was, among many other things, the story of how Russia went in a few years from being the world's largest oil producer to a mere middle ranker. Between 1987 and 1996, Russia's production almost halved.[103] The fall was caused by a combination of flagging investment in the later Soviet period, a depletion of the productive West Siberian wells that had been discovered in the 1960s, a drop in world oil prices from 1986, and the collapse of state funding at the end of the 1980s.

After the collapse of the Soviet economy, the new private companies did not have the resources, the personnel or the management structures to launch exploration programs for new sources; under the old system, this enormously costly business had been taken care of by the Soviet state. When state funding collapsed in 1989–91, producers were not able to rely on the world market as they were hampered by price caps on the domestic market, while export was undermined by tax and transport tariffs imposed by a Russian state that was desperate to drum up some revenue. Almost 80 percent of crude oil production was consumed within Russia and sold at internal prices that were initially not much more than one-fortieth of world prices. There was some increase to 1995, but prices were still too low to bring the oil industry the profits needed for investment. What mainly took place during the 1990s was "extension exploration"; but the law of diminishing returns had already set in. In 1999, world oil prices began to climb steeply, and new money entered the coffers for consolidation and development. In addition, the devaluation of the ruble in 1998 suddenly made Russian industry of all kinds more competitive. Production rose by 40 percent between 1998 and 2003. By 2004, Russia was on a par with Saudi Arabia as an oil producer.

Yet there remained a nagging suspicion that Russia's economy was too reliant on oil to maintain robust health. The suspicion hardened into certainty with the global economic crisis of autumn 2008, which hit Russia harder than most. Within a few months, the Russian stock market lost 80 percent of its value. The vaunted political stability of the Putin era was about to endure ordeal by recession. Petro-authoritarianism was good at maintaining its political hegemony, but it did need high oil prices in order to flourish and keep up its popularity. Ruling without popularity was possible but undesirable for a ruling class accustomed to a "managed democracy" that delivered 70 percent approval ratings.

Conclusion

We end, then, with a conclusion that might have gratified the Bolsheviks: almost a century after their revolution, economics remains the only appropriate lens through which to view political developments in Russia.

The Bolsheviks diagnosed bourgeois domination of capitalist societies through monopoly ownership of major assets. The theory of Marxist revolution was that it should bring about a long-term transition to a much more widely disseminated ("proletarian") sense of ownership where all members of society would have an equal stake in economic life and equal incentives to take part in it. The reality of Marxism-Leninism was that the state took upon itself the functions of ownership.

This, however, was a crushing burden even for such an overcontrolling regime as the Bolsheviks. In reality, economic life was controlled by a number of institutions with their own sets of interests (which might not correspond to those of the central plan). In the first instance, that meant the bureaucracies charged with managing specific branches of the economy: the people's commissariats (later ministries). State power over economic life was exercised in its most brutal form in the 1930s, when millions of peasants were dragooned into collective farms or exile, and millions of others poured into the construction sites of the first and second five-year plans. Industrial managers were kept on their mettle by a terror campaign. But this was sheer coercion to bring about an economic transformation, not a viable long-term management strategy. Even before the 1930s were over, the people's commissariats started to regain their equilibrium, and their security and (within limits) autonomy were only confirmed by the war years. At the same time, the traditional economic victims of Soviet power – unskilled workers and, above all, peasants – were subjected to unremitting exploitation.

Over the longer term, however, the drawbacks of this Stalinist economic model became apparent. This was an austerity economy dedicated to extracting surplus from the population. But what happened when there were no more resources to take, and when surplus extraction required not brute force but less tangible qualities such as motivation and innovation? The collective farm had been effective as a means of crushing the independent peasantry, but it was no guarantee of agricultural productivity. Ministerial officials and factory directions might have their primary loyalty to their own branch of industry or their enterprise, not to the overall cause of increasing Soviet productivity. Workers, moreover, might lack dedication to the task in hand – especially since recurring labor shortage put them in a strong position, and the post-Stalin state lacked the means to force them to work. Rising expectations over the postwar decades meant that the state had to take its redistributional responsibilities more seriously than in the Stalin period: instead of feeding just party-state functionaries and workers in valued sectors of production, it was now necessary to feed everyone else as well – and not only to feed them, but to house them, educate them, even pay them old-age pensions.

Following the comprehensive failure of numerous reform efforts from the late 1950s to the mid-1980s, the Soviet/Russian state finally, from 1988 onward, set a course for market reform: half-hearted to begin with, gung-ho from 1992 onward. The short-term results were disastrous. The introduction of limited market principles while the state pricing system remained largely in place and the institution of private ownership did not exist led to the complete breakdown of distribution. In 1992, the first of these problems was addressed by price liberalization (even if anomalies remained due to the discrepancy between internal and external prices for certain commodities). The second problem – ownership – was rather thornier. Although the privatization campaigns that began in 1992 and continued for much of the 1990s seemed to offer a radical solution, the institution of private property was still contaminated by politics to an extent unthinkable in a secure liberal democratic society. Control of medium-sized enterprises was in practice dominated by the old bosses who remained plugged into their nomenklatura networks. The major assets of the economy – the oil, gas and metals companies that were auctioned off in the second half of the 1990s – fell into the hands of new men whose most distinguishing feature was not business acumen but close association with the Yeltsin regime. The suspicion that privatization was little more than a cover for the continuing reality of state-bureaucratic power was only confirmed when the Putinist state quickly asserted itself and effectively renationalized sections of the "commanding heights" of the economy. Russia was a redistributional "resource state" more than a capitalist economy: control over resources – whether raw materials or manpower or political patronage – and their allocation to favored clients counted for more than legal ownership and extraction of surplus value.[104] Russia's very political economy was certainly inefficient and excessively reliant on world oil prices. It also seemed likely to give rise to further insider skirmishes over control of lucrative assets. Whether all this made the Russian polity of the early twenty-first century unviable for the medium term was, however, rather less certain.

4

Structures of Society

The title of this chapter is counterintuitive, given that one of the distinguishing features of Soviet society might seem to be its lack of structure. First in the civil war period, and then in the era of collectivization and crash industrialization from the late 1920s onward, Soviet people were subjected to an extraordinary – or horrific – degree of chaos, violence, and displacement. In a famous formulation, the social historian Moshe Lewin dubbed the interwar Soviet Union a "quicksand society" where no one could stand on firm ground.[1] The German invasion and its consequences put further tens of millions of people on the move; many of them had no home to return to at the end of hostilities.

This enormous disruption and indeterminacy forms a stark contrast with the rigidity of Soviet social description. Following the Stalin constitution of 1936, Soviet society was deemed to consist of two "classes" – workers and peasants – and one "stratum" (the intelligentsia). Ideology decreed that the class conflict of the revolutionary period – which had pitted proletarians and peasants against remnants of the "bourgeoisie" – had come to an end. The Soviet Union now had a homegrown educated class – a socialist intelligentsia – that enjoyed a harmonious relationship with those engaged in manual labor. Likewise, any antagonism between the urban population and the village had died out. It hardly needs saying how little this assessment of the situation corresponded to any empirical reality. The cleavages in Soviet society by the end of the 1930s were enormous: between the incarcerated and the free, between the collectivized village and everyone else, between university graduates and the poorly educated, between the party-state administrative elite and the rest.

The task of this chapter is to find an adequate set of categories for describing the development of Soviet society after the war. How can we begin to make sense of this hungry, impoverished, but victorious society? In the second half of the

1940s, the Soviet population once again faced extreme hardship, but over the following three decades it would enjoy the closest thing to normality that it would ever know. This fact gives us at least a prima facie case for arguing that Soviet civilization only reached a stable and recognizable state in the second half of the Soviet era.

Social Exclusion

The most important structuring division in Soviet society, for about half of its existence, lay not between workers and peasants, or urban and rural, but simply between those who were "in" and those who were "out." There were always categories of the population defined by the Soviet state as lying beyond the boundaries of legitimate society: "kulaks," criminals, Trotskyites, and assorted "enemies of the people," sometimes even entire ethnic groups that were considered guilty of disloyalty.

But the criteria for distinguishing an enemy from a friend of Soviet power were often opaque. Labels like "kulak" and "Trotskyite" were often used to settle scores or to meet arrest quotas, not because they corresponded to real offenses against the Soviet regime. There was also ambiguity in the fate of individuals under Stalin. People could go from socialist hero to enemy of the people, from prisoner to prison guard, from incarceration to freedom (though less often than in the other direction).

These peculiarities of Soviet repression were abundantly evident during the war and just after it. The war against an external enemy did not diminish the scale of internal repression. Death rates in the Gulag were at their highest in 1942–3, and hundreds of thousands of new prisoners streamed into the camps to replace the million or so released in the first three years of the war. This dynamic corresponded to a general pattern of fluidity in the Gulag population in the Stalin years. Somewhere between 20 and 40 percent of inmates were released every year in the period 1934–53, while the total number of prisoners released was probably well in excess of 6 million. An estimated 12–14 million people passed through the camp system in the period 1934–44, and a further 10–13.5 million between 1945 and 1954. The Gulag, then, was an experience that affected vast numbers of Soviet people and belongs near the center of any social history of Russia in the Stalin years. The already close relationship between the camps and "ordinary" Soviet society was only strengthened in the immediate aftermath of the victory, when Stalin for the first time granted a mass amnesty. More than 600,000 prisoners (or nearly 40 percent of the total Gulag population) were released at a stroke. Most of them had been sentenced under draconian wartime legislation (in many cases, for leaving factory jobs without permission). The length of sentence and the prisoner's past record were the main criteria for release: recidivists were excluded from the amnesty. No less a figure than Lavrentii Beria, the head of the NKVD and the main overseer of the Gulag, found it hard to perceive an economic rationale for the policy. The amnesty did not target invalids for early release, and the overall effect was to shrink the pool of skilled labor in the Gulag. The immediate mass release created huge administrative and transport problems. Most likely, the amnesty had the ideological function of marking the Soviet victory and a foreign policy objective of improving the international image of the USSR on the eve of the Potsdam conference.[2]

Beria need not have worried. Within three months of the amnesty, almost half of those slated for release had been replaced by people convicted of similar infractions of labor discipline. The Gulag continued to grow over the next few years: shortly before Stalin's death, the camp and colony population reached its peak figure of 2.5 million.[3] The Gulag had changed its character since the 1930s: it now contained a new generation of political prisoners – former Red Army soldiers, Polish officers, Ukrainian and Baltic partisans, German and Japanese POWs – who had strong collective identities and were more awkward for the Soviet state to handle than prewar "politicals." But the main factor in the postwar growth of the camp population was the activity of the criminal justice system. The antitheft legislation of June 1947 brought a further wave of new prisoners, and they were serving longer sentences than petty criminals earlier in the Stalin period. Theft of state property (irrespective of the amount) carried a minimum sentence of seven years and a maximum of 25. Over the period 1946–52, around 5 million people received terms in prison or labor camps for criminal convictions. For comparison, rather less than 10 percent of that number was sent to the camps for political crimes.[4]

Since its creation in the early 1930s, the camp system had always had an economic as well as a punitive rationale: to provide labor for construction and mining projects in remote areas that would struggle to attract free labor. It soon became an economic empire of its own. Of the 2.2 million prisoners held in labor camps at the end of 1947, almost 1.7 million were put to work on projects under the auspices of the Ministry of Internal Affairs. More than 700,000 worked in agriculture and light industry, 273,000 in the timber industry, nearly 250,000 on "special construction projects" in the Far North, 216,000 in railway construction, and 179,000 in mining and metallurgy. The "leftover" half a million inmates were leased out by the MVD to various industrial ministries.[5]

But the Gulag was only the most substantial of several sources of unfree labor for the Stalinist state. The Soviet Union in 1945 faced a serious labor shortage. Following the war, heavy industry had a deficit of about 1 million workers. The solution was to draw new workers into the labor force, mostly from the countryside. If they did not come of their own accord, they were coerced through forms of labor conscription. The measures made an impact: by Stalin's death, the industrial workforce had risen by 75 percent. Soviet conscripts were supplemented by German and Japanese POWs, who numbered about 1 million in 1947. "Special settlers" (people exiled from European Russia, whether as kulaks or as members of "repressed" national groups) provided another million workers – mostly in agriculture, but also in coal mining, the timber industry, and metallurgy. Repatriated Soviet citizens from central and eastern Europe were yet another source of manpower: about 5.4 million of these had been brought back to the Soviet Union by the end of 1947. Perhaps 20 percent of them were deprived of their liberty in some way: some were imprisoned, but the majority were placed in "labor battalions" under the auspices of the Ministry of Defense. In March 1946, more than 600,000 Soviet people were indentured workers of this kind. Prisoners on early release from the camps constituted a second major category of indentured worker. In such cases, release might be conditional on a term of labor service in particular factories or construction projects.[6]

In addition, the Soviet government drafted new people into the industrial workforce. In 1946, for example, it recruited more than 2 million peasants, demobilized soldiers, and urban residents. Over the period 1946–52, 5.8 million workers were hired in this way (and even this fell short of the target of more than 6.5 million). While these workers were notionally free, their labor contracts placed severe restrictions on them: if, for example, they quit before the end of their contracted term (usually five years), they were liable for prosecution as labor "deserters." The Soviet regime also had a special institution for drafting teenagers into undermanned areas of the economy. A "Labor Reserve" system of effective conscription for young people between 14 and 17 had been set up just before the war, and after 1945 it assumed major importance in sending youngsters into priority sectors of the economy. Over the period 1946–52, more than 4 million young people went into the Labor Reserve schools, even if many of them never reached the industries for which they had been designated: many fled back to the village, or into sectors of the economy with less harsh working conditions.[7]

So Soviet reconstruction and heavy industry depended enormously on coerced labor. But that is not even to mention the most substantial excluded group in Soviet society: the collectivized peasantry. According to 1932 legislation designed to clamp down on social disorder following collectivization and on spontaneous rural–urban migration, all people living in towns, urban settlements, state farms, and certain other sensitive areas such as border zones were to be issued with internal passports, which were henceforth to be the only valid identification document. This automatically excluded tens of millions of newly collectivized peasants and created in a very real sense a "second serfdom."

The war had brought demographic crisis to the Soviet village, as men departed for the front. Toward the end of the war, women of working age outnumbered men by four to one on the collective farms; a year after the end of the war it was two to one (and three to one in the RSFSR). Given the poverty of rural areas, many demobilized peasants had little inclination to return to agriculture after the war. But no account was taken of the diminishing productive forces in the village when the state set its targets for food deliveries. A famine of 1946–7, which killed well over a million people, was cataclysmic evidence of the plight of the *kolkhoz* peasantry and of the government's indifference to it. Even in 1947–8, the state was claiming half of all grain produced on the collective farms and more than half of their milk and meat. The prices the state paid for these products were often vastly below their production cost (not to mention their value on the *kolkhoz* market). The currency reform of December 1947 was a further blow to peasant well-being, as it wiped out rural savings. Agricultural taxes hobbled the peasant household, causing many people to dispose of precious assets such as livestock. Little wonder, then, that the collective farm population in Russia fell precipitously in 1948–9 without ever having climbed back to prewar levels. Over a million peasants of working age left the village in these years.[8]

The Stalin era, moreover, ravaged the population not only in a physical sense. It placed millions of Soviet people in a twilight zone of stigma and displacement. Even if many people in the 1940s found that their term in the camps came to an end, they had to live with its consequences for their civilian life. Smooth reintegration of former prisoners into society was a very low priority for the Stalinist state. Tens of millions of people had their life-chances impaired and their credentials permanently damaged. The war added further categories of suspect or stigmatized individuals. Soviet people who had been on occupied territory or in enemy captivity were called on to account for themselves before the authorities. In the Vinnytsia region of Ukraine, at meetings to "verify" wartime conduct, Party members were presented with the brutal question: "Why did you choose to remain on occupied territory?" Very few of them were able to give satisfactory answers. In 1946 and the first ten months of 1947, 60 percent of the region's top brass (nomenklatura) lost their positions. About 90 percent of Ukrainian Party members on formerly occupied territory who were subjected to verification had been expelled by 1948.[9]

Society in Flux

An awareness of the coercion employed against the population should not make us overestimate the rigidity and order of postwar Stalinism. This was a society constantly on the move, one that existed in conditions of desperate chaos and poverty. Wartime disruptions did not end with Victory Day in 1945. The enemy had occupied territory with a prewar population of 85 million (or 45 percent of the total Soviet population). Millions of Soviet people had been displaced by the German advance or by later waves of evacuation. The best part of 10 million demobilized soldiers had to be absorbed rapidly into an employed labor force that grew by 12 million between 1945 and 1950. Despite continued draconian legislation, labor turnover continued to be high as people quit jobs in search of better housing or a more adequate food supply. By the early 1950s, migration out of the village had become a flood. Between 1950 and 1954, around 9 million people moved permanently to the towns, especially from the rural areas of central Russia.[10]

The next major case of population dispersal came in 1953 as a direct consequence of government action. An amnesty announced on 27 March 1953 flung more than 1,200,000 people (or almost half of the Gulag population) back into Soviet society. The beneficiaries included women who were pregnant or with children under ten, minors, men above 55 and women above 50, and those convicted for specified less serious offenses.[11] To the extent that the amnesty was discussed in public, it was presented as a sign of the Soviet state's magnanimity and of Soviet society's robustness.

In reality, however, the effects of the mass release were hugely destabilizing. By the late summer, officials were pinning the blame for a crime wave on the amnestied prisoners. Even though the police took special measures to ensure that the release did not cause disturbances, the authorities could not keep pace with population movement on this scale. Resettlement provision was inadequate, and in any case some former prisoners did not want to take up the work they were offered in "free" society. The situation was exacerbated by the fact that many serious criminals had been released. The amnesty decree, as well as releasing immediately certain categories of prisoner, had also halved sentences for all prisoners, which meant that even prisoners serving a 25-year sentence might be released on the spot. More than a third of those released had been serving sentences of more than five years. These people, it was assumed, lay behind an increase in violent attacks of 66.4 percent, a 30.7 percent rise in murders, and a 27.5 percent rise in rape – not to mention a substantial increase in the rate of common theft. The rest of Soviet society responded with apprehension and antagonism to a group of people who were regarded as troublemakers.[12]

When prisoners returned to society, they faced everyday problems even more acute than ordinary Soviet citizens. The main problems were finding a job and somewhere to live. Even people with good contacts, such as the wife of the prominent Finnish Bolshevik Otto Kuusinen, might face months of legwork before they found a flat. The restoration of property was also fraught with difficulty. Certain categories of Gulag inmate – notably former POWs – found that they received distinctly unfavorable treatment from local authorities on their return to civilian life. Little effort was made to grant the rehabilitated symbolic reintegration into

Soviet society. Between 1953 and 1958, only 2,125 citizens were granted permission to regain medals of which they had been stripped during the Stalin period (this accounted for well under 10 percent of the total).[13]

Gulag returnees were an especially difficult case of a key social phenomenon in the post-Stalin era: migration. Until the 1974 passport reform, the freedom of movement of collective farm workers remained severely circumscribed on paper, but this did not prevent continued heavy rural–urban migration. Departure from the *kolkhoz* was in principle dependent on the authorization of the farm chairman. Permission might be granted to leave for specific periods of time (for education or military service), which might then lead to further opportunities outside the village. The only almost certain way to gain permanent release was to marry someone outside the *kolkhoz*.[14] Nevertheless, opportunities for geographical mobility increased after Stalin. New legislation of October 1953 lengthened the period of validity of the internal passport, which previously had been five years in almost all cases. For those aged between 20 and 40, the period was extended to ten years, and for those over 40 passports became permanently valid. There was also a slight softening of the restrictions on collective farm workers: rural people were now allowed to spend up to 30 days in passportized areas provided only with permits from their rural soviets.[15]

The urban proportion of the population duly crossed the threshold of 50 percent in 1962. In the 1960s, on average, about 1.5 million people each year left the village for the town. And, because the small-town economy of the Soviet Union was weakly developed, most of these people flocked to the big cities. Between 1959 and 1970, the rural population fell in absolute terms by 3.1 million, while the 1970s brought it down by a further 6.9 million. The biggest drifts away from the village were found in Russia and the Ukraine; these were partially compensated by Central Asia, where the rural population continued to grow. If agriculture accounted for half of Soviet employment in 1939, it fell to 39 percent in 1959 and 21 percent in 1979. By the 1970s, moreover, over half of the rural population was employed directly by the state, whereas a decade earlier it had largely worked on collective farms.[16]

If rural–urban migration was the dominant trend in Soviet mobility, there were also high-profile cases of movement in the other direction. From the very beginning, the Soviet project had required not only the consolidation and expansion of major industrial centers but also the dispersal of the urban population in order to develop and "civilize" the remoter parts of Soviet Eurasia. The early Khrushchev period saw one of the great campaigns in this vein. The Party plenum of February–March 1954 announced a scheme to develop hundreds of thousands of hectares of land in Kazakhstan. Internal memos reported a surge of popular enthusiasm. Within ten days of the plenum, nearly 25,000 volunteers had departed. In due course, the Belorussian republic alone would deliver 37,000 volunteers (far in excess of the 1,300 it was allotted in the plan). Recruitment in the second year of the scheme was even greater than in the first; all told, the Komsomol delivered more than 363,000 recruits to the scheme between 1954 and 1960. But the Virgin Lands were settled not only by clean-cut Communist youth. Other contingents included peasants from collective farms in other regions, people repatriated from China, "special settlers" (mainly members of ethnic groups deported under Stalin), and Gulag inmates. Between 1954 and 1956, 34 state farms in the Virgin Lands were built by prisoners. Living and working conditions, especially in the first two years, were dire. Little wonder that the Virgin Lands scheme was characterized not only by self-sacrificing labor but also by mass violence (often ethnic) and high rates of workforce turnover.[17]

The Virgin Lands might be seen as a microcosm of the entire Soviet experience from the late 1920s to the late 1950s: large numbers of people thrown together in an unfamiliar location, some willingly but many under duress, and left to fend for themselves. This was a society characterized by a large amount of mobility – both geographical and social. Even at the very end of the Soviet period, most Soviet urbanites were of rural origin.[18] How, in this light, can we impose analytical fixity on a situation of enormous social flux?

Class and Developed Socialism

The tripartite division adopted in Soviet sociology – workers, peasants and intelligentsia – did a poor job of concealing the hierarchies that structured this notionally egalitarian society. The life-chances of Soviet people depended enormously on where they happened to be born, what kind of education they received, and in what institutions they spent their adult life. The Soviet ideology of popular enlightenment and empowerment always stood in an uneasy relationship to the reality of a rigid political order with its own privileged caste of functionaries. Public discourse was consistently evasive or mendacious on these matters, but the regime periodically adopted policies to adjust the balance between elite and "masses."

The key institution for such social engineering was the Communist Party itself. Party membership was a passport to social and professional advancement in most desirable spheres of Soviet existence. Army or police officers or state functionaries could not be without it. Throughout its existence, the Party had veered – with sometimes drastic results – between phases of mass recruitment and phases of mass expulsion and restrictive admissions. Affirmative action policies were desirable as they increased proletarian and peasant representation in an institution that spoke in the name of the working class; but they also risked compromising the ideological purity and integrity of the USSR's dominant organization.

This dynamic continued to be much in evidence during and after the war. During the period 1941–4 the Party threw open its doors: hundreds of thousands of men were admitted straight from their army units. The result was that the Party membership at the end of the war was dominated by raw recruits: in January 1946, only one-third of members had been in the Party before June 1941. The government duly moved to tighten up procedures. A Central Committee resolution of July 1946 stipulated stricter individual scrutiny of applications for candidate membership. In some areas, admissions practically ground to a halt, which brought an absolute fall in Party membership of 38,000 in 1948 and 12,000 in 1949. Membership then rose by about half a million between 1950 and 1953, but even this was a low rate of increase compared to earlier phases of Party expansion. Moreover, the Party continued to expel unworthy members from its ranks: at least 100,000 people a year, a rate topped only in the notorious purges of the 1930s. Aggressive affirmative-action policies were eschewed in the late Stalin era: worker and peasant recruitment suffered as a result of postwar restrictions, and emphasis was placed on drawing into the Party "the best people," whatever their social background.[19]

Restrictive recruitment policies continued for about a year after Stalin's death, but then Khrushchev opened a new phase of easier access (especially for those of worker and peasant background). Party membership actually fell in 1953, but it went up by 92,000 in 1954 and 166,000 in 1955. In the de-Stalinizing year of 1956 the Party admitted a total of 381,000 new candidate members. After that, the trend was upward until 1964, when 879,000 new candidates were admitted. The year after, total Party membership reached 12 million. And the Party could claim to have become less of an intelligentsia preserve. Between the 20th and 22nd Party congresses, two in five new recruits were classified as workers when they joined the Party and a little more than one in five were collective farm workers.[20]

Khrushchev's egalitarian and anti-intellectual inclinations were indulged not only in policy on Party admissions but also in the sphere of education. In 1954, lessons in basic manual skills were introduced for the first five years of school; the 1955 curriculum brought in two-hour practical classes for years 8–10. In December 1958, the Central Committee issued a decree "On the Strengthening of the Link of the School with Life" which mandated a much larger element of "work education" for schoolchildren. The aim was to make school graduates better fitted for the manual employment that still awaited most of them – and, conversely, to give intelligentsia children a taste of working-class life. The reformed RSFSR curriculum of 1959 greatly increased the time spent on manual skills: in years 5–8 this rose by two or three hours a week, and in the later years of school it took up as many as 12 hours.[21]

Even more problematic were Khrushchev's interventions in the intelligentsia preserve of higher education. The late Stalin era had seen the prestige of high

FIGURE 4.1   Party committee meeting at car factory, Ulyanovsk, 1960.
Source: © Nickolai Bobrov / PhotoSoyuz.

academic achievement rise ever higher. The war had boosted the state importance of science, and in the late 1940s research workers with higher degrees could expect to be well rewarded. In relative terms, this was the high-water mark of earning power for those employed in higher education.[22] The prestige of universities – especially the major institutions in capital cities like Moscow and Kiev – rose greatly. The new building of Moscow State University on the Lenin Hills, in a spectacular location overlooking the Moscow River, was perhaps the most eye-catching construction project of the late Stalin era.

The universities admitted a proportion of working-class and peasant applicants that would have been remarkable in western Europe in the same era, but the overall trend had been downward since the affirmative action era of the early 1930s. In 1936, around 45 percent of students in Ukrainian university were classified as being of "employee" (white-collar) background; by 1953, that figure had risen to 53.5 percent.[23] The increasing number of school graduates in the late Stalin era caused a bottleneck in university admissions. Strict academic selection criteria meant that children of the intelligentsia were more likely to gain admission to the elite institutions of higher education. In the mid-50s, only 30–40 percent of students at Moscow University were of working-class or peasant background. Here was the context for Khrushchev's controversial interventions in university admissions and curriculum design. The Soviet leader set about rectifying the social imbalance, above all by creating a fast-track admissions system for candidates with two years' experience in industry or agriculture. By the end of the Khrushchev era, such students accounted for almost two-thirds of the higher education population.[24] A further egalitarian provision of Khrushchev's education reforms stipulated that students who lacked production experience should work full-time in their first year of study, attending to their academic work only in the evenings.

The universities, especially the prestigious and well-established ones, were less than eager in their adoption of these measures. In the USSR as a whole, 63.7 percent of the higher education intake of 1958 consisted of veterans and students with production experience. But in Moscow and Leningrad Universities, for example, the proportion was well below 50 percent. Official statements left unclear how and where students were to gain their production experience, and universities exploited the ambiguity. Administrators showed little interest in policing the system rigorously, and many students found undemanding casual employment as caretakers or cloakroom attendants. Universities were also willing to connive with students to evade the stipulations of the unpopular job placement scheme. Students felt that they deserved better than the manual occupations into which they were being steered by Khrushchev's policies of social engineering, and it seems their lecturers often sympathized.[25]

These radical measures were largely discontinued after Khrushchev's fall. As early as autumn 1964, universities were once again left to run admissions more or less as they saw fit. The change was dictated partly by a reluctance to disrupt and antagonize an important feeder institution for the Soviet elite, but also by the fact that Khrushchev's insistence on vocational training was now somewhat anachronistic. Higher education was no longer, as in the industrializing 1930s, a mere conveyer belt for "specialists" in heavy industry who needed hands-on experience as well as technical expertise. Close to a third of higher-education graduates were absorbed back into the expanding education system. This was partly a consequence of the marked feminization of higher education: women made up around half of the student body by the 1970s as compared with well under a third in the late 1920s. Many of them left their university or institute for a career in teaching: 80 percent of teachers in secondary schools were women. Another heavily feminized – and relatively poorly paid – profession was medicine, where as many as three-quarters of doctors were women.[26]

The value of academic excellence and the principle of specialization gained ground in the school system after Khrushchev. The system of specialist schools for high-achieving children expanded over the next ten years. By the late 1960s, the Soviet Union had 50 full-time specialist art schools, and by 1973 it had reached a figure of 36 music schools. The system of schools with some degree of academic specialization also grew: as of 1967, there were 700 language schools. The most desirable professions for Soviet school-leavers included research worker, engineer, and pilot. For all the rhetorical emphasis placed on the dignity of manual labor, the ambitions of the Soviet population were directed elsewhere.[27]

Realizing those ambitions was, however, another matter. Until the late 1950s, "complete secondary education" (to Grade 10) had been a mark of high educational achievement and close to a guarantee of entry to higher education. Stalin had introduced fees for Grades 9 and 10, creating a financial bar to the educational progress of working-class and peasant children. Under Khrushchev the bar was substantially removed, and by 1970 a large majority of Soviet youngsters were enjoying a complete secondary education. But this did not bring an end to class stratification: it meant that the threshold of high status was located not in the transition from Grade 8 to Grade 9 but in the move from school to higher education. Competition for university places was fierce, and tended to be dominated by intelligentsia offspring, whose expectations were set higher and who enjoyed greater parental support. One survey of the mid-60s, conducted at the Ufa Aviation Institute, found that 83 percent of students of white-collar background could expect parental assistance as compared with 70.1 percent from blue-collar families and a mere 31.6 percent of peasant background.[28]

In its system of social stratification, the Soviet Union was apparently converging with other parts of the industrialized world: social occupation and status were strongly hereditary. The majority of unskilled workers were of peasant origin, while more than half of skilled workers had a working-class background. Senior managers, in the Soviet Union as in western Europe, had a good chance of seeing their children emulate their success. The transmission of occupational privilege was less a matter of property and income than of less tangible advantages. In the post-Stalin period, wage differentials between skilled manual workers and "engineering-technical" personnel tended to fall, but the latter nonetheless enjoyed a

higher standard of urban living: they had more living space, were more likely to
have a separate family apartment, and owned more labor-saving domestic appliances. Most important, given that Soviet life made impossible the accumulation
and intergenerational transmission of large quantities of wealth, they were able
to give their children educational opportunities. In short, it was clear that
Khrushchev's experiments had not done away with fundamental inequalities in
access to education.[29]

The regime had taken a decisive step back from the radical egalitarianism of
its early days: ever since the early 1930s, "levelling" (*uravnilovka*) had been a dirty
word. By the post-Stalin era, this tolerance of wage inequality might be justified
on the grounds that several decades of Soviet power had done enough to provide
equality of opportunity, and that the demands of a modern economy required
the principles of specialization, mechanization, and the growth of the white-collar
classes (the effective disenfranchisement of the peasantry, and the subordination
of meritocratic principles to a politicized bureaucracy, were passed over in
silence). The result was that the Soviet Union in the 1960s saw a growing cult of
professionalism (as opposed to the sheer self-sacrificing enthusiasm for toil that
was expected of earlier generations).[30] One of the signature films of the era was
Nine Days in One Year, whose physicist hero is so absorbed in his work that
he exposes himself to mortal danger. Another was *Colleagues* (cf. Chapter 6),
whose hero similarly puts his life on the line; the film ends up as a paean to the
ethos of professional service and expertise and to the ties of brotherhood between
practitioners.

The intelligentsia – the Soviet equivalent of an educated middle class – was
enjoying a phase of unprecedented stability, status, and growth. If we take higher
education as the measure of the intelligentsia, then just over 6 million members
of this class were employed in the Soviet economy in the autumn of 1968. All in
all, including all family members, this Soviet intelligentsia probably numbered
15–20 million.[31] In Soviet culture, the overtly plebeian was on the retreat. The
values and behavior of the "old" (pre-Stalin) intelligentsia were now becoming a
cause for pride rather than apology. One revealing index of *intelligentnost'* as a
publicly approved virtue was the advice literature on "cultured speech" (*kul'tura
rechi*) that first appeared in the early 1950s and gathered momentum in the
Khrushchev era. This "purist" campaign against slang and other kinds of linguistic
vulgarity may be seen as symptomatic of the rise of a Soviet version of class snob-
bery.[32] The ambition of Soviet ideology to overcome divisions between "mass"
and "elite" tastes was increasingly belied by the realities of Soviet cultural production. A good illustration is the completion in the anniversary year of 1967 of two
contrasting cinematic accounts of the civil war. One, Aleksandr Askol'dov's *The
Commissar*, was perhaps the most powerful and nuanced Soviet film on the revolutionary period; it was put on the shelf until the glasnost era. The other, *Wedding*

in Malinovka, was a musical romp in which Whites and Mensheviks serve as pantomime villains. As Irina Shilova, later a well-known film critic, recalled of her youth in the 1950s, she adopted the values of her intelligentsia milieu by affecting "snobbish" disparagement of certain kinds of comedy and melodrama (even if she secretly enjoyed them). Even in the Thaw era, it was clear that Soviet culture was coming to be structured by a divide between "serious" and "trashy" films that was reminiscent of the capitalist world.[33]

If the advantages of being educated and professional were so manifest in the Soviet Union of the 1960s and 1970s, we might well ask how the rest of society was kept in its place. The traditional Soviet answer would have been coercion, but following the mass amnesties of the Khrushchev period and the softening of the criminal justice system it was no longer available to Stalin's successors. Instead, the regime was able to offer modest but genuine improvements that alleviated some of the most gaping inequalities in Soviet society. From around 1950 onward, the Soviet population did not experience famine, and from the early 1960s to the mid-1980s it enjoyed stable fixed prices for the basic commodities. The rising educational levels of the postwar decades were not just a matter of the expanding intelligentsia. In the 1930s, compulsory schooling had amounted to only four years, but in 1949 it was raised to seven, and in 1959 to eight. The average number of years spent in school by the economically active population rose from 6.8 in 1959 to 8.1 in 1970.[34]

All the same, it is clear that not all Soviet people by any means were becoming office workers. Of the 56 million people active in the economy in 1968, more than half were classified as "workers" (24 million in industry and 5 million in construction). The level of mechanization remained low: in 1962, nearly half of all Soviet workers were still doing manual work without machines. The low-income sectors were clear enough: light industry, textiles, public services – not coincidentally, the spheres that were dominated by women. The number of men employed in warehouses increased by a factor of three between 1948 and 1965, while the number of loaders went up by 70 percent. A charitable explanation would hold that these figures were a sign of the growing Soviet economy, but they do indicate the continued prominence of the unskilled sector. Although some Soviet people were able to achieve significant upward mobility while remaining in manual occupations – by moving from unskilled to skilled work over the course of their careers – those with ambitions for intelligentsia status were more likely to be disappointed than fulfilled, given the bottleneck that was higher education in the Brezhnev era.[35]

The limited prospects afforded by many forms of work in the Soviet Union were mitigated by a substantial relaxing of labor discipline. By a decree of June 1940 workers had been forbidden to change jobs without permission (even if, by the 1950s, this rule was not enforced as rigorously as before). Within a year of the revocation of this law in 1956, about half of all workers changed jobs. From the late 1950s, the annual rate of turnover stabilized at around 20 percent (and this figure excluded certain significant categories of job change such as military service). Perennial labor shortages meant that workers often had opportunities to seek better conditions elsewhere.[36] The obligation of each Soviet citizen to work had its coercive implications – a law against "parasitism" meant that people might face imprisonment for failing to take up any job – but it also had enabling aspects for the population. It meant, in the post-Stalin era, that job security was close to absolute, and that if workers decided to quit one job they could be confident of finding another one. Rather than acting as pawns of state labor policy, Soviet people could make informed and rational decisions to move to factories or branches of industry where they could improve their earning power, benefits, and work conditions. It was important to make a good choice, as enterprises dominated infrastructure and housing provision in many parts of the Soviet Union. In 1985, ministries (which stood above particular branches of the economy) controlled almost half of state housing, while local government (the soviets) owned just over a quarter. In one district in the Urals in the first half of the 1970s, ministries procured more than 1,600 buses – ten times as many as the public transport system managed to obtain in the same period.[37]

The more tolerable labor relations of the later Soviet period were complemented by measures to maintain the social order. The principal socializing institution for working-class male youth was the army, which was a route out of the collective farm for millions of village youngsters and a means of upward social mobility. (Party membership, for instance, was much easier to obtain after a period in the armed forces.) Even in an era largely free of "hot" wars with direct Soviet participation, the Soviet Union remained a highly militarized society. In 1967, a reform of military service reduced the standard term of conscription from three years to two but also introduced twice-yearly rather than annual call-ups. The implication was that a higher proportion of each cohort would serve, though for a shorter time, and the number of trained reservists would be boosted. Young men were granted certain categories of deferral (family hardship, higher education, health), but about half of the males in each age group would serve. In 1982, moreover, an amendment to the military service law restricted the number of higher education institutions whose male students were granted deferral. By the mid-1980s, the Soviet Armed Forces numbered almost 6 million people (and around 25 million reservists), which made them the largest military in the world. After a phase of demobilization under Khrushchev, the troop level had risen steadily from the 1960s, reaching its peak only in 1985.[38]

Soviet young people were subjected to a substantial program of military training even before they were called up. The main preparatory organization was the Voluntary Society for Assistance to the Army, the Air Force and the Navy

(DOSAAF), which increased its program of pre-draft training following the reform of 1967, thus reducing the time required to train conscripts when they entered the armed forces. Between 1967 and 1970, DOSAAF put up 560 new buildings for purposes of military training, and by 1973 it had 9,000 sets of premises to its name. In the early 1970s, the organization claimed an active membership of tens of millions.[39]

Once they had performed their military obligations to the Soviet state, Soviet people were quite literally kept in their place by a system of territorial zoning. The Soviet space was structured by a system of geographical stratification that was headed by major republican capitals and "closed" cities, which were better provisioned, better connected, and more richly endowed with educational institutions and employment opportunities than other parts of the USSR. Access to these desirable cities was governed by a system of residence permits (*propiska*). If a migrant worker wished to make the jump from the provinces to the capital (without marrying a Muscovite or Leningrader or gaining access to an institution of higher education), he or she might have to accept many years of uncomfortable existence in a de facto shanty settlement as a *limitchik* worker (see Chapter 6).

The single greatest social and territorial divide, in the 1960s as previously, lay between the collectivized village and the rest. Until a reform of 1974 finally stipulated that collective farm workers be issued with internal passports, many rural people continued to labor under the terms of a "second serfdom." But the situation was not as static as it might appear. Well before 1974, the post-Stalin regime showed its intent to modernize the village and to bring it in line with the Soviet version of industrial modernity. Once established in power, Khrushchev had the opportunity to put into practice one of his long nurtured schemes: to "industrialize" the village, in other words to increase the size and production capacity of agricultural units at the expense of their number. (See Chapter 3 for more detail.) Here was a departure from the Stalinist policy of brutal exploitation of the village. For the first time the Soviet regime had a genuine rural "policy," even if its implications were still coercive. Khrushchev's goal was to trim back household plots, forcing peasants to devote their energies to collective agriculture, giving them a money wage instead of paying them in kind for their "labor days," and turning them into rural proletarians. The obvious way to go about this was to reduce the number of collective farms and make them resemble their larger and more monetized counterparts in the state sector. Amalgamation and liquidation duly brought a reduction in the number of *kolkhozy* of more than a half between 1955 and the early 1960s, while more than 23,000 of them had their status changed to that of state farm (*sovkhoz*). The impact was felt as far away as Buryatia, where the number of collective farms fell from more than a thousand in the aftermath of collectivization to fewer than sixty by the 1970s.[40]

FIGURE 4.2   A new village in central Russia, 1960: The Khrushchev ideal of rural transformation.
Source: © Arkady Shishkin / PhotoSoyuz.

The implications of post-Stalin agricultural policy were not simply exploitative. The village too was affected by the social modernization of the era. Before the war, five years of schooling had been the limit of the ambitions of many rural people, but by the late 1950s more than half had eight years of schooling (as compared with less than 10 percent in 1938).[41] Education became the key to professional advancement in the village as in the city. Even the *kolkhoz* was recruiting its leading personnel on the basis of their formal qualifications. Occupational change in the direction of professionalization affected even the most "backward" sections of Soviet society. By the 1970s, the Buryat *kolkhozniki* studied by Caroline Humphrey were for the first time able to live on their wages; before that, subsistence agriculture on their private plots had been critical for their well-being. The rural family was now "no longer *primarily* oriented towards production"; it was, rather, the "unit of consumption."[42] The village also became much more connected to the institutions of Soviet life. Just before the war, only one in eight collective farms had had its own Party organization, but by 1953 the proportion had risen to five out of six.[43] The rise was due in part to the redistribution of communized peasants from the armed forces, and also to the enlargement of collective farms in the early 1950s. There were now more rural Communists to go around fewer farms.

Generation and Gender

Although Marxism-Leninism saw class as the fundamental structuring principle in human society, the Soviet Union always gave much prominence to a biological, age-based frame of reference. Generation had figured large in the public discourse of the 1920s and 1930s, when references to the heroic mission and special historical worth of the revolutionary cohort alternated with anxious suggestions that the "first Soviet generation" might not be up to the challenge. A preoccupation with spoiled and degenerate youth was no less a constant of Soviet culture than the presumption of the special commitment of youth to building Communism. Attitudes to old people were also ambivalent. In the very early Soviet period, the older generation very often connoted undesirable "remnants of the past"; there was no question that certain categories of older people – peasant women, ex-bourgeois – were among the most backward or retrograde in Soviet society. In the longer term, however, Soviet society needed the source of symbolic authority that was provided by an "old generation." By the mid-1930s, certain categories of old person – famous scientists, patriarchs of worker dynasties – were shown to be thoroughly worthy of respect.

In the postwar era these ambiguities in Soviet thinking on generation were still palpable. But Soviet generational discourse also changed its contours. To some extent, generation moved into territory formerly occupied by class. The Stalin Constitution of 1936 decreed that class antagonism in Soviet society had come to an end. The two classes of peasants and workers, along with the stratum of the intelligentsia, would henceforth work together to bring Communism closer. Class conflict had previously been the main motor of history in a Marxist understanding. Now generation could provide a fresh source of momentum. It is in this light that we should see the appeals to youthful enthusiasm launched by Khrushchev in his Virgin Lands scheme.

But ambivalence about youth did not go away. If anything, it became more acute, as the war served as an enormous historical caesura between everyone who had experienced it at first hand and everyone who had not. The danger was that later generations might prove to be unworthy of the heroic cohorts who saved the Soviet Union in its hour of mortal danger. Conversely, the prestige of the older generation was greatly raised by its contributions to the heroic phase of socialist construction in the 1930s and to the victory of 1945. To an ever increasing extent, the Soviet Union had its very own old people: cohorts who had grown up in the 1920s or later, and hence been comprehensively socialized as Soviet.

The discursive salience of generation was underlain by demographic changes. Before 1945, it had been hard to make firm judgments about Soviet demographic trends given the succession of cataclysmic blows to the well-being of the population: the Soviet Union had suffered perhaps 40 million unnatural deaths due to collectivization, resettlement, terror, and world war between the late 1920s and 1945. But the relative stability of the postwar era meant that firmer conclusions could be drawn.

At least some of them were reassuring. Life expectancy in the USSR went up by more than twenty years between the late 1930s and the late 1950s from around 47 to more than 68. The increase can be ascribed to general improvements in the standard of living (better housing, diet, and sanitation) as well as to more specific improvements in health care such as the wider use of antibiotics. Infant mortality in the RSFSR rose sharply during the 1946–7 famine, but the overall trend was downward: from 159 per 1,000 live births in 1943 to 73 in 1953 and 50 in 1956. Soviet life expectancy in the early 1960s was reckoned to exceed that in Austria, Belgium, Finland, and Japan. By the early 1980s, however, the USSR had lost ground in demographic terms. The Soviet system had exhausted the improvements possible by basic public health measures: it might have won the battle against TB, but it was not capable of averting a high level of cardiovascular disease. The Soviet health care system was looking underfunded and creaky. In 1980, 72 rubles were spent on health care for the average Soviet citizen, which compared unfavorably with the $1,064 spent on the average American. Between 1960 and 1990, male life expectancy actually fell – from 65.3 to 64.3 years. The Soviet healthcare system – like the Soviet system as a whole – was good at "campaigns" but much less effective at differentiated solutions or at encouraging people to take a more active part in their own fortunes.[44]

Another crucial demographic development in the postwar decades was the decline in Soviet fertility. The process had started in earnest in the late 1920s. The following three or four decades saw a demographic transition that had taken

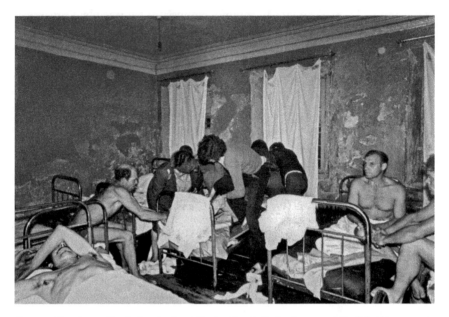

FIGURE 4.3   A very Soviet institution: The inside of a "sobering-up station" in Cherepovets (Vologda region), 1980.
Source: © Yury Rybchinsky / PhotoSoyuz.

centuries in western Europe: by the 1950s, the birth rates in the European parts of the USSR were broadly in line with those in the West. One hundred women born in Russia in the last five years of the nineteenth century bore on average 408 children, while their contemporaries in France managed only 210, and those in America 253. The female cohort of 1940 in the RSFSR produced fewer children than their counterparts in many parts of the West: only 189 births per hundred women, as compared with 238 in England.[45]

These changes put the Soviet Union broadly in line with trends elsewhere in the developed world, with two important qualifications. First, the worrying dip in life expectancy from the mid-1960s onward pointed to profound drawbacks in the Soviet social and economic order and made for a sorry contrast with other late modernizing countries (notably Japan). Second, the transition from high to low fertility was extraordinarily accelerated. It was linked to levels of female participation in the labor force that by the 1970s were reckoned to be the highest in the world. It gave young adults unprecedented personal freedom, as they had fewer children at later ages. It also had implications for the structure of the Soviet family, as parents and grandparents lavished more attention and resources on far fewer children and grandchildren. One scholar has drawn attention to the phenomenon of "serial only children," as career imperatives and cramped housing led Soviet people to space their children much more widely than was customary in the West.[46]

Social attitudes were often not able to catch up with demographic realities. Although the Soviet order, on one level, was encouraging women to be low-fertility citizens dedicated to productive work outside the home, on another level it retained its earlier pronatalist instincts: family planning was practically unknown in the Soviet Union, and abortion remained a primary method of birth control. For all the talk of women's equality (for example in the 1977 constitution), employment remained highly segregated by sex, and women remained low-status and low-income workers. Ever since the start of Soviet industrialization, they had been concentrated in heavy, hazardous, monotonous, and often "pre-industrial" work. As late as 1978, a survey of the southern city of Taganrog found that 44 percent of female workers were engaged in labor of this kind (as compared to 30 percent of men).[47] At the other end of the occupational hierarchy, their representation was correspondingly weak. In 1961, only 2 percent of collective farm chairmen in the Soviet Union were female, though the 1959 census had delivered a figure of 19.8 million women employed in agriculture (of whom 15.8 million were unskilled).[48] Although the post-Stalin decades saw a great influx of women into professional and semiprofessional occupations – the number of women technicians, statisticians, economists, and engineers rose by a factor of more than three between 1955 and 1968 – women's earnings remained on average around 70 percent of men's.[49] The 1970s and early 1980s saw some advances in the provision of maternity leave and other benefits for women, but these tended only to confirm the notion that women were second-class employees. They also reflected the demographic panic of the time: the birth rate in the European parts of the USSR was dwindling to an alarming extent, while in Central Asia it remained undesirably high. The government encouraged Russian and Estonian women to take more time off work and have more children, while it urged Tadjik and Uzbek women to take a more active part in the labor force.[50]

Another consequence of sudden demographic shifts was that notions of a generation gap became even more plausible. Not only had younger Soviet people avoided the hardships of the war, they could also confidently expect to avoid the infectious diseases that had carried off many children in earlier cohorts, and to receive plenty of attention and resources from their devoted parents; they could then look forward to decades of increasingly prosperous urban life where they would face increasing temptations from decadent Western mass culture and consumerism. No wonder Soviet journalists and caricaturists constantly returned to the stock figure of the spoiled youth.

The stereotypes corresponded, at least to some extent, to a real difference in outlook between younger and older generations. The Soviet Interview Project (conducted in the early 1980s) delivered results that were a neat inverse of those produced by the Harvard Interview Project (which was conducted in the early 1950s, but pertained to the prewar period when informants had last lived in the Soviet Union). In 1940, it was the younger people who were more accepting of the Soviet order; by the 1970s, it was the older cohorts.[51]

By the early 1980s, Soviet sociologists were pointing firmly to more consumerist attitudes among the younger generation. Those in their early twenties were far more likely to take an interest in stereos and gold jewellery – not to mention cooperative apartments and cars. The over-25s took more of an interest in furniture and fashionable clothing. But the Soviet wage hierarchy placed firm limits on the earning power of younger workers. The Soviet media expressed periodic concern that the parents of teenagers and twenty-somethings were too ready to help them out. An All-Union survey of 1978 found that more than half of parents were ready to buy their children shortage items even if their own needs had to be neglected.[52]

Even conscripts were not as pliable as they once had been. As a result of the reform of 1967, military service became more universal, but it was a rather different phenomenon when conscripts became overwhelmingly urban and at least moderately well educated. If in the Khrushchev era, conscripts had been split fairly evenly between the working class and the peasantry, by the mid-1980s the proportion of workers had increased to more than two-thirds, while peasants accounted for only 13 percent.[53]

The Soviet institutions of youth socialization remained in place and even extended their reach. Membership in the Young Pioneers became practically universal for Soviet children. In 1960, the organization numbered 15.4 million members out of a total cohort of 16.6 million; in 1970 the equivalent figures were 23.3 million out of 24.9 million. The organization was now for the first time gaining a real presence in rural areas. By 1977, Moscow could boast seven "Pioneer palaces" and thirty-two "Pioneer houses," which together ran more than 4,300 clubs and pastimes with almost 75,000 children participating.[54] By the mid-1980s, the Communist Youth League (Komsomol) could claim a membership of 40 million.

But the Komsomol was itself emblematic of an ageing political system where the gap between elderly leadership and youthful rank-and-file widened. At its 13th congress in April 1958, 52 percent of delegates were older than 26 (the notional maximum age for membership in this organization).[55] The graying of the Soviet youth organization gained momentum in the early Brezhnev era, when a 40-year-old was appointed Chairman with a view to hardening the Komsomol's core of (sometimes rather mature) Party activists.[56] The Party, too, "aged" as an institution. At the end of the war, Party members of more than ten years were a small minority of about 15 percent; by 1956 the proportion was already well over half. The temporarily high recruitment rate during the war and under Khrushchev, along with the absence of major upheavals (such as wars and purges), meant that the traditionally youthful membership began in the late 1960s to age significantly.[57]

Anxiety over the backwardness and religious belief of old people (especially village women), which had still been strong in the Khrushchev era, gradually receded to make way for a cult of seniority in Soviet society. Ex-soldiers received little official support or recognition in the immediate postwar period, but commemoration of the war became a mainstay of Soviet public life from the mid-1960s onward. Veterans received state benefits and awards, and their example was held up as an inspiration to youngsters.[58]

The general prominence of the older generation was further bolstered by the emergence of the mass Soviet pensioner. Old-age benefits had been woefully inadequate in the Stalin era, and in practice many old people worked until they dropped. In 1956, however, the Soviet government announced a new "comprehensive" pensions law. Although this legislation left out the sizable section of the population that worked on collective farms (this group would finally be covered, on less generous terms, in 1965), it meant that for the first time millions of Soviet urbanites could expect a decent level of state support in old age (even if, as many did, they kept working for a few years). For a country with a low birth rate and an ageing population, the implications were enormous: by the collapse of the Soviet Union, there were almost as many pensioners (30 million) as Komsomol members.[59]

Reclassing Russia: Society in the Transition

By the early 1970s Soviet Russia had attained a reasonably stable social order with its own occupational, age, and gender hierarchies. All of this came under threat as the country lurched from reform to disintegration in the late 1980s. The collapse of the Soviet Union and the ensuing period of economic reform dealt a colossal blow to the population's real and perceived well-being. The clearest index of the malaise was a demographic crisis. Besides an unprecedented peacetime increase in mortality, fertility dipped alarmingly. Between the 1989 and 2002 censuses, the average number of children per woman in Russia fell from 1.83 to 1.25 in cities, and from 2.63 to 1.5 in rural areas.[60] The result was a colossal strain on welfare services that were already tested beyond their limit by the economic crisis of the 1990s. In 2002, 32 million people were drawing a pension (not including invalidity pensioners), and the median age of the population had risen since the last census in 1989 by four years to 37.1.[61] Pensions were paid late for much of the 1990s, and for many people they were set at poverty level. At its nadir, in the wake of the economic crisis of August 1998, the average pension fell below the official subsistence line.[62]

Nor was this the only way in which the older generation was weakened by the economic transformation. Senior workers might find themselves first in line for demotion or redundancy, and lacked the time to re-skill. Sheer physical energy was a prerequisite for success in areas of the economy such as small retail business or "shuttle" trading. Jobs in commerce seized the prestige once reserved for professions like engineer or scientist. The impression of hierarchies upturned was confirmed by a sharp downturn in higher education in the 1990s. A university degree from a Soviet institution now had limited value on the labor market, and many people with such a qualification suddenly found themselves vulnerable. According to one 1993 survey, nearly 50 percent of the "mass intelligentsia" were poor.[63] Unsurprisingly, enrolments fell. In 1990, 30 percent of the school-leaving cohort entered tertiary education, but by 1993 that figure had fallen to just over 26 percent.[64]

This was an era when "survival strategies" were rather more than a sociologist's turn of phrase. Tens of millions of urbanites relied – whether materially or psychologically – on garden plots where they grew potatoes and cabbages. Even by the miserly official definition of poverty, at least one-third of Russians were poor in 1992–3 (about three times the rate found in 1991). In 1992 the average wage was three times the poverty line; by 1995 the ratio had fallen to 1.8. In 1999 more than 38 percent of the population were officially poor.[65] Government figures revealed a level of inequality that would have been pathological at the best of times and was all the more traumatic for a country emerging from egalitarian state socialism: the top 10 percent of the population earned about four times as much as the bottom 10 percent in 1990, but 15 times as much in 1994 and 13 times as much in 1996.[66]

In times as bad as these, widespread social unrest might have been expected. In July 1989 the self-belief of the Soviet regime was badly shaken by a strike wave in the mining industry, the first such organized working-class resistance since the 1930s. Over the next two years, industrial action reached alarming proportions: in the first nine months of 1990s alone, strikes took place at 1,700 different Soviet enterprises. But, with the notable exception of the miners, grievances remained localized and failed to cohere into a more general political agenda. In due course, shop floor confrontation petered out.[67] In the 1990s, many people took the option of remaining at their workplaces, even if they had to wait months for wages that were ravaged by inflation. Their decision was partly based on habit: Soviet traditions of workplace paternalism died hard, and the possibility of unemployment held terror for workers raised on Soviet traditions of guaranteed work. But there was also a sound economic rationale for the decision to stay put. Post-Soviet enterprises may not have paid much, but their provisioning networks and social benefits were too important to be abandoned in the absence of appealing alternatives. For their part, the ex-Soviet enterprises laid off relatively few workers and did the best they could to procure resources and contracts following the demise of the Soviet centralized economy.[68] A major research project of 2002–6, which collected information from 52 different enterprises in several branches of the economy and seven different regions, found that, even in relatively successful companies, management structures had changed rather little since Soviet times. Paternalism lived on, which meant a failure to delegate powers to middle management but also the practical necessity of allowing line managers to mitigate the effects on the workforce of production targets imposed by top management.[69]

The 1990s, then, were a decade of desperate "making do" when many people were stuck in a Soviet occupational rut that was fast becoming a trough. Despite the indeterminacy, however, there were glimmers of a new social order. One of the constants of social commentary in the first years after the Soviet collapse was the notion of the "crisis" of the intelligentsia. The educated elite brought up under Soviet power was seen to be ill-suited to the new challenges of democratic politics and capitalism. The Soviet intelligentsia was too habituated to comfy cultural hegemony and jobs for life to make an adequate response to the turbulent but exciting phase of "transition." All they were able to do was issue plaintive cries about the declining prestige of high culture and the plummeting circulation figures of their beloved literary journals.[70]

Such a diagnosis was perhaps a touch facile, not least because it underplayed the strenuous efforts made by many educated professionals to find a place and a purpose in the new Russia. But it did clear the way for serious study of Russia's new professional classes and educated elite. The Russian middle class became the main analytical quarry of post-Soviet sociology and journalism: its existence and well-being were treated as a measure of the success of Russian "transition." After the collapse of the currency in August 1998, there was much speculation that the new middle class had been killed in the womb. In due course such talk appeared to have been premature. Tertiary education, the primary feeder institution for the Russian mass intelligentsia, recovered after the collapse of enrolments in the 1990s. By 2004–5, the proportion of students in the population had more than doubled since 1990–1.[71] By the end of 2007, a Google search for "Russian middle class" generated around 3 million hits. Even the government made morale-boosting statements on the subject. In April 2007, German Gref, Minister for Economic Development and Trade, announced that, by 2010, 30–35 percent of Russians would belong to the middle class (up from 20 percent in 2006).[72]

By the early twenty-first century, Russians were identifying themselves as middle-class in much the same way as people in the West, with income the prime indicator of such status. Avowedly middle-class people were more socially active

and more optimistic. Their growing confidence was underwritten by unprecedented spending power and opportunities to travel. Educated professional
Russians were now citizens of the world to an extent that would have seemed
remarkable as recently as the late 1980s. Now, a Russian who took up residence
in North America or western Europe was not an émigré but a migrant like any
other. Back in Russia, professionals' level of affluence still lagged behind – the per
capita income requirement for a Russian middle-class family in 2006 was no more
than $600–700 per month (with regional variations) – and they still worried about
material and social welfare issues that would not concern their counterparts in
the West. Income, occupation, and self-identification as "middle-class" did not
always match up: this was still an extremely fluid society where social markers
remained unstable. But Russia had acquired an urban mass consumer society
vastly more recognizable to an inhabitant of Manchester or Philadelphia than had
been the case even in the mid-1990s.

The impression persisted, however, that the class descriptors adopted in
Western social science did not quite fit Russian reality. In large parts of nonmet-
ropolitan Russia, the lines between urban and rural population, between peasants
and professionals, were far from clear. An extensive fieldwork project of 2000–3
revealed myriad ways in which people in the Russian regions might combine salaried work with commitment to an agricultural household-based economy. One
village informant spent her days working in the local library for a minuscule
salary, but got up at five to feed and milk her cow before sending it off to join a
herd that was taken out to graze by a specially hired shepherd; then, in her lunch
break, she would rush back for the second milking. According to 2002 census
statistics, 36 million Russian households were engaged in agriculture, and less
than half of those were located in rural areas proper.[73]

Figures such as these have led many historians and sociologists to ponder the
nature and the extent of the social transformation that Russia underwent in the
twentieth century. On the one hand, the persistence of "traditional" forms of
subsistence agriculture was only too clear. On the other hand, post-Soviet Russia
had many of the hallmarks of "modern" state–society relations. A case in point
was the elaborate system of social benefits which the Soviet Union bequeathed to
the new Russia. Many of the 50 million or more urban people cultivating household plots were "pensioners": an identity defined completely by the modern state.
They were both anachronistic reminders of Russia's peasant ancestry and living
evidence of the Soviet social contract.

The welfare system itself, while impressive in its scope and scale, was full of
ambiguities. In the Soviet period, social benefits were not primarily designed to
alleviate hardship. Pensions, for example, were granted to men at the age of 60
and women at the age of 55 (earlier still in "harmful" occupations that might
affect workers' health). The absence of means testing was reasonable enough in

Soviet conditions of stable scarcity, but it was a serious flaw in the 1990s, when the combination of ageing population and economic crisis made the pensions system catastrophically underfinanced and unable to target the worst cases of poverty. Another fundamental problem was the system's lack of transparency. By 2003, at the federal level alone, Russia had 236 different categories of benefit entitlement; when other administrative levels were taken into account, the figure was in excess of 1,000. A new law on benefits that came into force in January 2005 was designed to increase transparency and create a more clear-cut division of welfare responsibilities between the federal center and the regions. While these goals were admirable in principle, the reform did not meet its stated objectives: Russia was left with a hybrid of Soviet-style untargeted benefits and liberal means-tested provision, while regional inequalities only increased. The law also provoked the widest social unrest of the Putin era: thousands of pensioners came on to the streets in cities across Russia in protest at the "monetization" of benefits – such as bus passes and medical prescriptions – that had been crucial to the well-being of lower-income sections of the population.[74]

A similarly mixed picture can be seen in the postcommunist development of that crucial Soviet institution, the army. Since the 1930s, militarization – with conscription its crucial element – had been a defining feature of Russian society. In the post-Soviet era it was for the first time put under serious question. From 1989 onward, "committees of soldiers' mothers" established themselves as the most successful nongovernmental organizations of post-Soviet Russia. Their exposés of bullying and mismanagement were only strengthened by the military misadventures of the Yeltsin era. In 1994–6 the army received the worst publicity it had ever known as its equipment, personnel, and organization were discredited by the disastrous campaign in Chechnya. Confronted by powerful images of the corpses of Russian conscripts, public opinion moved strongly in favor of a contract army. Civilian policymakers began to realize, if they had not already, that the Russian army was a Cold War anachronism poorly prepared for the challenges – above all counterinsurgency – that it was likely to face in the postcommunist era. However, the Russian military establishment was as conservative as military establishments everywhere, and the Yeltsin administration lacked the political will to break its resistance, adopting for the most part a policy of none-too-benign neglect.

Early signs in the Putin era were no better. The regime responded to the sinking of the nuclear submarine *Kursk* in August 2000, which killed all 118 crew members, with a Soviet-style campaign of misinformation. It was not until almost two weeks after the tragedy that Putin began to make public gestures to assuage public dismay and the grief of the submariners' families. Hazing of conscripts remained a problem so acute that tens of thousands of families were paying bribes to gain their sons exemption from military service: in 2005 alone, 6,000 soldiers were admitted to hospital after injuries inflicted by bullying, and 16 lost their lives. All the same, in 2006 the State Duma introduced measures against draft deferment, and alternatives to military service were made as unattractive as possible.[75] Although the early phase of Medvedev's presidency suggested renewed government commitment to the idea of a contract army, reform of this kind still faced strong opposition from the General Staff. There were also limits to the extent to which the population was capable of a radical challenge to the military orthodoxy. The armed forces permeated Russian society. According to the most commonly cited figure – which may be an understatement – Russia had around 1.4 million serving military and paramilitary personnel in 2002. This was approximately the same number as served in the United States, a much wealthier country with twice Russia's population. When we add to this figure the millions of men who had passed through military service, and take into account the long tradition of military training for the school-age population, it is no wonder that pacifism was frowned on in Russia. The national Union of Committees of Soldiers' Mothers achieved its successes partly because it did not attempt any radical challenge to the importance of the armed forces in Russian life, eschewing rights-based argument and drawing attention instead to cases of brutality and corruption.[76] If demilitarization is a corollary of postindustrial civilization, Russia in the early twenty-first century was still some way off achieving it.

——————— Conclusion: Modernity Manqué? ———————

Russia's twentieth-century social history seems to meet all the criteria for rapid modernization. The Soviet/Russian population became vastly more urban, secular, and educated. It had better health care, lived longer, and reproduced more slowly. Women went out to work in their tens of millions. People lived in "gridded" cities that were recognizably a variant of urban modernity. Tol'iatti, the major new center of the Soviet automobile industry in the 1970s, might be said to be Detroit, Michigan without mass car ownership.[77]

Perhaps, however, the carlessness of the Russian provinces is more significant than any surface resemblances between American and Soviet industrial modernity. The Soviet experience placed severe restrictions on the extent to which people could become autonomous, mobile, modern citizens. Nor does one need to try too hard to identify further limitations of Soviet/Russian modernization. More than a few traces of the traditional patriarchal order persisted through the twentieth century. Women might have gone to work, but they were concentrated in low-status occupations and were not absolved of the lion's share of domestic responsibilities. People might have moved to the cities but they retained connections to the village, whether through family ties or their own cultivation of rural or peri-urban plots of land. Life expectancy improved, but only up to a point well below that of Britain or Japan. The barriers between particular parts of the country, or particular walks of life, were as high as ever. Metaphorically speaking, there were in ex-Soviet Russia a great many Detroits where people might remain stranded in an attenuated version of industrial modernity. Perhaps, in Russia, the modern sociological concept of "class" has still not thrown off its unwanted ancestry in the system of social "estates" whereby people were assigned to arbitrary status groups with particular duties and privileges.[78]

The abundant paradoxes of Russia's social development have led one prominent sociologist and demographer to speak in oxymoronic terms of Russia's "conservative modernization."[79] While accepting the heuristic value of this formulation, however, we must defer judgment for a few more pages. The next chapter will swap broad sociological categories for a closer analysis of Russian society in practice.

5

Public and Private

The Soviet Union was by all appearances ruled by a political system whose mission was to break down the barriers between public and private. In setting itself this aim, the Soviet regime was seeking to master an area of life that was resistant to state-led solutions. It was also defying a trend found everywhere else in developed societies in the second half of the twentieth century: as Europeans moved to cities, became better off, acquired more free time, and developed extensive and fluid social networks, they became much less interested in the forms of solidarity and collective action that the Soviet regime wished to encourage. They also gained more of a sense of their own value and autonomy as individuals – and this was reflected in areas of behavior from voting to reproduction. The Soviet objective, by contrast, was to drive forward modernization without permitting its more individualizing effects.

There has long been a sense of intellectual and moral unease in applying the categories of public and private to Russia. As used in the Anglophone world, these words tend to presuppose a set of laws and institutions that were conspicuously lacking in the Soviet Union. In liberal states, the private sphere has been protected from undue outside intervention by the institution of private property and by a shifting set of other laws relating to the individual, some of which were codified and internationalized in the middle of the twentieth century as "human rights."

None of this was remotely true of the Soviet Union. Here was a country where the individual citizen was poorly protected by the law. Even if the threat of arrest receded considerably after 1953, harassment and discrimination without redress remained routine. Conversely, access to the means of public communication was very tightly controlled even at relatively unbuttoned moments of Soviet history such as the Thaw of the mid-1950s.

Commentators on Soviet society have drawn a number of contrasting conclusions from all this. The most widely held view is that the state was all-powerful and there was very little privacy (as we would understand that word) in Soviet society; such private life as people did manage was hard-won and squirreled away from the intrusions of the police state. The most severely oppressed members of society could not permit themselves to open up even to their family and friends, and would sometimes remain guarded and self-censoring for decades after they returned from prison or labor camp.[1] The small majority of Soviet citizens who did not have brushes with incarceration had to engage in obfuscation and self-delusion as they sought to square their individual interests and preoccupations with the demands of social participation. The result was the unlovely Soviet faculty of "doublethink," according to which people could say one thing in the company of those they trusted and quite another in public – without necessarily noticing any discrepancy. One wry British scholar observed that the time-honored Russian practice of *vranyo* – embroidering of the truth, or elaborately performed falsehood that stops short of a barefaced lie – had gained additional purchase in the Soviet period.[2]

The point can be bolstered linguistically. As is often remarked, there is no word in Russia for "privacy" – unless one counts the ugly loan-word *privatnost'* that has been adopted by the post-Soviet social sciences. The word used in Soviet times as an equivalent for the Western "private" was *chastnyi* (related to the word for "part"), which had pejorative connotations of bourgeois atomization and special interests. As one ex-Soviet observer has noted, "'Private life' is often synonymous not with 'real life' or authentic existence but with foreign, inauthentic behavior."[3] The Soviets did have notions of "personal life" (*lichnaia zhizn'*) and "personality" (*lichnost'*), but these were regarded as legitimate targets for intervention and supervision by the general public (*obshchestvennost'*). The implication drawn by one theoretically minded scholar is that, in Soviet Russia, "private life did not shrink to intimacy in the sense of a legitimate and protected sphere of privacy. Both privacy and particularism were completely rejected and stamped out by the social."[4] The counterpart term *publichnyi*, nearly three centuries after its adoption in the Petrine era, still had a neologistic and vaguely obscene ring: it was most commonly encountered in the phrases *publichnyi dom* (brothel) and *publichnaia zhenshchina* (prostitute). *Obshchestvennost'* – a term derived from the word for "society" that had connotations of "community" and "public opinion" – was the greatly preferred alternative.

Another, less negative, view is that Soviet people were not, by and large, the suffering victims of constraints on private freedom. Perhaps, in fact, the political pressures on Soviet people, far from destroying private life, made it all the more valuable, enjoying, and fulfilling. One noted émigré sociologist has gone so far as to argue that Soviet Russians had more rewarding friendships than Americans of the same era. When Vladimir Shlapentokh left the Soviet Union for North American academia in 1979, he was astonished to find that the members of his new professional community "were closer to the tribal-family type communion and that blood ties were more important than intellectual and emotional sympathies". He went on to bemoan the fact that "a festive meal with a circle of friends and intellectual conversation is a phenomenon absolutely unknown in America".[5] His general position has also been elegantly stated by an American anthropologist: "In contrast to truncated political and public realms ... the realm of the private flourished in Soviet life; moreover, the freedoms experienced in this private realm gained a particular depth and resonance – were gracefully cloaked in a sense of intimacy – precisely because of their location in a wider system of falsity and prohibition".[6] Put in starker historical terms, this interpretation would amount to the argument that the postwar decades saw a clear bifurcation of public and private – a "privatization" of Russia *avant la lettre*.

To these two approaches – one highly skeptical of Soviet people's opportunities for private life, the other extremely bullish – we can add a more nuanced third. On closer inspection, the binary opposition of public and private turns out to be a blunt analytical instrument. As historical investigation of Soviet private life has broadened to include topics as diverse as home-making, pet-keeping, friendship, domestic violence, and car maintenance, the boundaries between public and private in the Soviet Union have come to seem porous and shifting. One recent account recommends thinking in terms of a "multiplicity of layers rather than a flat or unitary conceptualization of the private sphere."[7] It is possible to conceive of a Soviet life that was deeply embedded in various types of "collective" yet not necessarily antipathetic to small-group solidarity and personal self-interest. Ethnographic accounts of late Soviet society find little tension or incompatibility between public and private. Caroline Humphrey shows that the distinction had no meaning for Buryat collective farm workers in the 1970s as they strove to maintain or improve their material lot. In his study of the "last Soviet generation," Alexei Yurchak takes a milieu as far removed from East Siberian agriculture as could be imagined – the upwardly mobile Komsomol circles of Leningrad in the 1970s and 1980s – and finds that his subjects were able to reap the practical and emotional rewards of public participation without doing violence to their inner being or their friendships. This was less "doublethink" than "flexithink."[8]

This chapter replaces the liberal public–private dichotomy with a different model for understanding historical change in postwar Soviet society. From the 1940s onward, in law, public discourse, and social and economic policy, a peculiarly Soviet notion of "personal" life took shape. The authorities now increasingly recognized that the individual citizen had a right to "personal" property (*lichnaia sobstvennost'*), to single-family housing, and to attributes of modern life such as domestic appliances and autonomous leisure travel. This legitimate consumption was of course far more circumscribed than in the "bourgeois" world, but still represented a major innovation of the era; it was the socioeconomic corollary of the "emancipation" of the Soviet population after Stalin. Yet, if this personal sphere was sacrosanct in theory, the reality was that, in order to obtain their due, Soviet people still had to engage in energetic lobbying of the authorities, use whatever informal networks and contacts they had at their disposal, and cultivate their superiors at the workplace. However hard they tried, Soviet life remained frustrating, exhausting and – given its lack of transparency – profoundly unfair. Yet it also gave rise to myriad sub-"public" allegiances and forms of behavior that made Soviet socialism viable – at least for a while. When market relations were unleashed on Soviet society in the late 1980s, there was reason to believe that the power of money would make life in Russia more transparent and help to institute a more secure public–private divide. As the final section of this chapter will suggest, the reality has been far less straightforward.

Stalinist Starting Points

World War II, to an even greater extent than Russia's previous wars, placed limits on people's opportunities to take decisions as individuals. Most Soviet citizens, whether or not they were actually at the front, were subject to military discipline. Memoirs convey the terror that people had of being late for work or of committing some misdemeanor at their factory or office: labor "deserters" and other miscreants were at risk of draconian punishments. All this made the discipline of the 1930s seem positively lax. In addition to the Gulag population proper, hundreds of thousands of Soviet people were "labor conscripts," living and working on terms little better than those of convicts. Rural people, for their part, toiled under the crushing burden of requisitioning and taxation that left them in even more desperate straits than in the prewar Stalin era.

But there was more to Soviet people's subjective experience of war than coercion. At the same time as certain categories of the population were oppressed and stigmatized, other groups participated full-bloodedly in the national cause, finding it possible, for perhaps the first time in their lives, to assess events on terms congruent with the public "script." For the millions of young men who poured into the armed forces from rural areas, the war years represented a break with their earlier experience of Soviet power. In the newly collectivized village they had been at the bottom of the social order and could expect little from the state other than taxes and grain quotas. Now they were given uniforms and rations and told they were the vanguard of the Soviet cause. Perhaps, even, they joined the Party. Something similar might be said of Soviet women, a second-class gender in the 1920s and 1930s, who now had the chance to overcome their presumed social and political backwardness as they toiled in farm and factory or took up arms.

The wartime ethos of public service and sacrifice was most obvious among those who were engaged in articulating it to the rest of the population. Members of the educated elite, even those who had hitherto lacked obvious civic engagement, threw themselves into the fray with panache and conviction. Intellectuals and artists wrote for the press, spoke on the radio, gave performances at the front, or simply joined up to fight. War poetry was perhaps the first Soviet literature that truly fulfilled its socialist realist mission of being "popular" (*narodnaia*) as well as ideologically correct. The Soviet literary milieu also produced a number of war journalists – Konstantin Simonov, Ilya Ehrenburg, Vasilii Grossman – whose energy and eloquence made them supreme exponents of the genre.[9]

Wartime patriotism was not, however, a matter of high-flown sentiments. Various kinds of emotional glue were required if the generality of the Soviet cause was to adhere to the consciousness of individuals and small groups. The building blocks of state patriotism were not abstractions like socialism or nation but rather family, community, and locality. All this came with a large admixture of rage – mostly directed at the German invaders, but also at the accumulated deprivation, humiliation, and repression of the previous twenty-five years.

Propaganda during the war showed itself flexible in using symbols and motifs for their raw emotional power rather than any obvious compatibility with Marxism-Leninism. One of the more resonant such symbols, and certainly the most jarring for a Marxist-Leninist, was religion. The struggle with Nazi Germany was quickly christened a "holy war," and everyday religious practice made a strong comeback after the Church was taken under Stalin's nurturing wing in 1943. The newly created Council for the Affairs of the Russian Orthodox Church reported that almost 150,000 people had attended Easter services in Moscow in 1944, while two or three times that number had been present for the traditional midnight procession. In a single church in the important evacuation city of Kuibyshev, the number of weddings held rose from 139 in 1943 to 403 in 1944 and 867 in 1945.[10]

The rapprochement with religion was a striking innovation of wartime public culture, but the defense of family and home was its key thematic component. War poetry permitted an intimacy that would have been regarded as lyrical excess in the 1930s. The civic dimension of Soviet life became personalized as never before. Broadcasters read out hundreds of letters "to and from the front" where soldiers and their families sent greetings and exhortations to each other and passed on personal news.[11] Feature films made during the war contained relatively little frontline fighting (partly because this was too disturbing and difficult a subject, partly because the film studios were evacuated in haste and operating under material constraints). Instead, in the genre of "home-front melodrama," the stakes of war were transferred to the domestic arena. The emblematic *Wait for Me* (1943), which evoked the enormously popular poem of the same title by Konstantin Simonov, showed women negotiating the moral perils of wartime – the temptation not to "wait" for the return of long-departed husbands – in implausibly well-furnished interiors.[12]

During the war, women, and motherhood came to the fore as patriotic symbols. The culture of the industrializing 1930s had been overwhelmingly masculine and proletarian – much as the Soviet regime might claim to have revolutionized gender relations – but during the war women were rhetorically upgraded. They fought and served in auxiliary capacities at the front, they slaved in munitions factories and in the fields, they kept home fires burning. But most crucial to their symbolic value was their function as mothers. "Motherland" (*rodina*), not Stalin, was what most Soviet soldiers thought they were fighting for. And this term was backed up by any number of poster images and film depictions of ardent, patriotic, and female heads of family.[13]

At the level of public discourse, then, we find an unprecedented fusion of the public with the personal and intimate. Something similar was happening at the level of everyday life. One of the paradoxes of Russia's war is that, while high levels of coercion were applied in the rear as on the front line, Soviet people were obliged and even encouraged to take more control over their lives. Even military discipline was not quite as it appeared in the decrees of the State Defense Committee when transferred into the milieu of the army unit, where group solidarity might keep the NKVD at arm's length. In civilian life, moreover, disorganization and forced self-sufficiency were central to the wartime experience. State capacity to provide its population with food and shelter, never enormous in the Stalin era, came close to collapse, especially in 1941–3. People had to grow food on urban plots and buy what they could at markets where prices at other moments in Soviet history would have been prohibited as "speculative." The household became the fulcrum of economic life, and it was defined more loosely to include non-kin as people came together to maximize their chances of survival. The workplace was a center of provisioning as well as a unit of production. People's life-chances depended to a critical extent on where they worked. Food might be monotonous and inadequate in factory canteens, but it was – at least sometimes – enough to keep workers alive. Enterprises were better able to provide housing than municipal authorities. They could also help workers with their household economies – notably by providing seed for planting.[14]

Soviet people, then, were obliged to act as individuals as well as citizens; and they had various places – above all, the household and the workplace – where they could shelter from overintrusive central government. They were also prepared to engage the center directly. The sacrifices borne in the war gave rise to a sense of entitlement. Hundreds of thousands petitioned the authorities in Moscow. Their grievances were sharpened by the greater transparency of life in wartime:

FIGURE 5.1   "For the Motherland!" (1943).
Source: akg-images / RIA Nowosti.

people could see (or think they saw) who was contributing to the war effort and who was not, and draw conclusions as to whether they were receiving their due.[15]

Given the immense release of social energy the war had brought, the question was how order was to be restored: how the private was to be prevented from taking over the public. An important part of the answer came with a series of campaigns to strengthen the role of state agencies in supervising economic life. Audits and inventories in the immediate postwar period revealed a mass of irregularities in the ways enterprises had allocated resources and households had registered (or failed to register) plots of land and dwellings. The reality was that discretionary semilegal arrangements remained widespread at least into the early 1950s, but the government was now signaling its intention to do something about the situation. An important real and symbolic marker of the Soviet state's growing control of the everyday economy was the antitheft legislation of 1947 which, besides rounding up hundreds of thousands more slave laborers for the Gulag, may be seen as the foundational moment of a stable socialist property regime.[16]

The key actors in this regime, however, were not officials in the Ministry of Justice but the managers and administrators who had real day-to-day control over resources. While such people had to bear in mind the new disciplinary measures, they did not need to fear for their lives in the manner of their 1930s' predecessors. Their position had only been strengthened by the war, when Party officials and industrial managers became valued plenipotentiaries instead of potential scapegoats; for those bosses who survived with an unblemished record, the prospects in the mid-1940s were better than ever. Highly placed officials, moreover, were able to provide institutional shelter for any number of lower functionaries and attached workforce. The result was what might be called Stalinist corporatism. As during the war, individual citizens' prospects depended less on their relationship to "the state" than on their particular institutional affiliation; here was an effective form of mediation between household and central authorities that bolstered the stability of the Soviet order.

This, more or less, was the situation on the ground, but as ever it needed to be "spun" by Soviet culture. The key discursive tool for reconciling public and private, in the late Stalin era as before the war, was "culturedness" (*kul'turnost'*). The precepts of "cultured" behavior were a mélange of public health, self-cultivation, and consumerism. In general, over the first three decades of the Soviet era, lifestyle recommendations moved from the rudimentary (literacy, clean underwear) to the more advanced. What stands out from a survey of material from the late Stalin era is the extent to which restrictions on the depiction of consumer comfort had been lifted. Novels served as "a material inventory of embourgeoisement," providing extensive accounts of households with parquet floors, pink lampshades, and knickknacks.[17] In the newspapers, retail workers were enjoined to engage in "cultured trade" (a slogan first introduced in the 1930s) by ensuring a reasonable selection of goods and delivering acceptable service to consumers. The director of TsUM, the showcase department store in the Soviet Union, asserted in 1949 that culturedness and customer service were even more important than plan fulfillment for the shop's mission. TsUM was even able to offer imported goods, such as stockings, that were in high demand.[18] Out of the public gaze, the elite was developing a strong sense of entitlement to the material attributes of civilized modern life. Functionaries traded military uniforms for smart civilian suits. Prominent members of the cultural intelligentsia sent in a steady stream of requests for material assistance to Party and state officials. Cars were a common object of desire, on the grounds that public transport did not work well or that vehicles previously at the disposal of writers and performers had been requisitioned during the war. The most proactive petitioners went so far as to send in a list of building materials they needed for repairing their dachas. If in the 1930s such requests had generally been addressed to the executives of the "creative unions," by the late 1940s they were going straight to the government.[19]

As these examples begin to suggest, the finer things in life were only available to a well-connected metropolitan elite. For those less favored, the hardship of the postwar years made comfortable – or indeed "cultured" – existence quite unthinkable. Besides chronic lack of food, the population had to contend with a shortage of housing that was desperate even by Soviet standards. When the war was over, Soviet people, like their counterparts elsewhere in the world, desperately wanted to return to a "normality" that, in truth, had never existed in the prewar USSR: to find a spouse and a place to live, to settle down, to have children, to enjoy stable and fulfilling work lives. In practice, however, domestic happiness was hardly achievable for many people in the Soviet Union. Millions of Soviet women had lost their men, and the chances for unattached females of finding a partner were greatly reduced by the sex imbalance in the postwar population. The catastrophic state of housing acted against the establishment of anything approaching a normal life. The urban housing stock fell by around a quarter over the war years. Even five years after the war, the average Soviet urbanite had well less than 5 square meters at his or her disposal. Outside the capital, running water, sewerage, and central heating were luxuries.[20] There was also the problem that millions of Soviet people were still on the move in 1945 and 1946. Many of them did not get home for years – by which time they effectively had no home. Furthermore, millions of peasants were fleeing the collective farm. How were they all to be accommodated?

The answer, of course, was with great difficulty. Yet, precisely because of the collapse of prewar infrastructure, attitudes and practices were beginning to change. Millions of urban people had to appeal to the authorities to reclaim property that they had been forced to abandon, thus asserting rights and ownership in a way they had not been called on to do before.[21] During the war, the Soviet state was forced to acknowledge as never before the importance of housing built and maintained outside the framework of state, enterprise, or municipal authorities. A decree of May 1944 offered encouragement for individual construction in the form of cheap state loans and assistance with building materials. Soviet legal theorists now had an overarching concept to cover the results of such activity. The notion of "personal property" included housing that was individually owned but did not exceed a citizen's legitimate requirements. This term had figured in early Soviet legislation and had been part of the Stalin Constitution of 1936, but its implications had never before been so extensively tested in practice.

The quantity of urban housing in the USSR classified as personal property rose by almost 70 percent between 1944 and 1950 to more than 125 million square meters. Housing controlled by local soviets showed a more modest rise over the same period of 23 percent (or a total of 85 million square meters). Much of the individual housing went up in a hurry, without the necessary authorization. The authorities in Stalingrad, one of the most high-profile sites for reconstruction in the postwar Soviet Union, reported that about one-sixth of new individual houses between 1945 and 1950 fell into this category.[22]

But the individual was not the sole or even the principal subject of personal property. The family, a subject of furious debate in the interwar period, was now firmly established as Soviet society's primary grass-roots institution. Public discourse blithely championed the family, even as it also subordinated it to the "Great Family" of the Soviet people. More concretely, the family's right to distribute household resources was recognized in a new 1945 law on inheritance, which expanded the legal definition of the family circle in response to the wartime growth of interdependence between soldier sons, parents, and grandparents.[23] The value of the family was also boosted by a pro-natalist campaign launched as the country's leaders began to think of replenishing war losses. A new Family Law of July 1944 increased aid to women with several children: provisions ranged from financial support to medals for "hero mothers." At the same time, the new legislation stipulated state support of unmarried women with children. Single mothers had never previously been treated so well by the Soviet state, though the law – with its diminishing of male responsibility for children – was an encouragement for men to create more of them.[24] In 1946, 752,000 children were born out of wedlock, and by 1949 the figure had risen to close to a million.[25]

For all the squalor and hardship of these years, there is some evidence that the relationship between state and society was shifting even in what is considered the most rigid and dismal time in Soviet history: the late Stalin era. Whether we look at family policy, at property discourse, or at the consoling myths of novels and films, there are signs that a Soviet personal sphere was becoming at least conceivable. But was it achievable?

The Rediscovery of the Personal

The dignity of the individual quickly became a central preoccupation of the post-Stalin era. Writers were the first to give it public expression. As early as April 1953, the poet Ol'ga Berggol'ts bemoaned the absence of true lyricism in Soviet literature. At the end of the same year, *Novyi mir*, the main literary journal of the time, published Vladimir Pomerantsev's article "On Sincerity in Literature" which criticized the tendency of Soviet writers to "varnish" reality. In 1954, the cosmopolitan and savvy Ilya Ehrenburg seized the moment by publishing a novella, *The Thaw*, which gave the name to a whole epoch of Soviet culture. The work pitted an engineer hero against a self-serving and emotionally limited factory director, a battle that was fought largely for the affections of the latter's wife. Besides this basic narrative interest, it offered an extended rumination on the balance to be struck between personal and public life, and on the ways that should be rendered in art.[26]

In due course literary works would become more forceful in showing the conflict between the morally upright individual and a political system usually embodied by obnoxious functionaries. The most important work of 1956, Vladimir Dudintsev's *Not By Bread Alone*, described the struggle of a talented inventor, Lopatkin, to have his new design for a centrifugal pipe-casting system adopted by industry in the face of vested interests and bureaucratic opposition. The negative hero of Ehrenburg's *The Thaw* still had some compensating qualities, but Lopatkin's principal antagonist is a downright scoundrel. Lopatkin himself is an ascetic who subjugates all other aspirations to his invention; in the Soviet 1950s and 1960s, the role of romantic hero was more likely to be taken by an engineer (or physicist, or geologist) than by a musician or an actor.

This turn to human interest made perfect sense to the literary and artistic intelligentsia. In addition to offering writers and filmmakers more latitude, individual narratives made better stories if they were released from the obligation to nod in the direction of the Communist Party. Cinema, as a medium predisposed to personal stories, was quick to respond.[27] From 1954 onward, the output of Soviet studios included ever more films with sympathetic and nuanced portrayals of heroes (often heroines) whose lives threaded together the public and the personal. Some of them were rather less than heroic in their actions and choices, and their lives might unfold out of the direct gaze of the Party or the Soviet workplace. Such protagonists were not straightforwardly admirable, and redemption did not always await them. *Different Fates* (1956) was perhaps the first Soviet film to feature a loathsome heroine who – in a striking violation of the Soviet norm that sins should be redeemed or punished – does not perceive her moral turpitude even when given a golden opportunity to do so in the final scene.

The turn to the personal affected even that paragon of patriotic topics, the war. The international calling card of Soviet cinema in the late 1950s was *The Cranes Are Flying* (1957), a wartime love story where the central couple are only briefly together: the hero disappears from view early on, as he is killed at the front near the beginning of the campaign. Instead, the film follows the heroine, Veronika, through her marriage (under duress) to the hero's cousin and her difficult life under evacuation through to the final scene of welcoming the soldiers back at the railway station (when Veronika finally has to accept that her beloved is dead).

The film's plotline, its Gothic style and swirling camera angles leave the viewer in no doubt of the war's emotional dimension. A more down-to-earth, but in some ways more affecting, treatment of the impact of the war on personal relationships was Lev Kulidzhanov and Iakov Segel's *The House I Live in* (also 1957), where the characters are forced to set aside their prewar preoccupations. A somewhat *exaltée* intelligentsia girl shelves her acting ambitions and becomes a nurse, later meeting her death while on service. The war is seen to cast a harsh light on the concerns of peacetime, but it does not invalidate them. This is a world of flawed but likable individuals.

Similar preoccupations – but from a masculine perspective – inform the two other most celebrated war films of the Khrushchev period. In *The Ballad of a Soldier* (1959), the amiable young hero is granted leave for a battlefield exploit and spends the rest of the film making his way home for what turns out to be a very brief meeting with his mother. *The Fate of a Man* (1959) contains scenes of stirring patriotism – the best-known coming when the hero avoids summary execution in a POW camp by showing the German commandant that a Russian soldier can hold his drink – but it also tells the story of a man who is profoundly damaged by the loss of his family and other traumas of war.

At the tail end of the Thaw era, Larisa Shepit'ko's *Wings* (1966) brought a still higher degree of nuance to the war theme. This time the military conflict is already two decades in the past. The heroine is a renowned former bomber pilot; in the present she is the director of a vocational training college. Unable to overcome her brusque military manner, she struggles to form satisfactory relationships with her adopted daughter, with a troublesome student at the college, or with potential male partners. But she remains a complex, sympathetic, and in many ways fulfilled person.

As the above examples indicate, Soviet cinema of the Thaw was not championing the personal entirely for its own sake. It would be more accurate to say that it was debating the relationship between the personal and the social spheres. *The Cranes Are Flying* was stylistically of a piece with *Breakfast at Tiffany's* (1961), but rather different in its preoccupations. Whereas Audrey Hepburn's Holly Golightly is engaged in self-discovery through jewelry-gazing, Tat'iana Samoilova's Veronika has to worry about her duty to her country, to her adopted family, and to her man at the front.

Perhaps, however, stylistic resemblances are more significant than they seem. In the Khrushchev era, the media of Soviet culture were beginning to influence its messages as never before. Radio-listening had changed greatly since the 1930s, when most people's access to broadcasts came through wired receiver points, usually set up in public places or communal flats, which precluded channel-switching. Now, vastly more Soviet families had radio sets of their own that could be used to tune in to more than one station. Broadcasters also had to bear in mind

FIGURE 5.2   A consumer from the Leningrad region tries out the latest model of radio set (the Rodina-47), 1947 or 1948.
Source: Courtesy of A.S. Popov Central Museum of Communications, St Petersburg.

the greater claims on the attention span of their listeners: in the early 1960s they began to experiment with more interactive forms of programming.

The big media innovation of the post-Stalin era was television. The Soviet regime threw its weight behind the new technology. Television sets became required items for Soviet people much sooner than one might expect in a country with such a poor record in household gadgetry. While television seemed to deliver the Soviet propagandist's dream of total audiovisual penetration of every home, it also came with drawbacks. How could one be sure that Soviet people were watching in the right way, given that they were doing so out of the public gaze? Was not television a recipe for social passivity?[28]

Beyond the mass media of the press, radio and television – which, for all the concerns they caused Soviet propagandists, were always heavily monitored – the modest liberalization of the post-Stalin period opened up other venues for cultural activity that were practically uncensorable. The literary journals that had carried such daring material in the 1950s and early 1960s were increasingly subject to restrictions, and by 1970 were muzzled. But the intelligentsia of the major cities turned instead to the theater, where productions of even the most canonical works could draw knowing responses from audiences well schooled in Soviet "Aesopian language." Outside the major cities, where professional companies were more thinly spread, amateur theater flourished between the late 1950s and the late 1960s. Official figures put the number of amateur troupes across the USSR at 150,000 in 1958. These groups adopted varied, even experimental, repertoire, and some of them found ways around the official prohibition on ticket sales, managing to build around them a like-minded audience.[29]

Amateur musical performance took off in the institution of Houses of Culture in the late 1950s, and by the mid-1960s guitar poetry was an established genre of Soviet cultural life. Its rise proved to be perfectly synchronized with that of the open-reel tape recorder, which first reached the Soviet market in significant numbers in 1960. By the mid-1960s, annual manufacture had quadrupled to half a million, and by the end of the decade it exceeded a million. The guitar poets (or "bards") brought new versions of intimacy to a listening audience that expanded from small apartment gatherings to a national audience thanks to the tape recorder. Even after their art received mass dissemination through unofficial recordings, the bards clung to their amateur persona. Bulat Okudzhava (b. 1924), the first of the guitar poets to come to prominence, made no claim to proficiency on his instrument – he even drew attention to the inadequacies of his guitar technique and his voice, offering these as tokens of his sincerity and drawing a clear line between his own output and official professional song.[30]

Building a Soviet Personal Sphere

The realm of cultural expression provided the Khrushchev era with one of its key labels ("Thaw"). But to pay too much attention to literary journals or even cinema is to risk downplaying more practical measures that had much greater impact on the quality of life of Soviet people. In the late 1950s, *homo sovieticus* saw astonishing changes in his everyday habitat. A mass housing campaign brought tens of millions of Soviet people out of communal apartments (or worse) and into single-family dwellings. The usually five-story prefabricated housing that sprang up on the rapidly incorporated outskirts of Soviet cities gave the era one of its signature terms: the *khrushchevka*. These housing blocks themselves formed new kinds of estates which were known as "micro-districts" (*mikroraiony*). Between 1955 and 1970 more than 35 million apartments were built, and more than 130 million Soviet citizens moved into new housing.[31] The housewarming was one of the iconic images of the Thaw era, especially in cinema. In *The House Where I Live*, for example, the story begins with people of various social backgrounds moving into apartments on the same stairwell. As it happens, the action is set in the 1930s, but the scene is pure Khrushchev.

FIGURE 5.3   The interior of a worker's apartment, Baku, 1950s. A Soviet image of cosy domesticity, complete with TV set and knickknacks.
Source: © Eugeny Khaldei / PhotoSoyuz.

Practical problems for new residents were legion. Economy and speed were the watchwords of the housing campaign, and building standards were often low. The development of transport networks could not keep pace with the new construction, so many families found themselves displaced from city-center *kommunalki* to remote concrete shanties. The design of the new apartments was not generous. Kitchens were felt to be poky, and residents resented not having the toilet separate from the bathroom. The dimensions of the rooms were disappointingly small.

All the same, the Khrushchev housing campaign brought a substantial improvement in many people's living conditions and a huge boost to the morale of Soviet urban society. This was the largest housing project anywhere in postwar Europe and the Soviet version of slum clearance. In many cities, low-rise housing was demolished to make way for new five- and nine-story blocks. Most of the construction was done under the auspices of soviets and other organizations. The category of individual housing, which had been so prominent in the chaotic postwar years, now faded: in 1959 it made up just over a quarter of new urban construction, in 1964 only 16 percent, and its decline would continue in the 1970s and 1980s. Moreover, regulations on individual houses became more restrictive. A decree of July 1958 placed limits on their size in square meters (60), whereas previously the only restrictions had been number of rooms (five) and stories (two). Then, in 1963, it was forbidden to build individual houses in cities larger than 100,000 people.[32]

But the decline of individual housing did not mean that Soviet people were losing control over their homes. If anything, the opposite. Personal property, perennially subject to arbitrary restrictions, had been a precarious category for living space in a Communist state. Now, however, people would enjoy tenure in the more secure structures of housing owned by municipal soviets or organizations. One indication of growing security was the greater number of officially sanctioned flat exchanges (27,000 in Moscow in 1961, following the establishment of exchange bureaus). Soviet urbanites might also become members of housing cooperatives, which were again encouraged, after a twenty-year hiatus, from 1958 onward. By the end of the Khrushchev era, housing cooperatives across the USSR numbered around 225,000 shareholders – still a modest number – but their presence in Soviet society would steadily increase in the 1970s and 1980s.[33]

As a result of continued mass construction between the late 1950s and the late 1980s, 53 percent of all Soviet families (including rural) came to live in separate apartments, and more than 83 percent of the urban population could boast separate apartments or houses. All told, more than 76 million apartments were built between 1956 and 1989.[34] For generations who remembered far worse, it was a remarkable transformation. In the prewar era people had regularly found themselves displaced, settled, and resettled. They often had to live with a changing cast of neighbors in a *kommunalka* of several rooms. Now, however, they were able to look forward to a more untroubled, if usually cramped, existence. Problems quickly arose if a family wanted to expand its living quarters or to move. But, while they were able to stay put, life was relatively good. The scope for individual construction was now less than it had been in the years of postwar reconstruction. But the state was producing so much new housing that this did not matter. American researchers conducting a major interview project with Soviet citizens who had left the USSR in the 1970s noted to their surprise that these people – who, given their decision to leave, might have been expected to think poorly of life in the Soviet Union – expressed a "relatively high degree of satisfaction with housing."[35]

Housing was not the only policy sphere where the relationship between state and society was changing. The 1950s saw a more general shift to policies based on a notion of entitlement. The Soviet state was beginning to recognize in practice

FIGURE 5.4 Calling cards of later Soviet civilization: Mass housing overlooked by the Ostankino TV tower (completed 1967).
Source: Author's photograph, August 2007.

that it had obligations to its citizenry. Theoretically, it had made this concession earlier, notably in the Stalin Constitution of 1936 which had introduced a concept of citizenship without discrimination. But the constitution belonged to the realm of Stalinist fantasy; it brought no policy commitment to popular well-being, and it did nothing to impede the mass terror campaign of the late 1930s. Following the war, ordinary people might have felt that they deserved more from the state, but the Stalinist regime remained notably indifferent to popular welfare. Priorities finally began to change in the 1950s. As we have seen, the government took upon itself the rehousing of tens of millions of families. It also gave greater heed to the hundreds of thousands of letters from citizens eager or desperate to improve their lot. Petitions to the authorities in the Khrushchev era reveal a powerful sense of entitlement based on war service or lengthy work record; people were impatient for the "socialist contract" to be renewed and expanded.[36]

Even the right to labor can be seen as part of the entitlement discourse. In the war and the late Stalin period, of course, this was odious and obfuscatory rhetoric:

in practice people had the "right" to be conscripted into labor battalions. By the late 1950s, however, the balance had shifted. The notion that the personal rights and fulfillment of Soviet people depended on their work had enabling as well as coercive dimensions. In practice, workers and management had time-honored ways of frustrating government efficiency schemes – especially when the threat of terror was lifted. Workplaces were centers of provisioning networks and sources of sociability. Above all, given the government insistence on the obligation to work, Soviet people did not need to worry about being fired.

The new relations between state and society were reflected institutionally in Central Committee decrees of January 1957 and August 1958, which increased the degree of citizen empowerment possible through local government. District soviets were duly inundated with letters from constituents: one district in Moscow (with a population of around 240,000) received almost 12,000 letters in the first third of 1962 alone.[37] The soviets were not resurrected as institutions of popular democracy, but they did provide an important new focus for petitions regarding welfare. Here was a powerful statement about the grass-roots connection between the individual citizen and the state.

In Moscow, the municipal administration took steps to take control of housing distribution and set up a fair centralized system (rather than the departmentally dominated housing economy of Stalinism). Greater enrolment on the municipal housing queue – from under 40,000 families in January 1953 to almost 200,000 in January 1964 – may perversely be seen as a sign of success: as a meaningful gesture toward egalitarianism. The system may not have been satisfactory or transparent in practice – special interests remained strong, and Soviet people were as always adept at bending the rules – but it did institutionalize a notion of fairness.[38]

The introduction of a new minimum wage reduced the gap between white- and blue-collar earnings. Average wages showed a healthy rise from 715 rubles per month in 1955 to 778 rubles in 1958. At the same time, working conditions became more tolerable: the standard work week shrank by two hours, while maternity leave and disability benefits were extended.[39] Such measures were not just a matter of egalitarianism: they also represented an absolute improvement for the whole of the Soviet population. In the 1950s the leadership recognized the importance of popular well-being in ways that were wholly unprecedented in Soviet history; the Soviet Union was going from a "warfare" state to something beyond the limits of a Western-style welfare state. Besides the housing campaign – which, for all its failings, was the most ambitious of its kind in the world – the Soviet government in 1956 carried out a reform of social benefits that established near-comprehensive pension coverage for urban people and established the lowest pensionable ages in the world: 60 for men, 55 for women, lower still in certain more hazardous branches of the economy.

The post-Stalin regime also recognized the legitimacy of aspirations to modern consumer culture. Indeed, the state took the lead in helping to design a stream-lined "modern" interior to go with the new separate apartment.[40] By the early 1960s, the government was trapped by its own promise of modest but steadily improving prosperity. When it violated its implicit undertaking to maintain low prices (as occurred in the summer of 1962), it faced serious popular unrest.[41]

The apotheosis of the Soviet welfare discourse came in the "Brezhnev Constitution" of 1977, whose provisions were notably more elaborate than those of their Stalinist predecessor (if also at some remove from reality). In article 39, as a token of "developed socialism," it delivered the promise that socialist society would "expand rights and freedoms and constantly improve citizens' living conditions." Article 44 went into some detail on the types of housing available to Soviet people and the means of their distribution. Further articles specified the "right to enjoy the achievements of culture," the "freedom of scientific, technical and artistic activity," the freedom to "take part in the management of the affairs of state and society," and the protection of individual freedoms (telephone conversations were now specified as secret, whereas previously only correspondence had been mentioned).[42]

Policing the Personal

Post-Stalin ideology had a great deal to say about what citizens might expect from their state; but it also, as before, insisted that people owed much in return. Entitlement to various social benefits came tightly bound up with obligations and moral norms that liberal democracies would balk at imposing on their citizens. One of the most fundamental concerned that cornerstone of the Western liberal order: property. Soviet people were not permitted to own property that exceeded their needs, and deriving unearned income from housing was not legitimate.

In reality, however, there was and could be no blanket prohibition on the private rental market. People rented out parts of their dwellings while they continued to live there; paying guests, in a society beset by housing shortage, were never in short supply. An even grayer area was the beloved and increasingly available Russian version of the "second home": the dacha. Before the war, such out-of-town houses were largely restricted to the privileged few who worked in organizations that could provide access to such an amenity; the less fortunate had to try their luck on a private rental market supplied largely by the population of villages within range of the major cities. In the 1950s, however, the dacha phenomenon started to become a broader social phenomenon. One factor was the postwar growth of "garden plot" settlements, which started as a desperate subsistence measure but became more elaborate over time, offering people not only a potato patch but also a shack in which they might stay the night. The other contributing factor was the increasing number of institutions and organizations – notably the proliferating workplaces of the post-Stalin professional classes – that could assist their employees to set up dacha "cooperatives" or "associations." Many of these settlements were extraordinarily modest compared with those of the Stalinist dacha-frequenting classes, but they did much to alleviate urban over-crowding in the summer months.[43]

This expansion of exurban domesticity was, however, a source of great anxiety in a political order that placed a taboo on individual self-enrichment: how could the guardians of Soviet probity be sure that people would not build dachas larger than they "needed" or rent them out for inflated sums? Accordingly, the Khrushchev regime placed new restrictions on the size and design of dachas: dwellings were to have no more than 60 square meters of living space, while the size of plots in many settlements was capped at 600 square meters.

The same ambivalence was evident in the attenuated Soviet adoption of consumer values. Consumerism was never wholeheartedly embraced but always hemmed in by all kinds of restrictions. The agencies of the state were required to make discretionary judgments as to how much, and what kind of, consumption was legitimate. The Khrushchev era saw a publishing boom in the field of advice literature, but the recommendations it dispensed often betrayed the difficulty of drawing clear lines between acceptable and excessive consumption. How were Soviet people to be discerning modern consumers and austere and virtuous collectivists at the same time?[44]

Thus, while from the mid-1950s onward advice on home furnishings and polite conduct became more elaborate, apprehensions of moral decline did not die away. The dangers of materialistic urges were a recurring preoccupation in mass culture to the very end of the Soviet period. Several of the films of the well-loved comedy director El'dar Riazanov took a dark look at the demeaning effects of consumerism on human beings. In *The Zigzag of Fortune* (1968), one member of a work collective wins the lottery and comes close to losing his friends and his woman. In *Watch Out for the Car!* (1966), the mild-mannered hero turns out to be a crusader for justice outside the law: he is a vigilante thief who steals cars acquired by corrupt Soviet citizens, then selling the vehicles and donating the proceeds to an orphanage. In *The Garage* (1979), Riazanov draws a disturbing picture of a group of (intelligentsia!) people losing their human dignity in the rush to acquire secure parking spaces.

Soviet policy on consumerism is but one of several indicators of a central paradox of the Khrushchev era: in a period that has gone down in many accounts as the most liberal phase of Soviet history before Gorbachev's glasnost, the agencies of the state policed the boundaries between public and private more obsessively than ever previously or subsequently. The Soviet notion of the "personal," which was given unprecedented practical and material support in the 1950s, was not an absolute value but was overlaid by a moral code concerning the individual's relationship to society. Increased prosperity was good, but it should not be allowed to turn fine Soviet people into selfish atomized individuals such as were to be found under capitalism.

Accordingly, the Soviet state enjoined society to monitor closely the use citizens made of their new entitlements. A study of policy and institutions might even lead us to see the Khrushchev era as the apotheosis of the Soviet takeover of the private domain. The revived institution of comrades' courts claimed jurisdiction over a large number of minor infractions. Although they did not have powers of arrest and conviction, they could require offenders to make a public apology, issue public reprimands, levy modest fines, and cause offenders trouble both at work and in the apartment block. Another notorious institution of the time was the "people's patrol" (*druzhina*), which had a reported 2.5 million members in 1960 and 4.5 million in 1965. On average, the patrols numbered around 30 members, and in parts of the RSFSR as much as 3 percent of the population was enlisted. The ambition to achieve total collective surveillance was given striking expression in Khrushchev's speech to the Central Committee in November 1962: "We have 10 million Party members, 20 million Komsomol members, 66 million members of trade unions. If we could put all these forces into action, if we could use them in the interests of control, then not even a mosquito could pass unnoticed."[45] As one political scientist puts it, the purpose of Soviet community organizations of this kind was "to make the regime your neighbor by having your neighbor represent the regime." The comrades' courts and the patrols constituted "an effort to give an appearance of a self-policing community in which social norms have the force of law and each citizen is accountable to his neighbor." By 1965, Moscow was reported to have 5,580 comrades' courts involving more than 50,000 people. New regulations of October 1963 and January 1965 allowed these institutions to expand their remit from public disorder issues such as drunkenness and hooliganism to minor civil cases, small-scale embezzlement, and certain other criminal cases.[46]

The mantra of public surveillance left numerous traces in the mass culture of the time. In Iulii Raizman's *But What If It's Love?* (1961), a courting teenage couple is subjected to public humiliation on their housing estate for developing a tentative attachment to each other while playing hooky from school. Only after the girl is driven to attempt suicide is the situation resolved. Here the *khrushchevka* came face to face with the *charivari*. The Khrushchev regime's more interventionist ethos may also be seen to lie behind the single most destructive campaign of the post-Stalin era: the crackdown on religious life from 1958 onward that closed thousands of churches and a large proportion of the USSR's seminaries and monasteries. Priests were harassed, propaganda was venomously atheistic, and the financial basis of church life was attacked, notably through a sudden increase in taxes on production of candles. For a political culture with ambitions to create virtuous activists out of the population there was no more offensive reminder of earlier (Stalinist!) compromises with backwardness and obscurantism than the persistence of religious observance in the homeland of atheist socialism.[47]

Besides repressing deviations from socialist norms, the regime also proclaimed its ambition to release the civic energies of the population. For all that Soviet society was undergoing pan-European trends in the privatization of daily life, it also retained forms of semicompulsory public participation that made it quite distinct from Western democracies. Soviet elections were a case in point. Voting remained a prominent civil ritual, even if the outcome was never in doubt. Soviet citizens were required to turn out for a variety of elections: to the USSR Supreme Soviet, to the Supreme Soviets of the individual republics, and (most frequently) to local soviets. Candidates were selected after a close scrutiny of their political reliability and work record but also with an eye to their social "representativeness." Between 1961 and 1975, for example, the proportion of women deputies increased steadily from 40 percent to almost 50 percent. By 1975, women made up more than 40 percent of deputies at all levels of the local soviets.[48]

The elections were preceded by campaigns that yielded little in collective man-hours to the equivalents in liberal democracies. For the two or three months preceding elections, millions of "agitators" were charged with checking names and addresses in person, expounding the issues of the day to the electorate – and, not least, bringing them out to vote. Their efforts were deemed successful: for the 1975 elections to the Supreme Soviets of the republics, a turnout of 99.98 percent was reported. Even citizens who found themselves in hospital, on a ship, or on a long-distance train found special polling stations at their disposal.[49] The elections served their purpose of demonstrating the unity and civic-mindedness of Soviet society, even if there is abundant anecdotal evidence that they were regarded by the population as an excuse for a holiday rather than a political event.

It is easy to exaggerate the importance of surveillance and civic participation from a study of the Soviet public record. The situation on the ground was much less clear than in normative statements. One study has shown that judges from the mid-1950s onward chafed at Stalin-era legislation that put substantial obstacles in the way of divorcing couples. Instead, legal practitioners tended to take a relatively liberal view of marriage breakdown, allowing husband and wife to go their separate ways without asking unnecessary questions.[50] The comrades' courts were initially designed not as a means of collective surveillance but as a cost-cutting measure. While they undoubtedly provided a home for thousands of busybodies, they hardly seem to have shaken Soviet society to its core. The same goes for the people's patrols, which probably served as an outlet for the aggression of young males but whose nominal membership was almost certainly far in excess of their active membership.[51]

Without terror, state-directed *obshchestvennost'* was not a serious threat to the Soviet personal domain. On occasion, however, it could cause Soviet people anything from mild inconvenience to extreme hardship and suffering. The most notorious of various ugly examples was the case of the Leningrad poet Iosif Brodskii, who in 1964 was sentenced to five years of hard labor for the crime of "parasitism." The most obvious effect of such clumsy and brutal efforts to police the personal was the alienation from public life of those who were most visible and audible in the "Thaw" period. In the 1950s and early 1960s, much informal interaction within the intelligentsia had a soapbox character, as people transferred the idiom of civil engagement to their private discussions. At times such patterns of behavior could be observed in public. The landmark Picasso exhibition in Moscow in December 1956 was quite literally a clamorous occasion, as viewers gesticulated and held forth as they stood before the paintings.[52] By the mid-1960s, and especially after 1968, the Soviet chattering classes had withdrawn to their kitchens and their informal discussion circles. Instead of forming the opinions of society in general, they had to make do with the members of their social circles (*kompanii*). In fact, the Soviet ideal of *obshchestvennost'* was writ small in the key milieus of the intelligentsia: in their *kompanii*, communal frequenting of cultural events (exhibitions, theaters and concerts, both public and "underground"), and shared consumption of cultural artifacts (above all books). As one scholar has noted of the *kompanii*, "their choice of attributes, rituals, and spaces indicated that they were searching for something that went beyond 'privacy.'"[53]

The same point can be made of the quintessential feeder institutions for the metropolitan intelligentsia – the major higher education institutions such as Moscow State University. University life provided students with the ready-made structure of the *kollektiv*. Students attended lectures together in a close-knit "academic group" of about fifteen on the same "specialty." Each such group had a leading nexus of three: the Komsomol representative, the union representative, and an academic monitor whose task was to keep the deans informed of students' academic progress. Komsomol activists made up a significant minority of the student body: at Moscow State University, for example, they numbered 1,700, or 10 percent of the student population. It appears that, at least until the de-Stalinizing year of 1956, these activists were not treated with cynicism or disrespect by their fellow students; the latter were probably conscious that Komsomol work was no sinecure, taking up as much as 30 hours per week among leading activists. The *komsorgi* did, however, face resistance if they tried to impose on their classmates forms of discipline that conflicted with longer-standing forms of mutual aid and group loyalty (this generated conflict in the postwar era, as activists were very often army veterans who had military notions of discipline that were out of keeping in the university milieu). Overall, the evidence is that the officially recognized *kollektiv* accommodated more independent social groupings (again known as *kompanii*) without seriously threatening them. The collectivism of public life was not at loggerheads with informal friendship ties but rather, for the most part, dovetailed with them. In the late Stalin and early Khrushchev periods, student activity continued to conform to official norms even if it was not adequately characterized by those norms. It was only in 1956 that student life took a turn to more autonomous discussion of public issues, but even that was couched in terms entirely loyal to Soviet socialism.[54]

The Late Soviet Period: The Maturation of the Personal Sphere

Perhaps even to a greater extent than in other societies, intellectuals have shaped our view of what it was to live in the later Soviet era. They tell a story of disengagement and doublethink, of inner opposition and withdrawal into the realm of intense intellectual interaction with the like-minded. The impression is one of uneasy and often antagonistic coexistence between "state" and "society."

If we cast our social net a little wider, however, it seems that the notion of the personal, first fully elaborated in the 1950s and early 1960s, worked rather well in the post-Khrushchev decades. It became more capacious, but it did not change fundamentally, and it enjoyed widespread acceptance. The government, for its part, somewhat relaxed its vigilant policing of the personal sphere. The social turbulence of the Khrushchev period, with its amnesties and outbreaks of mass unrest, largely subsided. Educational experiments ceased, and the result was a much larger Soviet white-collar class. People now enjoyed well-defined career structures and stable jobs. The workplace, moreover, was far more than a source of income. It provided a ready-made social network that people relied on to negotiate the many problems of Soviet life. The respondents of the Soviet Interview Project of the early 1980s (admittedly a group of higher than average occupational status, but also one that had voluntarily left the Soviet Union) expressed general satisfaction with their jobs. Only 6 percent had been "very dissatisfied"; overall, work was reported to be the most satisfying area of life in the Soviet Union.[55]

Accordingly, the white-collar or intelligentsia workplace was one of the preferred settings for Soviet cinema on contemporary themes. Protagonists were shown to be engrossed in the affairs of their workplace, but they were far from being the heroic overachievers of Stalinist culture. Rather, their work activities were counterpointed – often humorously – by less than heroic personal lives. The translator hero of Georgii Daneliia's *Autumn Marathon* (1979) misses deadlines as he juggles mistress, wife, and jogging expeditions with a Danish colleague. In El'dar Riazanov's popular comedy *Office Romance* (1977), a mousy male statistician wins the heart of his stern and dedicated boss.

The strengthening of Soviet professions and other occupational cultures had the effect of drawing a clearer divide between work and leisure. Work was no longer something that was meant to fire all parts of the Soviet soul. In the late 1960s, the Soviet economy moved to a two-day weekend. Organizations became more generous with paid holidays and tickets to resorts. An early public opinion survey on the subject, conducted in 1966, revealed much interest in holidays. Forty-five percent of respondents thought that holidays were to be spent with the family, while almost as many (41 percent) thought that it was preferable to spend this time with friends and colleagues.[56] By the end of the 1970s, 60 percent of Soviet citizens were going on holiday, and on average they spent about 8 percent of the family's annual income. The average holiday provision was almost 21 working days (ranging from 12 days for collective farm workers to more than 33 for teachers).[57]

Foreign travel – primarily within the socialist bloc in eastern Europe – picked up in the Khrushchev era. In 1963, for example, more than 50,000 Soviet people were able to travel to eastern Europe courtesy of their trade union organizations; a further 10,000 went under the auspices of the Komsomol tourism organization.[58] The rise in domestic Soviet tourism was even more striking: figures doubled from 1965 to 1980, and in the Brezhnev era the number of individual tourists (known as "wild" tourists, or *dikari*) began to exceed those who traveled on package holidays (*putevki*).[59] Certain Soviet holiday locations – especially Black Sea resorts such as Sochi – acquired reputations not far removed from those of the mass holiday resorts opening in Spain in the same era.

The increasing recreational autonomy of Soviet people was also recognized in policy on that icon of twentieth-century selfhood, the car. In the Khrushchev period, the Soviet economy served up an average of only 61,000 vehicles per year to individual purchasers. In 1965, however, came an announcement that annual production would shoot up from 200,000 to 800,000 in the eighth five-year plan. By 1975, with the help of a major new enterprise opened with Italian investment in Tol'iatti, production reached 1.2 million.[60]

When Soviet people were at home, their "free" time was likely to be taken up with domestic rather than civic affairs. Household chores remained extraordinarily time-consuming, and they continued to consume far more of women's time than of men's. In one 1963 study, women were revealed to spend on average 6.5 hours on housework on Sundays; men managed just one hour. Laundry took an average of 6 hours per week. A Kiev study of 1965–6 revealed that only one in five households spent as little as half an hour per day shopping; two in five spent 1–1.5 hours, while the rest spent more than two hours.[61]

As late as 1976, only two-thirds of Soviet families could boast refrigerators or washing machines; other labor-saving devices – vacuum cleaners, food processors, pressure cookers – were minimally represented in Soviet households. Nor did this take into account quality, which for many Soviet goods was appalling. The indicators for TV sets were slightly better: 223 per thousand residents as compared with 571 in the US. But the gap in car ownership was a chasm: 98 million in the US compared with 5 million in the USSR. Other technologies of everyday life were even more pitifully developed. The average Soviet person made 3.4 long-distance phone calls in 1976; the equivalent figure for the US was 76. The situation was hardly more comforting if a Soviet observer turned to consumer basics, which were traditionally the benchmark of the regime's economic success. At then current levels of growth, meat production in the Soviet Union of 1976 was due to catch up the American figure of the same year in 2033.[62]

No one could reasonably dispute that Soviet people did not live well by Western standards. But it might be argued that the relevant benchmark was not the contemporaneous United States, but rather the Soviet Union of even a few years previously. Here the Soviet population could observe slow but steady progress. Before the war, families in collective farms would spend two-thirds of their income on food, but in the Brezhnev period the figure was only one half. People were putting more money aside: the amounts held in savings accounts rose from 157 rubles per savings book in 1960 to 1,189 rubles in 1980, and the number of such savers in rural areas went up from 13.9 million to 35.5 million.[63]

Of course, the increase in savings reflected in large part the unavailability of desirable goods. Another telling statistic of the same era was that working-class and agricultural families spent more on drink than they did on paid services.[64] Yet signs of consumer aspiration could be detected even in the Soviet village. The villagers of Viriatino in Tambov region, the focus of a major ethnographic study in the 1950s, were showing an increasing interest in fashionable garments, making greater use of specialist tailors instead of sewing their own clothes. The headscarf was still universal attire for women, but the younger ones liked wearing one-piece dresses (which had first appeared in the village only in the 1940s) rather than the traditional skirt and blouse (*kofta*). Young people made a point of changing into clean clothes when they got back from work. People also increasingly ironed their clothes and preferred to store them not in trunks, as had always previously been the case, but in wardrobes.[65] Complementary evidence can be found among the more urban and professional informants of the Soviet Interview Project. While more than half of the sample expressed dissatisfaction with the supply of goods in the USSR, less than 15 percent declared themselves "very dissatisfied" with their overall standard of living.[66]

The dissatisfaction may partly have been due to the fact that consumers had become more discriminating. In the late 1960s, Muscovites might hold back from purchasing washing machines until automatic models were available, while visiting provincials swooped on the manual machines. An all-Union survey of 1980–1 showed that color TV sets, furniture suites, fancy tableware, carpets, stereos, books, and fashionable clothes were in especially high demand. The Soviet Union remained anything but a throwaway culture, but by the late 1970s it was at least conceivable for household items to be disposed of because they did not look nice: by 1980, two-thirds of consumers buying new lampshades did so because the old ones had lost their aesthetic appeal, not because they were actually broken.[67]

Up-to-date consumer items required money, and sociological data of the Brezhnev era confirmed that earning power was an important criterion for Soviet workers, be they manual, white-collar, or even intellectual. Their aspirations were to some extent being met by the Soviet economy. The average annual wages for workers and employees more than doubled between 1960 and 1980 to over 2,000 rubles. The average expenditure on clothing and footwear of urban families increased by a factor of four between 1964 and 1979: this was a much faster increase than that of expenditure on food, which in the 1970s fell as a proportion of household budgets from just over to just under 40 percent. Greater purchasing power meant more discriminating consumption. Soviet shoppers were increasingly willing to express dissatisfaction with the offerings in state shops. One survey in Ukraine in 1970 found that almost half of customers wishing to buy a shirt left an amply stocked shop without making a purchase. Ten years later, in a Union-wide survey, a third of the 5,000 respondents declared themselves dissatisfied with the selection of women's clothing (and a quarter with men's). When the Moscow Trade Department had to explain a sharp reduction in clothes sales in 1971, it referred to a "dramatic change in fashion" to which factories had not had time to respond. Even sociologists and philosophers were called on to make sense of the fashion phenomenon. In 1973, a collection of articles entitled *Fashion: Pro and Contra* was the first full-length treatment in the Soviet Union of a subject that had previously been associated with meretricious Western consumerism.[68]

The rebarbative public discourse of the Khrushchev era had softened by the 1970s. Of course, Soviet journalists and intellectuals routinely pontificated about the devastating effects of excessive "Western" individualism and consumerism (ignoring the fact that it was precisely the Soviet system, with all its defects, that was turning people into obsessive procurers of consumer goods), but not with the interventionist intent of the late 1950s. Moreover, the Soviet population's increasing preference for the domestic sphere over more "cultured" and "active" forms of leisure such as sport and theater attendance sprang directly from Khrushchev's own housing policies: it was evidence that, for the first time, tens of millions of people truly had a home – a single-occupancy dwelling – to make. Many urban people even had a second home: a dacha or a house in the village made available to them by relatives.

A home – whether a *kolkhoz* dwelling, a dacha, or an urban flat – had to be furnished. Here expectations were rising even in the apparently more benighted corners of the Union. By the 1970s, Buryat collective farm workers were able to buy standard modern furniture and wall hangings.[69] The Viriatino study of the mid-1950s revealed that in half of houses built since collectivization the stove was positioned in the corner by the door, separated by a partition from the rest of the interior, instead of dominating the peasant home as was traditionally the case. This allowed the creation of a specially designated bedroom area. Families with connections to the city had urban furniture in their homes; even furniture made by local carpenters followed urban models. These collective farm workers were also showing a taste for decorating their interiors: they put up on their walls postcards, posters, cuttings from magazines, artificial flowers, and carpets with illustrations that the ethnographers found tasteless. The former distinctions between rural and urban houses were being erased.[70]

Household spending on furniture increased in the 1970s in line with other forms of consumer expenditure. Furniture remained expensive: a sofa-bed could easily cost an average monthly salary, while a carpet might cost two or three. Despite the prices, furniture acquired through the state system almost tripled from 1960 to 1970, and had tripled again by 1985. Furniture buyers of the 1970s were also more sophisticated than their 1950s predecessors: they placed a premium on aesthetic coordination throughout a flat, and scoured the shops for comfortable three-piece suites (a concept that had barely existed twenty years earlier).[71]

The Soviet domestic environment of the postwar decades was profoundly different from that of the 1930s. The stability – and, within limits, increasing well-being – of Soviet life made the family a secure bastion of the personal sphere. According to the 1970 census, nine out of ten Soviet people lived in a family; of the rest, almost half were only temporarily away from their families (because they were studying, doing military service, or traveling for work purposes), which meant that only 6 percent of Soviet people had no family.[72] The sprawling arrangements of the hungry 1940s, when the family was an economic association more than a tight-knit kin unit, had faded. The aspiration of Soviet people was increasingly to set up a nuclear household. Parents were able to lavish more time and resources on fewer children: the reigning ethos was "children first." Adolescents were treated more leniently by the criminal justice system. According to legislation of December 1958, 14–16-year-olds were to be prosecuted only for especially serious crimes, and courts in practice tried to avoid criminal sentences. Child rearing received medical supervision at least in the more developed areas of the Soviet Union: by the late 1950s, in the major cities, nurses were visiting as many as 98 percent of mothers in at least the first month of the baby's life. By 1970, more than 90 percent of all babies were seen by a nurse at this stage, although only two-thirds of mothers across the USSR attended prenatal consultations. Although the Soviet order retained – and indeed extended – its forms of obligatory socialization, these did not contradict the child-centered trend of the postwar era. In 1960, the Young Pioneers organization numbered 15.4 million members (out of a total cohort of 16.6 million), while in 1970 it expanded its membership to 23.3 million (out of a possible 24.9 million). By now, however, the focus of the organization was shifting from political education to the kind of pastimes laid on for children in all developed societies. In 1977, Pioneer organizations in Moscow ran more than 4,300 clubs and provided for nearly 75,000 children.[73]

The greater stability of family life meant, for example, that the concept of "personal property" could include more people. It was now legitimate for parents to join construction cooperatives and build not only for themselves but "for our son." Alternatively, they might leave a grandmother behind in a communal flat while the rest of the family moved to a cooperative or enterprise-provided apartment. Conversely, many urban families now found themselves the proprietors of a "house in the country" on the death or migration of elderly relatives.

There were, however, limits to nuclearization. One was that the continuing shortage of living space often did not permit couples to live separately from their parents. In the less well-endowed cities, such as Leningrad, the proportion of three-generation households was as high as 25 percent. Even where grandparents did not cohabit with parents, Soviet urban households often remained heavily dependent – for home help, child care, or simply money – on the older generation (especially grandmothers). Later on in the family life cycle, the dependence of children on parents lasted longer than hitherto. The Soviet Union was subject to similar demographic trends to those found elsewhere in the developed world. Age at first marriage rose through the Soviet period: according to the 1926 census, 12.2 percent of men were under 20 when they married, whereas the same figure in 1973 had fallen below 5 percent. The equivalent figures for women in the RSFSR fell from 29 percent in 1926 to 19 percent in 1970. In Central Asia there was an even more dramatic fall: from around two-thirds in the early twentieth century to about a quarter in 1970.[74]

Late marriages were accompanied by falling fertility: the average Soviet household had 2.8 children in 1959 but only 2.4 in 1970, and there were considerable differences between the more fertile Central Asian republics and the less fertile Slavic regions of the USSR, between urban and rural areas, and between the blue-collar population and the intelligentsia. Seven in ten young couples lived with their parents before they had children, and at least half of them were prepared to be financially dependent on them. For more and more young people, the chronological boundaries of personal life were being pushed back: the period before the onset of full child rearing and financial responsibilities came five or ten years later than it had done in the early postwar period.[75]

Soviet family policy remained full of contradictions. On the one hand, the Soviet ideology of modernization and female emancipation implied a fall from the traditional exceptionally high birth rate found in prerevolutionary Russia. On the other hand, a high birth rate was considered indicative of rising prosperity and national well-being. The USSR took a strong pro-natalist turn in the 1930s. Abortion was outlawed in 1936 (having been fully legalized in 1920), and almost nothing was said publicly in the Stalin period about means of contraception. In practice, abortion remained the primary means of birth control even before its re-legalization in 1955. But even the 1955 legislation was not accompanied by any serious policy on family planning; all it did was provide further encouragement for abortion. The sexual revolution of the 1960–1970s – with its underlying principle that women might make their own reproductive choices – passed the Soviet Union by. Around 8 million abortions were registered annually from the mid-1960s onward. An overwhelming majority of women having abortions were married: they cited reasons such as money problems, inadequate living conditions, and difficulties with their partner (often as a result of drinking). The age group most prone to abortions was 25–34, which again indicates the extent to which abortion was a routine and repeated method of limiting fertility. Even at the very end of the Soviet period, there were around two abortions in Russia for every one birth (close to twenty times the rate in West Germany or the Netherlands).[76]

Even if it had not fully adopted modern methods of contraception, Soviet society was following the Western trend toward more liberal views on sexual activity. Soviet research into sexual attitudes and behavior was tentatively revived after a hiatus of three or four decades in the mid-1960s. Pioneering post-Stalin surveys of Soviet sexual habits, conducted primarily among students and professionals, indicated a moderately high tolerance of premarital sexual activity. Only about 20 percent of Leningrad students surveyed in the mid-1960s were willing to condemn sexual relations before marriage, not least because to do so would have meant to condemn themselves: 85 percent of the men and 47 percent of the women stated they had already had such sexual experience. Follow-up studies of the 1970s revealed increasingly liberal attitudes, though there was much variation from the liberal capital cities in the western part of the Soviet Union to the more conservative small towns, villages, and Central Asian and Caucasian republics. The leading sexologist of the time has claimed – on the base of evidence from youth surveys of 1965, 1972 and 1995 – that Soviet sexual relations were increasingly of the "loving" type rather than the "recreational"

FIGURE 5.5   Postcard "I Love You," 1950s.
Source: © PhotoSoyuz.

type. It was hard to avoid the conclusion that, despite or because of the increasing amount of sexual contact before marriage, the quality of sex in Russia was improving.[77]

Soviet people's practice in their intimate relationships bespoke a new commitment to the values of individual fulfillment. According to data from the early 1980s, a third of couples who lived with their parents before marriage moved out immediately after marriage. Only 25 percent stayed living with the older generation after the first ten years of marriage.[78] While these figures were extremely high by British or American standards, they represented a significant change from earlier Soviet norms.

Soviet spouses were also able to exercise greater personal agency by choosing to divorce. After a liberalization of legislation in 1965, the rate went up from 1.6 per 1000 inhabitants to 2.8 per 1000 in 1966; it then rose further to around 3.5 per thousand (all this compared strikingly with the rate of 1.1 per 1000 in 1940). In many big cities, one in every two marriages would end in divorce. Not only did the divorce rate escalate in the later Soviet period, so did the rate of repeat marriages. According to figures from 1978–9, 40 percent of men and 34 percent of women would marry again after a divorce. There was some talk, by the 1970s, that the divorce law was too liberal and made it too easy for women to opt out of a marriage (women initiated divorces in about 70 percent of cases, often on the grounds of their husband's alcohol abuse). "Family consultation services" were set up in major cities from the early 1970s onward at least in part as a means of resolving marital difficulties.[79]

Another contributing factor to the high divorce rate was the equalization of the sex balance following the decimation of the male war cohort. By the late 1960s women did not need to worry so much that, if they were to divorce, they would never find another partner. They also had a high degree of economic autonomy (relative to other European countries) given their high level of workforce participation. At the 1970 census, two-thirds of households had at least two economically active members (the figure was even higher in urban areas). Only one in five households had just one earner. Of course, none of this amounted to women's emancipation, as household chores remained a feminized corvée. In collective farms, women had only half as much free time as their husbands, while in urban working-class families the proportion was only slightly higher.[80] All the same, the perennial conflict in Soviet family policy between encouraging a higher birth rate and encouraging female labor had substantially been resolved in favor of the latter.

As we have seen, families became smaller and better housed over the post-Stalin decades. Soviet life remained exhausting and stressful, and its stresses were borne disproportionately by women, whether working mothers or child-minding babushkas. Even with this important qualification, however, we cannot say that late Soviet life had been "privatized" in a Western understanding. Soviet people could not go to work, draw their salary, and then automatically count on a decent quality of life as "private" individuals. They were – and had to be – virtuoso informal operators. Given that money was in short supply and in any case did not buy many of the things that citizens of market democracies take for granted, people sought other ways. They were able to tolerate gray areas between professional and personal loyalties and allegiances that most Westerners would find intolerable.[81] While they made the best of the situation – cultivating "friends" wherever they could, whether in a grocery store, a hospital or a garage – we find here evidence less of heart-warming social cohesion than of a forced response to the idiocies and power imbalances of Soviet life. By the 1980s, the difficulty of living under Soviet socialism was sapping the morale of the population – especially those urban and educated people who, in a more liberal society, might have hoped for a greater level of status and material reward. Such people would provide the natural constituency for market reform when this came on the agenda in the late 1980s, even if they were often dismayed by the version of capitalism that it in due course produced.

─────   Post-Soviet Russia: The Hegemony of the Private?   ─────

In the late 1980s, the monopoly of the Communist Party and affiliated organizations on public expression was suddenly lifted. In the short term, this brought a
sharp increase in the population's level of political engagement. It also meant that
state intervention – still strong as late as the mid-1980s, when the government
enacted policies to reduce the population's consumption of drink and improve
its work habits – finally lifted. Soviet-era taboos were removed, and Russians had
the opportunity to become fully-fledged private citizens.

Although self-enrichment was not always viewed as a matter for celebration
– the Soviet habit of stigmatizing ill-gotten gains was compounded by the visible
excesses of nouveau riche "New Russians" – Russian mass culture soon became
vastly more laissez-faire. Sex scenes in films went from taboo to de rigueur
within a year or two of *Little Vera* (1988), the high-water mark of sexual glasnost.
The magazine *SPID-Info* quickly turned itself from a public health periodical
(*SPID* is Russian for AIDS) into the vanguard of Russian pornography. The
naked female form was ubiquitous in Russian cities of the early 1990s, most
prominently on reusable carrier bags that were very often sported, disconcert-
ingly, by women.

After the initial boom in sexually explicit material, pornography became "nor-
malized" and kept to its own market. A more pervasive addition to Russian print
culture was advice literature that instructed Russians on how to dress, behave,
and generally observe the public/private divide after the fashion of an imagined
Westerner. Russia rapidly assimilated a how-to heritage that ranged from Dale
Carnegie to *The Joy of Sex*.[82] Gender relations were subject to public discussion
and partial redefinition. After decades of neglect, women were recognized as a
crucial element in the reading audience. Romantic fiction – most of it translated
– made a huge impact on the book market. Certain other genres were to a significant degree feminized. Critics took to speaking of a distinct subgenre, the "female
detective novel," written by women and featuring a woman as the main character.
In a category of her own stood the most successful detective author of the 1990s,
Alexandra Marinina, who sidestepped Russian convention and made her central
protagonist an emphatically unglamorous woman who combined crime-solving
with a gently chaotic everyday life.[83]

Television, too, saw a turn to the quotidian. In the early days of Russian adaptation to Western TV formats, escapist dramas, such as the Mexican *The Rich Also
Cry* and *Santa Barbara*, were compulsive viewing for the Russian audience. After
a few years, the soap opera began to migrate to native settings. A trailblazer in
this regard was the publicity campaign for MMM, the most notorious pyramid
scheme of the post-Soviet era, in which a Russian everyman, the construction

worker Lenia Golubkov, comes to terms with his magically expanding wealth in a linked series of everyday encounters.[84]

While the mass culture of the 1990s raised the profile of fine living and self-cultivation, mentalities and social practice did not change as fast. "Private" life, in the serene Western sense of that word, was scarcely achievable in conditions of hardship and economic instability. Many people remained tied to their Soviet-era enterprises and associated provisioning systems (such as they were). The onset of economic crisis caused the population to engage in coping strategies familiar from earlier periods of Soviet history.[85] It was telling that the most valued outlet for post-Soviet domesticity, the dacha, combined the urge to home-make with the need to guarantee subsistence in conditions of post-Soviet uncertainty. Moreover, Soviet-style social capital – rather than occupational status or even current level of earnings – continued to matter a great deal, even if networks of reciprocity were now more likely to have a monetary dimension.[86]

By the early Putin era, the sense of perpetual material crisis had finally abated. Many people remained poor by Western standards, but even they did not worry about starvation. More to the point, those Russians who were not immediately concerned with subsistence could raise their aspirations. A dacha might be turned from a shack into an exurban home with electricity and even plumbing. Potato patches might be converted to flower beds or even lawns. Urban apartments might be kitted out with new kitchens or stylish lighting. Glossy magazines accordingly made fine profits from dispensing fashion tips and life-style recommendations.

The home now had not only a symbolic value but a price. Private ownership of property was not only de facto (as in the municipal and cooperative housing of the late Soviet period) but also de jure. People could buy and sell property freely; in conditions of oil-fueled economic boom, that meant a rise in prices that would have been astonishing to a British home-owning public, let alone to ex-Soviet Russians accustomed to price stability. By the late Putin era, apartment prices in Moscow were such as to make visiting American academics blanch. Inhabitants of the big cities negotiated the market with the assistance of family housing that had been privatized cheaply in the 1990s or else took their chances on the rental market. By Putin's second term, some of them were taking out mortgages, although investment in the housing sector remained low and cash-strapped local government was still responsible for maintaining much of the urban housing stock.[87]

So much for the post-Soviet private. But what of its bourgeois corollary, the "public sphere"? The mass political engagement of the late 1980s and early 1990s could hardly be sustained – revolutions do not last for ever – and the question was what kind of civic engagement would be possible in postcommunist Russia. To what extent would the closed power structures and institutions of Soviet

Russia now open up to public scrutiny and discussion? The corollary of *lichnost'* in Soviet times had been *obshchestvennost'*, but what would it be in these very different social and economic conditions?

An obvious starting point is the media and communications technology that had the potential to change how Russians related to each other and to the public good. Post-Soviet Russia started from a low technological base. In 1994, Russia had only 162 telephone lines per 1,000 people (as compared with 602 for the United States). As of early 2000, estimates of the number of Russian net users ranged from 1.5 to 6 million.[88] By the end of 2007, just over a quarter of the population, or almost 30 million people, were reckoned to have used the internet in recent months. The number of domain names grew by 66 percent in 2007 to reach the figure of one million. But web use was overwhelmingly concentrated in the major cities: in Moscow it took in over half the population, as compared to less than a quarter elsewhere. The penetration of internet technology in Russia had, moreover, lost momentum in 2007 after several years of steady growth.[89]

In comparative perspective, then, Russian internet adoption was modest. But even without this qualification there were good reasons to doubt the capacity of the new technology to bring into being an engaged public opinion. What the internet gained in coverage relative to the print media it lost in political impact and thematic concentration. The illiberal government for the most part did not need to engage in heavy policing of the internet, relying instead on the medium's tendency to fragmentation and the population's low level of trust in much of the information obtainable online. The Runet had its greatest impact in apolitical activities such as social networking. In sites like odnoklassniki.ru (which allowed former schoolmates to get in touch) and vkontakte.ru (the Russian version of Facebook), long-standing forms of social capital made the transition into the computer age.

Russian television provided even more conclusive evidence that mass audio-visual technologies are not incompatible with an illiberal political system. The genre of the political debate was notable for its absence on state-controlled TV, while the interview and press conference formats were completely dominated by incumbent politicians. A good chunk of the national evening news was devoted to making the president look tough, well informed and businesslike: a standard scene was for Putin to subject some sweating plenipotentiary in the regions to aggressive questioning about the latter's performance in office. Before and after the news bulletin, however, the schedule was much less hectoring: Russian viewers could find there all they liked about celebrities, sport, cooking, gardening, and love-making. The quotidian reigned supreme, and it had been indigenized. Now, if the Russians needed a soap opera, they did not look to South America or even to California but made it themselves.

Any number of observers have pounced on such phenomena as evidence of the failure of a vibrant "civil society" to materialize in post-Soviet Russia. An alternative view might see the tameness and everydayness of mainstream media content as a very reasonable, and healthy, corrective to the Soviet experience of enforced collectivism and public intervention in personal life. One might also ask whether Russia is so very different from Western liberal democracies. Although the economic base line is lower in the former Soviet Union, a story of materially preoccupied middle classes, crisis of trust, and disengagement from politics is prima facie familiar from discussions in Britain and the USA.

The answer, however, is that Russia *is* different. The British media bemoan a crisis of trust precisely because the general level of trust in public institutions is so high, and because journalists' role is to be seen to be making life difficult for office-holders. Material concerns are much less preoccupying in societies with long-established legal systems and large per capita GDPs (the recent crisis not-withstanding). In Russia, by contrast, we can point to a paradoxical but apparently enduring Soviet legacy: the prominence of the personal and informal dimensions in a society that was in theory entirely subordinated to the public and political.

——————— Conclusion: The Personalization of Russia ———————

As this chapter has attempted to show, "private life" is not the best framework for understanding what took place in Soviet society over the postwar decades. Rather, between the late 1930s and the mid-1960s a coherent and distinctively Soviet notion of the "personal" took shape. Although the term *lichnost'* had con-notations of Bolshevik self-fashioning, the personal sphere of the mid-Soviet period was underpinned not by self-improvement or collective surveillance but rather by notions of property, welfare, and entitlement. The Soviet personal sphere included those parts of life – emotional fulfillment, consumption, the home – that Soviet people could legitimately call their own. It differed from the private sphere in the West in that it was not absolute. Soviet people did not have an inalienable right to retain their apartment, or to build a dacha, or to engage in nonillegal economic activity, or to spend their money as they saw fit. Work, ownership, economic activity were all regulated by strong moral norms; the rights enjoyed by Soviet people were fuzzy, existed at the discretion of state agencies, and came bound up with obligations and responsibilities. Conversely, Soviet society allowed little or no space for discussing important areas of private life that would receive an airing in Western liberal democracies. The Soviet Union remained to the end a prudish place where abortion was a routine form of birth control, and where many women were left to believe that the contraceptive pill put them at risk of cancer.

By the late 1960s, state agencies and individuals had reached an unprecedentedly stable modus vivendi. Soviet people knew almost instinctively how far the "personal" could be pushed, not least because the limits often corresponded to their own notions of fairness and propriety. The state, for its part, began to behave less harshly and capriciously than in earlier phases of the Soviet period. The Soviet personal sphere, which formed between the late 1930s and the mid-1960s, represented a hard-won equilibrium – the "steady state" of the Soviet order. Over the 1970s and 1980s, its boundaries shifted in line with developments in the consumer economy but its essence remained intact. State supervision kept the personal in check but still allowed it room for growth. The point is best illustrated by the two greatest objects of desire for Soviet consumers – cars and dachas – which became significantly more accessible in the later Soviet period, even if car ownership remained low by European standards and most dachas were so modest as not to merit the designation of "second home."

One might, however, ask how far quantitative change can be pushed before it becomes qualitative. How many families could experience the autonomy and mobility of personal car ownership without rebelling against the terms of the Soviet "personal sphere"? How many failures and frustrations inflicted by the Soviet economy could people endure? How much exposure to Western goods and mass culture could Soviet society sustain without being won over to bourgeois commercialism?

The answer is that we will never know: it was not Pepsi-Cola or Snickers bars that brought down the Soviet Union. But, once the Soviet political and economic system had imploded, it was clear that taboos on excessive and conspicuous consumption, as well as exhortations to uphold the common good, had no chance of withstanding the onslaught of "private" (read: antipublic) values and behavior. Before very long, Russians were driving cars as large as they could afford and retreating behind the steel doors of their apartments.

The result, however, was not a new stable divide between public and private. Because public institutions were so disastrously weak in the 1990s, they were vulnerable to takeover by private interests and personal networks. In Russia's "privatization" phase, the gap between private and public was too poorly defined for asset redistribution to be anything other than a cut-throat struggle where the difference between state and special interests was close to meaningless.

When we arrive at the new order of the early twenty-first century, it still seems appropriate to speak of continuities and Soviet legacies. Of course, the range of legitimate consumption and ownership is now far broader than it ever was in Soviet times, but the principle that it is subject to fluid, discretionary, nonlegal notions of legitimacy has not gone away. People can now own several apartments in Moscow, but oil and gas companies, not to mention other profitable areas of the economy, are reserved for the select few. We can usefully apply to contemporary Russia an insight acquired by a Norwegian anthropologist during his fieldwork in Leningrad in the early 1980s. Rather than being structured by a public/private distinction and mediating between its two poles, Russian society consists of a multiplicity of "islands," which defend their prerogatives against outsiders and do not communicate well.[90] On the island of Gazprom the public good is construed rather differently than in the archipelago of the healthcare system or the rustbelt.

6

Center and Periphery

Russia's sheer size has long been central to its national identity, and never more so than during the Soviet period. The "Song of the Motherland," with the signature line "Broad is my native land" at the start of its refrain, became the unofficial national anthem of the USSR on its composition in 1936.[1] The myth of the boundless North maintained its firm grip on the Russian imagination in the twentieth century. Siberia gave rise to a "state superiority complex," born of the myth of "limitless supplies of land, wealth and strength," which no Russian could properly resist.[2] In the Cold War era the complex became if anything more acute. As Hedrick Smith noted of Soviet Russia in the 1970s, "bigness and power are admired almost without qualification."[3]

Russia's enormous territory lent power and prestige to the state that oversaw it, but it also presented rulers with immense practical difficulties. Soviet leaders could not afford to ignore a problem that had confronted their predecessors over the previous few centuries: how to ensure even minimal control over territories that might be as many as ten time zones from Moscow?

The Bolshevik answer to this question was to set up a highly centralized system of government whose notionally federal principles were disregarded in practice. Resources and population poured into Moscow, which had been made the new capital in March 1918. The socialist metropolis cast an imposing shadow over the rest of the country. Even Russia's former capital and new second city, Leningrad, was treated with suspicion lest it show any signs of political or cultural autonomy. The Stalinist project, as it emerged from the late 1920s onward, was one of ruthless exploitation of territory, of internal colonization where dekulakized peasants and various other categories of the population served as slave labor for socialist construction.[4]

The notion of hyper-centralism and crushing state domination of the expanses of the USSR needs, however, to be qualified on at least two scores. First, the ambitions of the Soviet state went beyond the mere crushing of dissent and resistance. They also included civilizing "backward" territories, modernizing them, making them economically productive. Second, any political project that was to be sustained over such a vast land mass faced formidable technical difficulties. How was Moscow to establish routine control, who were its plenipotentiaries to be, how could their loyalty and effectiveness be ensured, how was coordination between regions, and between regions and center, to be achieved?

In this light, it is hardly surprising that the relationship between "center" and "periphery" was an acute preoccupation of the Soviet regime in its formative period of the 1920s–1930s. The immediate challenge, in the wake of revolution, was for a small conspiratorial party to achieve effective political control of a vast space. The solution was to establish close relations between the Bolshevik rulers in Moscow and Party leaderships around the country. The Communist elite – the membership of the Central Committee – contained a substantial number of regional bosses whom Stalin co-opted and used to build his power. These men had very often earned their stripes in provincial committees during the revolution; their background, unlike that of the central Party elite, was overwhelmingly non-émigré. Personal networks forged in the years of revolution and civil war were all-important, and they tended to be tightest in areas where the fighting had been fiercest. The result was precisely not a transparent bureaucratic state; it is better described as patrimonial.[5]

The new regime ended up with a workable system of rule, but not one that necessarily served as a smooth transmission belt for commands issued by the center. In the short term, the state became more dispersed and localized as a result of the revolution. The 64 provinces in 1917 had grown to 93 in 1921 (with corresponding increases in the number of lower-level administrative units). A proposal in March 1921 to reduce the complexity of these arrangements met resistance from the regions.[6] On the whole, over the 1920s, the circulation of personnel between different regions, and between Moscow and the regions, increased the coverage of Bolshevik government. But there remained the nagging problem that the regions were in a position to subvert – or even defy – Moscow's instructions. Provincial bosses clashed with the center on the practical details of collectivization, though not on the principle. Even when there was no direct conflict, leadership networks in the provinces tended to obstruct the smooth implementation of central policy. Lack of transparency was an increasing concern for the Bolshevik leadership, especially when crash industrialization raised the stakes of economic management in the 1930s. Provincial leaderships wasted few opportunities to advance the interests of their region in the "center," but their efforts often put the center–periphery relationship under strain. In some cases they lobbied for balanced "complex development" that would make their region self-sufficient; Moscow, by contrast, tended to envision regional economic specialization, which would make Soviet territory more amenable to central planning and wholly dependent on the center for resources.[7] The converse problem arose when regions manipulated central objectives with a view to raising their own status. As industrialization gathered speed, bosses from the Urals region requested the raising of their targets with a view to securing a good chunk of capital investment. In the short term they were successful, but in the medium term they had driven themselves into a difficult position: the targets of the five-year plan were far out of reach, and from now on the Urals leaders would have to find ways to resist Moscow's pressure to deliver.[8]

A cycle of accommodation and confrontation between center and periphery was one of the constants of Soviet politics. At moments of crisis – war or succession – the leadership in Moscow badly needed to forge reliable links with leaders in the regions. Later, however, the regions might become too self-assertive for Moscow's liking, or might simply get in the way of central policy. The "problem" of the provinces was resolved in the 1930s by violence: many regional bosses lost their heads in the Terror, and the center rammed through its agenda for economic development. Yet, although personnel changed, the overall patrimonial principles of the Soviet system did not. There simply was no other way to govern the enormous Soviet periphery (without conceding significant amounts of self-rule to the regions, which of course the Bolsheviks were not prepared to do).

Personnel policy was not, however, the Bolsheviks' only means of keeping their enormous land mass under control. They were also engaged in what might be termed Communist colonization – a project to spread routine political practices and Bolshevik civilization to all corners of the country. On these counts they were unprecedented among Russian rulers in the scale of their ambitions. If the tsars had been content to let parts of their empire run themselves – as long as they delivered their taxes – the Bolsheviks were not so laissez-faire. The very word "periphery" was Sovietspeak: it was designed to avoid the undesirable connotations of conquest, subjection, and benightedness that were present in words like "provinces" and "colonies," but at the same time it left little doubt that outlying regions were subservient to the designs of the state and had some catching up to do.

Here the "center" (i.e. Moscow) would come to the rescue. "Mastering" new territory was a heroic Soviet cause in the 1930s, and for a long time thereafter. Newspaper articles and newsreels exhorted people to head for the major construction sites of the first five-year plan. Explorers and aviators became some of the cultural icons of their age as they used modern technology to bring new territory under the sway of Soviet civilization.[9]

But the Soviet treatment of the periphery had a much darker side. Exploration was motivated not only by the quest for new resources, or by the urge to demonstrate the strength and unity of the socialist state, but also by national security concerns. The border guard was another heroic figure of 1930s mass culture: he was a protagonist in dozens of films, set in locations from Poland to the Pacific, with evocative titles like *A Border under Lock and Key*.[10] Conditions on the periphery were even worse than in other parts of the Soviet Union. When migrants arrived on construction projects far from Moscow, they found life unforgiving: the nascent socialist city offered them dark streets, open sewers, and accommodation in tents, barracks, and mud huts.[11] Most importantly, the greater part of center–periphery migration in the Stalin period was coerced. Hundreds of thousands of peasants and other undesirables from European Russia were exiled as "special settlers" or Gulag inmates to remote mines and construction sites, where they were left to freeze and starve or were worked to death.

The Gulag may usefully be seen not as a separate universe but rather as the lowest extremity of an administrative-territorial hierarchy that structured the Soviet Union. At the other, more desirable, extreme lay "closed" or "regime-zone" cities such as the capitals and major industrial centers: these were better provisioned than the Soviet average, offered greater employment opportunities, and required special permission to live in them. "Open" cities, to which access was less restricted, were by definition of lower status. A few rungs lower came the collective farms (where many people were left immobile by the lack of an internal passport), and lower still came the "special settlements" for deportees, which placed strict limits on the mobility of inhabitants. Only then came the Gulag – which itself was divided into different categories of camp and degrees of unfreedom.

But a description of the fixed structures and hierarchies of the USSR fails to do justice to enormous amount of movement that took place in this country from the early 1930s onward. The system of hierarchical "zoning" in large part emerged as a response to the challenge of controlling a society that was drastically uprooted by collectivization and industrialization. As one historian has described the situation: "Like a wall of water broken through a dyke, 12 million people went into motion without the powerful channeling force of private property to guide, control, restrict, redirect, and curtail them."[12]

Dispersal and Recentralization: The War and After

By the end of the 1930s, the Soviet system of territorial zoning had established only precarious control over population movement. Then it was thrown into greater turmoil – first by the temporary expansion of Soviet territory, then by the

German invasion. At a time of European war, the perennial Soviet fear of fifth columns went to new extremes. Between 1939 and 1941, hundreds of thousands of Ukrainians, Poles, Lithuanians, Latvians, and Estonians were deported from the western borderlands, whose conquest by the Red Army had in the short term only undermined national security. When the war with Germany started, the Soviet regime carried out mass repression in European Russia against ethnic Germans, more than 850,000 of whom had been "preventively" deported to Kazakhstan and Siberia by the end of October 1941.[13]

Before long, however, the western borderlands were overrun and even the capital came under threat. It took shockingly little time for the Germans to land direct blows on the real and symbolic center of Soviet power. As early as 28 June 1941 the authorities concluded that Lenin's Mausoleum was not bombproof, and within days a special train was organized to take his body to safety in Tiumen in Western Siberia. On the night of 21–22 July, exactly one month after the start of the Soviet–German war, Moscow suffered its first bombing raid; even the Kremlin suffered damage. In October the military commander of the Kremlin requested 4,000 kilograms of explosives with a view to booby-trapping the government complex.[14] However, while the Bolshevik founding father was evacuated, the current dictator stayed. Although preparations had been made for his departure, Stalin chose not to quit the capital.

Here was a powerful symbolic commitment to maintaining the citadel of Soviet power, but it did not change the fact of mass population movement in the face of the Nazi threat. Almost immediately after the German invasion, the decision was made to organize large-scale evacuation. Important archives and valuables were moved east. Much of the economic administration and educated elite found itself in Kuibyshev (formerly Samara) and other population centers on the southeastern Volga. Writers and their families left in a first wave of evacuation in July to Kazan, and then on to Chistopol, Elabuga, Naberezhnye Chelny, and other towns on the Kama river. A second wave in October took people to Kuibyshev, Kirov, Kazan, Chistopol, Sverdlovsk, Molotov, and Tashkent. The Kiev film studio went to Ashkhabad, where four short films were in production by early September. Moscow and Leningrad filmmakers were sent to Alma-Ata, a city that had a remarkable wartime concentration of artistic talent: Sergei Eisenstein, Mikhail Zoshchenko, Sergei Prokof'ev – to name but three.[15]

The largest component in evacuation, apart from children, was labor to support the war industries that were moved east. By the start of 1942, 2.2 million people had been evacuated from Moscow since the start of the war, leaving the population of the capital at 2,370,000.[16] The current best estimate puts total wartime evacuation in the range of 12–17 million. These were mainly urban people: qualified workers, engineers and technicians, women, children, and old people. Life in evacuation was almost invariably hard, though the degree of its severity varied.

Evacuees attached to factories and organizations were in general better housed and provisioned. Those who traveled without such a work placement might end up in poor and remote rural areas. Those who were evacuated earlier under calmer circumstances, and who had the chance to grow food through the summer months, were relatively advantaged. Best off, as ever, were the families of employees of central organizations, Red Army commanders, and members of creative unions.[17]

The concentration of population in particular regions placed enormous strains on everyday life. By the start of 1943, evacuees made up almost 10 percent of the population of the Urals region, which had had an acute housing shortage even before the war. This was now greatly exacerbated by the sudden influx: in urban areas of Sverdlovsk oblast (the industrial heart of the Urals), average housing was 3.1 square meters per person as of 1 March 1942 – not far above the "sanitary minimum" of 2.5 square meters. Unsurprisingly, tensions sometimes ran high between the local population and the evacuees, who were unwanted guests and competitors for scarce resources. Although many hosts treated evacuees with compassion, it was all too easy – for a population reared on Stalinist enemy rhetoric – to brand them as cowards and traitors when domestic tensions came to a head.[18] Evacuation had brought an unceremonious and unprecedented confrontation between the metropolitan center and the benighted periphery. As the son of one Soviet writer observed, "in Chistopol we have arrived in the nineteenth century, if not further back." Roads were appalling, motor vehicles were nowhere to be seen, and modern plumbing was absent. For their part, the locals found plenty to resent in the influx of guests from the center: writers' wives arrived in the town with large amounts of spare cash and set about buying up food.[19]

Another problem was labor discipline. Draconian legislation had been introduced in 1940, and sanctions were enforced even more rigorously in wartime, but that did not stop tens of thousands of workers "deserting" factories during the war years. In 1943, at one aircraft factory in the Volga region, more than 3,000 workers were classified as "deserters," and two-thirds of them faced criminal prosecution. Here, as elsewhere, the problem was not just poor work conditions but also the mass injection of untrained rural people into the industrial workforce.[20]

Then, when the war turned in the Soviet favor, these people had to be sent back. A Soviet government decree of February 1942 had confiscated much housing owned by local soviets and enterprises in evacuated areas (thus effectively depriving thousands of evacuees of their homes, and offering them a disincentive to return ahead of time). But most people who had been moved east had a strong sense that evacuation was temporary and home was elsewhere. According to official statistics (which were probably an underestimate), about 1 million people were "re-evacuated" in 1943, more than 2 million in 1944, and more than 1.2

million in 1945. The process dragged on to 1948, and hundreds of thousands of workers were kept at their wartime workplaces longer than they expected.[21]

The most traumatic population displacement was, of course, inflicted by the Germans. In total, almost 9 million Soviet people (civilians and POWs) were moved to the territory of the Reich and its allies: 3.25 million POWs, 4 million civilians deported as forced laborers, 350,000 *Volksdeutsche*, and a further million people classified as refugees and evacuees. The vast majority of those found alive at the end of the war, 5.7 million, were repatriated to the USSR. A propaganda campaign assured them that they would receive a warm homecoming, but the reality was that any repatriated citizen was to be carefully screened. At its peak in mid-1945, the Soviet filtration system had 150,000 employees, almost 400 centers at various administrative levels, and a capacity of 1.3 million repatriates. A heavy weight of suspicion fell on deportees, who had to prove that their departure had not been voluntary. Even when they left the filtration camp, repatriates remained under surveillance by the local NKVD and faced numerous obstacles to full reintegration into Soviet society.[22]

Repatriates took their place among the many, sometimes interchangeable, categories of suspicious misfits in postwar Soviet society: POWs, other displaced people, the unemployed, "speculators," petty criminals. Whatever the human misery created by such stigmatization, it was a dismally predictable response from a closed and militarized state that was facing the disturbing fact that tens of millions of its citizens were on the move, many of them returning from encounters with the nonsocialist world. The challenge to party-state hegemony was equivalent to a second collectivization. How was the center to re-establish firm control?

The first step was to take stock of the administrative arrangements that had formed during the war. Center–periphery relations were a matter of regime survival between 1941 and 1945, when a network of strong regional representatives had carried out the bidding of the State Defense Committee (GKO). The exigencies of wartime required a reduction of bureaucracy and a simplification of decision-making. In Moscow the five-man GKO issued commands of a general kind, while regional bosses were left in charge of operational matters. This was a practical arrangement, but it represented a significant devolution of authority. Once the war ended, the Soviet regime took measures to recentralize the economy. In 1946 the commissariats (now called ministries) were given back their powers, and the central government (the Council of Ministers, under Malenkov) dominated economic policy. Postwar centralizers had plenty of work to do. The economy was severely lopsided. The eastern part of the country had a disproportionate number of military enterprises that now had to be converted to other functions. The west of the country was devastated and desperately needed reconstruction.

This was the context for a discussion of economic development priorities in the late 1940s. The war years had seen a considerable relocation of people and industries to the east, but investment had of course been skewed to the defense sector. The question now was whether Soviet economic policy should be aiming for a more rounded development of these regions or should instead focus on aiding the recovery on the traditionally more developed parts of the country. All the while, the western parts of the Soviet Union were making insistent demands on resources. As early as 1944, the areas liberated from German occupation were sucking up more than 40 percent of Soviet investment (as compared with only 16.3 percent in 1943).[23]

In 1945, the central authorities conducted a debate on the merits of "regionalization" – in other words, the channeling of resources to ensure the harmonious development of particular regions rather than simply to maximize short-term output. The advocates of regionalization and "complex development" achieved success in principle with the establishment of a new commission on regionalization in July 1945. In practice, however, ministries retained a great deal of power to direct resources as they saw fit in order to maximize production in their sector. The Soviet planning system gave them every incentive to do so. As a consequence, the output from the eastern parts of the USSR (the Urals, Siberia and the Far East) fell substantially as a proportion of overall Soviet industrial output: from a third in 1945 to less than 20 percent in 1950.[24]

Despite the recentralizing trend, Moscow still perceived autonomous regional networks as a threat. In the postwar Stalin era, however, it mostly found less violent ways of dealing with the threat than had been the case in the 1930s. The one large exception was the Leningrad affair of 1949 which brought a bloody purge of that city's leadership. Turnover in regional elites at this time was generally quite high: according to a Malenkov memo of March 1950, 31 out of 106 Party secretaries at oblast, krai and republic levels had been appointed in 1949 or early 1950. But this was still not a return to the 1930s. The post-1938 generation of Party bosses was more loyal to Stalin than the previous one – and the ageing dictator, for all his tendency to suspicion, was capable of perceiving this.[25]

No one questioned the hegemony of the center. Resources had begun to flood to Moscow in the 1930s – witness the construction, to much fanfare, of the first metro stations, or the specification in the 1935 General Plan that apartment blocks should have a minimum of six floors.[26] In the postwar years, however, the economic clout and symbolic prestige of the socialist capital reached a new peak. In September 1947, in a speech on the occasion of the 800th anniversary of the city's founding, Stalin hailed Moscow as the political center that had gathered the dispersed Russian territories of the feudal age into a single state and then defended this state against foreign aggressors. Moscow's great achievement was that it had been and remained "the founder and initiator for the creation of a centralized state in Rus." In Soviet times, moreover, the city had assumed further significance as the center of world socialism.[27] The most eye-catching demonstrations of Moscow's primacy were the seven skyscrapers that were projected for prominent sites around the city center; in their steeples and "wedding-cake" design they were quintessential expressions of the Stalinist fusion of baroque and classical styles. In the very late Stalin years, construction of the Moscow Metro proceeded to the Ring Line (completed 1954), which not only included the most grandiose station architecture of the whole subterranean network but also encompassed the center of the ultimate socialist city.[28]

───────── Geographical Stratification after Stalin ─────────

De-Stalinization did a good deal to disturb the stable hierarchy between center and regions that had taken shape in the Stalin period. Early signs came even under Stalin. In 1952, a ten-year plan for the construction of Moscow was noticeably less of a hymn to monumentalism than its 1930s' predecessor. After Stalin's death the most grandiose of all Stalinist projects – the construction of a gigantic Palace of Soviets on the site where the Church of Christ the Savior had previously stood – was finally dropped. The corresponding high-profile project of the era – the Palace of Soviets that went up in the Kremlin complex – was low-key by comparison. In a further break with monumentalism, new residential blocks in Moscow were to be limited to a mere five stories.[29]

Center–periphery relations in the Soviet Union were a matter not only of symbolic politics but of population management and economic exploitation. The coercive dimension of the USSR's human geography was most evident in the camp and colony network of the Gulag. From the late 1920s to the early 1950s, forced labor was the main means of colonizing inhospitable but resource-rich parts of the periphery. In the process, new cities and populations took shape, and the Soviet Union's system of incarceration became to a significant extent its method of settlement. On the ground, the transition from Gulag to "free" settlement was not at all clear-cut. Vorkuta, one of the most notorious prison camp destinations of the Stalin era, was also officially a city whose population grew from under 25,000 at the start of 1945 to almost 200,000 in 1965. In 1940, the Politburo took the decision to develop coal-mining in the region, and during the war the Vorkuta labor camp (*Vorkutlag*) became a crucial supplier of coal to besieged Leningrad. Vorkuta was connected by railway to the national network in 1943, and coal production was greatly increased from 1943 to 1947 – at enormous human cost. The prisoner population rose to 62,688 at the start of 1948 (this despite the release of more than 15,000 in the amnesty of 1945). While this rapid expansion depended on a constant supply of slave labor, the nonprisoner popula-

FIGURE 6.1   Moscow as thrusting modern metropolis: Kalinin Prospekt under construction, 1965.
Source: © Mark Redkin / PhotoSoyuz.

tion was also growing. By 1953 the city of Vorkuta had almost as many inhabitants as the local camp complex: 68,553 as opposed to 72,312. The city was acquiring the appurtenances of Soviet civilization: its own Victory Boulevard (in 1945), a noncamp newspaper (1952). The boundary between inmates and non-inmates was friable, as some prisoners were permitted to live outside the "zone." A notable example was Vorkuta's most famous prisoner, Aleksei Kapler, who had been imprisoned for an affair with Stalin's daughter. He was permitted to live relatively comfortably in the city and serve as the city's photographer. Some inmates remained in Vorkuta after release: this was the closest they had to a home. In addition, the population of Vorkuta was swelled by an influx of migrants who had never been prisoners.[30]

Not everyone, however, regarded the Gulag and its conglomerations as home, and the mass releases in the mid-1950s presented a major challenge to the territorial arrangements that underpinned the Soviet order. Hundreds of thousands of ex-convicts were on the move, and Soviet society was gripped by fear of a crime wave. As early as 7 March 1953, some ill-wisher broke off the arm of a Stalin statue in the Magadan Park of Culture and Rest. In December 1953 Magadan district gained administrative status, but over the next two years more than a quarter of its population – above all camp inmates from the notorious Kolyma complex – fled the region.[31]

Besides posing a threat to public order, the post-Stalin amnesties caused chaos in the system of labor distribution. The mass releases caused acute manpower shortages in regions whose whole development had been predicated on the supply of unfree labor. Just before the amnesty of 1956, there were 112,238 people in the camps of Perm oblast. By 1961, the number of camp administrations in the region had fallen from eight to two, and the population of the labor colonies to around 30,000. But this left a huge labor shortage, as production targets for the region's timber remained high.[32]

The traditional Stalinist solution to such problems was the system of labor conscription called *orgnabor*. But post-Stalin methods had to be less coercive, and the mid-1950s saw a shift to methods of mass mobilization. The most impressive example was the Virgin Lands project (described in Chapter 4), but inhospitable Gulag outposts were also beneficiaries. In Perm, the short-term solution was to launch recruitment campaigns and to seek redistribution of labor from other regions. By these methods almost 15,000 more workers entered the Perm timber industry in 1962.[33] More generally, contraction of the armed forces was releasing hundreds of thousands of young men into the labor supply, and departing for a sub-Arctic mining town was for many of them a reasonably promising opportunity. Life in Vorkuta might be hard, but it was often preferable to life back on the collective farm where there was no excitement, no travel, and no bonus wages. While conditions were squalid in the 1950s and labor turnover high, in the longer run Vorkuta proved a surprisingly attractive place to settle as one of the more privileged "open" cities in the Soviet Union.[34]

Other remote corners of the USSR were even more attractive to migrants. In the 1960s, Chukotka had the highest rate of in-migration in the entire country, and by the fall of the USSR the native population made up only 10 percent of the population in that region. Chukotka had special kudos as a border territory within sight of America, but it also offered generous salaries and other benefits. By the late 1960s, food and drink shortages were practically unknown for the northern

FIGURE 6.2   Snapshot of the Russian periphery: Settlement in North Urals, Sverdlovsk
region, 1958.
Source: © Yury Krivonosov / PhotoSoyuz.

settlers, housing was good by Soviet standards, and the settlers had the time and
the spare cash to travel more freely than any other non-elite category of the Soviet
population. For a combination of economic and security reasons, the Soviet state
was to lavish on the circumpolar North subsidies that amounted to 6 percent of
GDP.[35]

Yet Soviet popular culture continued to insist that migration from center to
periphery was a heroic undertaking. The Thaw era saw some attempt to recapture
the pioneering exploratory spirit of the earlier Soviet period. The geologist was a

romantic figure: a free spirit untrammeled by the spatial constraints of ordinary Soviet life. This profession had among its screen representatives charismatic actors such as Mikhail Ul'ianov (in *The House Where I Live*, 1957) and Vladimir Vysotsky (in *Brief Encounters*, 1967). A special aura of adventure attached itself to Siberia and the Far East. In *The Boss of Chukotka* (1966), set during the civil war, a young Bolshevik outsmarts predatory American capitalists and travels halfway round the globe to deliver to the Soviet authorities the million dollars he has extracted in customs duties.

For many young people, however, the move "to the periphery" was a matter neither of monetary incentive nor of popular mobilization but of obligation. The Soviet system of labor allocation (*raspredelenie*) remained committed to the idea that many educated specialists from the major cities should spend at least the initial period of their career a long way from Moscow or Leningrad. Graduates were given the security of a job and housing for three years, but they were meant to go wherever they were sent. A romanticized version of the system was presented in the film *Colleagues* (1962), which follows three medical graduates as they take up their first jobs. The most dedicated and principled of them goes to the back of beyond to become a village doctor. His two friends turn up to visit just in time to operate on him after he has been stabbed in the street by a jealous local.

Away from the big screen, however, the system of *raspredelenie* was resented and evaded by those who had the connections to do so. The planning system struggled to match up the output of higher education institutions with the requirements of various branches of the economy, all the more so when the number of graduates grew constantly with the expansion of higher education. In 1980, *raspredelenie* had to process 49 percent more young people than in 1970. By the 1980s, according to state figures that were almost certainly an underestimate, around 10 percent of graduates were failing to turn up at their assignments (though levels of compliance varied greatly between republics: graduates in the Caucasus and Central Asia were the least obedient). Conversely, enterprises – which were habituated by the planning system to request more human resources than they needed – might turn away graduates who had dutifully arrived for their three-year assignments, or reassign them to unskilled work. It was little surprise that *raspredelenie* rapidly unraveled in the late 1980s when the authority of planning agencies was drastically curtailed.[36]

The spread of Soviet civilization to the periphery was sometimes given a push by central investment. One striking example was the creation in the late 1950s of a major new academic center, Akademgorodok, just outside Novosibirsk. The new town quickly became a haven for the liberal intelligentsia, even if ideological constraints tightened after 1968.[37] Another case of resources pouring outward from Moscow was the last great mobilizational cause of the Soviet period: the campaign to build a railway from Lake Baikal to the Amur River (BAM). This project has gone down as the greatest white elephant of the late Soviet period, but a study of its participants suggests a slightly different picture. Workers on BAM were drawn by the lure of high wages and other benefits but were also, to judge by memoirs written later in life, caught up in the general enthusiasm fostered by the project. The romantic appeal of "mastering nature" and collectively overcoming obstacles had evidently lived on into the late Soviet period, as had the appeal of sociability, unselfishness, and mutual reliance at the workplace. BAM also had freedom to offer: many of its young workers valued their larger wage packets not just for consumer reasons but also because they gave them the opportunity to explore parts of the country they would never have reached otherwise.[38]

Long-distance travel within the Soviet Union was still a substantial undertaking. The country was afflicted by the perennial Russian condition of "roadlessness," and large areas were cut off from major transport routes.[39] Nonetheless, the long-haul rail journey – whether to visit relatives, to investigate tourist sites, or to take a holiday in the South – was an increasingly accessible (and enjoyable) ritual of Soviet life. Air travel, too, was now doing much to make Soviet people mobile. The journey time for a flight between Moscow and Leningrad fell from 3 hours in 1949 to 1 hour 5 minutes in 1969, while the duration of the Moscow–Vladivostok route fell from just over 44 hours to just over 13 hours. In 1949, the Black Sea holiday resort of Sochi was directly connected by air to 28 Soviet cities; by 1969 that number had risen to 77. By this time, moreover, long-distance journeys were more likely to be made by air than by rail: in the peak holiday month of August in 1969, 109,000 Muscovites flew to Sochi, while only 91,000 took the train.[40]

The most desirable kind of mobility, however, took Soviet people from the provinces to the capital. In the post-Stalin era, as before, making it to the "center" was the surest way for an ambitious outsider to achieve self-advancement. Although the housing shortage made it difficult for young people to move away from their home town to study, by the 1950s there were opportunities for provincials to make their way to a larger city or republican capital. In fact, university halls of residence could not cope with the expansion: in 1953, 45,000 students in Ukraine alone rented rooms (or, more likely, parts of rooms) on the private market.[41] A 1950s hall of residence in Moscow is the main setting for the first half of the prizewinning 1979 film *Moscow Does Not Believe in Tears*. The three main protagonists are all young women who have come to Moscow to make good: they act out (with varying success) the "Soviet dream" of upward and inward mobility.

Over the post-Stalin decades, millions of Soviet people were claiming their part of the dream by moving, if not to Moscow, then at least to the nearest urban center. Mass rural–urban migration continued to be a defining demographic fact of the Soviet experience until the late 1970s. In the two years preceding the 1970 census, almost 14 million people – about 6 percent of the population – were classified as migrants, more than two-thirds of them of working age. Russians were the ethnic group most ready to move from one part of the USSR to another, while Central Asians and Caucasians were the most sedentary. More than 5 million people had moved from one urban location to another, and 4.4 million from rural to urban location. Unsurprisingly, urban locations in the RSFSR were the most popular destinations for migrants. In the 1960s, Central Asia and Kazakhstan had been the beneficiaries of campaigns to increase in-migration from European Russia, but this trend was now going into reverse.[42]

The strong impulse of the Soviet population to head for the major centers was partially held in check by the Soviet system of zoning, which created a basic distinction between "open" and "closed" cities. In the latter, the residence permit – *propiska* – was especially hard to come by. Tightening up the passport regime (in other words, increasing residence restrictions and their policing) was a standard response by the Soviet authorities to social unrest. In July 1962, at a time when the authorities were acutely preoccupied with manifestations of "anti-Soviet" sentiment, the list of cities that barred categories of ex-convict was expanded to include Krasnodar, Rostov-on-Don, Groznyi, and various towns in the Stavropol and Rostov regions.[43] The 1979 census indicated that just over 50 million people – almost a third of the urban population of the USSR – lived in closed cities, where they could expect to be better supplied with consumer goods and find more fulfilling employment. Naturally, many members of Soviet society who lived outside the closed cities strove to move to them, but the Brezhnev regime tried to steer them to open cities. Soviet migration specialists continued into the 1980s to argue that the *propiska* system was the way to manage migration. The problem was that markets did not operate, and housing costs and wages were very similar across the Soviet Union irrespective of how desirable a territory was. The result was that people strove to get round the rules and obtain a *propiska* for a higher-status territory.[44]

In Moscow, the city authorities struggled – for the most part unsuccessfully – to keep down demographic growth: their fear was that the showcase city of the USSR would all too easily become overgrown with shanty sprawl. A crackdown on passport violations brought some reduction in the rate of growth from the late 1950s to the mid-1960s. Then, however, growth consistently exceeded the plans drawn up to contain it. Moscow's population reached 8 million in 1979, a full 11 years ahead of projections. Admittedly, the *propiska* system kept the capital's rate of growth lower than that of other major Soviet cities. But there were always ways round the regulations. Individuals could bribe officials or contract fictitious marriages. Some organizations – important enterprises, the Party, the KGB – could put their employees on the fast track to the capital. The single greatest source of expansion was the system of "limits" for migrant labor allocated to particular enterprises. The workers, dubbed *limitchiki*, who came to Moscow on these terms were little better than slave laborers for the years of their contract. Their reward, however, was a Moscow residence permit. Between 1971 and 1986, 700,000 *limitchiki* were let into Moscow. The consequence of the unplanned population growth, however, was that Moscow was acquiring some of the sprawl that Soviet ideology attributed to the unplanned capitalist city: by the 1980s, some 650,000 people were commuting in daily from outside the city.[45]

Soviet administrative structures, in the post-Stalin period as previously, struggled to cope with a period of rapid social transformation and population movement. Order was maintained, even if at the cost of discretionary arrangements and bureaucratic gray areas. The question was how such a system could ever be liberalized without leaving millions of people in abandoned outposts of socialist civilization and, conversely, turning Russia's main cities into shanty agglomerations. Could the periphery ever have a life of its own without the constant intervention of the center?

The Rise of the Soviet Regions

The extent to which the Soviet provinces could become autonomous depended, above all, on relationships within the political elite. The perennial tug-of-war between center and regions entered a new phase with the power struggle following Stalin's death. In the early stages of his leadership career, while he was consolidating his position and beating off his rivals, Khrushchev carefully cultivated regional elites and promoted his own men wherever possible. Between March 1953 and February 1956, 45 out of 84 first Party secretaries of republics and oblasts were changed.[46] It was largely thanks to support from regional bosses on the Central Committee that Khrushchev was able to come out on top when he faced a leadership challenge in the "Anti-Party Affair" of 1957. He also strove to make the working relationship between Moscow and the regions more productive and to improve the economic coordination of the Soviet system. Soon after the crisis of summer 1957, he launched a radical structural reform by setting up regional "economic councils" (*sovnarkhozy*) to challenge the dominance of the branch ministries. Nor was this the end of the upheaval for regional bosses. In 1960 and 1961, 57 of the 101 regions in the RSFSR and the Ukraine had their first secretaries changed. By the 22nd Party Congress of 1961, one-third of the full members of the Central Committee were new arrivals since 1957.[47]

Khrushchev's commitment to regionalism was driven as much by political tactics as by any set of economic principles. He was doing what all Soviet leaders did: he made sure people loyal to him were installed in positions of authority around the Soviet Union. His decentralizing credentials also seem dubious on grounds of political principle. At heart, like all Soviet leaders, he remained an overcontroller. When he found that the priorities of regional leaders differed from his, he set about a further reorganization, creating separate agricultural and industrial divisions. By the end of his period in office, Khrushchev had thoroughly antagonized the regional bosses in the Central Committee who had helped him consolidate power and had failed to develop any compensatory power base in the ministries.

The 1950s saw considerable turnover of regional leaders, but this did little to change the modus operandi of the Soviet system: the bedrock of Party functionaries (approximating to British civil servants) remained in place. It would appear that the regional Party apparatus was left in relative peace through all the leadership reshuffles. Provincial Party life had its stable rituals and forms. Oblast Party organizations held conferences every two years; these events ended with the "election" of a new oblast Party committee with more than 100 full and candidate members. The committee contained a few token workers and farmers, but it mainly comprised a selection of the area's elite: Party officials at various levels, state officials, enterprise directors, and a few other categories (military officials, newspaper editors, writers, scientists, and so on). The plenary meeting of the Party committee elected a bureau to serve as the day-to-day executive organ. The latter body was dominated by full-time Party officials – the various obkom secretaries, the chairman of the regional executive committee, the first secretary of the Party committee in the capital city.[48]

After Khrushchev's fall, the balance between regional and "branch" (i.e. ministerial) principles of organization predictably tipped back in favor of the latter. Brezhnev quickly reversed the bifurcation of regional organizations that had been Khrushchev's last significant contribution. The *sovnarkhozy* were abandoned in 1965, and the ministerial system was restored in a way that was meant to give more rights to individual enterprises. Regional leaders countered by lobbying for administrative forms that would allow enterprises still greater autonomy. The result of their efforts was the creation in the early 1970s of production associations that would allow groups of factories to resolve more issues on a local level. It was clear, however, that real power lay in Moscow.[49]

Just how much power was devolved to regional Party secretaries has been a question of great interest to political scientists. On the one hand, the provincial first secretary seemed to be a viceroy in his own domain; yet, on the other, he had to follow the agenda set in Moscow and was dependent on the center for power and resources. At times of stress, provincial bosses could still, as in the 1930s, be scapegoated, even if the sanctions were less bloody than in the Stalin period. As oil output in Western Siberia dipped alarmingly in the early 1980s, almost the entire administration of Nizhnevartovsk (the crucial region for the industry) lost their jobs, and the personnel purges soon spread outward to Tiumen.[50]

The relationship between central authority (the ministries) and the regions continued to be the central problem of Soviet economics. Coordination of economic activity at the local level was always a weak point, given the vertical chain of command from Moscow downward. In theory, local Party officials were supposed to improve economic coordination in their regions, but they never had the same political leverage as the officials in the center. Large industrial enterprises under all-union jurisdiction were more likely to take orders from Moscow than to follow the instructions of local agencies. The only example in the later Soviet period of a coordinated regional plan came in Western Siberia, the most important area of the Soviet Union for oil and gas production.[51]

Yet, at the same time, regional bosses had some freedom to interpret plan targets and other central directives in the light most convenient to their interests. They were constantly engaged in energetic lobbying of the center for increased investments and decreased output targets. They also put down roots that would never have had time to grow in the turbulent prewar era. It was symptomatic that the two dominant figures of the later Soviet period were Party bosses with a long-term personal and professional attachment to their native regions. Boris Yeltsin had spent his entire career in the Urals until 1985, when he was summoned from Sverdlovsk to enter the Central Committee apparatus. Mikhail Gorbachev returned to his home region of Stavropol after graduating from Moscow State University in the mid-1950s and did not leave until he made his breakthrough in Moscow politics in 1978. The contrast with Nikita Khrushchev, who shuttled back and forth between Ukraine and Moscow at Stalin's whim, could not have been clearer.

With the approval (or at least acquiescence) of such regional leaders, some cities and regions were able to acquire a sense of local patriotism that would have been frowned on (or stamped out) earlier in the Soviet period. The most prominent example was the Soviet Union's second city, Leningrad, whose distinctive social and cultural profile was viewed as a threat to the Muscovite centralism of the Stalin era. Any suspicion of political autonomy had been ruthlessly suppressed in the "Leningrad Affair" of 1949. In the post-Stalin era, however, the city made a comeback, thanks largely to its important place in the military-industrial complex.[52] Its prominence was reflected in the more intensive fostering of war memory, which could be at once impeccably patriotic yet individualized and localized. The city had its own version of the pan-Soviet cult of the war, which culminated on Victory Day 1975 in the unveiling of a Monument to the Heroic Defenders of Leningrad (placed on the main route from the airport into the city). But Leningrad also had its own compelling stories to tell of sacrifice and suffering. Popular memory of the Blockade was not allowed public expression in the late Stalin period but, following the Secret Speech, the war memory of Leningrad was effectively rehabilitated. In 1957 a replica of the wartime street signs warning of the danger of shelling was placed at no. 14 on Nevsky Prospekt. The famous Piskarevskoe war cemetery was dedicated on Victory Day 1960. Before the war it had been a military cemetery, but it was now the burial place for all the victims of the Blockade (above all starvation victims).[53]

Leningrad was an unusually striking place: a former capital, a city with a rich cultural heritage that had been damaged but not destroyed by the war. Other places were less fortunate: the Soviet Union abounded in grimly standardized suburbs, worker settlements, and municipal architecture. All the same, a certain degree of "localization" was occurring, in perhaps less eye-catching fashion, in many other areas of postwar reconstruction. The port city of Sevastopol had been devastated by bombing; by the time of liberation, only 3,000 of the city's 110,000 prewar inhabitants were left. As architects and planners set about rebuilding the city, they attempted to retain something of the city's prewar heritage. The Leningrad-trained municipal architect aimed to preserve as much as possible of the city center, and otherwise to take account of the specific population and geographical location of the city. Local architects, moreover, were able to make their own small contributions – for example, by adding Corinthian facades to reflect the close proximity of the ancient Greek city of Khersones. Planners avoided including monuments to current leaders with no particular connection to the city. Heroes of the Crimean War had precedence over Stalinist grandees.[54]

The post-Stalin era saw a rediscovery of cultural memory in a broader sense. The concept of "conservation zone" was introduced in 1949, but a historical conservation movement only really came alive in the mid-1960s. Its mass organization was the All-Union Society for the Protection of Monuments of Art and Culture (VOOPIK), which was set up in 1965 and numbered 92,400 primary organizations by 1980. Through the 1960s and 1970s new museums were established, memorial plaques were put up, and many cities worked hard to display and celebrate their heritage. Here was one of the few kinds of legitimate nonparty civic activity after the end of the Thaw period.[55]

The cause of national heritage also broadened to include the Russian countryside. From the late 1950s onward, writers increasingly turned their attention to the village as a repository of timeless Russianness. Ideologically orthodox novels of collective farm life gave way to a new literary trend called "Village Prose." Its leading representatives, themselves of rural background, delivered nostalgic, though also unvarnished, depictions of a rural world that Soviet modernization had put under threat. In the works of writers like Vasilii Belov, Valentin Rasputin, and Viktor Astaf'ev, the northern region of Vologda or the Siberian Altai challenged the near-monopoly of the major cities on Russia's cultural memory.[56]

A largely congruent development was the emergence of a public ecology movement. The post-Stalin intelligentsia turned against the gigantism of Stalin-era construction projects, asking awkward questions about the costs they imposed on the environment. A *cause célèbre* of the late 1950s was the campaign to oppose a grandiose plan to increase water flow from Lake Baikal to hydroelectric stations by detonating a vast explosion at the mouth of the Angara River. The first resistance came at a conference in Irkutsk in August 1958 where scientific arguments were bolstered by moral, aesthetic, and nationalist motivations. Although this manifestation of Siberian patriotism was duly noted by Party watchdogs, the plight of Baikal received much coverage in the press. An article in *Literaturnaia gazeta* in October 1958 on the plight of the lake quickly elicited more than a thousand letters from around the country. The temperature of public discussion rose still higher with the news that two substantial military-industrial factories were planned for construction on the south shore of Baikal. Over the next few years, coverage expanded from newspapers into intellectual "thick journals," as Siberian scientists put up spirited opposition to the opening of the new plants. The cause of nature protection in the later Soviet period has been called a "surrogate for politics"; it was also a means of raising regional consciousness.[57]

Nonetheless, the unpopular industrial facilities at Baikal did in fact open in 1966–7, and their toxic effluents were soon reckoned to have caused substantial ecological damage.[58] The stirrings of public environmentalism constituted a powerful statement in defense of the periphery, but whether they made any political difference at the center was another matter. This would not have been the first time that the Soviet system had allowed cultural tokenism that did not threaten the basic power relations. In the 1980s, however, those power relations changed of their own accord, which vastly expanded the room for maneuver of the Soviet provinces.

Post-Soviet Regionalism

Boris Yeltsin was one of the few people to have considered the regional problem seriously while the USSR was still in existence. As the Party boss of a major industrial region in the RSFSR, Yeltsin nursed a robust sense of resentment that he was obliged to report directly to central Soviet officials without the facilitating intermediate structures that were to be found in the non-Russian union republics. In the early 1980s, he was apparently pondering ways in which the Soviet federation might be made more responsive to its more economically powerful regions. In addition to giving Russia more institutional clout in the union as a whole, this might involve streamlining the overelaborate federal structure of the RSFSR so that it would comprise seven or eight powerful regional republics (one of which, naturally, would be Yeltsin's own patch of the Urals).[59]

This was not an idea Yeltsin could make public while the existing Soviet federal system remained strong. But, once he became RSFSR president in 1991, he had every reason to fear the disintegration of the Russian Federation – its Balkanization or, perhaps more precisely, its "Caucasianization." The Russian Federation contained a number of "peripheries" that, once the organizational structure of the Communist Party was removed, were worryingly undergoverned. In theory, power was transferred to state institutions: the Supreme Soviet and the executive committees (ispolkoms) of local soviets. The question was how these regional executives would operate in the new political conditions and how they would relate to the center – above all in the enormous Russian Federation, with its 89 territorial "subjects." Under these circumstances, it was legitimate to ask where the periphery ended and the center began. Skeptics argued that the threshold lay only at the border of Moscow oblast (or even at the Moscow ring road).

Even more disturbing for the cause of the integrity of the Russian state was the significant number of ethnically defined "republics" within the federation: how viable would a multinational nation prove to be? In July 1991, the Russian Supreme Soviet raised four of the five existing autonomous oblasts to the status of republics. This brought to 20 the total number of republics, and it would rise again to 21 in June 1992 when Checheno-Ingushetia was recognized by the Supreme Soviet as having split into two. In addition to the republics, the Russian Federation contained one autonomous oblast and ten autonomous okrugs that were also defined in ethnic terms. But even these ethno-territorial divisions did little justice to the intermingling of national groups in practice. Fewer than a third of the ethno-territorial units – mostly small republics in the North Caucasus – had an absolute majority of the titular population. Russians were strongly represented almost everywhere else. Even in the self-assertive republic of Tatarstan they made up more than 40 percent of the population (only a few percentage points below the Tatars, who also did not constitute an absolute majority).[60]

It was hardly surprising, then, that the precise terms of the federation were a controversial topic of debate in the Russian Congress of People's Deputies from the start of that institution's working life. All the while, political events were moving fast. Yeltsin's RSFSR itself set the tone by declaring sovereignty on 12 June 1990. Similar declarations come from the more independent-minded republican leaderships in the RSFSR later in the summer – though it was as yet unclear what all this would mean in practice.

Moods in the regions varied enormously – from separatism to passivity and loyalty to Moscow. With the exception of Chechnya, which revolted against the Soviet state and declared independence in September 1991, the most insubordinate Russian region in the first half of the 1990s was Tatarstan. In the late Soviet period the titular nationality (Tatars) had made significant strides in the regional nomenklatura and the upper echelons of economic administration. In the late summer of 1990, the capital of Tatarstan, Kazan, had been the scene for one of Boris Yeltsin's more famous declarations in his struggle against Soviet institutions: "Take as much sovereignty as you can swallow."

A contrasting case was Yakutia (renamed Sakha in 1990). This remote mineral-rich province had seen intensive in-migration over the previous three decades. Its leaders had the economic leverage to be forthright in their dealings with Moscow. After briefly ceasing to deliver gold and diamonds to the central Soviet authorities, they obtained a better deal from the Russian government: the republic would retain 10 percent of its diamonds. Although negotiations over the diamond industry were complex, Sakha remained a loyal member of the Russian Federation through the constitutional upheaval of 1992–3. President Yeltsin and the local elite had agreed an acceptable division of the spoils, while the local population was happy to turn out and vote for leaders who were seen to have defended the region's interests.[61]

A number of republics (including Kabardino-Balkaria, Mordovia, Tatarstan, and of course Chechnya) had rapidly acquired strong local executives that would not accept any fiat from Moscow. Accordingly, the new Federal Treaty of March 1992 established a status distinction between republics and the rest: the republics were defined in ethnic terms (even if the titular nationality did not make up a majority of the population), and were to be granted their own constitutions and elected legislatures and executives. Only Tatarstan and Chechnya refused to sign.

This was a messy but at least temporarily viable arrangement. The new national government had not attempted a direct attack on the prerogatives of regional bosses, but it remained for the foreseeable future in thrall to Soviet ethno-territorial arrangements that had themselves come about haphazardly and were not conducive to transparent and democratic government. This "asymmetrical federalism" left the way open for endless wrangling over taxation and control of economic resources.

Admittedly, soon after the defeat of the August coup Yeltsin set up a new institution – that of presidential representative – as a means of creating an effective transmission belt between center and regions. But this office did not always serve in practice to bolster presidential power. In some cases the representatives had a stronger allegiance to the region they oversaw than to the president who had appointed them and were able to use the position to build up a regional power base. Over the next two years, Yeltsin increasingly found that regional autonomy constituted a problem rather than a solution. In 1992–3 the regions (including Yeltsin's home oblast of Sverdlovsk) took the side of the Russian legislature in its standoff with the president. In October 1993 the conflict was resolved by force, and the president was able to drive through a constitution that gave him substantial powers and permitted him to rein in the ambitions of regional leaders. In the new constitution, the word "sovereign" was eliminated from the description of the republics' prerogatives, and Russian federalism (in theory, at least) was made more symmetrical.

But this still did not mean that the president could impose his will on the regions. Several of the republics and oblasts had genuine economic leverage over the center. Regional executives, moreover, soon found that elections could give them legitimacy and a power base that they had lacked under the Soviet system. What this meant was that Russian federalism in the 1990s remained profoundly asymmetric. Whatever the constitution might have promised, the central government was prepared to negotiate bilateral treaties with individual regions and republics. More than thirty such agreements were signed in 1996–7. The proactive Tatarstan secured such a treaty only a matter of weeks after the Constitution was passed in December 1993.[62]

The corollary of asymmetric federalism was "segmented regionalism." Regions differed greatly in their political and economic outcomes. In general, obkom bosses made a smooth transition to heading regional administrations. New heads of regional administrations were appointed by the president in 1991–2, while the republics had more leeway in how they chose their chief executives. There were some high-profile early elections – for the position of mayor in Moscow and St. Petersburg and for that of president in the republic of Tatarstan – but regional elections started in earnest late in 1995. Forty-seven regional chief executives were elected in 1996. Between 1995 and 2000, 44 percent of incumbents were ousted in a total of 148 elections. By 2003 Dagestan was the only region in the Russian Federation that had never held a direct election for its chief executive. More to the point, the chief executives elected in the regions were not guaranteed to bend to the president's will.[63]

Regional executives had a rather unclear relationship to their legislative counterparts, which were also elected. The first round of regional legislative elections came in March 1990, when new regional soviets were elected. These remained largely in place until the autumn of 1993, when the president dissolved them by decree in all regions apart from those that enjoyed the status of republic. The end of 1993 and the beginning of 1994 saw a wave of new legislative elections; the winners were to enjoy a two-year term. From 1996–7 onward, regional legislative elections took place on a regular basis.

Regional elections did not necessarily make local politicians more accountable. For one thing, the political system lacked the transparency (or at least readability) provided by truly national political parties. Party development in Russia's regions was extremely weak. According to the Central Electoral Commission, the 12 largest parties in Russia accounted for only 10 percent of deputies elected to regional legislatures between 1995 and 1997; about 80 percent had no party affiliation whatsoever.[64] Parties, where they did develop a regional profile, tended to be just a symptom of conflict within the local elite.

Although there were some cases where relatively liberal oligarchies came to power, in general the tendency was for the establishment of strong executives whose debt to Soviet traditions was only too clear. Variations in policy were a matter less of ideology than of social and economic realities. Different regional administrations faced very different challenges, depending on their access to communications and markets, their demographic and ethnic profile, their political leverage, and above all the economic resources they had at their disposal. Russia remained a "fragmented space" where communications were poor and many regions still hoarded resources as in Soviet times. Movement around the Russian Federation was notionally free under the more liberal 1993 constitution, but in practice there were severe economic barriers to migration and successful adaptation. Moscow, in defiance of the constitution, continued with a Soviet-style *propiska* system. The residence permit could be bought – but only for a sum as high as 500 minimum monthly salaries. The crisis period of 1991–4 brought a growth in the rural population that was comparable only to the de-urbanization that followed the 1917 revolution. But the status quo was restored in 1995: the larger and richer settlements tended to attract population and resources, while others continued to decline. On average, in *European* Russia, cities of more than 250,000 inhabitants were 314 kilometers away from the nearest settlement of similar size – double the figure for western Europe. Settlement in Russia tended to be heavily concentrated in regional capitals: on average, a third of the population lived in such cities. The Russian Federation had only 27 km of paved roads per 1,000 square meters of land. Even the most densely paved region in the country – Moscow – was some way behind western Europe.[65]

Even the Russian welfare state was becoming decentralized. Administrative responsibility for distributing pensions was increasingly resting with regional governments – a convenient way for the central government to lighten its load and pass the buck for inadequacies in provision. Those regions with substantial claimant populations – who might cause political difficulties if their entitlement was not met – tended to be more zealous in performing this responsibility.[66] Poor regions, however, were often unable to meet their welfare responsibilities. The sphere of social benefits was just one of many examples of the lack of legal transparency and equity in the Russian Federation. An inspection of regional legislation by the Justice Ministry in 1997 found that nearly half of 44,000 legal acts were out of line with the Constitution.[67] In the second half of the 1990s, it was plausible for a keen observer of regional politics to predict that Russia was on the verge of a "dismantling of the state."[68]

Yet, within a few years the incipient disintegration of the Russian Federation was not only checked but thrown into reverse. Following the 1998 financial crisis, which had only strengthened the trend of regional autarchy and fragmentation, previously divided political constituencies in Moscow came together behind a new agenda of bringing the subjects of the federation to heel. The federal elite had too much to lose if it conceded effective control over the regions. The trend of the next ten years – associated primarily with the presidency of Vladimir Putin – was to increase Moscow's power at the expense of elected executives in Russia's various republics and oblasts. Precisely because the regions were so diverse and so autarchic, they were unable to put up adequate resistance to recentralization. In one reading, this was a complete throwback to the Soviet nomenklatura system whereby regional bosses were appointed by Moscow even if they were notionally approved by their local elite. The key quality required of any provincial executive was the ability to lobby the center for resources.[69]

The early Putin era saw a determined effort to rein in the regional governors: in a decree of May 2000 that bypassed the constitution, seven new "federal districts" were established (Central, Northwestern, Volga, North Caucasus, Urals, Siberia, and the Far East). They were headed by presidential envoys with a broad supervisory brief, which notably included monitoring the implementation of federal law. Five of the seven envoys came from a military or security background – a clear indication that Putin was intent on re-establishing the "power vertical." The heads of the federal districts were to be the president's regional enforcers.

The results were impressive. Only a year or so after the decree, the justice minister was able to report that 94 percent of regional laws had been harmonized with federal legislation; a further law of 2003 imposed a deadline of mid-2005 for removing any remaining discrepancies. The era of multiple bilateral treaties between center and regions was brought to an end: between the end of 2001 and the middle of 2003, more than 30 such treaties were abandoned. Taxation powers were recentralized, though the delivering of state responsibilities was another matter: a new 2005 law on social benefits only increased regional welfare inequalities.[70]

The Putin government also sought to consolidate the Russian party system: by reducing the number of parties, it could make political life across the many regions of Russia more stable, transparent, and amenable to central control. A Law on Political Parties (adopted in June 2001) imposed much stricter conditions for registration: parties were now required to have a larger membership that was more evenly spread over the country. They were also required to participate in elections. In 2002 came a law that reformed electoral systems in a way designed to increase the role of party lists (and thus the influence of central politicians). In April 2003, a further amendment required a second round of voting if no candidate obtained more than 50 percent in the first round – another consolidating measure.

The most striking centralizing measure of the Putin era was a federal law of 11 December 2004 that stipulated presidential appointment of governors. Even before that Putin had been interfering in gubernatorial elections – in one notable case the incumbent Aleksandr Rutskoi in Kursk oblast had been disqualified from running – but this was a step further in the drive to put an end to what one nationalist politician called "matreshka federalism."[71]

New institutions were set up to increase coordination and consultation between the center and the regions. The State Council (established September 2000) was a forum for the president and the governors, and had more than 20 attached working groups. A Legislative Council (set up in May 2002) was an equivalent body for heads of regional assemblies and representatives of the upper chamber (the Federation Council) of the Russian parliament. But consultation took place very much on the center's terms, and Moscow remained hostile to forms of inter-regional association. Troublesome regional leaders – such as Tatarstan's Shaimiev – were co-opted into the federal elite rather than permitted to form a permanent counterweight to presidential power. All in all, there was every reason to suspect that the pendulum had swung back too far from the asymmetrical federalism of the 1990s: the overcontrolling center seemed to be back in charge.[72]

While the results of the recentralizing drive were impressive, it remained open to doubt whether these changes would in fact make the Russian state more streamlined and efficient. In practice, the role of presidential discretion remained considerable, and the likelihood was that the state would remain in thrall to cliques and interest groups (even if the balance had shifted firmly to cliques based in Moscow).

Nor did the increased role of presidential discretion do much to threaten entrenched regional elites. There was a good deal of continuity from the 1990s – and even before. Plenty of late Soviet bosses enjoyed lengthy tenures in the new political conditions – none more so than Vladimir Mikhailov, who ran the Siberian city of Kemerovo from 1986 to 2006. Regional newspapers and government websites made no distinction between Soviet and post-Soviet eras: Communist first secretaries were seen as regional figureheads in just the same way as post-Soviet mayors and governors. Nor was there much difference in age profile: one study of the period from the mid-1950s found that post-Soviet officials were actually a little older when they took up their positions than their Soviet predecessors: 46½ rather than 45. Even though it was too early to draw firm conclusions, some post-Soviet officials were well on the way to accumulating tenures as long as officials in the "stagnation" era. The same pattern of monopolization of high office by a self-enclosed elite, and of promotion and rotation within a closed circle, was in evidence. The contested elections of the period 1991–2004 had made surprisingly little difference.[73]

It is worth asking why the regional governors did not put up more resistance to the trimming of their powers under Putin. For many of them, it was more comfortable to receive direct presidential appointment instead of running for election. Their regional power did not diminish, even if their dependence on

Moscow increased. The new law, moreover, removed the limit on the number of terms they could serve, which meant that tried-and-tested regional bosses could be left in place. The continuation of Soviet-style patronage politics made the Russian federal system predisposed to corruption and also reduced the president's prospects of undertaking fundamental reform (by, for example, streamlining the elaborate ethno-federal system that the new Russia had inherited from the USSR). It appeared that the Soviet pattern of rule was becoming re-established: an over-controlling center that found it convenient in practice to cut patronage-based deals with regional elites. Federalism still did not have firm procedures for regulating the relationship between central government and regions in a fair and transparent way. And the center always had to contend with the possibility that particular regions would strike deals that evaded Moscow's revenue-collecting capacities.[74]

If the political relationship between center and periphery combined the trappings of federalism with some Soviet-style patterns of government, the view "from below" presented a similarly mixed picture. The legacy of Soviet spatial zoning, of Soviet economic projects, and even of the Gulag, was palpable at the end of the twentieth century. Many people were stuck in unlikely parts of the periphery where they or their parents had been deposited by the Soviet experience. In the Russian Far East, 10 percent of the Soviet-era population moved away, but the region remained poor and unemployment high.[75] Government and economists conceived the notion that the population of northern outposts would naturally adjust downward after the Soviet collapse, given the nonviability of such regions in market conditions. But this did not always happen at the rate anticipated. The reasons often lay in a combination of the residents' attachment to what was now their home and the absence of viable alternatives. For middle-aged and elderly people especially, social capital was what counted, whether it was accumulated in Kaliningrad or Magadan.[76]

In addition to Soviet overextension into the Far East and north, the new Russia had to face the long-standing phenomenon of "dying" settlements. Nor was this a phenomenon restricted to rural areas. Although Russia could claim to be a three-quarters urban country, many settlements were no more than pseudo-urban. The Russian Federation was a vast patchwork of small and medium-sized towns whose histories, economic functions and prospects varied enormously. Many of them were heavily reliant on Soviet economic structures – the local *raion* (district) center, a nearby small factory, state employment (in the local school, medical center, or post office). Practically all inhabitants – even those who self-identified as the local "intelligentsia" – were heavily committed to garden plot agriculture. The local economy of such places was boosted by injections of cash from relatives in the big cities and by state disbursements: in some small towns, half or more of the population were pensioners. However resourcefully their

FIGURE 6.3   Gulag settlement turned regional center: Lenin Street, central Magadan, 2007.
Source: © Sergei Potapov / PhotoSoyuz.

inhabitants might respond to postsocialist conditions, Russia's towns clearly varied in their long-term viability: some would go the way of depopulated villages, while others would grow and find a place in new social and economic networks.[77]

For all the palpable continuities with the Soviet experience, postsocialism did much to transform the relationship of Russian citizens to their territory. Geographical mobility now faced vastly fewer restrictions. In the 1990s, this largely took the form of substantial permanent migration: 5 million people moved to Russia from the ex-Soviet "near abroad," and more than 1 million left the inhospitable north of Russia. These vast migration flows dried up in the early twenty-first century, and Russia was left with a substantial amount of routine labor migration. Many temporary workers came to Russia from Ukraine, Moldova, Central Asia, and China, but a lot were moving within the Russian Federation itself. As was to be expected, the Central Federal District (which included Moscow) was the biggest magnet. After an early post-Soviet dip, rural–urban migration recovered to its late Soviet levels. As in Soviet times, higher education and a move to the nearest substantial center were the surest ways to achieve self-advancement and self-fulfillment. Although migrants were still legally required to register – and so the Soviet system of *propiska* lived on in fact if not de jure – it did not seem to act as a brake on migration. Many migrants chose not to register because they were prepared to gamble that they would not need to call on local services but also because they returned home often enough that they could count as temporary visitors. The main obstacle to internal migration was not registration but the difficulty of finding affordable accommodation.[78]

It was also clear that some Russian regions were flourishing in post-Soviet conditions, whether by cultivating their historical memory or by taking their cut of Russia's relative prosperity in the early twenty-first century. As of 2009, IKEA's Russian network included, besides five outlets in Moscow and St. Petersburg, stores in Rostov-on-Don, Ekaterinburg, Nizhnii Novgorod, Kazan, Novosibirsk, and the Republic of Adygeia (with new openings planned in Samara and Omsk).

The idea of Russia's healthy regional diversity was widely promoted in the media. By the early twenty-first century, Russian mass culture was performing admirably the task of celebrating local variations while championing the idea of a strong united nation. Russia's best-loved game show, *Field of Miracles*, offered viewers an orgy of folksiness, as guests from all corners of the country went through the ritual of singing their local ditties (*chastushki*), displaying local artifacts to the camera, bringing along their own food and drink, and even dressing up the presenter in folk costume. As in Soviet times, Russia was presented as a large happy family, where differences concerned nothing more fundamental than recipes for pies and jam.[79]

Yet Russia remained an archipelago more than a properly integrated national territory. To be sure, the commuter belt now extended a long way, and the economic benefits of proximity to the metropolis were felt as far north as small towns in the Tver region. But power, resources, human capital, and knowledge were still overwhelmingly concentrated in the capital. In 2005, Moscow accounted for about 60 percent of titles and 85 percent of copies of books printed in the Russian Federation.[80] No degree of cultural hegemony, however, was going to resolve the age-old conundrums of Eurasian governance. As at previous moments in Russian history, centralization could not provide solutions to all of the problems of maintaining an overextended territory. Putin might have gained the upper hand in his dealings with the regions, but the center–periphery problem showed no sign of long-term resolution. Even in the president's second term, there were signs that certain regions were chafing at the strict terms imposed on them, and parts of Russia's borderlands – above all the North Caucasus – were still violent and undergoverned. There was little prospect that Russia's leaders or population would reconsider the principal axiom of Russian state-building: that territory, not human capital, is the principal guarantee of national security and prosperity.

7

National Questions

The Soviet era brought a new set of answers to a very old question: how was a multiethnic state dominated by Russia, but in which Russians made up at best a small majority of the population, to retain its political and social integrity? The issue became all the more urgent in the late nineteenth and early twentieth centuries with the rise of ethnic nationalism among the subject peoples of central and eastern Europe: above all Czechs, Poles, and Serbs in the Austro-Hungarian empire, and Poles, Finns, and Ukrainians in the western parts of the Russian empire.

National problems proved intractable in Austria-Hungary, and defeat in World War I brought the collapse of that state. The Russian empire was also defeated, but its successor state, Bolshevik Russia, managed through a combination of ingenuity and coercion to maintain most of the territory of the former empire under a different name and a different ideology.

Ingenuity was required above all to design a federal state with dozens of ethnically defined administrative units that would not compromise the integrity of Soviet power. Absolutely central to the Bolshevik self-image was the notion that the Soviet state had broken decisively with centuries of imperialism. The USSR was, on paper at least, to be a multinational entity that did not reduce territories and ethnic groups to second-class status. During the civil war, Lenin and his People's Commissar of Nationalities, Joseph Stalin, developed a federal system in which the notion of nationality would be closely tied to that of national territory. Each designated ethnic group was to have its homeland, whether that was a full union republic, an "autonomous republic" embedded within a union republic, a "territory" (okrug), or a mere "autonomous region" (oblast). In the 1920s this ethno-territorial system was taken to an extreme: "national" units might be formed wherever they occurred, even if that was the microscopic scale of the village. Soviet nationality policy also took a relatively moderate approach to cultural differences and the colonial legacy: the authorities promoted a policy of "indigenization" (*korenizatsiia*), which stipulated education and publishing in native languages and the training up of and promotion of "native" cadres. While these might sound like liberal multicultural measures, they had a thoroughly illiberal ideological rationale: according to the Bolshevik historical schema, all peoples had to undergo evolution from lower to higher forms of development, and national consciousness was a necessary step along the way, serving as a comforting delusion for societies undergoing modernization.[1]

This was the historical long term, but indigenization presented numerous short-term problems for Soviet state-builders. Given the intricate multiethnic mosaic that was the former Russian empire, the Soviet government could never satisfy the aspirations of all ethnic groups all the time. Indigenization was likely to make nationalities more conscious and resentful of their neighbors, to bring a heightened awareness of national particularities that was at odds with the broader Soviet project. Another problem was that it threatened to give too much power to national elites, who might use central policy to build up their own power base or to develop nationalism for its own sake. The Moscow leadership was especially alive to such concerns when making policy for sensitive border regions: the Soviet state could not afford national separatists or ethnic fifth columns in the event of a large-scale European war.

Here is where coercion came in. At the end of the 1920s, the Soviet leadership launched a violent crackdown on the most worrisome border region of all: Ukraine. This republic's leaders had indigenized too enthusiastically for Moscow's peace of mind, especially as the western frontier of the USSR ran through an ethnically mixed zone of eastern Europe that might form a focus for the territorial claims of several neighboring states. A show trial of Ukrainian nationalists in 1930 was followed two years later by a campaign of terror against the Ukrainian Party apparatus. From the mid-1930s onward, a succession of other Soviet nationalities – from Poles and Germans in the western borderlands to Kurds and Koreans in the east – felt the punitive attentions of the Soviet state. An obsession with national security was taking the Soviet leadership in the direction of ethnic cleansing.

Indigenization remained official policy in the 1930s, but there was no mistaking the general turn to Russian-dominated state patriotism (with nods in the direction of "friendship of the peoples"). Less clear were the long-term prospects of "Sovietness" as a new national identity that might transcend both Russian chauvinism and ethnic particularism: in the 1930s this was still a work in progress. Nevertheless, the putative Soviet nation was soon to face its greatest ordeal: a struggle for the very existence of the USSR that would test the loyalty of all ethnic groups in the Soviet Union from German to Georgian.

The War as Crucible of Ethnicity

The Russified patriotism and ethnic cleansing of the 1930s had in large part been the Stalin regime's response to the prospect of war. When the war actually entered Soviet territory in June 1941, the stakes of the USSR's many national questions were raised to a new level.

As regards state-promoted patriotism, the situation was relatively straightforward. The war only strengthened the turn to a distinctly un-Marxist Russian nationalism. The press instantly referred to the conflict with Nazi Germany as the Great Patriotic War, though this phrase did not become official until November 1944.[2] The authorities put out a call for popular accounts of the pre-Soviet past. Historians were instructed to concentrate on heroic precedents such as the expulsion of Napoleon in 1812 and Alexander Nevsky's victory over the Teutonic Knights in 1242. Tsarist generals such as Ermolov and Skobelev could now be included in the patriotic pantheon, while famous rebels against the tsarist order – Pugachev, Razin, Shamil – were no longer acceptable topics.[3] The result was to entrench an ethnic Russian identity that interwar Soviet culture had largely skirted around. By the end of the war, there was little doubt that Russians were not only first among equals; they were just first. Stalin sealed their dominance in a famous toast delivered to the commanders of the Soviet Army on 24 May 1945: the dictator drank to the "Russian people" as the "leading force" of the Soviet Union and a repository for "common sense, clear mind, sturdy character and patience."[4] All this woefully underplayed the non-Russian contribution to the Soviet war effort. The Soviet armed forces included more than thirty ethnically defined infantry and cavalry divisions: about twenty infantry divisions from the Baltic states and the Caucasus, and about fifteen cavalry divisions from the Central Asian republics. These units, moreover, absorbed only a small proportion of the total number of non-Russians who served in the Red Army. By summer 1943, there were 55 newspapers published for the front in non-Russian languages.[5]

The conflict with Germany was also dubbed a "holy war," and this was more than a turn of phrase. The authorities quickly put a stop to antireligious propaganda and allowed a few churches to reopen from late 1941 onward. In September 1943 came the closest point of rapprochement between the Kremlin and the Church: Stalin personally received religious leaders and instructed them to hold a Church council that would elect a patriarch. This rehabilitation of the Church during the war was not only a matter of Russian nationalism. It was also forced by the realities of conquest and occupation. The Soviet absorption of eastern Poland in 1939 brought the Soviet Union 1,200 Orthodox parishes. The occupation of the Baltic states in June 1940 brought another half million Orthodox believers and 300 more churches. Bessarabia and northern Bukovina delivered another 3 million Orthodox and more than 2,000 parishes. Even a state with the repressive instincts of the Soviet Union could not hope to stamp out the religion of some 6 million people. This was all the more true when the Soviet Union itself came under attack in 1941. Stalin's concessions may well have been a measure aimed at the primarily Orthodox areas that the Red Army still had to liberate. A Russian Orthodox Church loyal to Soviet power would help to regain control in the western borderlands and would be far preferable to the Uniates (Greek Catholics) or the Ukrainian Autocephalous Church.[6]

The milder policies on organized religion outlasted the war. A decree of 22 August 1945 spelled out the rights of the Church as a legal entity. It was allowed to own houses and vehicles and to set up shops for the sale of candles and other religious items. Local authorities were to help houses of worship to obtain building materials for repairs. By the spring of 1946, the patriarchate was firmly established in Moscow, and the reach of the Church had extended from the central USSR to much of the rest of the country; several thousand churches were operational, and seminaries and convents had reopened. Between 1944 and 1947, 1,270 churches opened in territories that had never been occupied during the war, while more than 3,000 churches survived in the territories occupied by the Soviets in 1939–40 and reclaimed at the end of the war. The USSR gained a few thousand more churches from newly incorporated territory in Western Ukraine and from the territories occupied by the Germans, where parishes had sprung up in 1941–3. The best estimates give a figure of just over 14,000 Russian Orthodox churches in January 1947; the center of gravity of Orthodoxy had shifted firmly to Soviet Ukraine, which is where almost two-thirds of parishes were located.[7]

The Ukrainian focus of operations, after 1945 as before, had a national security rationale. The orientation of the Uniate Church toward the Vatican caused the Kremlin acute concern, and the transfer of hundreds of its churches to the Russian Orthodox Church made impeccable political sense. The Soviet regime took a pragmatic and instrumental attitude to religion, although pragmatism coexisted uneasily with the visceral hostility to organized religion that remained strong among party-state functionaries. Between May and July 1944, for example, regional Soviet authorities turned down almost 90 percent of applications to open churches. Only the most persistent and well-organized communities of believers had any chance. Between 1944 and 1947, only about 14 percent of petitions to open churches in the Moscow region were granted. In 1948 came a shift back to a more repressive policy on a national level.[8]

Inhabitants of the western borderlands would never have been in any doubt of the coercive instincts of the Soviet leadership. For all its concessions in the field of religion, the USSR played a full part in the maelstrom of ethnic violence that swept central and eastern Europe during World War II. As we have seen, the mid-1930s saw a turn to large-scale repression against particular Soviet nationalities. At this stage the rationale was less ethnic than territorial: Poles, Germans, Finns, and Koreans were uprooted and deported because they were identified as potential weak links in sensitive border regions. Once the war started, the Soviet state began to take indiscriminate measures against certain ethnic groups in their entirety, irrespective of where they lived or what counterevidence there might be for their loyalty to the USSR. "Enemies of the people" were now construed in much more ethnic terms. In this respect, the Soviet war started not in June 1941 but in September 1939. The Soviet Union's borders shifted to the west with the invasion first of eastern Poland and then (in 1940) of the Baltic states and Bessarabia. In their efforts to crush any resistance to the occupation, the Soviet authorities arrested likely opponents, sometimes inflicting terrible punishment on them. In the worst case, of April 1940, 20,000 Polish prisoners were shot by the NKVD. The Soviets also adopted their standard practice of forced population transfer. Mass deportations – usually conducted in the space of a single night – started within months. Around 275,000 people were uprooted in 1940, mostly to remote parts of northern Russia; the total number of Poles deported by the Soviets in 1940–1 was somewhat over 300,000.[9]

The other major acts of socio-ethnic cleansing in the 1939–41 period took place in the Baltic states, Bessarabia, and Western Ukraine. The deportations in these areas took some time to organize, but they finally took place in May and June 1941 – shortly before the German invasion. The Ukrainian deportations were designed to remove "counterrevolutionaries and nationalists," while the measures taken in the Baltic states and Bessarabia targeted likely opponents of the Soviet regime: former members of nationalist parties, policemen, landowners, factory owners, prominent civil servants, and so on. All told, according to internal Soviet figures, around 90,000 people were deported in this final prewar operation. If we add in the figures for ethnic Poles, the Soviet state had deported close to 400,000 people from its new western territories in its initial phase of rule between September 1939 and June 1941.[10]

Soviet rule in the western borderlands was not just about violence; it also involved exploiting tensions between Poles and Ukrainians, Poles and Lithuanians, and Poles and Belorussians. Shortly after the Soviet occupation of eastern Poland in September 1939, Stalin granted Wilno (an overwhelmingly Polish city in culture and population) to Lithuania. The Lithuanian government promptly set about establishing political and cultural hegemony in the city (now called Vilnius), often denying citizenship to Poles and Jews. The experience of Soviet occupation from June 1940 to June 1941 only heightened ethnic tensions. This was the conflict-ridden environment that the Germans came upon in 1941; Lithuania saw the first mass executions of Jews in Germany's eastern empire. In 1939–41, many Jews in Soviet eastern Europe wondered whether they could possibly be worse off in German-occupied territory.[11]

The period 1939–41 was bad enough as regards Soviet ethnic violence. But the next phase of war, when the Soviet Union was fighting on its own territory, was even worse. After the German invasion, the first group to feel the punitive attentions of the Soviet state were the 850,000 or so Soviet people of German origin who were deported east by the end of October. Later on, the existing Soviet propensity to think the worst of groups located outside the Russian heartland was exacerbated by the fact that several of these groups had spent extended periods under German occupation. More than two-thirds of the territory occupied by the Germans had belonged to non-Russian territorial units (union republics or autonomous republics). It was only in these areas that the Germans established their own civil administration – which required participation from the local population. The German empire was a highly differentiated, and to some extent ad hoc, creation which made distinctions between racial groups of different status. Among the Soviet nationalities, apart from the ethnic Germans (*Volksdeutsche*), the Baltic peoples were near the top of the hierarchy. Tens of thousands of Latvians and Estonians took up arms on the German side.[12]

Ukraine, the largest and most crucial area of Nazi occupation, was a different matter. The territory held by the Germans contained 320,000 ethnic Germans (a further 100,000 had been deported by the Soviet authorities before the Germans reached them).[13] Beyond these *Volksdeutsche*, however, the population consisted largely of despised Slavs: the Nazis made few distinctions between Ukrainians and Russians. Parts of the Ukrainian population had welcomed the German invasion, but any enthusiasm was quickly tempered by the reality of brutal Nazi exploitation. Ukraine provided about a third of all the forced labor in the Reich. Of the 4.4 million Soviet deportees repatriated by 1 March 1946, 1,650,343 were classified as Ukrainians. Between 1942 and 1950, 1.85 million *Ostarbeiter* would return to Ukraine.[14] The main gift the Germans bestowed on the Ukrainians was training in ethnic cleansing that the latter would put to use against the Poles when they got the chance in 1943.[15]

German occupation had been most prolonged – 30 months – in the Crimea, and the Tatar population there had been treated better than the local Slavs. In the North Caucasus the period of occupation had been much shorter, but the local population had failed to mount any serious armed resistance to the Germans – which was itself a sign of treason in the eyes of the Soviet authorities. Counterevidence was disregarded. More than 17,000 Chechens and Ingush had gone off to fight for the Red Army in the first months of the war, and a total of 137,000 Crimean Tatars had served in the Soviet Armed Forces (of whom 57,000 had died by 1944). All told, more than 60 million Soviet people spent at least some time under occupation, which made it gruesomely unjust to single out small peoples in the Caucasus for punishment.[16]

Nevertheless, when the moment came to reclaim territory, the Soviet authorities had far more evidence than they needed to convict entire ethnic groups of treason. The ensuing wave of repression also served as a convenient opportunity to break the resistance of groups – notably the Chechens and Ingush – with a long record of frustrating rule from Moscow. Retribution was summary. In the North Caucasus and southern steppe, the Karachai were deported in November 1943, the Kalmyks in December 1943, the Chechens and Ingush in February–March 1944 and the Balkars in April 1944. Shortly afterward, in May 1944, almost 200,000 Crimean Tatars were sent east. Of those who reached their place of exile in Uzbekistan, almost 20 percent had died by the end of 1945.[17]

Deportation was not just a form of punishment; it was also, in the wake of genocidal war, a means of nation-building. As the Red Army swept west in 1944, Stalin's attention turned to ethnic engineering in the western borderlands of the Soviet Union. The Soviet regime decided to resolve the ethnic problems of the region by ensuring the homogeneity of national republics. Mass population transfer was the main way of achieving this. The main task was to shunt the Polish population west, thus leaving "Western Ukraine" and "Western Belorussia" to their titular nationalities. Between 1944 and 1946, about 780,000 people classified as Poles or Jews were moved from Soviet Ukraine to Poland. Any Poles who avoided this "repatriation" had to fear ethnic cleansing by the Ukrainian nationalist army (UPA). Conversely, almost half a million "Ukrainians" were repatriated to the Soviet Union between October 1944 and June 1946; about two-thirds of them were forced to move.[18]

Nor did this exhaust the list of cases of ethnic violence within the Soviet Union as a result of the war. As Khrushchev later remarked in his Secret Speech, the only reason the Ukrainians were not deported was that there were too many of them. There was no doubting the resistance to Soviet domination in the newly annexed territory of Western Ukraine. Collectivization of this region was forced through between 1948 and 1950, but the Soviet authorities had to combat Ukrainian nationalist partisans until the early 1950s. People in the Baltic states were also ready to take up arms against Soviet power: around 30,000 Lithuanians, between 10,000 and 15,000 Latvians and 10,000 Estonians belonged to the partisan movement at its peak in 1945–8. Lithuanian partisans executed perhaps as many as 13,000 collaborators; according to Soviet sources (presumably an underestimate), Soviet and partisan casualties were equal at around 20,000.[19]

A further wave of deportations in the Baltics occurred in 1948–9. The largest came in March 1949, when almost 95,000 people were removed from Estonia, Latvia, and Lithuania in a single coordinated operation. This was a measure to crush the remaining "nationalists" and "bandits," as well as to crush resistance to collectivization in the Baltic republics. All told, between the annexation of the Baltic states in 1940 and Stalin's death, the Soviet authorities deported more than 200,000 people from the Baltics.[20]

Summary figures on the exiled population give some sense of the cumulative effect of ethnic deportation. The number of people in exile ("special settlers" in the Soviet terminology) was 2,342,506 at the end of 1945, having more than doubled since 1938, but it did not reach its maximum – 2,753,356 – until the start of 1953. The single largest national group in exile was Germans: those sent east in 1941 were now joined by *Volksdeutsche* from Ukraine and those repatriated from Germany and Austria to produce a figure of 1,224,900 at the start of 1953.[21]

Besides the forced removal of social and ethnic undesirables, "Sovietization" included the importation of new population to fill the gaps left by the exiles. From 1945 to 1949, an average of 20,000 Soviet immigrants per year arrived in Estonia. After the lifting of travel restrictions in 1946, many people from Pskov, Novgorod, and Leningrad oblasts crossed into Estonia to buy food – to the displeasure of the Estonians.[22] The postwar period also saw a crackdown on all manifestations of national culture that were out of keeping with the Russian-dominated state patriotism of the time. The second half of the 1940s brought a vicious campaign against non-Russian historiography. Republican Party organizations from Kazakhstan to Armenia were attacked for "nationalist" deviations. Even the Russian nationalists were slightly affected. The extravagant historical parallels that had been permissible in wartime were now trimmed back. The Great Patriotic War was now reclaimed as a Soviet national triumph, as an epic feat unrivaled by any prerevolutionary Russian exploits. The Soviet state imposed its own version of Russianness that once again downplayed the significance of the Orthodox Church and instead emphasized devotion to the state and high achievement in approved fields of culture and technology. The 150th anniversary of Russia's national poet, Aleksandr Pushkin, was celebrated in 1949 with much pomp, while most of mankind's more significant inventions – the steam engine, the radio, the airplane, the light bulb – were attributed to Russians. Several scientists and writers figured in the twenty or so films made in these years about notable prerevolutionary Russians.[23]

The most virulent manifestation of Soviet chauvinism in the late 1940s was an anti-Semitic campaign initiated at the highest levels of the state. In a grotesque irony, the Soviet Union – a country that had just faced a threat to its existence from an anti-Semitic adversary and had seen half of its Jewish population (or 2.5 million people) perish in the Nazi genocide – started a campaign of repression against its own Jews. During the war, Soviet Jewish public figures had been permitted to raise their profile by creating a "Jewish Anti-Fascist Committee." This body had outlived the war until it was suddenly disbanded in November 1948.

Its members faced arrest, torture, prolonged incarceration, closed trial, and – in most cases – execution. The persecution of the JAFC was accompanied by a purge of Jews in public life and the professions.[24]

The timing of the anti-Semitic campaign was determined by broader factors. One underlying factor, undoubtedly, was time-honored prejudice. This had taken ugly new forms during the war, when anti-Semitic folklore alleged that Soviet Jews only did service on the "Tashkent front." In the late 1940s, Harrison Salisbury observed the anti-Semitic story to be part of the standard Russian joke repertory (the other elements being the Georgian toast and the Armenian joke).[25] Anti-Semitism had become more pervasive and more acceptable in the Soviet Russian Party apparatus since Stalin's patriotic drive of the 1930s. Systematic ethnic discrimination seems to have started in earnest in 1937–8, and from 1938 Jews found that posts in the Central Committee were closed to them.[26]

Jews also suffered from their anomalous position in the Soviet ethno-federal system. The Soviets had told people insistently that they must have an ethnic identity, and that ethnic identity went along with a particular territory (a republic or an "autonomous region"). The Jews were problematic precisely because they were so well integrated into Soviet society and so little associated with any particular territory. In this light, it was all too easy for Soviet Jews to be targeted on grounds familiar from earlier Soviet ethnic violence: as potential fifth columnists, as an ethnic group whose loyalties might lie with a nation-state outside the USSR rather than with its Soviet homeland. Suspicions of this kind became far more acute with the creation of the State of Israel in 1948 and the enthusiastic response to this event by Soviet Jews. The visit to Moscow of Golda Meyerson (later Meir) that September brought thousands of Soviet Jews onto the streets, a fact that caused immense alarm to the Soviet authorities.[27]

The Soviet Union's Jews were the latest in a succession of ethnic groups to have suffered systematic violence at the hands of the Soviet state that formed a Communist counterpart to Nazi imperialism. The war had left deep scars on the multiethnic Soviet population, and these scars were laid bare by the Soviet ethno-territorial system. To what extent could they heal after the death of the dictator who had inflicted so many of them?

The National Dimension of De-Stalinization

The implications of de-Stalinization for state–society relations were immense, and perhaps nowhere more so than in the field of nationalities. Khrushchev's policies signaled a change in relations between "center" and "periphery" that was likely to open new opportunities for national self-assertion. They brought back into the Soviet fold almost all of the pariah nations of World War II. And they released from exile and prison camps tens of thousands of "nationalist" opponents of Soviet power.

A notable sign of change came in August 1954 with a decree lifting restrictions on former kulaks and on German labor conscripts: a total of 118,000 people. The key decrees on rehabilitation of deported ethnic groups then came in 1955–6. On 17 September 1955 the Soviet government announced an amnesty for citizens convicted of collaboration with the occupying forces in World War II. Then, in December 1955, legal rights were restored to the Germans in exile and their families. Over the following months a succession of other peoples were done the same courtesy: in March 1956, the Kalmyks were restored to Soviet citizenship, in April came the turn of the Crimean Tatars, Balkars, and Meskhetian Turks, and in July that of the Chechens, Ingush, and Karachai. The decrees still did not grant these peoples the right to return to their former homelands, but that too would soon change. In January 1957, five of the repressed peoples were given back their autonomous territories, while the Germans and Crimean Tatars were still denied any restoration of territory. Changes in boundaries meant that the Chechens and Ingush (and to a lesser extent the Kalmyks) were not returning to exactly the same homeland; the Ingush in particular resented the loss of one district to neighboring North Ossetia, and the resulting tensions would help to trigger an ugly burst of ethnic violence in the early 1990s. By 1959, not more than 60% of Chechens and 50% of Ingush had returned – a slower rate of return than in the case of other repressed peoples. By 1970 the figures were up to 90% and 85% respectively.[28]

A similar process brought back into the fold deportees from the western parts of the USSR. The first wave of Gulag amnesties in 1953–4 excluded people deported on political grounds from the western borderlands, but from 1954 onward tens of thousands of inmates were released back to the Baltic republics, Belorussia, Moldavia, and Ukraine. Many of them were genuine nationalist opponents of the Soviet regime. In October 1956, the Ukrainian Ministry of Internal Affairs recorded a total of more than 45,000 former nationalists and sympathizers who came back to the western part of the republic.[29]

The beneficiaries of the new turn in nationality policy were not only the ethnic pariahs of Soviet society. In June 1953 a Central Committee resolution proclaimed the ending of "distortions in Soviet nationalities policy." This implied in the first instance personnel changes. Ethnic Ukrainians were restored to positions of power in their republic, while representatives of the titular nationalities were installed as second secretaries in the three Baltic republics. Similarly motivated reshuffles brought "indigenes" promotions at middle and top levels of state structures. Khrushchev's reform of government along regional lines (through the institution of the *sovnarkhoz*) had the effect of giving more power to the elites in non-Russian republics. In 1960, the three largest republics – the RSFSR, Ukraine, and Kazakhstan – were even granted economic councils of their own to supervise economic activity on their territory.[30]

But Khrushchev's policies on nationality issues were as inconsistent as those in other areas. The softening of repression empowered local elites and awakened expectations of cultural liberalization that were not always met. Decentralization was an administrative and economic measure designed to improve the performance of the Soviet system. It did not betoken a new tolerance of national particularism. The differences between Moscow and the localities came to a head in 1958 in a controversy over an education reform. Between 1958 and 1961, indigenous bosses across the USSR were removed from their posts for having overstepped the mark. Especially affected were Azerbaijan and Latvia, the two union republics that had done most to resist the new legislation.[31]

There was more than met the eye even to the regime's grandest gestures on matters of nationality politics. In 1954, to much fanfare, Khrushchev donated the Crimea to the Ukrainian republic. But this was less an enlightened and generous act than yet another heavy-handed piece of Soviet ethnic engineering. Besides marking three hundred years of Russian–Ukrainian "friendship," the gift served to strengthen the Slavic hold over the peninsula as it brought tens of thousands of Ukrainian settlers pouring in. It also decisively weakened the territorial claim of the deported Tatars, who were left to embark on almost three decades of lobbying for restoration of their rights. In 1967 they were finally absolved of collaboration with the Germans, but even that did not give them the right to return to their homeland.[32]

Nationality policy, even when it softened, continued to have the core goals of the regime close to heart. Policies with a bearing on nationality issues were usually conceived as a means to some other end. This meant, however, that Soviet leaders – from Khrushchev to Gorbachev – consistently underestimated nationalism as an autonomous political factor. Soviet authorities were caught unawares by the unintended consequences of ethnic engineering. Large-scale population movement might create ethnic tensions and spark social conflict. Chechens and Ingush who returned to their homeland were soon fighting the incumbent Russian population in the North Caucasus for property they had been forced to relinquish in 1944. Everyday ethnic tensions were especially pronounced in Kazakhstan, which saw the peak of Russian in-migration in the early 1960s.[33]

Khrushchev-era policy also underestimated the extent to which national symbols might step into the void left by the Stalin cult. In Armenia, for example, a huge Stalin statue was removed in 1962 from a prominent position overlooking the capital Yerevan, to be replaced five years later with a similarly imposing statue of Mother Armenia that faced Mount Ararat. In a concession to Soviet patriotism, a museum of the Great Patriotic War was accommodated at the base of the statue. The most militant expressions of Armenian nationalism in these years were

FIGURE 7.1   Tallinn, 1947: An early postwar song festival.
Source: © Eugeny Umnov / PhotoSoyuz.

caused not by antagonism to Soviet Russia but by commemoration of the Ottoman genocide, which entered Armenian public discourse in 1963–4 and sparked mass demonstrations in April 1965.[34] In nearby Georgia, by contrast, de-Stalinization had been the trigger. Khrushchev's Secret Speech brought thousands of protesters on to the streets in Tbilisi, but the motivation was nationalism rather than Soviet loyalism: Georgians objected to the denunciation of their most famous son. Georgia's antagonistic relationship to the new party line was hardly soothed by the heavy-handed repression that ensued. In 1963, following the anti-Stalin resolutions of the 22nd Party Congress in 1961, six Georgian poets were arrested for distributing anti-Soviet leaflets. The Georgian Party leadership acquiesced in the efforts of its intelligentsia to resist Russification.[35]

As the contrasting examples of Georgia and Armenia – two Christian neighbors in the South Caucasus – begin to indicate, national movements around the Soviet Union sprang from different sources. In some cases a struggle for political independence was uppermost, in others the struggle for rehabilitation after Stalinist oppression. Some groups had an identity that was religious or cultural, while other national communities might have economic, demographic, or ecological grievances to unite them. As often at moments of national self-assertion, history could be a particularly explosive issue. The biggest nationality-related scandal in the

Soviet history profession concerned the figure of Shamil, who had led decades of Caucasian resistance against Russian rule in the first half of the nineteenth century, but whose reputation had fallen foul of the Great Russian nationalist tendencies of the Stalin era. In March 1956, taking advantage of the more liberal signals coming from the top, the journal *Issues in History* published an article with the eloquent title "On the Struggle of the Caucasian Mountain People with Tsarist Colonizers." In the autumn of the same year, two conferences on Shamil were held in quick succession. The first, in Dagestan, comprised an attempt at full rehabilitation of Shamil, while the second, in Moscow, offered a corrective. The matter was firmly settled by Party intervention over the following winter.[36]

Undoubtedly the most politically troublesome national groups were those recently incorporated into the USSR. De-Stalinization gave a green light to forms of national self-assertion in the Baltics. Song festivals in the Baltic republics became mass events. One such occasion in Latvia drew more than 7,000 participants and an audience of 70,000; the program even included songs by émigré composers. This was outdone by a 1965 festival in Estonia with 26,000 singers and an audience of 120,000. Once again, the nationalist thrust of the repertoire was clear. Local elites were seizing post-Stalin opportunities to revive the flagging cause of indigenization. In the political uncertainty following Stalin's death, Russians were nervous about remaining in or moving to the Baltic republics. Between 1952 and 1956, the non-Estonian contingent in the Estonian Communist Party declined from 13,374 to 12,138 – the first time it had fallen since 1945. At the same time, immigration of nonnatives ground to a halt, while tens of thousands of Baltic deportees returned to their homelands between 1956 and 1959. Expectations of far-reaching political change rose with the events of 1956 in the Eastern bloc; student riots in Vilnius accompanied the Hungarian revolt.[37]

Yet there were still clear limits to indigenous autonomy, and these would soon be reasserted by Khrushchev. A countermeasure against Baltic nationalism was Russian in-migration. According to the 1959 census, only a third of the inhabitants of the Lithuanian capital Vilnius were Lithuanians; in Riga, Latvians made up around 45 percent of the population. The all-important security forces and police were, moreover, dominated by non-indigenes.[38] Relations with the "center" in Moscow required care from republican elites. The Lithuanian and Estonian leaderships remained circumspect and managed to avoid the punitive attentions of Moscow. The Estonian Party had a particularly high proportion of "native" cadres who had lived much of their lives in Soviet Russia before being "imported" to Estonia in the postwar period: they were dubbed "Yestonians" because of the Russified pronunciation they had picked up. Less careful was the Latvian Party, which took measures to indigenize its executive and other key institutions and then publicly resisted Khrushchev's language reform. It was duly purged.[39] The regime's commitment to Sovietization (read: Russification) had hardly weakened.

─────── Modernization and National Consciousness ───────

From the mid-1950s onward the era of partisan warfare faded into the past, and ethnic identities and relations in the USSR unfolded in a more gradual and less overtly conflictual way. They were conditioned by two main factors: first, the structure of the Soviet ethno-federal system which granted particular national groups (or their elites) cultural salience and economic leverage; second, the long-term processes of social modernization, which notably included migration from villages to cities, the move to universal secondary education, and the extension of other social provisions. The paradox was that the USSR – which had been responsible for some of the worst ethnic violence of the mid-twentieth century – also gave tens of millions of people the cultural and economic tools to become more aware of their national identity. In the later Soviet period, 53 of the basic territorial units in the USSR were defined in terms of ethnic homelands: all 15 union republics, 20 autonomous republics, 8 autonomous oblasts and 10 autonomous okrugs.[40]

Soviet people were obliged to identify themselves in terms of nationality: the internal passport was the crucial document for every Soviet person, and its "fifth paragraph" (on nationality) was the section people paid most attention to. A reform of 1974 – which finally extended the internal passport to all Soviet people including collective farmers – offered an opportunity to remove the nationality clause, and there were in fact some indications in the Soviet press that this option was being considered, but it was not taken. By all accounts, the measure would have been unpopular with many non-Russians, for whom the passport clause offered a safeguard of their national prerogatives.[41]

Nevertheless, Soviet ideology continued to cling to the assumption that national differences would become less salient as socialism became more developed. The new Party Program of 1961 delivered an upbeat message on the nationality question: it claimed that national borders in the Soviet Union were losing their former significance. Khrushchev spoke of the inexorable "fusion" of national groups; the ideology of the Brezhnev era used the less categorical term "rapprochement," but the implications were similar. There were reasons to believe that social and demographic convergence between the Soviet Union's national groups was occurring. Levels of education, urbanization, and social mobility were evening up, even if great disparities remained. For the first four decades of the Soviet period, the Russians were the prime beneficiaries of the economic development occurring in the USSR: not only was such development concentrated in the RSFSR, Russians could also migrate to developing urban centers in other parts of the union. In the 1960s and 1970s, urbanization gathered speed in the other republics.[42]

FIGURE 7.2 Soviet modernity reaches Central Asia: A new city in Uzbekistan, 1968.
Source: © Nikolai Bobrov / PhotoSoyuz.

Whether this brought "rapprochement" in the sense of greater ethnic mixing is, however, questionable. Urbanization brought a greater concentration of the indigenous population in the cities of its own republic rather than accelerated migration across republican boundaries. Between 1959 and 1989, the proportion of ethnic Russians declined in the cities of all the union republics except Estonia and Latvia (which were flooded with Russian migrants); by 1989, the indigenous population made up the majority in the cities of all republics except Kazakhstan and Kyrgyzstan. A similar, though less marked, indigenization took place in most autonomous republics and autonomous oblasts.[43] Soviet-style modernization was having the effect of concentrating the titular nationality in the cities of its own republic, of consolidating rather than diluting the sense of a national homeland within the socialist union.

Migration between national homelands was relatively high between 1959 and 1970, as the Soviet population recovered from the effects of Stalin-era policies, but the 1970s and 1980s were characterized by stability. People were showing every sign of attachment to the national homeland they were allotted by the Soviet state. Georgia was the champion of national consolidation: between 1959 and 1979 the population of the republic grew by 25%, but the Georgian share more than kept pace, rising from 64.3% to 68.8%; this was the only union republic that saw an absolute decline in the Russian population. More than 96% of Georgians lived in Georgia, the highest degree of ethnic concentration in a homeland to be found in the Soviet Union. The neighboring Armenians were the most dispersed national group in the Soviet Union: the 2,725,000 Armenians living in "their" republic represented a little under two-thirds of the total number of Armenians in the USSR. But they too followed the trend of consolidation in the home republic: in 1979, almost 90% of the population of Armenia was Armenian.[44]

The Soviet Union was also giving people the cultural and intellectual tools to articulate a national identity. Between 1959 and 1979, five national groups at union republic level and 18 more at autonomous republic level narrowed the gap in educational attainment between themselves and the Russians; in 1979, Georgians, Armenians, and Ossetians could claim to be better educated than Russians. Then, between 1979 and 1985, all 14 of the other union republic nationalities achieved more rapid educational development than the Russians, and the Azeris joined their neighbors in the Caucasus to be among the highest achievers in the USSR. Conversely, the Jews, not endowed with a homeland in the Soviet federal structure, were subject to de facto quotas for university admissions. In 1970, people holding Jewish nationality made up 2.3% of students in higher education. Although this proportion was higher than their overall proportion of the Soviet population (0.89% at that time), it represented a striking fall from the 13.3% of the student body that was officially Jewish in 1935.[45]

Certain republics were taking great care to recruit members of the titular nationality into the intelligentsia. Affirmative action in higher education was carried to the point of outright favoritism. Georgians, for example, made up two-thirds of the population of the Georgian republic in 1970 but more than 80 percent of the student population in higher education. The rate of higher education in Georgia was extremely high by all-union standards: of every 1,000 people, 62 men and 85 women were graduates (as compared with 41 and 63 respectively in the RSFSR). Between 1950 and 1975, in the 14 non-Russian union republics, the number of people with higher research degrees (candidate of science or doctor of science) grew at an average annual rate of almost 10% (that is to say, more than 50% faster than the same figure for the Russians). Georgians, Estonians, and Armenians joined the Russians as national groups overrepresented in white-collar employment relative to their proportions in the overall Soviet population; by 1987, five national groups had intelligentsias – educated professional classes – that were larger in relative terms than that of the Russians. The increased indigenous representation extended to the upper echelons of the party-state and to other elites. Despite the purges of republican leaderships in 1958–61, over the period 1955–72 the titular nationality was proportionately overrepresented in the leadership structures of eleven of the non-Russian union republics. Writers, trade union functionaries, and prominent academics were also increasingly likely to come from the titular nationality.[46]

There is also evidence that indigenous people felt proprietorial over their "own" republic, and resentful of outsiders who appeared to challenge their dominance. One interview survey of Soviet Germans from Kazakhstan and Central Asia found that, at moments of conflict, native people would often throw at local Russians the phrase "Why don't you go back to your Russia?" People also felt resentment at the status of Russians in everyday communication: customers in shops and restaurants might be ignored if they addressed the local staff in the Soviet lingua franca. In May 1969 in Tashkent, antagonism went as far as violent unrest under the slogan "Russians get out of Uzbekistan," while analogous incidents were reported in Tajikistan and the Baltic republics in the 1970s. Although it is hard to judge with certainty, it seems that the 1970s saw a growth in everyday ethnic antagonism. Russians, for example, objected to what they saw as a Caucasian takeover of the food markets in their major cities.[47] The late Soviet city was a place where people might become more, not less, conscious of their ethnic identity; it was an excellent site for "inventing" traditions. As one scholar puts it, Caucasian customs of exaggerated hospitality were redeployed in the Soviet city as a way for people to add a "socially elevating native cultural twist to their newly acquired roles in a modern industrial environment" and thus to resist "Soviet proletarianization."[48]

Nonetheless, the limits to ethnic equalization remained palpable. The first was that the Russians, as ever, could still consider themselves first among equals. For them, a Soviet national identity could operate more coherently alongside a more ethnically and linguistically defined Russian identity. Surveys conducted in Moscow, Kishinev, and Tashkent in the late 1970s and early 1980s found that more than two-thirds of Russians in those cities regarded the whole USSR as their homeland. Russians were ready to migrate outside their "home" republic because they had much less to lose, and much more to gain, from such mobility. By 1959, ethnic Russians made up 20% of the Estonian population as compared with well under 10% before the war. More than half a million immigrants flooded into Latvia, bringing the population of the republic from 1.4 million at the end of the war to 2 million in 1955. Migrants formed a particular concentration in the important urban centers. By the end of the Soviet period, the Latvian proportion of the population of the capital Riga was only a little more than a third. The first two-thirds of the twentieth century were a period of extensive Russian migration beyond the territory of what became the RSFSR in Soviet times. According to the 1979 census, about half of the Russians in the non-Russian republics were those who had moved to these areas in the Soviet period (as well as their offspring). In 1926, 5 million Russians had lived outside the RSFSR; five decades later the figure had increased fivefold.[49]

The main indicator of Russian cultural primacy was the position of the Russian language. Russians could afford not to learn other people's languages but expect others to learn Russian. According to the 1970 census (the first to include such information), only 3 percent of Russians in the USSR said they were fluent in another Soviet language, and in most cases the language in question was Ukrainian. The teaching of indigenous languages in the autonomous regions of the RSFSR declined markedly as Russian strengthened its grip. The only non-Russian national groups in the RSFSR with schools that offered a full secondary education in their native language were the Tatars and the Bashkirs (within their respective autonomous republics). Non-Russians located outside their home republic often found themselves deprived of the opportunity to study in their native language, or even to take their language as an optional subject at school. Native-language education was relatively strong in rural areas with a strong concentration of indigenous language speakers, but much weaker in the more prestigious urban centers in the non-Russian republics. The population of the Belorussian capital Minsk was two-thirds Belorussian in the early 1970s, but the city had no schools where children were taught in Belorussian. Native languages at the union level increased their representation in the school system in the 1960s, but the 1970s and 1980s saw a clear increase in linguistic Russification in the schools of the non-Russian union republics, which caused significant cultural tensions.[50]

Language was an explosive political issue in the Soviet Union as it has been in many other multiethnic states. The educational reform of 1958, which gave parents the right to choose in which language their children would be educated, was interpreted by many people as a Russifying measure: in practice, far more non-Russian parents would send their children to Russian-language schools than the other way around. The 1977 Constitution spoke of the "opportunity for" rather than the "right to" education in one's native language. In 1978, Moscow attempted to reverse clauses in the new constitutions of the Transcaucasian republics that installed Georgian, Armenian, and Azeri as the state languages of their respective republics. Thousands of Georgians took to the streets to defend the status of their language.[51]

Certain union republics were more successful than others at maintaining a system of native-language primary and secondary education. Rates of native language education for indigenous children were lowest in Kazakhstan, Belorussia, and Ukraine. Latvia and Kyrgyzstan were in the middle of the range, while the three Caucasian republics, Lithuania and Estonia were successful at maintaining the status of their native languages. Russian became much more of a lingua franca in higher education, though Georgia, Armenia, and the Baltic republics were again quite successful at maintaining universities that taught in the indigenous language.[52]

The same tendency to Russification was reflected in print culture. Between 1960 and 1980, the proportion of all Soviet books published in Russian rose from 72.7% to 77.8% of all titles, and the percentage of all copies published also increased marginally to more than 82%. The Central Asian nations, the Ukrainians, and the Belorussians saw the native-language share of publications in their republics decline markedly over the same period. Even the less linguistically disadvantaged nations – Georgia, Latvia, Lithuania, and Estonia – voiced complaints about the danger of linguistic Russification. Much as nationalists might protest, there was no doubting the fact that Russian was crucial for social and professional advancement in the Soviet Union, especially for those who found themselves outside their home republics.[53]

The cultural and political resources available to particular ethnic groups depended greatly on their position in the Soviet ethno-territorial hierarchy. Ethnic groups that existed at the level of the autonomous republic or region had fewer opportunities for self-affirmation, and faced greater demographic threats, than the union republics. Overall growth in the indigenous populations of the eighteen autonomous republics slowed in the 1970s and 1980s. By 1989 they averaged 42.3% of the population in their home republics. The autonomous okrugs were in an even weaker position: their indigenous populations fell in the 1980s from 18% to 16% of the population of their territories, while the Russians averaged just over 60%. By contrast, the nations with union republics to their name averaged just over two-thirds of the population of their home republics in 1989.[54]

Creeping Russification also took place through intermarriage and the passport system. By the 1970s, about 15% of marriages in the Soviet Union were ethnically mixed, the rate having risen by 50% in the 1960s.[55] Offspring of such marriages could choose between the nationalities of their parents when determining their passport nationality at age 16. If one parent was Russian, that tended to trump the nationality of the other, especially in the Slavic republics of Belorussia and Ukraine. Similarly, the vast majority of children of Russian–Jewish marriages would choose Russian nationality.

The primacy of the Russians was also reflected in that key institution of Soviet life, the army. Russian was the sole language of the armed forces, and non-Slavic personnel found their upward mobility blocked. Slavs dominated in the combat units, and the different national groups tended to hang together in their units. All this undercut any sense of the army as a crucible of Soviet identity.

Yet, considering all the factors in its favor, the Russian language made rather little headway in the postwar period. In 1959, 10.2 million non-Russians (or

10.8% of non-Russians in the USSR) stated that Russian was their first or native language. By 1989, the numbers had risen noticeably, but not exponentially, to 18.7 million (or 13.3%). Given the pace of urbanization over these decades and the Russification of the education system, this was a modest return. Gains in Russian language adoption were found among the indigenous peoples of the autonomous republics (such as the Karelians, Komi, Mari, Mordvins, Udmurts, and Chuvash). The more culturally robust union republics successfully resisted Russification (Georgia, Tajikistan, Turkmenistan) or even de-Russified (Estonia, Armenia). The westernmost and heavily Slavic republics – Ukraine, Belorussia, Moldavia – experienced significant Russification.[56]

National differences, then, were not dying out – but did they present a threat to the political stability of the USSR? Some movements for national rights in the 1960s and 1970s took forms that went far beyond what was normally permissible in the Soviet Union. Armenian nationalism, first manifested on a mass scale in the demonstrations in 1965 on the occasion of the fiftieth anniversary of the Ottoman massacre, took a more troublesome – from a Moscow perspective – turn in the 1970s. In January 1974, a member of an underground nationalist party burned a portrait of Lenin in central Erevan; in January 1977 came a terrorist bomb in the Moscow metro; and a Helsinki human rights group was set up in Erevan in April 1977. The situation of the predominantly Armenian population of Nagornyi Karabakh, an enclave in Azerbaijan, was a particularly sore issue; ten years later it would lead to war as the Soviet federal system weakened.[57] The Lithuanian nationalist movement sought ostensibly nonpolitical instruments of self-assertion: the Church (an especially powerful source in Catholic Lithuania, which could feed off events across the border in Poland) and the cause of national and human rights. The most widely circulating petition in Lithuania, which collected 148,149 signatures, concerned the opening of a church in the city of Klaipeda.[58] The largest national dissident movement was to be found in the Ukraine. Even though post-Stalin Ukrainian nationalists had swapped insurrectionary tactics for the promotion of human rights and "national revival," they were subdued by waves of KGB repression in 1965–6, 1972–3 and 1976–80.[59]

The elites of the union republics were more indulgent to such manifestations of cultural nationalism than their less indigenized predecessors. Native-born elites for the most part observed the limits imposed by the Soviet system on national self-assertion. While some of them had sympathy for the nationalist cause, they were more often concerned to advance the economic interests of their region like any other Soviet boss. They were not about to undermine the system that fed them. The Ukrainian Party boss Petro Shelest managed to increase and Ukrainianize the Party membership in the 1960s, but did not try to prevent repression of Ukrainian nationalist dissidents and was not able to check the Russification of the education system in his republic. All the same, in 1972 he was removed for his nationalist leanings: the signs had been that he was preparing to rehabilitate the Ukrainian Party leaders who had perished under Stalin.[60]

The removal of a republican first secretary was a striking event precisely because it was fairly untypical of relations between Moscow and the republics by this stage of the Soviet period. Heads of the national republics were generally adept at promoting the interests of their territory at the all-union level and at ignoring Moscow's instructions when it suited them. In the early 1960s, for example, leaders in Georgia and Latvia successfully resisted the idea of expanding heavy industry in their republics, seeing this as a measure with Russifying implications. Elites in the less developed republics of Central Asia were able to lobby for greater investment by levelling at Moscow the charge of internal colonialism. Gently blackmailing their Russian comrades, they frequently referred to Central Asia as the "cotton colony" of the Soviet Union. Striking examples of longevity and cadre stability could be found among national elites. Between 1953 and 1988, the post of first Party secretary in Armenia had only four incumbents, and all of them had risen through the Armenian Party apparatus. The Armenian elite represented a tight network bound not only by common institutional background and career trajectory but also by social and kin ties.[61]

In the early 1980s, nationalism did not present an imminent threat to the Soviet order; it was contained by the Soviet political system. But Moscow had few grounds for complacency. If that system were ever to weaken, national issues were ready to come to the fore. A reservoir of discontent was accumulating at the middle and lower levels of Soviet society that might easily take ethnic form at times of stress. Newly educated indigenous populations did not always have a suitable supply of rewarding and high-status employment. There was a possibility that the Soviet Union would fall victim to a version of the disease that beset late industrial society elsewhere in Europe in the second half of the twentieth century: a compound of xenophobia and *ressentiment*.

There was also the problem that in the Soviet Union, as in many other places, the strongest driving force of nationalism was not language or culture, or even economics, but rather dislike of other nearby ethnic groups: nationalism was very often "anti-neighborism." And the Soviet federal system – which gave more than fifty ethnic groups territories of their own – had given everyone far more grounds for such antagonism. The greatest concentration of fractious neighbors came in the Caucasus, where Georgians looked askance at Abkhazians and South Ossetians, and Armenians and Azeris competed for the disputed territory of Nagornyi Karabakh. "Caucasianization" – the Soviet equivalent of balkanization – was the specter that haunted the Soviet ethno-territorial state.

---------------------------------- The Socialist Orient ----------------------------------

To a Russian ear, the Caucasus was a watchword for ethnic discord and fragmentation. But it also contained some of the more mobile and successful groups in the Soviet Union, many of whose members had reasons to be grateful to the Soviet system. What, though, of Russia's greatest cultural Other: the East? The Soviet project of ethnic fusion faced its greatest challenges in the parts of the USSR that were most culturally alien to the Slavic mainstream: the "backward," primarily Muslim, areas to be found on the southern and southeastern periphery. That meant, above all, the Central Asian republics of Turkmenistan, Tajikistan, Kyrgyzstan, and Uzbekistan.

Russia claimed a longer and more intimate relationship with Islam than the Western great powers. The throwing off of Muslim hegemony over central Eurasia was a central foundation myth of the Russian empire. In 1552 Ivan IV took the Tatar city of Kazan, and from that moment on Russia was by definition a polyconfessional entity. A further wave of Russian expansion into the Islamic world took place in the second half of the nineteenth century and was harder to distinguish from the kinds of colonization practiced by the French or the British. In the early Soviet period, however, the Russians flourished their anticolonial credentials as they set about building "indigenous" nations in the same way as they did in the western borderlands at the same time. The difference was that, while Ukrainians might have had some degree of national consciousness, Turkmens most certainly did not. Indigenization in Central Asia was shaped by a strong sense of this region's "backwardness" and failure to conform to Soviet civilizational norms. Efforts to accelerate the Bolshevik version of historical progress had some dire consequences – worst of all in Kazakhstan, the republic that straddled Russia and Central Asia, where a campaign to sedentarize and collectivize agriculture caused the deaths of more than a million people.[62]

In the postwar period, the Soviet regime faced a familiar challenge in Central Asia: to continue and complete its civilizing mission while remaining true to its anticolonial self-image. The situation in the East in the late 1940s was more promising than that in the West. Unlike the deported peoples of the Caucasus and the western Soviet Union, Central Asia could claim not to have had a bad war. Hundreds of thousands of Muslims fought in the Red Army. The center of gravity of the Soviet war effort shifted to the southeast in 1941: more than a million evacuees ended up in Kazakhstan, Kyrgyzstan, and Uzbekistan, and many factories were transferred to Central Asia (as was much of the Soviet culture industry). Historical accounts of the late Stalin era emphasized the affinity through the ages between Muslims and Russians: the word "conquest" was banned from accounts of Russian–Muslim relations.[63]

By some statistical measures, Soviet modernization achieved significant progress in Central Asia over the postwar decades. In 1959, only 30% of people aged ten and over had obtained even partial secondary schooling; by 1970 that figure had risen to 40%, and by 1979 to almost 60%. Overall, however, the impression was that the region was retaining a robust separateness. Perhaps the main reason was its explosive birth rate, which, for Soviet policymakers, made for a worrying contrast with the demographic stagnation in the Slavic republics. In both the 1959 and the 1970 censuses, more than 80% of Central Asians were under 50. Between 1959 and 1970, the Soviet population increased at an average of 1.33% per year. But the Muslim average was 3.19%, far in excess of the Russians' rate of 1.12%. From 1970 to 1979, Soviet population increase dipped below 1% per year, but Soviet Muslims were still far ahead of the Russians with an annual growth rate of 2.17%.[64]

Despite continuing migration from the European parts of the USSR, Central Asia was becoming more Muslim. Central Asians by and large stayed put: in 1979, around 99% of Turkmens, Kyrgyz, Uzbeks, and Tajiks lived in the Central Asian republics. Assimilation to Russo–Soviet culture was limited: in the 1979 census, 97–8% of the Turkmens, Tajiks, Uzbeks, and even Kazakhs named their own national language as their "mother tongue." The population of Central Asia was weakly integrated into key Soviet institutions. Young men were reported to engage in draft-dodging to a greater extent than other ethnic groups. Party organizations in Central Asia still had disproportionate numbers of Russians. In 1974, for example, the Tajik Communist Party was two-thirds Central Asian in its membership when the republic's population was more than 80% Central Asian. In 1927, membership of the Communist Party across the Soviet Union had been 3.5% Central Asian, which meant these republics were underrepresented by a factor of two. In 1986, Central Asians made up 6% of the Party membership, still not much more than half of their share of the Soviet population (which stood at more than 10%).[65]

Yet, at the very top level, Party bosses in Central Asia showed enviable longevity, thus confirming the impression that Central Asia was a world of its own. Sharaf Rashidov became Uzbek first secretary in 1959, remained in his position for more than 20 years and presided over a great expansion of indigenous Party membership in the 1970s.[66] The established pattern was for first Party secretaries to be indigenous, but for Slavic second secretaries to exercise a firm supervisory role. In many areas, however, supervision appears to have been lax. Everyday life in the Central Asian republics was less closely monitored than in the European heartland of the Soviet Union. Central Asians were much more likely to have private homes than the Soviet average. From 1977 onward, collective farmers could claim a 1,500-ruble loan to build themselves a house. Per capita living space was significantly higher in Central Asian cities than in those of the RSFSR.

The population could also benefit from an expansion of the private sector in agriculture. Output from private plots in Uzbekistan rose until it accounted for a quarter or more of collective farmers' income in the late 1970s. The Brezhnev regime's relatively laissez-faire rule in Central Asia has been dubbed "welfare colonialism."[67]

The main cultural factor that set Central Asia apart from the Slavic mainstream was religion. By the mid-1950s, Islam was a global political and cultural force; and, for all that it was best known for its impact in the decolonizing Middle East, its center of gravity lay not there but in (largely Soviet) Eurasia. By 1989 the Soviet Union contained 54 million Muslims, of whom two-thirds were in Central Asia. Soviet Muslims, like their Christian compatriots, were granted increased institutional representation during World War II. In 1944 the Soviet government set up a Council for the Affairs of Religious Cults, which had jurisdiction over all confessions other than the Russian Orthodox Church; in 1965 this would be replaced by a Council for Religious Affairs responsible for all religions including Orthodoxy. The mainly Sunni Muslim population of the USSR was given four "spiritual directorates." The largest of them was based in Tashkent and had authority over Central Asia and Kazakhstan. The others were in Ufa (for European Russia and Siberia), Makhachkala (for the North Caucasus and Dagestan), and Baku (for the Transcaucasus).[68]

The period 1947–54 saw a retreat from wartime policies more encouraging of organized religion – the number of mosques fell to 337 at the beginning of 1955 – while 1955–8 was a period of renewed liberalization. Then, from the late 1950s to Khrushchev's fall came a further crackdown which saw the virtual elimination of mosques, especially at the village level. The number of mosques was brought down to a postwar low of 309 in 1964, and measures were taken to ban religious ceremonies in private homes. Official Islam began to revive again in the late 1970s. As of April 1979, 200 large "cathedral" mosques were recorded as existing, but the state of grass-roots Muslim life was less clear. In 1974, for example, 27 working mosques were reported in Dagestan, while in 1978 the Chechen-Ingush autonomous republic had only two (both of which had just opened). In 1976 the whole of Azerbaijan had only 16 working mosques.[69]

Much religious life, however, did not show up in Soviet statistics. The "parallel Islam" of unofficial prayer-houses seems always comfortably to have outnumbered registered mosques. In 1945, when representatives of the Council for Affairs of Religious Cults began sending Moscow reports on religious life in their localities, they had much to say about unregistered worship. In many districts the faithful were able to make use of abandoned or dilapidated mosques. Chechens and Ingush started building prayer-houses without authorization when they returned to their homeland after 1957. In 1957 their autonomous republic was reckoned to have more than 1,000 unregistered prayer-houses for 398 registered ones. The role of mullah was often taken by elders with sufficient knowledge of Islam to perform rites. Across the Soviet Muslim world, the gap between official and unofficial Islam seemed to be widening. One estimate holds that there were at least 1,800 unofficial mosques – found in such places as tea-houses and bakeries – at a time when there were only 230 registered places of worship in Central Asia.[70]

The wider implications of grass-roots Muslim activity are less clear. Islam was a pattern of life rather than a religious doctrine or (still less) the conduit for a political ideology. Religious observance had a strong generational dimension: surveys of the Tajik rural population in the late 1960s and 1970s found that it was mainly pensioners who prayed the full five times per day, but that around a third of Muslims in the age range 40–60 prayed two or three times. Greater piety appeared to be a sign of a stage in the life cycle rather than an attribute of a historical cohort.[71] If Islam provided Soviet Muslims with an overarching identity, it was an extremely capacious one. There were many different ways of being Muslim in the Soviet Union – from the more devout in Dagestan and Uzbekistan to the considerably less so in Tatarstan.

This diversity is a large part of the reason why the "Islamic threat" to the Soviet Union, a subject of much speculation in the 1970s–1980s, failed to materialize as the USSR entered a critical condition in the late 1980s. Being Muslim did not prevent people from also taking on the new national identities of Uzbek, Kyrgyz, or Turkestani. Nor did it necessarily mean disaffection from Soviet Communism. The extreme "otherness" of the Muslim part of the USSR was not a threat to that country's existence or even its stability. When the Soviet Union did finally collapse, many members of the Central Asian elite were among the most reluctant to see it disappear.

Being Soviet: A Viable Identity?

In spite of all the evidence that the Soviet Union was an ethnically and culturally diverse place, it would be wrong to reject out of hand the possibility of a Soviet identity that overrode, or at least combined with, other national identities. The Soviet regime emerged from World War II with a readiness to employ terror against diehard opponents – such was the case with the campaigns against "nationalists" in the Baltic republics and the Ukraine in the late 1940s – but also with a confidence that non-Russian parts of the union could be "Sovietized." This made for a distinct contrast with the 1930s, when terror had been the option of first resort when dealing with obstreperous regional elites or with ethnic groups of dubious loyalty. Before the war, Sovietness had been rough and raw, and indigenization had rubbed along uncomfortably with Russian chauvinism and xenophobia. Now, perhaps, Soviet nationalism was approaching the finished article.

Nikita Khrushchev may be seen as the leading apostle of Sovietness. Thanks to his early years in the Donbas, Khrushchev could claim to embody the Soviet dream – as a provincial worker who had made good, but also as a person who had moved readily from one national republic to another. Admittedly, the republics in question – Ukraine and Russia – were ethnically and linguistically congruent to a greater extent than most in the USSR, and Khrushchev still took the primacy of Russian culture as a given, but he could nonetheless see himself as a person committed to the Soviet "fusion" of peoples in deed as well as in rhetoric. Directly after the war, before his transfer to Moscow in 1949, Khrushchev was in charge of the cleanup operation and reconstruction effort in Western Ukraine. In his memoirs he recalled the patriotism of the Ukrainian people, the warm reception he personally received, and the achievements of Ukrainian agriculture. He also reflected bitterly on the famine of 1946–7, caused by the ruthless exploitation of the village for the benefit of the industrial economy, and his own powerlessness to avert it. Practically absent from his account, however, was the more coercive side of his career as Stalin's Ukrainian viceroy: the (re-) imposition of collectivization and the de facto war against Ukrainian nationalists that lasted until the early 1950s.[72] Ukraine, as a large and economically powerful republic that had spent much of the war under Nazi occupation, was the crucial test case for postwar Sovietization; anyone who stood in its way was to be eliminated or forcibly resocialized.[73] In later years, too, Khrushchev would combine presumably genuine professions of affection for Ukraine with a steely commitment to Sovietness. As we have seen, his famous "gift" of Crimea to the Ukraine in 1954 may be interpreted less an act of favoritism toward his "home" republic than an archetypal Sovietizing gesture. Following the expulsion of the Crimean Tatar population in 1944, the peninsula was a social and economic disaster zone; what better way to repair it than by strengthening the bond between the Ukrainian and Russian peoples and by flooding Crimea with Slavic migrants?

When Khrushchev came to power in the mid-1950s, his faith in the strength of the Soviet identity would receive an even sterner test than in the de facto Soviet–Ukrainian war of the late 1940s. In 1956–7, tens of thousands of nationalist opponents were released from the labor camps and allowed to return to their former places of residence in the Baltic republics, Moldavia, and Western Ukraine. The local administrations and police forces were, unsurprisingly, against the idea, but Moscow gave them no choice. The Soviet leadership was putting its faith in indigenous cadres, many of whom owed their rise to the postwar struggle against nationalism in the western borderlands. Their loyalty was to Moscow, not to their co-national troublemakers who were returning from the Gulag.[74]

The repercussions of 1956 in the western borderlands were contained before they became system-threatening. But that still leaves the question of whether

Khrushchevian Sovietness caught on to any meaningful extent. While its successes were extremely limited in the Baltic republics, the Slavic republics were a rather different matter. Eastern Ukraine, the RSFSR and much of Belorussia do seem to have become substantially "Sovietized" in the postwar era. This new Soviet identity was a rather different matter from the official patriotism promoted between the early 1930s and the war, which had drawn extensively on Russian chauvinism and taken long looks back at the glorious national past of imperial conquest and expulsion of foreign aggressors. After 1945, milestones such as the defeat of the Tatars at Kazan in 1552 or the expulsion of Napoleon in 1812 were replaced by one much closer to hand: the Great Patriotic War itself.

In general, post-Stalin Sovietness was anything but backward-looking. It was self-assertively "modern," setting great store by the latest achievements of Soviet civilization: postwar reconstruction, expanding welfare provisions, cultural and sporting achievements and – perhaps above all – achievements in science and technology whose crowning glories were *Sputnik* in 1957 and the manned expeditions that started with Iurii Gagarin's in 1961. Its core values were social justice, collective purpose, technological modernity – all with a healthy admixture of national one-upmanship.

Sovietness also had mass socializing institutions that operated far more effectively than before the war. The Pioneers and the Komsomol came much closer to achieving saturation of the younger age groups. Rituals – from weddings to parades – provided enjoyable and engaging forms of social participation; even if people marched on May Day for the camaraderie and the free food rather than for the cause of international socialism, they did at least turn up. Documents and administrative procedures constantly reminded people of where they were and who they were. On a visit to remotest Siberia in the late 1990s, the travel writer Colin Thubron encountered an alcoholic Entsy, a man about as far removed from mainstream Soviet life as can be imagined, who, with his house burning down, rescued one item only: his passport.[75] A more Soviet reflex it would be hard to imagine.

Even food and drink performed an integrative function in the Soviet Union. Sovietness had its own consumer brand, which encompassed Soviet champagne, boxes of chocolates, and a number of apparently more humble concoctions. A mainstay of home cooking in the later Soviet period, and an essential accompaniment to any festive occasion in the 1970s or 1980s, was the Salade Olivier (usually known in English as Russian salad), which typically consisted of peas, ham, salted cucumber, potato, and hard-boiled eggs mixed in mayonnaise. Although the salad had a French genealogy – it was supposedly invented by a certain Lucien Olivier, head chef at a fancy Moscow restaurant, in the 1860s – it was so well loved precisely because of its quintessential Sovietness: its ingredients were appreciated as emblems of the indomitable capacity of *homo sovieticus* to get round shortages and put something tasty on the table. Paradoxically, evidence of Soviet economic dysfunctionality could serve to bolster a kind of everyday patriotism.[76]

Conversely, the main social obstacle to the spread of Sovietness – the existence of a large rural population that had little reason to thank the Communist Party – had been substantially alleviated. The Russian village had become a better educated and less benighted place, and the "second serfdom" endured by the Soviet collective farm population was finally lifted with the passport reform of 1974. More importantly, rural people were simply a far smaller proportion of the population in the 1970s than they had been in the 1930s. The fate of the disappearing and neglected village was a central concern of the Russian nationalist intellectuals who gained a higher profile in the Soviet cultural elite of the 1960s and 1970s, but Russian society as a whole was more concerned with sport, space, and cinema.

Soviet mass culture found ways of processing the "otherness" found within the Soviet Union and making it unthreatening and even endearing. The locus classicus of Soviet orientalism was *White Sun of the Desert* (1970), an adventure set in Central Asia during the civil war. The hero finds himself having to escort a harem out of trouble. In spare moments he writes back to his trusty Slavic wife expressing his longing to return home. If we add bawdy humor and subtract a small amount of moral seriousness, the film may be seen as the Soviet equivalent of the almost contemporaneous *Carry on up the Khyber* (1968). The difference is that the Khyber Pass was at some remove from British state interests by the 1960s, while Central Asia remained part of the successor state to the Russian empire.

Outside Central Asia, non-Russian ethnic groups were allowed to laugh on more equal terms. Georgii Daneliia was a Georgian filmmaker who had to his credit *I Stroll Around Moscow*, an iconic movie of the Soviet 1960s. In 1979 he brought out *Mimino*, which tells the story of a pilot from a Georgian backwater who dreams of giving up short helicopter rides between mountain villages and working instead on long-haul and international flights. He sets out for Moscow to further his ambition and falls in with an Armenian truck driver. The two of them have various misadventures which culminate in a court appearance for Mimino: he has assaulted the man who once reneged on a promise to marry his sister. He is let off with a fine, and through a chance acquaintance is able to fulfill his professional dreams. In due course, however, he realizes that international airlines are not for him and returns to bucolic backwardness in his home village.

On one level, the film confirms stereotypes of Caucasians as hot-blooded, erratic, and comically oblivious to Russian cultural norms. But it also offers a sympathetic portrayal of the two main protagonists, and shows that they have something to envy: a strong sense of roots that does not prevent them from being Soviet. These two provincials are not so very different from other Muscovites in the ways that they try to get by through personal connections and native wit.

In the post-Stalin decades such interethnic encounters became all the more frequent as the Soviet Union followed the global trend of allowing increased migration from the ex-colonial "periphery" to the metropolitan "core." In the 1950s, Moscow had a modest but significant Muslim population of tens of thousands, above all Tatars. From the 1960s onward, Caucasian and Central Asian migrants started moving to the RSFSR in respectable numbers. What they found on arrival depended to a predictable extent on class background. Students and budding functionaries had a rather different experience from that of construction workers; the latter in turn need to be distinguished from market traders who were swapping the collective farm for a more lucrative occupation. Even for lower-status migrants, however, the Russian experience had a good deal to recommend it. They had to contend with everyday racism, to be sure: a Central Asian man with a Slavic woman on his arm was liable to draw aggressive attention, while the term "blacks" seems to have gained currency in the 1960s as a general Russian pejorative for Caucasians and Central Asians. Against that, racism in Britain or America in the same era was certainly no less acute, and many Soviet migrants could reflect on countervailing acts of kindness from the "host" population. They generally felt they were treated fairly by officialdom, while the Russian city was a land of opportunity in the eyes even of a *limitchik* worker, for whom a cash wage, guaranteed (if squalid) housing, and the promise of a residence permit represented a large improvement on life-chances back home.[77]

Central Asians in the RSFSR faced the universal migrant conundrum: how to assimilate fast without losing their original identity. As usual, the arrival of children precipitated hard decisions: what passport nationality to give them, how to educate them (given that native-language schooling was not available in the RSFSR), even what name to give them. Such questions could more easily be fudged by the large majority of the Soviet population that lived in the Slavic republics of Russia, Ukraine, and Belorussia. For many of these people, Sovietness was a capacious umbrella identity that had room for other kinds of allegiance: family, religion, region, ethnicity. It was even possible for Soviet people to acknowledge the superiority of Western culture in certain areas, and to be fascinated by that culture, without losing their sense of belonging to a Soviet nation. The notion of the USSR's historical backwardness was a helpful escape clause from all kinds of awkward comparisons.

The Soviet Union, then, had a supraethnic civilizational identity that in many ways was analogous to that of its multiethnic superpower counterpart, the USA. Whereas Americanness placed a premium on liberalism, self-reliance, and individual achievement, the Soviet Union valued collectivism, social justice, and progress. The fact that the Soviet Union would soon fall apart does not contradict the notion that tens of millions of people, even in the mid-1980s, felt themselves to be securely and patriotically "Soviet." Certainly, Sovietness tended to exclude certain ethnic groups, being strongly Slavic in orientation. But then again, who would dispute that Americanness was white, Anglo-Saxon, and Protestant?

Nonetheless, the Soviet multiethnic state had fault lines that were lacking in America. It contained national territories with histories as non-Soviet nation-states: most recently and obviously the Baltic peoples but also, for short periods during the Russian civil war, the Caucasian republics and Ukraine. The structures of the Soviet ethno-federal state would give these groups political tools to seek secession if the Soviet system were ever to weaken.

An even bigger problem was that the inclusive, modern, supraethnic "Soviet dream" was undermined from within by the nationalism of the dominant ethnic group, the Russians. For most of the postwar era, Russian nationalism served the regime well by forming a symbiotic relationship with Soviet patriotism. The Russian cultural canon – Pushkin, Tchaikovsky, Chekhov – clearly helped to burnish the Soviet self-image. In the postwar decades, however, Russian national-ism shook itself free of Soviet multinational patriotism in two contrasting ways. First, it provided the impetus for a cultural revival that paid close attention to pre-Soviet history, to local heritage and to the shrinking world of the Russian village, thus implicitly calling into question the Soviet modernizing project. Second, Russian nationalism might take overtly chauvinist forms and undercut Soviet rhetoric about the "rapprochement" of ethnic groups.

The chauvinist version of Russian nationalism had been well represented in the Soviet system from the late 1940s, if not before. From the 1960s onward, however, it became more prominent. Leonid Brezhnev was less colorful than Khrushchev, but he, like his predecessor, had roots in the Ukraine and was a Soviet patriot in a similar vein. But, while Soviet multinationalism remained the belief-system of many apparatchiks, and the required idiom of political discourse in the Soviet Union, there were plenty of powerful functionaries – mainly in the RSFSR – who took a more Russian supremacist view.

As so often, the main litmus test for Russian nationalism in public life was institutional anti-Semitism. Violent campaigns against "cosmopolitanism" (i.e. Jewishness) were discontinued after Stalin's death, but discrimination against Jews remained a fact of life in the post-Stalin decades. It seems to have spiked again in the 1970s, when Soviet Jews were allowed to emigrate in significant numbers but also found themselves thrown out of prestigious professions. Sergei Lapin, head of the State Committee for Television and Radio, conducted an anti-Semitic purge of the media. Writers, for their part, weighed in on the side of solid Slavic virtues. In literature of the postwar era, Jewish and Russian characters regu-larly competed for the heroine's affections.[78]

To what extent did the racism of parts of the elite correspond to wider attitudes and behavior? It is certainly true that the Soviet Union was no paradise of mul-ticultural toleration. Even in Leningrad, the Russian city generally thought of as being most "European" (i.e. open to the outside world), newcomers with the wrong skin color and an inadequate sense of local decorum were liable to be branded yokels or savages. It did not help, from a Russian perspective, that many African students in the 1970s were receiving their grants in dollars and living rather better than their impecunious classmates.[79]

Ethnic humor offers an oblique indication of changes in grass-roots mentality. From the late 1950s, as people from the Caucasus started selling their produce at Russian urban markets, Russians started telling more jokes about Georgians, presenting them as oversexed wide boys. Then, in the 1970s, began an unending series of jokes about the ingenuous Chukchi people from northeastern Siberia: these jokes may be regarded as a very "Soviet" genre, since they depended on – whether they subscribed to or poked fun at – the civilizational hierarchy that put Russians at the top and reindeer-herders at the bottom. Perhaps the most nationalistic jokes told by Russians in the later Soviet period were those about the Ukrainians, which allowed the target group no redeeming features whatsoever; at least the Jews were allowed to be clever.[80]

The case of anti-Ukrainian jokes indicates a truth about nationalism that Soviet ideology never acknowledged: the easiest and often most effective way for a nation to conceive of itself is not through a shared culture or even a homeland but through reference to a disliked Other. But – and here comes a crucial qualification – this does not mean that Russians and Ukrainians were actually at each other's throats. Mature industrial society had its frustrations for undereducated young males in the USSR as everywhere else. There were numerous flare-ups in the 1950s and early 1960s (especially in the Virgin Lands), but relatively few thereafter. Ethnic violence born of plebeian *ressentiment* was a fact of postcolonial industrial life around the world in this era; the Soviet Union had only a mild case of it. We must conclude that the coexistence of Soviet patriotism and Russian chauvinism did not in itself pose a threat to the stability of the USSR. It did, however, create a potential problem in the upper echelons of the party-state: it undermined the elite's capacity for concerted action on national issues in the event of any challenge to the ethno-territorial arrangements of the USSR. Such a challenge was about to arrive.

Fragmentation and Dispersal

How did this highly imperfect but workable system fall apart so quickly along national fault lines? The answers, as one might expect, lie with the Soviet Union's rulers in Moscow. Between the early 1960s and the early 1980s, the Soviet system had treated elites from the national republics rather well. Under Brezhnev, six non-Russian republics could boast a representative on the Politburo at some point, even if these were mostly candidate (nonvoting) members. This relatively welcoming policy ended in the mid-1980s, as the new Belorussian, Georgian, Azerbaijani, and Uzbek Party bosses were not – unlike their predecessors – made candidate members of the Politburo. Even the Ukrainian first secretary, traditionally the most powerful figure in Soviet politics outside Moscow, had his sails trimmed and was replaced. Moscow was now paying closer attention to the conduct of republican leaders. The anticorruption campaigns launched under Iurii Andropov and continued under Mikhail Gorbachev had a distinct national dimension. The overwhelming majority of the Uzbekistan nomenklatura was removed between 1982 and 1987.[81]

These disciplinary measures were, however, followed by a liberalization of public life that allowed for increased expression of national grievances and preoccupations. The trailblazers in 1987 were the Crimean Tatars. Members of this ethnic group had a long history of frustration, having petitioned for a return to their homeland since 1956. Following a series of mass demonstrations, decrees in 1967 had first lifted from them the charge of mass treason and then allowed them freedom of movement – subject to existing residency restrictions (the *propiska*). In practice, the *propiska* system was used by Soviet administrators to keep the Tatars out of Crimea. Between 1968 and 1979, only about 15,000 of them were able to secure residence permits in their homeland. The authorities still did their best not to acknowledge the existence of this group – by, for example, folding in the Crimean Tatars with all other Tatars in the census. Finally, in 1987, a State Committee on the Crimean Tatars was set up, and from 1989 onward came a wave of return to the peninsula. By the start of 1996, there would be more than 220,000 Tatars in the Crimea.[82]

The Crimean Tatars demonstrated the new opportunities for national politics afforded by Gorbachev's glasnost. These were then seized to most impressive effect in the Baltic republics. The ice was broken in summer 1987 by a demonstration in Latvia to draw attention to the Molotov–Ribbentrop pact of August 1939 that gave the Soviet Union carte blanche in the Baltics. Another demonstration later in the year, to mark Latvia's independence day in 1918, was attacked by the police. After Moscow came clean about the Nazi–Soviet pact in the summer of 1989, any remaining legitimacy of Soviet rule in the Baltic region drained away. "Popular fronts" (to begin with, less overtly political than pro-independence nationalism) were eliciting impressive levels of social participation. In the most striking example, two million citizens of the region stood in a 370-mile chain from Vilnius to Tallinn to form a "Baltic Way" on 23 August 1989. Elections in the Baltic republics in early 1990 revealed a predictable split between pro-Soviet opinion in Russian-speaking areas and national separatist voting elsewhere, though the Latvian Popular Front also received many Russian votes. Lithuania declared its independence on 11 March 1990, which drew a pro-Soviet demonstration with around 30,000 participants. Beyond that, however, there was strikingly little mobilization of the pro-Soviet population, and no mass violence.[83]

The authorities in Moscow were not able to reconcile themselves to their unaccustomed powerlessness. After the Lithuanian declaration of independence, the Soviet center placed serious pressure on the republic: efforts were made to arrest Lithuanian deserters from the Soviet army, and an oil blockade placed serious strain on the local economy. Nonetheless, within weeks of the Lithuanian declaration, Estonia and Latvia had announced the start of transition to full independence. The final heavy-handed attempts to forestall Baltic independence came the following winter. Bomb attacks in Latvia seem to have been designed to destabilize the government there. In a conspiratorial but ultimately botched military intervention, Soviet troops killed 13 Lithuanians in Vilnius in January 1991 and injured several hundred more. A week later Soviet special forces launched an attack on the Latvian Interior Ministry. Yet, although the August 1991 coup brought a final short-lived attempt to regain Soviet control of Riga, the Baltic states were now too far on the road to independence to be held back.[84]

The Baltic republics became emblematic of national liberation struggles in the late Soviet period, but they were far from typical. Their combination of national consolidation and minimal bloodshed was not replicated elsewhere. National consciousness was a less straightforward affair in the westernmost Soviet republics of Ukraine, Belorussia, and Moldavia.

The story of Ukrainian politics is often told as a contest between a Ukrainian-speaking West and a Russian or Russified East. In reality, the notion of an East/West split fails to do justice to the country's regional diversity along ethnic, religious, and linguistic lines. In addition to "Russians" and "Ukrainians," moreover, there were plenty of people in the Ukrainian republic who were inclined to identify themselves as "Soviet." A survey of 1990–1 revealed that 43.4% of respondents who were officially "Russian" considered themselves Soviet, while another study of 1991 found that more than four out of five Russians in Ukraine referred to the Soviet Union, rather than Ukraine, as "their" country.[85] When the Ukrainian population voted overwhelmingly for Ukrainian independence in a referendum of 1 December 1991, this should not be mistaken for wholehearted endorsement of a Ukrainian national project; it was more a sign of the absence of viable alternatives to independence by that point. Likewise, when the incumbent Ukrainian elite turned in favor of independence in the autumn of 1991, this represented not a mass conversion to nationalism but rather an understanding that, following the failure of the August coup, the writing was on the wall for Soviet Communism. This political shift did not prevent corrupt ex-Communists retaining power in Ukraine into the early years of the twenty-first century.[86]

Nation-building turned out to be a more fractious affair in Moldova, a republic where ethnic and linguistic differences could less easily be fudged. The Soviet republic of Moldavia consisted largely of the territory of Bessarabia, which had first been annexed by the Russian empire in the early nineteenth century and had then, after spending the interwar period as part of Greater Romania, been taken over by the Soviet Union at the end of World War II. Moscow promptly took hard geopolitical measures to shore up the Sovietness of Moldavia, adding to the postwar republic a strip of territory across the Dnestr River (Transnistria) that had already been through two decades of Sovietization before the war as part of a "Moldavian Autonomous Republic" contained in the Ukrainian republic. Although accounting for not much more than a tenth of postwar Moldavia's population, Transnistria played a leading role in the republic's economy and political life. Suggestions of Moldovan national mobilization started in the 1960s, as Romania drew attention to its historical and linguistic affinities with its neighboring Soviet republic and hinted that the Soviet annexation was not altogether benign. On the Soviet side a battalion of Marxist theorists got to work proving the ethnic and linguistic separateness of the Moldavian nation from Romania, even if nothing more than the Cyrillic alphabet and a scattering of Russian loan words distinguished Moldovan from Romanian. The phase of ethnic mobilization in the 1980s brought a predictable outcome: the Moldavian elite – with the Bessarabian contingent more vocal than hitherto – argued for the Romanianness of Moldovan culture and pushed for independence from Moscow. A Popular Front mobilized in the late summer of 1989, as Moldova took its turn to protest against the iniquities of the Molotov–Ribbentrop Pact. But, while linguistic and historical concerns might be good for short-term mobilization, they could not overcome the basic ethnic and territorial divides of the country. Tensions between the Russian population and the Moldovan authorities brought armed conflict in Transnistria in 1992 that left a thousand dead and well over 100,000 displaced persons. Thereafter, Transnistria would have an uneasy but relatively stable existence as a Russian-backed enclave in the Moldovan state.[87]

This, however, might be considered a successful outcome compared to the Caucasus, a region that has become synonymous in the Russian imagination and in much non-Russian journalism with ethnic conflict. But even here, to ascribe violence in the late Soviet period to primordial and long-suppressed ethnic discord would be a gross oversimplification. A large factor in the rise of nationalism in the Caucasus in the late 1980s was the activity of local elites in mobilizing national sentiment once Moscow's authority and political apparatus started to weaken. Furthermore, to the extent that there was pre-existing antagonism, it usually had to do more with aspects of the Soviet experience than with anything primordial.

The ethno-territorial arrangements created by the Soviet state left political communities fragmented and weak. There were plenty of patron–client relations in the Soviet elite in the Caucasus, but little sense of where and how the boundaries of new political communities might be drawn. A case in point was Georgia, a tiny republic where democratization did not solve problems but rather created them. It upset the delicate balancing act performed by Soviet nationalities policy whereby ethnic enclaves might achieve administrative recognition as "autonomous republics" without threatening the prerogatives of the overall "titular" nationality. If union republics were to become nation states, Abkhazians or South Ossetians might outnumber Georgians in large electoral districts. How a republic like Georgia would move from its Soviet-style administrative hierarchy to a liberal multiethnic state was far from clear. In the event, it did not: the scholar and former dissident Zviad Gamsakhurdia came to power by making common cause with a popular nationalism that had little time for the large minorities in the north and west of the country. He soon proved unable to meet the considerable challenges of governing at a time of state collapse, prevaricated incomprehensibly at the time of the August coup, and was chased out by a coup in December 1991.[88]

Thus, the collapse of Soviet power in the Caucasus was far from being an example of postcolonial liberation. Rather, this was a fragmented and weakly governed borderland where national sentiment had the power to mobilize but was not necessarily well defined. Where the lines between national groups were clearly drawn, they reflected not antagonism toward oppressors in Moscow but rather hostility to groups much closer to hand. The worst ethnic violence of the late Soviet period came in Nagornyi Karabakh, a disputed enclave in the Azerbaijani republic whose population was largely Armenian. This territory had been a sore issue for decades, but it came to a head in the glasnost era. In February 1988 the Armenian-dominated local soviet of Nagornyi Karabakh declared its desire to join the Armenian republic. Mass rallies and rising nationalist militancy in the Armenian republic led many ethnic Azeris to flee. The reports they brought to Baku of mistreatment by Armenians, accompanied by the general radicalization of public opinion in Azerbaijan, brought catastrophe: at the end of February, the population of the overcrowded industrial town Sumgait, a mere twenty miles from the Azerbaijani capital Baku, launched a pogrom against the local Armenian population that killed almost 30 people and injured hundreds more. The authorities in Moscow failed to understand the gravity of the situation; Gorbachev continued to interpret events in the idiom of class rather than that of ethnic mobilization. To the extent that Moscow intervened, it managed to inflame the situation further: in January 1990, in an attempt to restore order after an even bloodier anti-Armenian pogrom, Soviet forces killed more than 130 Baku citizens. By this time, the two neighboring republics were embarked on a cycle of violence and counterviolence that would bring outright war in 1991 and an uneasy ceasefire only in May 1994.[89]

While the appalling escalation of violence over Nagornyi Karabakh was due largely to the actions (or inaction) of political elites, there was also a genuine long-standing territorial grievance that separated two national communities. Elsewhere in the region, however, national political life was altogether inchoate. As Party structures weakened in the North Caucasus, the way was open for aspiring leaders to experiment in their styles of self-presentation and their appeals to "their" community. A case in point was the autonomous republic of Kabardino-Balkaria, where existing power relations were disturbed in 1986 by the appointment of a complete outsider as first Party secretary. While this sort of personnel change was standard practice early in the tenure of a new Soviet leader, it had radical consequences when the political system itself started to undergo decentralization and democratization. One eloquent demonstration of the resulting political opportunities is the career of a certain Musa Shanib, a Circassian native of Kabardino-Balkaria. Formerly a sociologist and member of Soviet academia, Shanib turned to ethnic nationalism with all its more exotic trappings; he was especially devoted to the Circassian sheepskin hat, the *papakha*. His aim, in his biographer's phrase, was nothing less than to make himself the "Garibaldi of the Caucasus." In the early 1990s, as President of the Confederation of Mountain Peoples of the Caucasus, Shanib led a volunteer army to fight in support of Abkhazian independence. Soon after that his career as firebrand came to an end, and within a few years he had moved back into academia. For other participants in the ethnic politics of the late Soviet Caucasus, however, the move from Soviet professionalism to nationalist militancy was less reversible.[90]

A similar story of contingency and political indeterminacy can be told of the nationalist movement in the Caucasus that would have the most painful consequences in the post-Soviet era: Chechnya. What started in 1990 as a declaration of the "state sovereignty" of Checheno-Ingushetia became a Chechen revolution following the August 1991 coup in Moscow and then developed into a radical nationalist movement. It was headed by Dzhokhar Dudaev, who experienced a rapid conversion from loyal Soviet soldier to national separatist firebrand with a taste for theatrical dress and behavior. A textbook case of Soviet upward mobility, Dudaev had made a brilliant career in the military and had spent very little of his life in his "home" republic. What he knew about nationalism he had gleaned from serving in Estonia in the late 1980s. Chechen identity, as it emerged in 1990–4, had rather little to do with Islam and "clan" loyalty. Its main causes lay rather in the political vacuum following the Soviet collapse and the radicalization of a secular nationalism in the face of the threat of Russian intervention.[91]

Central Asia was another predominantly Muslim and (from a Russian perspective) culturally remote part of the Union. But its political trajectory could hardly have been more different from that of the North Caucasus. With one exception (Tajikistan), the incumbent nomenklatura maintained stable power under a new guise, and Communist authoritarianism became strong presidential rule. Patronage politics and clan networks had proved fully compatible with – indeed, had to a significant extent been fostered by – the Soviet state apparatus, and they would work just as well under conditions of national independence and selectively adopted market economy.

Central Asian leaders were forced to change their stripes in this way because of threats to their power emanating from Moscow. An efficiency drive reduced subsidies to the outlying republics, while an anticorruption campaign removed tens of thousands of office-holders. By attempting to crack down on clan politics, Gorbachev put the symbiotic relationship between Central Asian elites and the Soviet state under threat.[92] The democratization of the political system gave the Uzbek elite tools with which to fight back. At the first Congress of People's Deputies in 1989, Uzbek officials articulated public criticism of Moscow; the economic focus on cotton was a particular grievance, as was the Aral Sea ecological disaster. As the Soviet Union unraveled in 1991, the Uzbek leadership remained prudent but alert to opportunities. The president, Islam Karimov, hedged his bets at the time of the August coup in 1991, but resigned from the CPSU promptly after the coup failed. He then nationalized the Ministry of Internal Affairs and the KGB, making these institutions subordinate to the president.[93]

Other Central Asian republics, while they might have particular grievances against Moscow, remained the most loyal members of the Union to the very end. Turkmenistan declared sovereignty in August 1990 and achieved independence just over a year later, but its regime stayed open to the idea of a Soviet umbrella state.[94] Nursultan Nazarbaev, the Communist leader of Kazakhstan since 1989, insisted on the sovereignty of his state but also remained the staunchest supporter – other than Gorbachev – of the Soviet Union as a unified economic space.[95]

Where violence did occur in Central Asia, it was caused by local, economically rooted ethnic tensions rather than by any decolonizing impulse. Riots in Uzbekistan's Ferghana Valley in June 1989 were triggered by a marketplace confrontation between the minority Meskhetian Turks and local Uzbeks; hundreds of people died. The following summer in Kyrgyzstan something very similar occurred. In the southern city of Osh, conflict erupted between the local Kyrgyz population and the Uzbeks who were perceived to control the region's resources; 230 people were killed in a week. Here again, ethnic tensions were to a large extent conditioned by demographic and economic factors. The region was desperately poor, and access to land was a perennially difficult issue. The rural population had doubled between 1959 and 1989 – a period when it declined substantially in the USSR as a whole. The unemployed and the landless formed shanties on the outskirts of towns that could turn volatile at moments of stress.[96]

——————————— Post-Soviet Nation-building ———————————

Ethnic violence in the period 1987–91 was contingent and haphazard rather than preordained. That did not mean, however, that it would not recur after the collapse of Soviet power. The Soviet state had done a great deal to mix ethnic populations, and the complex ethno-federal structure of the USSR left as its legacy many territories that were likely to become objects of dispute between rival ethnic groups. As we have seen, some disputes of this kind erupted as the Soviet state became critically weak in the period 1988–91. The first, and one of the bloodiest, was the conflict between Armenia and Azerbaijan over Nagornyi Karabakh. The cease-fire of May 1994 brought no basis on which to achieve conflict resolution. Instead, the two sides remained locked in a "slow suicide pact" that not only blighted their own prospects but also snarled up the entire economy of the Caucasus.[97]

Several other conflicts broke out in the Caucasus region in the wake of the Soviet collapse. An Ingush–Ossetian war was the long-deferred legacy of the Ingush return from exile. A new law on the rehabilitation of repressed peoples, adopted in 1991, allowed for returnees to reclaim their land without clarifying how the inevitable disputes with the new occupants could be resolved. The result was a conflict that killed hundreds and displaced tens of thousands more. Independent Georgia was the scene for two protracted conflicts that arose from Soviet ethno-territorial arrangements. South Ossetia, an autonomous oblast within the Georgian republic, declared its sovereignty in September 1990; the response of the Georgian government was to cancel its autonomous status entirely. Armed conflict broke out in late 1991, and a cease-fire under Russian supervision was agreed in June 1992. But South Ossetia remained for Georgia a threat to national integrity and a galling reminder of Russian hegemony. In August 2008 a very different political regime in Tbilisi, headed by an American-educated 40-year-old rather than a Soviet dissident nationalist, showed it was no better able to resist Russian provocation: Mikheil Saakashvili launched an attack on South Ossetia that brought death and terror to the local population, swift defeat for Georgia, and the blighting of the country's prospects for the foreseeable future. A second separatist curse on post-Soviet Georgia was Abkhazia, a scenic coastal region adjoining Russia which in Soviet times had enjoyed the status of autonomous republic within Georgia. With Russian support, Abkhazia declared its independence in July 1992. The ensuing war of 1992–3 created more than 200,000 Georgian refugees and led to a troubled peace under close Russian supervision. To complete the story of strife in the post-Soviet Caucasus, between 1994 and 1996 the Russian Federation fought an even more destructive war against its own separatist region: Chechnya.

But the Caucasus was perhaps the exception rather than the rule; we should remember the list of conflicts that did *not* erupt into violence after the Soviet collapse. There was every reason to suppose that the fate of diaspora populations in the Soviet successor states would be an acutely difficult issue. In the aftermath of the Soviet collapse, more than 40 million people (and 25 million Russians) lived outside their Soviet-defined "homeland." Such diasporas were likely to be especially troublesome in states where the indigenous people were in a demographically weak position and the diaspora nationalities were large enough to cause trouble: Kazakhstan (only just over 40 percent Kazakh), Kyrgyzstan, Latvia, and Estonia. Yet, in the event, the only place where the presence of a Russian diaspora brought violent conflict was Transnistria, where it was modest by the standards of South Ossetia (let alone Chechnya).

To be sure, relations between Russia and the new Baltic states were at best frosty, and the accession of the latter to the European Union did nothing to improve them. Latvia and Estonia were aggressive in their legislation against the local Russian population, which was largely disenfranchised in the elections of 1992 and 1993 by new citizenship laws.[98] They also committed numerous offenses against the renascent Russian cult of World War II. In the worst of several spats, the leaders of Estonia and Lithuania declined to attend the sixtieth anniversary celebrations in Moscow in 2005.

With most of the other eleven Soviet republics, however, Russia maintained close and reasonably harmonious relations which neither side was willing to jeopardize on account of diaspora issues.[99] The potentially troublesome situation in Kazakhstan was eased by the stable rule of Nazarbaev, a virtuoso political operator in a republic where the titular nationality made up well under half of the population. Nazarbaev defused ethnic tensions, insisting on a "nationalism by soil" rather than "'nationalism by blood." It helped that he had unchallenged political supremacy bolstered by vast natural resources that placed Kazakhstan second only behind Russia among ex-Soviet republics.[100]

Nazarbaev's was not the only Central Asian regime that had become a nation by default. But accidental birth did not make such states unviable. The high degree of continuity between Soviet and post-Soviet political elites brought these states what political scientists call "pacted stability."[101] Once established in their new offices, post-Soviet leaders could find their own ways to maintain their power, whether by cultivating national identity or through old-style patronage politics (or, most likely, by some combination of the two). Turkmenistan's Saparmurat Niyazov in due course opted for an old-fashioned cult of personality, complete with a rotating gold-plated statue of himself in the capital. Uzbekistan's Karimov was a master of Stalinesque "neopatrimonialism" who played different agencies off against each other (even if by 2005, a year of mass unrest in Andijan, this arrangement was apparently coming under strain).[102] Kyrgyzstan was somewhat less illiberal, combining the apparels of democratic life with strong presidential rule. The collapse of the country's first post-Soviet regime in March 2005 was quickly dubbed the Tulip Revolution, a tag that seemed to overstate the degree of fundamental political change that had occurred. Where there was strife in post-Soviet Central Asia – in Tajikistan – it was caused less by ethnic discord than by the fact that the clan most favored under the Soviet regime had monopolized power and resources. Moscow had channeled resources to the Leninabad region and allowed its elite to lord it over the rest of the republic. When Soviet power collapsed, this situation was no longer tolerated by rival elites. The ensuing civil war – which may have killed as many as 100,000 people – was "not an ethnic or religious conflict but rather an Afghanistan-style internecine struggle among various Tadjik warlords from different provinces."[103]

In the early twenty-first century it was clear that no state in Central Asia – with the partial exception of Kyrgyzstan – had done much to build a democratic nation-state where sovereignty would rest with a people rather than a ruling clique. Ostensibly more promising cases were to be found in the western republics, which had experienced a greater level of political mobilization and social participation in the Gorbachev period. Here too, however, hopes of post-Soviet national rebirth soon seemed overblown. In 1994 Belarus elected a president, Aleksandr Lukashenka, who would soon become the most unabashed authoritarian leader west of Turkmenistan. Lukashenka maneuvered effectively between Russia and the European Union in his efforts to shore up Belarusian statehood. In the domestic arena he fashioned an "egalitarian nationalism" that relied less on notions of ethnic distinctiveness – which, given the highly Russified Belarusian population, would have sent even the most talented spin doctor into contortions – than on an ideology of sovereignty, unity, and antiliberalism.[104] Where ideology reached its limits, any dissent could be – and was – violently suppressed.

In Ukraine, meanwhile, ethnic issues were harder to ignore. A survey of the whole country in 1993–4 found that just over a quarter of respondents identified themselves as Russian and Ukrainian simultaneously.[105] In addition to the divisions between Russians, Ukrainians, Russian Ukrainians, and Ukrainian Russians, the government had to contend with the large and contentious separatist peninsula of Crimea, which, as well as being ethnically mixed, was disputed territory between Ukraine and Russia. In the event, the solution to the standoff between the governments in Crimea and Kiev was elite bargaining, which, while messy and protracted, did at least prevent ethnic strife.[106]

The lack of violence was a great blessing, but it was bought at the price of the domination of political life by a closed group of ex-Soviet functionaries and their associates in the business and criminal communities. All the while, in the absence of effective economic policy, the country's fortunes remained heavily dependent on Russian energy subsidies. Thus, the first decade in the life of post-Soviet

Ukraine was not quite so far removed from the Central Asian pattern as geography might suggest. The situation changed in the early twenty-first century, as a challenge to the status quo emerged from within the political establishment – the only place from which it could realistically come – in the form of the liberal-minded and economically principled Viktor Yushchenko. In November 2004, an especially egregious attempt by the ruling establishment to steal the presidential election – having already attempted to kill Yushchenko – provoked peaceful but determined mass protest. In what was instantly branded the Orange Revolution, Yushchenko was brought to power by nonviolent means. Here, for sure, was a moment when a national community threw off the shackles of Soviet political networks and corrupt "virtual democracy." Questions remained, however, about the longer-term capacity of the fractious team of Viktor Yushchenko and Yulia Tymoshenko to transcend their own growing animosity, the fundamental flaws in Ukrainian political order, and the country's regional, ethnic, and political divides.[107]

The adequacy of the political system to build a national community was no less in question in the largest ex-Soviet republic. Russia, like other parts of the Soviet Union, experienced a national revolution in 1991: the institutions of the Russian nation asserted their legitimacy, threw off the carapace of the Soviet political system, and seized control of Soviet assets on Russian territory. Politics, however, was one thing; society and ideology quite another. Russian national identity, like its counterparts in Chechnya or Ukraine, was a work in progress throughout the 1990s. The tensions and ambiguities were so great, in fact, that Russian nationalism may be regarded as the laggard among post-Soviet identities. The Russian Federation that emerged from the Soviet collapse was a complex ethno-territorial entity. It contained several flashpoints in the Caucasus as well as the obstreperous Muslim republics of Tatarstan and Bashkortostan; its total Muslim population was around 15 million.[108] Russia also lacked a workable national ideology. It was far from clear how the country might conceive of itself in national, post-Soviet terms: Russian identity was so closely tied to the Soviet state, and the new Russian regime was overseeing so traumatic and unpopular a package of economic reforms, that civil war between Russians loyal to the "Soviet" version of Russianness and their more liberal "post-Soviet" counterparts was more than an abstract possibility. Was the new Russia to define itself ethnically, culturally, civically, or geopolitically?

The question was answered in immediate administrative terms by the passing of a liberal citizenship law in November 1991, which imposed no language requirement and allowed residents of other Soviet republics to move to Russia and claim automatic citizenship.[109] But Russian national identity remained vague and incoherent. Anti-Westernism simmered in the background, yet the reality was that Russians, thanks to their new freedom of movement and communication,

FIGURE 7.3   Overlapping identities: Muslim veterans of World War II at Friday prayers, Moscow 1999.
Source: © Alexandre Shemlyaev / PhotoSoyuz.

were able to feel citizens of the world to a wholly unprecedented extent; "the West" could no longer serve as bogeyman as it had done in Soviet times. Russia had a glorious superpower history, but one that was contaminated by awareness of the suffering inflicted by the Soviet regime on its own population. Russia was an Orthodox country where the Church and the government were entering a close embrace, but the reality was that the ex-Soviet population was overwhelmingly secular and church attendance remained low by American standards. Russia fought a war against Chechnya between 1994 and 1996, but the 1990s also saw a large public revival of Islam: by 1998 Russia had more than 5,500 registered mosques, of which more than a third were in Chechnya and almost as many in Dagestan. Tatarstan had about 5,000 Muslim clerics (as compared with only thirty in the late 1980s). In 1997, space was found for a mosque on Poklonnaia gora, perhaps the most sacred of Moscow's patriotic sites.[110]

Such contradictions were frustrating to would-be ideologues, but they made Russia a relatively pluralist and liberal place in the 1990s. The end of the decade, however, brought a sharp move toward a more categorical nationalist discourse. The trigger was a second war against Chechnya. This conflict may not have been a "small victorious war" any more than its forerunner, but the string of terrorist

atrocities that preceded and accompanied it led the majority of the Russian population to see themselves as a national community under threat. In their sensitive
early stages, and for some time thereafter, nationalisms need a defining Other
more than anything else; Chechnya served this purpose for Russia in the early
years of the twenty-first century. The war was accompanied in the state-dominated media by ferocious anti-Islamist rhetoric that combined awkwardly with
more tolerant policies toward the entirely nonradical Muslims to be found in
other parts of the Russian Federation. The very tragic irony was that militant
Islam in the Caucasus was the creation of Russia's first war with Chechnya,
which radicalized, brutalized, and "re-traditionalized" the Chechen national
community.[111]

Following the shift to state-led patriotism in 1999–2000, a number of other
constituent elements of a robust Russian identity slotted into place. Russia had
not become devout, but Orthodoxy was serving its purpose as a badge of cultural
identity – rather like Jewishness for many secular Americans.[112] The country was
emerging from ten years of practically unceasing economic crisis and could shed
many of its feelings of national humiliation. The crucial factor in the new Russian
nationalism, however, was the depoliticization of much of the Soviet past. As well
as an Other, nationalism needs a coherent and evocative narrative of common
origins. The rise of the Soviet Union to superpower provided just that. And,
whereas ten years previously an account of Soviet history had to acknowledge its
vastly traumatic aspects, now it could be recast as triumph and vindication: Stalin
was a war leader, not a mass murderer. The Soviet legacy, rather than casting a
shadow, provided ideological shelter for a revived Russianness.

8

Geopolitical Imperatives

On the question of Russia's long-term role in world politics, as on so much else, historical opinion is polarized. Any number of observers, both near and far, have seen Russia as a rapacious imperialist or a thug among Great Powers, always inclined to throw its considerable if shapeless weight around with the impunity granted by its geographical remoteness, its large resources, and its subservient population. Another view stresses Russia's perennial and paradoxical sense of vulnerability, seeing it as the victim of its own enormous land mass and consequent openness to unwelcome incursions. As the first sentence of one weighty treatment of Russian history in the *longue durée* puts it: "The north Eurasian plain is not only Russia's geographical setting, but also her fate."[1]

Both of these interpretations capture something important about Russia's political relationship to the wider world, but the second of them perhaps requires special pleading in a history of the Cold War era. Between the mid-1940s and the late 1980s, Russia went far beyond what foes and friends alike had seen as its destiny as a contiguous Eurasian empire. Besides its long-standing areas of non-European geopolitical concern (Manchuria, Afghanistan, Turkey, Iran), it devised ambitious policies for most of the rest of the globe. Even Latin America, marginal to its interests, became a focus of attention. From 1973 to the mid-1980s, for example, the Soviet Union sold more than $1.6 billion's worth of arms to Peru.[2] But Russia embarked suddenly on this forty-year era of superpower status following an interwar period when its geopolitical fortunes had come close to their nadir. The USSR had found itself in a tense and beleaguered international position throughout the 1920s and 1930s; its rulers braced themselves for a major European war that they regarded as inevitable (but strangely failed to anticipate when it finally arrived). The devastation wrought by the Nazis, it goes without saying, only heightened the Soviet sense of vulnerability.

Yet, by 1945, that notion of vulnerability was fast becoming counterintuitive: the Soviet leadership had armies of occupation deep in central Europe, and soon it would have the opportunity (or face the temptation) to influence political outcomes in many other parts of the world as well. It might seem that this global remit would come naturally to the USSR, given Russia's lengthy imperial past and the Bolshevik ideology of international revolution. But in fact this was empire in a different sense, and on a different scale, from any known previously. The USSR had to contend with centrifugal tendencies in various satellite states as well as with a new global order where the USA, not Europe, was the main rival.

The Postwar Disorder

The Soviet Union had eastern Europe at its mercy by the middle of 1945. In May 1946, the Americans estimated the figures of 700,000 troops in Romania, 65,000 in Hungary, and 280,000 in Bulgaria.[3] In February 1947, even after several waves of demobilization, there were still half a million Soviet troops in eastern Germany.[4] Never had there been a more propitious moment for Soviet socialism to bestride the international stage.

What this implied was a standoff between two revolutionary regimes (the American and the Russian, founded respectively in 1776 and 1917), both of them with strong messianic elements, but with radically different political cultures: in one camp stood the values of freedom, Christianity, commerce and the individual; in the other were gathered coercion, Marxism, centralization and the collective. Was not conflict preordained?[5]

Perhaps so. But the likelihood of conflict was also lessened by the genuine reluctance, on both sides of the ideological divide, to enter into further confrontations after the defeat of Germany and Japan. The Soviet Union had in fact been more messianic earlier in its life span, although even this had not prevented it from seeking to establish relations with the USA. The main obstacle to such relations had been America's reluctance to recognize the socialist state, which it finally did in 1933.

Above all, however, these were two unsuspecting superpowers. They were not afflicted by a fit of absence of mind, as the Victorian J. R. Seeley suggested was the case with the British empire, but nor were they obviously orientated toward the global imperial role. The USA had been the pre-eminent economic power of the planet since World War I, but its behavior on the international arena had been notably diffident. Woodrow Wilson redrew some borders and left the Europeans to their own devices. Later on, the Great Depression had merely exaggerated a pre-existing American propensity to isolationism.

The Soviets had much less far to look for an ideology of global domination. The Bolsheviks had come to power in 1917 on the confident expectation that their coup d'état, which most contemporary commentators regarded as foolhardy as well as egregious, would be lent permanence by a wave of like-minded social revolutions in central and eastern Europe. Otherwise, it was hard to conceive how a small core of revolutionaries could hold power in the face of huge internal opposition and in the midst of a world war that Russia seemed poised to lose.

The Bolsheviks, of course, did survive, for a variety of reasons. Their internal enemies were divided, poorly connected, and made serious tactical and strategic errors. The Bolsheviks were good organizers and propagandists, and gained genuine, if sometimes only short-term, support from many soldiers, workers, and even peasants. And the potentially predatory imperialist powers (notably Germany and Britain) were busy enough fighting each other that they did not have time to destroy a revolutionary regime that, given their undivided attention, would surely have toppled.

But the Bolsheviks, much to their chagrin, were not able to trigger an avalanche of European revolutions. There were socialist takeovers in Germany and Hungary, but these were soon suppressed. On its creation in 1922, the USSR had to face many new countries in central and eastern Europe that did not embrace socialism and would show little prospect of doing so in the interwar period. This regrettable state of affairs required significant doctrinal revisions in the Soviet camp. The outcome of the process of rethinking was "socialism in one country," Stalin's famous slogan of the mid-1920s: the overriding objective was now to defend the interests and the security of the one Communist state that actually existed. The Soviet regime did not give up on its long-term ambition of spreading socialism west. But it pursued this aim not through its own Foreign Ministry but through the Communist International (Comintern).

The Soviet Union thus pursued a two-track foreign policy through the interwar period. But the primary and undiminishing concern of this foreign policy was the survival of the socialist state, an outcome that seemed anything but guaranteed in 1927 (the time of a major war scare) or 1931 (the Japanese occupation of Manchuria) or 1938 (the Nazi annexation of Czechoslovakia). On the question of the future, Soviet ideology and statist pragmatism spoke as one (and spoke more presciently than, say, English liberalism): a future large-scale war, in which major hostile powers would attempt to destroy the Soviet Union, was inevitable. The task, as Stalin saw it, was to delay the war as long as possible so that the USSR could build its industrial war economy, and preferably to ensure that the "imperialist" powers attacked each other before they turned their attention to the Soviets. In this context, the Nazi–Soviet pact of 1939, which directly contradicted all recent policy and threw socialists (both inside and outside the Soviet Union) into confusion and dismay, made perfect sense.[6]

In September 1939, according to the spheres of influence agreed in the secret protocol to their pact, the Nazis and the Soviets began to carve up eastern Europe between them. The Soviet share was Eastern Poland, the Baltic states, Finland, and Bessarabia. The Soviet regime encouraged interethnic violence (notably between Ukrainians and Poles) and wasted little time in imprisoning, deporting, or executing "socially dangerous elements." It also perpetrated unspeakable war crimes (without the justification of the subsequent Nazi-inflicted brutalization of the Eastern Front). In the most notorious of these, the Kremlin authorized the murder of around 20,000 Poles, many of whom were later found buried in the Katyn forest near Smolensk. Soviet occupation was almost certainly more destructive than German occupation in the period from September 1939 to June 1941.[7]

But the arrests and killings, or the seizure of Polish territory that made them possible, were not driven by an ideology of transcontinental conquest or the international spread of socialism. Stalin's primary concern at this moment, as it had been for the previous decade, was security. And security, in his view, was best served by territorial expansion: by pushing the border of the Soviet Union west and using Poland and the Baltic states as a buffer zone against German aggression. The same considerations of border security underlay acts of ethnic cleansing that had started in the late 1930s and would intensify during the war: Koreans, Poles, Volga Germans, and several other national groups were deported en masse because they were thought to represent a fifth column in geopolitically sensitive regions of the USSR.

By creating punitive and exploitative occupation regimes in Poland and the Baltic states, the Soviets ensured that large parts of the populations in those regions would welcome the German invasion when it finally came. At this cost, Stalin bought himself somewhat less than two years' grace from Hitler. One of the more surprising misjudgments in history was this notoriously suspicious dictator's stubborn refusal, in the face of overwhelming evidence of German preparations for war, to believe in the impending attack until, in the early hours of 22 June 1941, it actually occurred.

Several reasons for this error can be adduced: the reluctance of a leader (especially a dictator) to acknowledge that a deeply controversial policy (of rapprochement with Nazi Germany) had proved misguided, or his inability to believe anything (especially the truth), or his fear of provoking the Germans into an attack, or the difficulty of processing intelligence effectively in a brutal dictatorship, where the regime has much information at its disposal but few good means of assessing its reliability.[8] But, if international history is our main concern, one reason for Stalin's oversight seems particularly worthy of attention: the Soviet leader, head of the leading ideocratic country in the world at that time, misread the ideology of his Nazi counterpart. If Hitler had been the kind of Western imperialist, hungry for political advantage and economic resources but unwilling to risk overturning the European state system, that Stalin knew from the classic Leninist writings, he would not have launched a full-scale assault on the USSR in the middle of 1941. In reality, as the Soviet people would soon discover, he was something rather different: an inveterate geopolitical gambler on an astonishing lucky streak, and also a racist colonialist who would seize the opportunity to subjugate the Slavs and destroy the Jewish–Bolshevik scourge in its heartland. Effectively, Hitler was to apply the most vicious methods of extra-European imperialism to the European continent.[9]

The German invasion quickly forced upon Stalin unprecedented ideological concessions. He adopted the rhetoric of national community in direct preference to that of internationalism or socialism. The Orthodox Church was granted a place of prominence in national life. And the USSR was forced into alliance with Western powers – notably the British – that before 1941 would have been regarded as imperialists of the same stamp as the Germans. Indiscriminate opposition to rapacious capitalists was dropped, and in 1943 the Comintern was disbanded.

This is not to say that the relationship between the wartime allies was free of tension. The Soviets resented the Anglo–American delay in opening a second front in the West, and worried constantly that the British would agree a separate peace with the Nazis. The British and Americans had exactly the same concern about the Soviets. But the alliance held together – because it had to – and from late 1943 onward the thoughts of the major powers turned to the nature of the postwar order.

Here we come up against all the key questions of the historiography of the early Cold War. How did this postwar order turn so confrontational so quickly? Why did the habits of wartime cooperation not prove more enduring? How important was ideology, and what role should we ascribe to contingency and pragmatism? Were individual statesmen making rational and informed choices, or were they swayed by prejudice, opportunism, or domestic considerations? Was the Cold War the product of accident or of design?

Of these questions, only the last seems amenable to a reasonably straightforward answer: accident played a much greater role than design. But all the other issues hang in uneasy balance. Whichever side of the Cold War divide we look, it would be ill-judged to rule out either pragmatism or ideology in historical causation. What does seem critical, however, is that ideology and Realpolitik were out of kilter for a formative period in the late 1940s. Habits of thinking, especially when they are backed up by huge armies and entrenched in bureaucracies, are extraordinarily hard to shift. The Soviet Union had just beaten off a threat to its very existence, losing nearly 30 million of its citizens in the process. In 1945 or even 1948 it was counterintuitive to see the USSR as one half of a global bipolar order. In the late 1940s, as in the 1930s, security was a pervasive preoccupation of Soviet thinking on international affairs. The overarching ideological framework was also substantially borrowed from the prewar period. Soviet Russia was again surrounded by intrinsically hostile capitalist powers, who in due course would again enter conflict with the USSR and with each other as they competed for world markets. The British were still not to be trusted, and the Germans would eventually remilitarize and cause further trouble. The Second World War would not be the last conflict of that scale. As Stalin is reported to have said in this era: "The First World War tore one country out of capitalist slavery. The Second World War created the socialist system, and the third will finish imperialism forever."[10]

The quest for security, then, lies at the heart of Soviet motives in the early Cold War. But security, to the Stalinist mindset, was best realized through the acquisition of territory: it went hand in hand with empire-building. Stalin's underlying somber assessment of global affairs was alleviated by the considerable geopolitical advantages of the Soviet position in 1945. The principal European aggressor, Germany, was militarily and politically broken for the medium term. The Soviet Union's favorite method of increasing security – territorial expansion – could now be indulged to the full. The Soviets now had a buffer zone far greater even than what they had obtained in the Molotov–Ribbentrop pact: in addition to the western expansion of the USSR, they could now unquestionably control political outcomes in Poland, Eastern Germany, Czechoslovakia, Hungary, Bulgaria, and Romania. Even in a worst-case scenario, the next global conflict would be a few years in the future, by which time the USSR would be in a more robust state.

Within the limits of this security-conscious imperialist ideology – the belief that the forces of liberal capitalism and state socialism could not avoid confrontation for ever, and that in the meantime all necessary steps must be taken to maintain the security of socialism – Soviet foreign policy in the late 1940s was relatively flexible. Stalin did not care to antagonize the Western powers where he saw no practical advantage in doing so. He had no interest in supporting the Communist side in the Greek civil war, and turned against the Yugoslavs in early 1948 when they took this line. He refrained from committing himself to the Communists in the Chinese civil war until a relatively advanced stage of that conflict. Even where Stalin did precipitate diplomatic standoffs with the West and its allies, he did so in an attempt to further Soviet security and territorial interests rather than to boost the cause of world Communism. In 1945, the USSR issued demands to Turkey that provoked that country to declare martial law and suppress both socialist parties. The main longer-term effect of the Soviet action was that it hastened Turkey's entry into NATO (which occurred in 1952). In Iran, Stalin disregarded calls from local Communists for a revolutionary insurrection and instead squeezed the Iranian government for oil concessions, increasing the pressure by backing Azeri separatism in the northern part of the country and leaving Soviet occupation forces in the country beyond the agreed withdrawal date at the end of 1945.[11] Here again, Stalin's tactical misjudgments led to long-term strategic losses: Iranian Communism suffered a severe setback, and the Iranians were thrust into the embrace of the Americans with whom they maintained close relations until the Islamist revolution of 1979.

Stalin undoubtedly made errors in the Black Sea region and the Middle East. But he invested effort and prestige into these areas because he viewed them as traditional and entirely legitimate areas for Soviet geopolitical concern. The ultimate confirmation of the primacy of time-honored geopolitical opportunism in Soviet thinking came on 18 May 1948, when the USSR, a state led by a hyper-suspicious anti-Semite, became the first country to grant formal recognition to the state of Israel. The desire to cause trouble for the British proved stronger in Stalin's mind than the world's oldest conspiracy theory (though this order of priorities would soon be reversed, when the objective of getting the British out of Palestine had been achieved and Jewish nationalism appeared to be having a resurgence in the USSR).

Soviet foreign policy had a superstructure of revolutionary ideology, but its base was old-style imperialism: the world was structured by a fundamental division between strong and weak states, and the strong would divide up the world as they saw fit, and with due concern for their own security. In the immediate aftermath of the war, however, Stalin did not realize that this view of the world was already anachronistic. It depended on the existence of several Great Powers of approximately equal strength, each with their own conflicting interests and spheres of influence. In such a multipolar world, the capitalist powers could be relied on to attack each other (a socialist state, by contrast, kept out of cut-throat global capitalist competition and so had a greater chance of being left in one piece). The problem, however, was that the formerly multipolar world had since 1945 become bipolar: the European empires that had previously been rivals of each other at least as much as they had been rivals of Russia were now allied with the USA and dependent on American economic and military muscle.

This shift to bipolarity meant that Stalin's Marxist–Leninist rhetoric and saber-rattling (in Turkey, Iran, and in due course Berlin) had more serious consequences than the Soviet dictator anticipated: the Western allies were increasingly inclined to see them as expressions of a radically hostile geopolitical agenda rather than as conventional (if often deplorable) maneuvers in the quest for influence and strategic advantage. By the time that Stalin's thinking had begun to catch up with this new global reality, much damage had already been done: Churchill had delivered his Fulton speech, and in March 1947 the American president had declared the "Truman Doctrine" of support for "free peoples" facing the threat of "subjugation." What finally led Stalin to understand that relationships among the Western powers were characterized more by collaboration under the American aegis than by competition was the Marshall Plan for economic aid, publicly announced and proffered to all European countries in June 1947.

The growing realization of a less complexly confrontational world order brought the Soviets little succor. From their perspective, bipolarity was far more dangerous than the alternatives: from now on, the forces of world capitalism would be arrayed against them rather than against each other. In 1947, the Soviets showed their readiness for the new order with two powerful public gestures. First, they declined the Marshall Plan and prevailed upon their bloc in eastern Europe to do the same. Second, they issued what would retrospectively be viewed as their Cold War manifesto, their equivalent of the Truman Doctrine: Zhdanov's speech at a conference of European Communist parties in Poland at the end of September, which imposed a rigid "two camps" model of international relations.

The main testing ground for the first phase of the confrontation between socialism and capitalism was central and eastern Europe. This was a very different matter from Turkey or Iran. That Poland and Czechoslovakia should subscribe to "democratic socialism" was an entirely nonnegotiable requirement of the Soviet regime. Western politicians might have felt betrayed by Soviet tactics in eastern Europe, though they had few good reasons for doing so: it was clear enough by 1934, let alone by 1945, what Stalinists meant by "democracy." Winston Churchill might have liked to think that he held the Soviets at bay by sketching out the notorious "percentages agreement," but by the time of this wartime summit Stalin had most of eastern Europe firmly in his sights and was not about to be distracted. The reality of Soviet troops on the ground was far more powerful than any diplomatic arguments. By the end of the 1940s, the rigid and coercive structures of Soviet socialism had been superimposed on the whole of the eastern bloc.

This is not to say that even Stalin had fixed notions in 1945 as to how he would arrive at this desirable outcome. He had no inclination to provoke anti-Communist resistance where it could be avoided without compromising on basic Soviet geopolitical goals, and every interest in sparing scarce Soviet economic and state-building resources. The Soviet occupation of eastern Germany, for example, was seriously hampered by the lack of suitable cadres.

There were also good reasons to suppose that at least some eastern European societies might go along with Soviet designs if they were not excessively provoked. With the exception of Czechoslovakia, these countries did not have previous experience of stable parliamentary democracy. Their peoples were hungry, desperate, and displaced (more than 11 million were on the move at the time of liberation, and even more than that would be forced to leave their homes over the next three years as ethnicity and state boundaries were made to match up), preoccupied more with food and shelter than with their democratic rights.[12] Landowning classes and middle classes had been destroyed, notably in Poland (where, for example, more than half of all lawyers, and nearly 40 percent of physicians, had died during the war).[13] Nor, finally, was it absurd to imagine that people might vote Communist if free elections were permitted: they could hardly look back fondly on the recent political alternatives. From June 1945 onward the Soviets could proclaim that they had been the first of the occupying powers in Germany to allow the formation of political parties in their zone (even if they had a very particular sense of what direction those parties might take).

However, elections in November 1945 in Hungary and Austria showed that Communism would not triumph in eastern Europe without a good deal of help from the Soviet Union. Two years of maneuvering mixed with sheer violence and skulduggery ensued. The main tactical operation was to gather all "progressive" parties into broad democratic fronts that in time would be converted into single-party regimes. Socialists and agrarian parties were "encouraged" to join Communist parties whose hard core was usually provided by hand-picked cadres who might have spent more of their political careers in exile in the Soviet Union than in their home countries. If this form of consolidation did not work on its own, then terror and fraud could complete the job. Thus were elections in Poland in January 1947 allegedly won by a "Democratic Bloc" with just over 80 percent. The leader of the main alternative, the Peasant Party, was forced to flee to the West in October 1947. The Czechoslovaks, who were less crucial geopolitically and whose Communists were quite successful in their own right, were allowed to go their own way for longer. In free elections of May 1946, the Communists received a respectable 38 percent of the vote, but the following year the Soviets lost patience, forcing Czechoslovakia to turn down Marshall Aid and then orchestrating a violent Communist seizure of power in February 1948. The Hungarians, among whom the Communist presence had always been far smaller than in Czechoslovakia, were allowed to have a free election in November 1945 where the Smallholders gained 57 percent and the Communists only 17 percent. By August 1947, despite intimidation and fraud, the Communist Party only had a little more than 20 percent of the vote in parliamentary elections. In March 1948, the Social Democrats were forced to merge with the Communists, and the triumph of the new socialist bloc was confirmed by the sham parliamentary elections of 15 May 1949.[14]

Following the rejection of the Marshall Plan, Soviet intervention became more direct and more violent. Local Communist parties fell into line, in the process organizing purges and show trials that were grim replications of practices introduced with less unseemly haste in Moscow in the 1930s. In classic Soviet style, the victims were often convicted of an ideological deviation personified by one man. In the first half of 1948, Tito suddenly became the postwar Trotsky, and Yugoslavia went very quickly from serving as the Stalin's enforcer in the Cominform (the postwar successor organization to the Comintern) to taking the role of bogeyman.

But that left the altogether less straightforward case of Germany. At issue here was not only the political orientation of the country's postwar system but its very borders. The key question was whether, following a period of four-power occupation, Germany should once again be unified. The wartime summits showed that Soviet plans for Germany were fluid and opportunistic (with the proviso that the USSR would always reserve a determining role for itself). But in 1945 Stalin's solution of preference was to maintain an undivided Germany by setting up a "democratic" regime that would be sympathetic to the Soviet Union. The impetus would, of course, come from the east. In their own zone of occupation, the Soviets pursued a typical policy of left-wing consolidation. In April 1946, under duress, the well-established German Social Democratic Party, a long-standing butt of hostile Soviet propaganda, fused with the Communist Party in a Socialist Unity Party (SED) whose day-to-day operations were under the close supervision of Soviet political officers. The notion that the SED could win Germany over to socialism soon came to seem highly questionable: the Eastern Germans, alienated by the Soviet invasion and occupation and by the SED's burgeoning reputation as a Soviet stooge, delivered a strong anti-Communist vote in local elections of autumn 1946.

By 1948, following the stiffening of resolve on both sides of the emerging Cold War, a divided Germany looked increasingly likely. But that left the question of Berlin, still under four-power jurisdiction. When the Western Allies announced plans for a new West German state, and soon after declared the introduction of a new currency on its territory, Stalin decided to use the de facto Soviet military encirclement of Berlin to force concessions: either the Western powers would give up their idea of a separate West German state or they would give up Berlin. The western half of the divided city was blockaded for eleven months, from June 1948 to May 1949, during which it was kept supplied by Allied airmen. Stalin's ill-considered confrontational policy had the effect of hastening the outcome he was keen to forestall – the permanent division of Germany – and also failed to secure Berlin for the Soviet bloc. Rather, Stalin's pursuit of tactical advantage had exacerbated tensions, ideologized the Cold War conflict in the eyes of opponents for whom the Soviets would stop at nothing to ensure their domination of central Europe, and guaranteed that the Americans would maintain a long-term military presence on the borders of the socialist bloc.

On the question of Germany, Soviet foreign policy came up against its own contradictions. The goals of geopolitical security and imperial expansion might have seemed mutually reinforcing in the western borderlands of the USSR, in Poland, and even in Czechoslovakia. To establish a Soviet client state in eastern Germany, however, was to take the Soviet empire into a part of central Europe that was bound to be vigorously contested and to assume a draining long-term military commitment in support of an otherwise unviable political entity. The alternative – to work with the Western powers to establish a single, demilitarized but nonsocialist German state – was distasteful to what Hannes Adomeit has called the Soviet "imperial and ideological paradigm." The result of this contradiction was that Stalin's Berlin policy was fundamentally ambiguous: was the German capital a "lever" for achieving the creation of a single German state on more favorable terms or a geopolitical "prize" in its own right? Stalin kept his options open until his own error of judgment over the Berlin blockade left him with only one.[15]

In sum, Soviet foreign policy in the early Cold War era was ideological and imperialistic, but the ideology was that of security and territory rather than world revolution. Although the rhetoric of Marxism-Leninism implied rigidity, it was not incompatible with opportunism and Realpolitik in matters geopolitical. The Western Allies can been forgiven for having thought differently at the time, but Stalin did not have visions of European conquest. He would push territorial expansion only so far as he could without risking armed conflict. Particularly indicative of his frame of mind is the extreme sangfroid with which he treated the nuclear imbalance that existed until the successful Soviet test of August 1949. Although Stalin spared no resources in developing the bomb in the USSR, he did not see that nuclear weapons might make a fundamental difference to the conduct of war. It was not the Allied arsenal that put Stalin off invading western Europe – or indeed West Berlin – in the late 1940s: military action of this kind went far beyond his security objectives. As far as Stalin was concerned, this was an old-style war of nerves, not a gamble with the future of humanity.[16] The acquisition by both sides of unprecedented weapons of mass annihilation was subsequently an important conditioning factor in the superpower confrontation, but these destructive capacities do not provide a satisfactory account of the origins of the Cold War. Nor do they do much to explain the raising of its temperature in the early 1950s.

----------- The Cold War Turns Global -----------

A crucial part in the early Cold War was played by the various "hot" wars that took place in Asia in the late 1940s and early 1950s. The first of these that required the attention of the Kremlin was the Chinese civil war fought from June 1946 between the nationalists of Chiang Kaishek and the Communists led by Mao. For the first year or more of this conflict the Soviets were noncommittal. They had already established relations with the incumbent nationalist regime, which they had relied on to oppose the Japanese; Mao, by contrast, had in 1941 declined Stalin's request to assist in fighting the Japanese. Stalin was, moreover, apprehensive of the international ramifications if the Communists were to take power in Manchuria.[17]

But the main reason for Soviet hesitancy on the Chinese question was that Stalin and Mao had different notions of what Chinese Communism was and what it might achieve. For Stalin, China – Communist or nationalist – was just another strategic element that he could manipulate in pursuit of his goal: Soviet power and security. Mao, by contrast, saw China as a central part of a vast "intermediate zone" between the two superpowers where the real conflict between capitalism and Communism would henceforth take place. For him, China was not a bit-player but a talented understudy with potential to take the leading historical role.

By the start of 1949, the Communist victory in the civil war was drawing near, and high-level contacts between the CCP and the USSR became closer. In January–February, Mikoian visited China and went back home with favorable impressions, although Mao's theory of revolution, with its emphasis on agrarian revolt, would soon start to seem heretical in Stalin's Moscow. The Soviet press, while it celebrated the Communist victory in 1949, was noticeably reserved about Mao's personal role in the triumph. And, when the People's Republic of China was founded on 1 October 1949, the Soviet Union neglected to send a message of congratulation (though one day later it was the first state to recognize the PRC). Press coverage in the USSR was subdued compared to the hullabaloo attending the creation of the German Democratic Republic one week later.

Besides doctrinal differences, relations between Communist China and the USSR were strained by an unresolved matter of immediate practical import. In 1945, nationalist China had concluded a treaty with the USSR that granted the latter substantial military and economic concessions on Chinese territory. Mao was not alone among his compatriots in finding the terms of this treaty unaccept-able and, in December 1949, after a degree of stalling on both sides, he set off for Moscow with the aim of renegotiating the treaty (and the official purpose of attending Stalin's 70th birthday celebrations). The resulting new treaty, concluded after Mao was forced to endure some minor humiliations as he waited to be sum-moned by Stalin, offered more significant compromises from the Chinese side than from the Soviet; it also included a secret protocol prohibiting commercial or industrial activities by citizens of third countries in Manchuria and Xinjiang. All this smacked of old-style colonialism to the Chinese leadership, but they were forced to acquiesce. The Soviet buffer zone on its southeastern frontier had swelled to a generous-sized cushion.

Nor was this the end of the geopolitical uses to which Stalin would put the Chinese. In 1949, tension was growing between the two halves of Korea that had been established in 1945 after the end of the Japanese occupation. By the end of 1949, it was clear to both Mao and Stalin that their Communist counterpart in North Korea, Kim Il Sung, who had served in the Soviet army in World War II, was planning to invade the American-backed South. Since 1945, Stalin had pursued a pragmatic balance-of-power strategy in Korea and was wary of risking confrontation with the American forces still stationed in the South. In April 1950, persuaded that the United States would not intervene and concerned to assert Soviet leadership in the face of a growing challenge from China, he yielded to Kim Il Sung's repeated appeals and gave his approval to the North Korean plan.[18] He was not, however, willing to commit Soviet troops to the fray, preferring to encourage the Chinese to carry the military burden of the international Communist cause.

Although Stalin did not correctly predict the American reaction, the short-term results of the war were advantageous enough for the Soviet Union. The Americans were caught by surprise by the North Korean attack of 25 June 1950, and the Soviets were able to sit back and let the North Koreans and the Chinese do their dirty work for them. In the longer term, however, the Korean War was a disaster not only for the Korean people but also for global superpower relations. This war by proxy was an unhappy precedent for future entanglements in parts of the world even further away from the Soviet border that would prove much more militarily and economically onerous for the USSR. Not only did the Korean War raise Soviet–American mistrust to a new level, it also ruined the Sino–Soviet relationship. In due course, Mao would amply repay Nikita Khrushchev for the humiliations he had received at Stalin's hands.

Yet it bears repeating that Stalin's foreign policy was characterized by its short-termism and by a certain caution. Stalin himself was loath to commit the USSR to conflicts that would risk undermining its security. Subsequent Western attempts to extrapolate from Soviet policy to Communist schemes for world domination credit Soviet geopolitical thinking with more ideological coherence and ambition than it in fact possessed. For all Stalin's manipulations, the USSR was reacting to circumstances in Korea, not creating them.

The same point emerges from Soviet policy on the other notable instance of Communist self-assertion in Southeast Asia: the uprising launched by Vietnamese Communists in 1945 that, after years of fighting between the Vietminh and the French, led to the division of Vietnam into two zones in 1954. Once again, Stalin was cautious, keeping the Vietnamese Communist leader, Ho Chi Minh, at arm's length. Stalin's successors remained concerned to avoid war in Indochina after 1954.[19] The USSR had little interest in the region; but, if the Americans were not so indifferent, the Soviets had in large part themselves – or Stalin – to blame.

The big difference between Stalin's reign and all subsequent Soviet eras was that the post-Stalin leadership found it far harder to take a detached and instrumental view of non-European conflicts. Stalin had made a cold-blooded assessment of the utility or otherwise of Soviet involvement in various non-European theaters. He had sometimes made tactical or strategic misjudgments, but always on his own terms. For Nikita Khrushchev, by contrast, the wider world was a source of prestige but also of strain and crisis.

This change was partly to do with the very different temperaments of the two leaders: Khrushchev was the last figure in Soviet politics who could be accused of being "cold-blooded." Another crucial factor was a set of international ideological and geopolitical factors that were beyond Soviet control. Before the 1950s, the parts of the globe that lay outside Europe and North America were, to use Soviet terminology, the pawns of imperialism. Their political and economic fortunes depended hugely on whether the global Great Powers, with their vast military-industrial complexes, deemed them worthy of attention. The weakness of the non-European world lay in its lack of a modern industrial economy – and also in its politically fragmented character. Even China, a huge country with vast population and economic potential, was so internally divided that it was no match for imperialists who continued until the mid-twentieth century to extract humiliating concessions from it (by the late 1930s, with the Japanese attack, the imperialists in question were at least not European, but that was small consolation).

Following World War II and the near-fatal weakening of the British, French, German, and Belgian empires, some of the larger and more economically advantaged non-European countries were able to assert themselves in a number of ways. They made efforts to build modern states. They sought to nationalize branches of the economy that might formerly have been dominated by foreign capital. And, with the benefit of new mass media, higher levels of urbanization, education, and military service, they sought to cultivate a modern nationalism. Pre-eminent among this group of countries was Communist China, but other notable cases included India, Iran, Iraq, and Egypt.

As well as developing their own nationalisms, these countries developed an overarching international identity. In the Western parlance adopted in the early 1950s, they made up the "Third World": the part of the globe lying beyond the First World of the West and the Second World of Soviet eastern Europe. More importantly, however, the emerging non-European nations were beginning to organize themselves as a coherent geopolitical bloc. In April 1955, representatives of Asian, African, and Middle Eastern states met in Bandung, Indonesia to set a postcolonial and anticolonial agenda, and at the Belgrade Conference of 1961 25 states, from Afghanistan to Yugoslavia, signed up to a common program of "nonalignment": members of this bloc could not be expected a priori to take the side of either superpower on any particular issue. All the while, the nonaligned movement was gathering momentum due to the sheer increase in the number of political actors in the Third World: 25 new states were created in the years 1957–62 alone.[20]

On one level, the Soviet regime was obliged to welcome – and did welcome – this development. The downtrodden peoples of the colonized world were rising up, constituting their own nations, and even forming an international bloc to stand alongside NATO and the Warsaw Pact. The clear expectation on the Soviet side was that the nonaligned would tilt to the socialist side in due course. The Soviet intelligence world seems to have swung decisively over to this point of view. From about 1961, the KGB started to draw up plans as to how the Cold War might be "won" in the Third World.[21]

Yet, at the same time, the nonaligned movement presented a considerable doctrinal challenge to Soviet socialism. The Bolsheviks had from the beginning subscribed to a "two camps" worldview: socialism would fight it out with capitalism, and the former would ultimately win. In this schema, the Third World (to use an anachronistic term) did not have independent significance. It would play a crucial part in forcing the capitalist world to unravel through imperialist overextension but, once that had happened, the developing world would naturally be on the progressive downtrodden side of history. Yet here was a group of non-European leaders demonstratively announcing their adherence to a "third way."[22]

Luckily, Soviet ideology had resources to adjust to this development. It could advance an argument that it had already used many times with respect to "backward" nationalities within the borders of the USSR such as the Kazakh or the Turkmen. The argument was evolutionary: according to the Marxist time line, a regime could only be as socialist as its socioeconomic foundation. All countries had to go through the necessary economic and political stages on the route to the final goal of Communism: industrialization would lead to modern nationalism, which in turn would give way to socialism.

This theory of stages of development made for tidy doctrine but untidy politics. It failed to take into account two large problems. The first was that it flew in the face of the experience of the two lodestar states of world Communism: the USSR and the PRC. The Russian empire in 1917 had been far too backward to qualify for socialist revolution, yet one had (purportedly) occurred. The same was abundantly true of the war-ravaged and agrarian China where Mao's Communist Party had consolidated power in 1949. The historical evidence was that cataclysmic state breakdown, not industrialization or nationalism, was the main precondition for "socialist" revolution. And, once this precondition was in place, a relatively small group of dedicated revolutionaries could work wonders. It was extremely likely that Third World revolutionaries of this kind would in due course draw similar conclusions and try their luck (not least because the Chinese would incite them to do so).

The second problem with a gradualist, evolutionary approach to the Third World was that the condition of the nonaligned countries did not correspond to the theories of Marx and Lenin in a number of fundamental ways. To be sure, these countries lacked the industrial base and the modern economy that Marxism-Leninism regarded as prerequisites for socialism. But they had certain attributes

FIGURE 8.1   Fidel Castro with Khrushchev on the Lenin Mausoleum, 1963.
Source: © Alexei Gostev / PhotoSoyuz.

of the modern world that Russia had lacked in 1917. One was the availability (in principle at least) of modern medicine, which meant relatively low mortality and impending demographic explosion. Another was mass access to modern communications: cinema, radio, in due course TV. But the most important difference is that the ruling elites, and aspiring elites, of the nonaligned countries could reflect on the intervening half-century of history and could draw on the patronage of three major powers (the USA, the USSR and – increasingly – China).

What this meant was that the USSR was increasingly unable to follow the historical script written by Stalin: to take a comfortable back seat as the imperialist powers dashed each other to pieces and the progressive developing world arose from the rubble. The capitalist powers were getting on disappointingly well with each other, while the emerging nations of the Third World required constant encouragement, chivvying, and restraining, and were in any case as likely to attack each other as their former imperialist overlords (as disputes between China and India, India and Pakistan, and Iran and Iraq would soon demonstrate). As it took on this thankless task, moreover, the USSR faced hostile competition from the economically powerful USA and the ideologically powerful PRC. With the Americans it entered an economically ruinous arms race, while the Chinese, with their utopian and apocalyptic Great Leap Forward of 1958–62, launched an ideological challenge to a Soviet regime that they viewed not as the vanguard of world revolution but at best as a staid, conservative elder statesman of the socialist camp – and at worst as a leftwing version of white-man's imperialism.[23]

By the early 1960s, Soviet socialism had been maneuvered into a position where the Third World was crucial to its self-definition and sense of purpose. This global mission was a far cry indeed from the geopolitical orientation of the late Stalin period. Stalinist thinking was displaced in the early 1960s by a more optimistic doctrine of international affairs holding that the Third World could make rather swift progress along its historical time line. The consequences of this revisionism were not bad to begin with. The early Khrushchev period saw a series of prestige-raising and morale-boosting visits from Third World leaders to Moscow, and a few reciprocal trips by Khrushchev. The Soviets were able to look on gloatingly as the British and French humiliated themselves in the Suez crisis, though here already Khrushchev overplayed his hand, blind to the fact that American pressure, rather than Soviet threats, had played the crucial role in the collapse of the Anglo–French cause.[24]

Khrushchev drew a dangerous conclusion from the apparent success of Soviet policy in the Middle East. He became convinced that he could bully his American opponents into key geopolitical concessions. Although initially horrified by the power of atomic weapons, he soon took the more optimistic view that they made war with the United States all but impossible – and, less plausibly, that they could be used to batter down American opposition to Soviet objectives. In one of the many paradoxes of Khrushchev's leadership, brinkmanship became the preferred means of achieving "peaceful coexistence." The problem, however, was that ultimatums failed to remove the main "bone in the throat" of international Communism: the capitalist enclave of West Berlin. They also failed to change the reality that the USSR still lagged behind the United States in the range and destructive capacity of its missiles. As Khrushchev's sense of frustration grew, his risk-taking proclivities were heightened by the arrival in the White House of a young and apparently lightweight new president. In 1962, the Soviet leader embarked on his most dangerous bluff of all. By secretly placing nuclear weapons in the new Communist client state of Cuba, he could establish the equivalent of American bases in Italy and Turkey and subject the White House to the same feelings of powerlessness and rage that had been building in the Kremlin since 1958.

The ensuing crisis certainly proved to be the most nerve-racking confrontation of the Cold War.[25] Nor could the White House be said to be an innocent party: Eisenhower had planned covert operations against the new Cuban regime (including the assassination of Fidel Castro), while the Kennedy administration sent American-trained Cuban exiles on the disastrous Bay of Pigs operation in April 1961 and soon resumed an intensive program of political subversion. But the outcome of the nuclear standoff in October 1962 was only too familiar: once again the Americans failed to succumb to Soviet bluff and intimidation, and Khrushchev was forced into the most sobering climbdown of his erratic career. Not only did the USSR take the world to the brink of near-annihilation and then suffer a serious blow to its prestige, the Soviet patron also had to endure lectures from its notional "client" as Castro remonstrated with Khrushchev about the Soviet betrayal. In the Cuban leader's view, the prestige of international socialism was worth more than the lives of tens of millions of people (Communist and capitalist). With friends like these, the USSR scarcely needed enemies.

Central and Eastern Europe Revisited

Yet enemies were not in short supply. The most troublesome of them were to be found in the recalcitrant Soviet-dominated societies of eastern Europe. The first clear signs of trouble in the Eastern bloc came in May and June 1953, when a set of mainly working-class material grievances led to rioting in Bulgaria, Czechoslovakia, and the GDR. But the astonishing political maneuver of February 1956, when Khrushchev at the 20th Party Congress distanced the present Party leadership from at least some of the crimes and excesses of Stalinism, created the conditions for more politicized protest. In June 1956, the Polish Communist leadership was confronted by a workers' uprising in Poznan. The new General Secretary Gomułka was able to restore order by making a number of concessions: de-collectivization, greater liberalism in intellectual life, and safeguards for the place of the Church in Polish society. At the same time, even more impressively, he managed to convince Moscow both of his loyalty to the Soviet system and of the Polish determination to resist any Soviet invasion. Khrushchev arrived in Warsaw at the beginning of October on an impromptu visit to browbeat his Polish opposite number, who showed, through a combination of suasion and toughness, that he could stand up to the pressure.

A far more serious case in 1956 was Hungary, which produced the iconic Cold War example of anti-Soviet resistance. Here the situation was destabilized by two factors that did not obtain in Poland. First, the protest that escalated out of control in October was not an expression of specific economic grievances but bespoke a more radical and intransigent opposition to Soviet overlordship and a national liberationist agenda. Second, the capacity of the Hungarian regime to maintain control of the situation was seriously undermined by rifts in its leadership. Ever since the death of Stalin, Hungarian politics had been marked by the opposition between the Party apparatus (headed by the Stalinist Mátyás Rákosi until he was removed by Moscow in July 1956) and the head of the state, the more reformist Imre Nagy (who served as prime minister from 1953 to 1955, when he was removed from his post for the sin of "rightism" and even expelled from the Party, before returning to the office of prime minister on the eve of the crisis). Nagy's conflicting imperatives and inclinations – to fight his local political opponents, to show his reformist credentials to Hungarian society, to maintain order, to preserve good relations with a Soviet leader (Khrushchev) with whom he apparently shared the reformist impulse – left him unable to act decisively or send out clear signals when a tense situation turned to crisis.

Student protest broke out across the country at the start of October. In desperation, the Hungarian Party leaders turned to Moscow for assistance in imposing martial law; the first of two Soviet invasions took place on 23 October. On 25 October, Soviet troops opened fire on a peaceful demonstration outside the Parliament building in Budapest, killing well over one hundred citizens. Soon afterward, the situation was stabilized by political reshuffles that brought non-Communists to high government posts. Now beginning to overcome the hesitancy he had shown in the opening phase of the unrest, Nagy ordered a cease-fire, sought the withdrawal of Soviet troops and began to move toward building a more pluralist political system. The Soviet leaders, although this outcome was not to their taste, showed willingness to negotiate and even to make some concessions. In the event, however, direct action precipitated a draconian Soviet intervention. On the morning of 30 October, insurgents stormed the Party headquarters and lynched several secret policemen. A few hours later, Nagy put aside his equivocations and threw in his lot with the revolutionaries by formally announcing the creation of a multiparty system. Only now did Moscow take the decision to crush the insurgency. Soviet tanks rolled in on 4 November, more than 2,500 people were killed in the conflict, nearly 200,000 fled to the West, and Nagy himself was executed two years later.

Given the photographic and memoir legacy of the "Hungarian October," it is hard to avoid interpreting it as the moment when Soviet Communism shed its de-Stalinizing glove to reveal its mailed fist. Certainly, that was the conclusion drawn by the hundreds of thousands of people who left Western Communist parties at that time. Yet, although the centrality of violence to Soviet strategies of conflict resolution can hardly be doubted, a closer reading of the evidence suggests a more nuanced analysis of the Hungarian tragedy. The day-by-day history of the crisis shows that, while military intervention was not a last resort for the Soviet regime, it was also far from being a first resort. The Khrushchev leadership showed a willingness to negotiate after the initial disturbances that was remarkable given their Stalinist background and the provocation: the toppling of the Stalin statue in Budapest, mass disorder with incidents of mob violence, public anti-Sovietism. This was not 1968, when the Soviets bullied a Czechoslovak leadership that was maintaining public order and sincerely professing socialist (as opposed to national-liberationist) credentials. As late as 30 October, it seems, the Soviets were prepared to make concessions in Budapest. But then a further burst of unrest – including the murder of secret policemen – and the prospect of Hungary quitting the Warsaw Pact provoked more drastic measures.

The Hungarian events of 1956, then, are eloquent not just because they demonstrate the propensity for violence of the Soviet regime. While that propensity unquestionably existed, the Soviet leadership, especially once it had taken its de-Stalinizing course, had no incentive to subject itself to the costs, the humiliation and the international condemnation that would inevitably accompany military intervention. This was especially true of a country like Hungary, whose strategic value to the Soviet Union was considerably less than that of Poland. What we are left with is a series of misjudgments – concerning the impact of de-Stalinization on Hungarian society, the internal dynamics of Hungarian politics, and the political trajectory of Imre Nagy in particular – that left the all-powerful Soviets as much the slaves of circumstances as their masters. The Hungarian tail was wagging the Soviet dog even as it was being bitten off.[26]

A less bloody but in the long term more sensitive and intractable issue for Soviet foreign policy was the German question. In the mid-1950s, as in the late 1940s, both sides in the Cold War were notionally committed to reunification, but in practice they were extremely unlikely to agree on the terms under which it would be conducted.

The best chance of a fundamental Soviet rethink on the German question came and went in a brief period of two or three months in the middle of 1953. After Stalin's death in early March, his successors were at pains to stress their peaceful intentions in world affairs. They were also becoming increasingly aware that the policies of the hard-line Communist leader of the GDR, Walter Ulbricht, were doing much to alienate the population and little to improve its economic well-being. At the start of June, Ulbricht was summoned to Moscow and instructed to adopt a "New Course" more accommodating to popular grievances than the rigorous socialist policies – collectivization, austerity – to which he was committed. Ulbricht reluctantly agreed, but soon afterward circumstances conspired to arrest the New Course. First, a wave of social unrest undermined the case for political liberalization. Second, Lavrentii Beria, the notorious Stalinist secret police chief who had been notable since Stalin's death for his liberal sentiments on the German question (even if the nature and the sincerity of his intentions remain obscure) was suddenly arrested by his fellow leaders.

Although the Soviet leadership tried for the rest of the decade to steer Ulbricht toward a softer line in domestic policy, this was a doomed undertaking. The stability of the GDR – the most sensitive outer edge of the Soviet bloc – was simply too important to risk, and Ulbricht was able to derive great political – and economic – capital in Moscow from the very weakness of his regime. The fact was that this outer edge was fraying badly: approximately 2.7 million people took flight from the GDR between its creation in 1949 and 1961.[27] A new East German passport law of 11 December 1957 had stemmed the overall outflow of refugees from East Germany, but it greatly accentuated the role of West Berlin in the exodus: by the end of 1958, more than 90 percent of refugees were taking this route to the West, and many of them were the kind of educated specialists that the GDR could ill afford to lose.[28]

Khrushchev's characteristically drastic solution to this problem was to issue an ultimatum to the Western powers on 27 November 1958: he called on them to make Berlin a demilitarized "free city" and gave them a six-month deadline for withdrawal. This initiative went against the better judgment of some of Khrushchev's colleagues, though it did not meet Ulbricht's demand for the GDR to have full control of Berlin. When the West agreed to four-power talks, Khrushchev relaxed his deadline. A further period of maneuvering ensued, during which Ulbricht applied constant pressure for a unilateral solution to the Berlin problem. His demands became even more insistent as the number of refugees rose steeply in 1960–1.

The situation was resolved in August 1961 by the Soviet decision to build the Berlin Wall, that symbol of Cold War confrontation and that source of misery for hundreds of thousands of German families. But the iconic ugliness and brutality of the Wall should not obscure two crucial facts about this resolution of the perennial German question. First, the Soviet leadership took this path out of weakness, not out of intransigence or defiance, and they were weak not only with regard to the Western countries that exercised such a magnetic attraction over millions of East Germans but also in their relations with the East German leadership. Second, the building of the Wall was not actually an undesirable outcome for either of the superpowers. It imposed rigidity, but also stability. It brought a medium-term resolution to a question of immense importance to both sides where fundamental concessions were inconceivable. For the next two decades, the focus of superpower geopolitical concern would lie much further afield.

Colonialism Soviet-Style

The mid-1960s saw a retreat from the interventionist policies that had led the world to the brink of destruction in the Caribbean in 1962. Khrushchev's foreign policy adventures were easily condemned by his successors, who were seeking to distance themselves from his erratic patterns of rule. The Soviet regime was as little inclined as ever to relinquish control of its bailiwick in eastern Europe – witness the notorious intervention in Czechoslovakia in 1968 – but Third World interventions seemed too costly and too risky. This was also the era when the

Americans were acting out a prolonged cautionary tale about the dangers of Third World entanglements as they became ever more deeply mired in Vietnam.

By now, the Chinese were regarded in Moscow as more of a threat to world security than the Americans. Communist China was a geopolitical loose cannon. It was regularly inciting untimely revolutions in the Third World and badmouthing the Soviet Union as a state that had traduced its original sense of revolutionary purpose. The Chinese had a point, though through non-Maoist eyes this Soviet doctrinal flexibility could be viewed as a blessing rather than a defect.

One of many sore points in Sino–Soviet relations in the 1960s was Soviet policy in India. Soviet geopolitical thinking on India had a long pedigree – it stretched back to Lenin – and had always veered between two poles familiar from so many other areas of Soviet ideology: at one extreme was an ultra-leftist commitment to backing the Indian Communist Party and hastening revolution by taking advantage of the political instability of the country in the early years of independence; at the other extreme was a gradualist evolutionary interpretation according to which India had to go through its allotted nationalist phase, presided over by the Congress Party that had ruled since independence, with the Indian Communists remaining as bit-players. The Chinese regarded the latter position as apostasy, all the more so when Khrushchev effectively backed the Indians in a Sino–Indian border dispute of 1959. During the 1960s, India played a large and growing role as a buffer for the Soviets against the Chinese, and it would have served this purpose far less well if it had turned into a hotbed of revolution. On India at least, Soviet thinking in the 1960s and 1970s was thoroughly "de-eschatological."[29]

The Vietnam conflict, which involved a straight fight between Communist insurgents and the capitalist superpower, did not permit such a laissez-faire Soviet attitude. But nor did it meet a gung-ho response from Moscow. Vietnam is in fact a telling indicator of how the eternal tug of war in Soviet strategic thinking between pragmatism and the ideology of the international spread of socialism was conducted in the 1960s. The Soviets had known about the plans of the Vietnamese Communists to launch a military takeover since the end of the 1950s. But, both in public and in their direct contacts with the Viet Cong (Vietnamese Liberation Front) that had formed in 1960, they urged restraint. One of the firebrand Khrushchev's last foreign policy gestures was the publication of an open letter to world leaders where he urged peaceful resolution of the three big unification problems facing the world at that time: Korea, Germany, and Vietnam. When leading representatives of the Viet Cong came to Moscow in 1964, they did so at the invitation of the Soviet Afro-Asian Solidarity Committee; they had no direct contact with the Soviet leaders, who kept their distance.[30]

Despite Soviet counsels of restraint, tensions rose in Vietnam by the end of 1964: naval skirmishes between Vietnam and the United States in the Gulf of

Tonkin were followed by more interventionist declarations by the Johnson administration. In February 1965, Anastas Mikoian flew to Hanoi and urged the North Vietnamese to refrain from further provocation of the US. On the way back to Moscow, he stopped off to see Mao, a meeting that suggested that his efforts were most likely doomed: the Chinese dictator showed no interest in Soviet offers to act as peace broker.

Soon after, the Americans launched a bombing campaign against North Vietnam. At this point, the Soviets switched to a pro-Vietnamese public position and demanded that the Americans call a halt to their military action. The Soviet contribution was by no means limited to words. Starting in 1965, the USSR sent to Vietnam military advisers, industrial and telecommunications equipment, vehicles, medical supplies, and much else. Its provision of aid initially lagged behind the Chinese contribution but soon caught up. The North Vietnamese, as a poor country entirely dependent on foreign aid in order to fight their war, were adept at playing the bitter Communist rivals, China and Soviet Russia, off against each other. This was not a comfortable position for the Soviet leadership to find itself in, but in general it emerged from the Vietnam conflict with credit and strategic advantage. It had enhanced its prestige in the socialist world by defending the North Vietnamese cause, it had held its own in the standoff with China (which took a further turn for the worse in 1969 as Chinese and Soviet troops clashed on their joint border), and it was in a position to benefit from America's loss of power and prestige.

Vietnam also helped to make possible détente, the most promising development in Soviet–American relations since World War II. By the early 1970s, Leonid Brezhnev was a self-confident and well-established leader who could keep his own hardliners at bay. He had presided over striking improvements in the relationship between the Soviet Union and West Germany. He also had (by Soviet standards) considerable personal charm, a loathing of Khrushchevian brinkmanship and a genuine desire to play the role of peacemaker. In Richard Nixon, moreover, he had an equally adroit opposite number. In May 1972 Nixon came to Moscow, and the two leaders struck up a remarkably cordial relationship.[31]

The achievements of détente were real but impermanent. They depended on the rapport between two leaders whose role in events would soon be seriously diminished: Nixon was disgraced in 1974, while Brezhnev around the same time began his descent into physical and mental incapacity. Much more enduring factors in superpower relations were the military establishments in both countries. In any case, Brezhnevian détente had always been more concerned to avert direct nuclear confrontation with the United States than to reduce armed conflict of other kinds around the globe. The militarized Soviet establishment in fact drew interventionist conclusions from the slight lessening of superpower tensions: not only could the USSR now exercise close control over the eastern European bloc (to Brezhnev's relief and gratification, the crackdown in Czechoslovakia had drawn remarkably little protest from Western leaders whose eyes were trained on Southeast Asia and on various university campuses), it could also take a fraternal supervisory role in the non-European world without fearing instant retribution from the military-industrial behemoth of the United States, which was depleted by the war in Vietnam and would soon take a further blow when world oil prices leapt upward in 1973.

The USSR thus slipped comfortably back into a two-track foreign policy that combined a notional commitment to improving superpower relations with a readiness to get involved in Third World affairs. An entirely predictable focus of its attentions was the Middle East, especially when that part of the world showed its capacity to hold the oil-poor West to ransom in the 1970s. That is not to say that relations with the Soviet Union's clients in the region were cloudless. They were anything but. The problem with countries like Egypt and Iraq – the main clients of the USSR in the Middle East between the mid-1950s and the late 1970s – was that they put ideology and pragmatism on a collision course in Soviet foreign policy. For a combination of strategic and economic reasons, these countries were becoming far more self-assertive and nationalist from the 1950s onward. They were strategically important to the Soviet Union, they were capable of causing trouble for the Americans, but they were also liable to act in ways directly contrary to Soviet interests and ideology.

The Soviets had taken a position of sour neutrality as the Free Officers made their successful bid for power in Egypt in 1952. Relations became much warmer in 1953 and 1954, as the new regime took a gratifyingly anti-British stance, and in January 1954 the Egyptian deputy defense minister paid an extended visit to the USSR. In September 1955 Egypt confirmed its new ties with the Soviet bloc when it secured a $250 million arms deal with Czechoslovakia. Soviet–Egyptian relations cooled in the period 1959–61, when Moscow became concerned about Nasser's apparent expansionism.[32] But Soviet economic and military aid to Cairo increased again in the mid-1960s and peaked in the crisis of 1967.[33] The Soviet leadership was mortified by the disastrous Egyptian defeat in the Six-Day War with Israel, ascribing this to Arab incompetence. Nevertheless, when Nasser came secretly to Moscow at the end of 1969 to request further military aid, the Soviets did not hold back, committing artillery, air defense, and air force units to bolster what they saw as a key Third World ally. More than 20,000 Soviet servicemen saw varying periods of service in Egypt in 1969–70.[34]

This investment failed quite spectacularly to pay off. Nasser's successor Sadat was less anti-Western than his nationalist predecessor, and quite unabashed in playing the Soviets off against the Americans in a bid to secure his military aims. And, whatever strenuous efforts the Soviets made, his inclination was to ally with the Americans. In July 1972, in an act of apostasy that turned Sadat into the KGB's main Third World object of loathing, the nearly 20,000 Soviet military advisers in Egypt were expelled from the country.[35]

By this time, Soviet attention in the Middle East was turning to Iraq, if anything a more strategically important country than Egypt (given its oil reserves and proximity to the Gulf) but also a troublesome one for policymakers. After World War II it had been ruled by a monarchy that had broken off diplomatic relations with the USSR in 1955. In 1963 a nationalist Ba'ath regime came to power and promptly attacked the Iraqi Communists. After a few years of political turmoil, the Ba'ath seized power once again in 1968 and took a more peaceful view of Communism. In recognition of this, and of the strategic importance of Iraq (given the pro-Western shah in neighboring Iran), the Soviet Union agreed to provide Iraq with arms and economic aid. By the mid-1970s, Iraq was the greatest Third World recipient of Soviet military aid (although as Soviet arms deliveries grew in absolute terms they declined as a portion of the overall military aid received by Iraq, which diversified its sources in the 1970s). The Soviets were also delighted to help the Iraqis deal Western capitalists a blow by nationalizing their oil industry in 1972. They underwrote the costs of this decision by agreeing to buy Iraqi oil at guaranteed prices until the country was in a position to trade on the international market. But the Ba'ath policies on the Kurdish question and (especially) the Iraqi Communist Party were less comfortable for the Soviets. Never sympathetic to the Communists, in 1978 the Ba'ath regime launched a campaign of violence against them that the Soviets were powerless to prevent. Soviet–Iraqi relations reached their nadir in 1980, when Iraq attacked Iran without prior consultation. In Moscow's view, this was a senseless conflict between two anti-imperialist nations (though the radical anti-Communism of the Islamist Iranian regime ensured that Soviet arms supplies to Iraq, halted at the start of the war, would resume in 1981–2).[36]

The inescapable conclusion is that the Ba'ath regime did far better out of the Soviet–Iraqi relationship than the USSR: it received vast amounts of military and other aid, while its freedom of action was very little constrained. As the killing of Communists and Kurds, and the invasions of Iran and Kuwait, would show, Moscow was subsidizing a regime that did indeed take inspiration from the Soviet example – but from Stalin, not from Brezhnev or Andropov.

By the 1980s, the Soviet Union's most reliable ally in the Middle East was Syria, whose authoritarian and violent ruler, Asad, was courted by Moscow almost as soon as he came to power in 1970. Asad did at least refrain from outlawing the Communist Party and even appeased the Soviets by including the odd Communist in the government. But Syria's propensity to send hit squads abroad, and its insatiable demand for Soviet arms, made it an increasingly unrewarding and embarrassing partner for the USSR.

To refrain from action in the Middle East would have been an act of heroic restraint from the Soviet Union, given the intertwining of superpower strategic interests in that region. In other parts of the globe, however, Soviet policy took ambitious new paths and started to abandon the relative prudence it had shown in the second half of the 1960s. The USSR became more global and interventionist than at any point previously, and in the process it lost both ideological coherence and cold pragmatism.

To be sure, theoretical backing could be found for the more interventionist new course. Rather than relying on the slow-burning social contradictions presumed by the theory of stages of evolution, Marxist revolutionaries in the Third World could exploit the weakness and instability of their young postcolonial states and bring about socialism in a hurry – much as the Bolsheviks had done in Russia in 1917. The high point of Soviet geopolitical optimism coincided with the rise of postcolonial movements in southern Africa. In 1970, the KGB informed Brezhnev that the region contained a number of liberationist movements with a Marxist coloring that were potential clients of the USSR. And there were other factors that spoke in favor of Soviet engagement. The West's sole policeman in the region was the internationally disreputable and isolated apartheid regime in South Africa. The Portuguese empire – notably Angola – was showing all the signs of terminal weakness. As it approached its death throes, three principal anticolonial movements gathered their strength. One of them, the MPLA, had a Marxist orientation and was the natural candidate for Soviet aid.

In April 1974, a coup in Portugal brought an end to the Salazar dictatorship, and in January 1975 the Portuguese announced their plan for withdrawal from Angola. A civil war soon started, and the MPLA was attacked by the nativist nationalist FNLA, its main rival. The FNLA and its ally, the Chinese-backed UNITA, were supported by covert US operations and by a South African invasion in mid-October. In the meantime, the Cubans, who already had a distinguished record of practical support for African Marxist movements and had re-established a reasonably harmonious working relationship with the Soviets following a rift in the 1960s, urged decisive action in support of the MPLA. In the event, the Cubans went ahead while the Soviets hesitated, but the latter overcame their reservations when the South Africans invaded and it became clear that the CIA was taking an active part in the conflict. Once the USSR threw its weight behind the MPLA, the military tide turned; in December 1975 the US ceased its covert operations, and the South Africans were left without superpower backing. By February 1976 the MPLA had been recognized by most African states as the new Angolan regime.[37]

The Angolan civil war was with some justification seen as a great triumph by the Soviet leaders. The Soviet Union had intervened quickly and decisively in a conflict more than 5,000 miles away and had defeated a superpower rival that was ostensibly more deeply entrenched in the region. The Angolan experience seemed to show that local Marxist insurgencies, if handled in the right way by Moscow, could achieve striking successes and tilt the global balance in favor of socialism. To draw these conclusions was understandable but misguided – and not only because the Angolan civil war was far from over. The MPLA was not the only Marxist-inspired movement in Africa in the 1970s, but the word "Marxism," in Africa as on other continents, covered a multitude of economic conditions, social movements, and political conjunctures.

The friable character of African Marxism was demonstrated in the Horn of Africa, where Soviet foreign policy entered some of its more elaborate convolutions.[38] This region was strategically placed on trade routes and close to the key oil states of the Middle East. The dominant local power was Ethiopia, the oldest and proudest nation in Africa. In the second half of the nineteenth century, when the British began to penetrate the area, tsarist Russia had encouraged Ethiopian nationalism. Twentieth-century Ethiopia remained subject to European aggression: in the 1930s it fell victim to a full-scale invasion by fascist Italy. But the outcome of World War II worked in its favor: not only were the Italians defeated, the British also withdrew completely from its territory and it started to receive substantial American backing (as much as half of all the military aid that Washington supplied to black Africa at that time). The USSR could do little except shrug and consign Ethiopia to the camp of American imperialism.

It began to shed this indifference in 1955 when Ethiopia backed the pan-African cause at the Bandung conference that launched the nonaligned movement. A Soviet–Ethiopian rapprochement duly ensued, to the extent that the Ethiopian Emperor Haile Selassie made a triumphal visit to the USSR in 1959 and received a vast $100 million loan – the largest credit that the Soviets had ever offered to a black African nation. At the same time, however, Selassie did not break his ties with the Americans and remained ideologically out of tune with Communism. His relations with Moscow were further strained in the 1960s by disputes between Ethiopia and Somalia over the border region of Ogaden: more than one million Somalis had been left outside the borders of the new independent Somalia that had been created in July 1960. Ethiopia, a multiethnic state that risked fragmentation if it recognized separatist claims, was not inclined to make concessions, and it was backed up by its American patron which turned down a Somali request for aid.

At this point the Soviet leadership saw its chance to raise its profile in the region. As early as September 1960, it established full diplomatic relations with Somalia, and less than a year later it concluded with that country an agreement for economic and technical assistance. This policy may have made tactical sense, but it placed the USSR before a strategic conundrum: how was it simultaneously to maintain cordial relations with two countries – Ethiopia and Somalia – whose levels of antagonism were rising all the time and increasingly taking militarized form? In practice, Soviet professions of friendly neutrality were satisfying no one, least of all the Ethiopians.

By 1966 it was clear that the USSR was according higher priority to Somalia, but the Horn of Africa was not a great geopolitical concern for the Soviets who at that time were more engaged by the Middle East. Their attention switched back to East Africa in October 1969 when a coup brought a Supreme Revolutionary Council to power in Somalia. Its early policies were certain to please the USSR: social justice, nationalization of foreign businesses, and expulsion of the US Peace Corps. Moscow wasted no time in recognizing the new regime and, although it maintained cordial relations with Ethiopia, its commitment to Somalia grew strongly in the early 1970s. About 1,400 Soviet experts assisted Somali ministries and government agencies as the USSR endeavored to bolster the "socialist orientation" that seemed so pronounced in Somalia.

But here developments in Ethiopia changed the pattern of alignments in the region yet again. In 1974, a revolution deposed Haile Selassie, and Ethiopia embarked on land reform and the nationalization of enterprises. The new regime also faced internal opposition and nationalist separatism that placed Ethiopia's very existence under question. In mid-1976, in desperation, it cast around for new arms suppliers – and found a partner in the USSR. At the same time, much to Soviet dismay, Ethiopia continued to draw military aid from the US: American arms supplies actually grew substantially in the three years following the revolution, totaling nearly $200 million over that period. Yet even that figure did not match the arms that the USSR continued to pump into Somalia (more than $300 million over the same period).

As tensions between Ethiopia and Somalia rose again in the mid-1970s, the Soviet Union found itself in a paradoxical, and indeed untenable, position: it urged restraint on two African nations that it had helped to arm to the teeth. The political payback on its massive investment in the region was hard to perceive: Somalia could by no stretch of the imagination be said to be taking a socialist path, and if anything its native Islam made its population hostile to the USSR.

When Somalia precipitated full-blown war by invading the Ogaden in July 1977, the USSR finally had to choose between the two sides. It threw its weight behind Ethiopia, where a Communist regime had come to power by a coup in February of that year. Early in 1978, the Somalis were forced to withdraw, and the long-standing conflict between these two nations, both of them at one time or another Soviet clients, found temporary resolution. From now on, the USSR would take the role of patron of Ethiopia, which received the vast sum of $7.5 billion in military aid between 1978 and 1988. But the Soviets emerged from this relationship both poorer and morally compromised. Not only had they effectively engineered a war in the Horn of Africa, they were also forced to do business with a murderous Ethiopian regime that had purged native Marxists in the mid-1970s. The devastation caused to the region, in combination with the policies of the Soviet-backed dictator Mengistu, were responsible for the famine of 1984–5 that provoked worldwide horror.

The Horn of Africa – where two Soviet clients fought it out – was perhaps the height of tragic absurdity in the Cold War. But, although the conflict raised superpower tensions at the end of 1977, the Soviet intervention that finally destroyed détente and propelled the USSR much further along the path of terminal decline would come only two years later, and it was less obviously absurd.

Afghanistan conformed to a pattern not uncommon in the Middle East. A modernizing but authoritarian ruler had failed to control a fractious society. Facing opposition from conservatives and Marxists, his regime was brought down in April 1978 by the more doctrinaire of the two factions in the Afghan Marxist movement, the Khalq. This coup came as a complete surprise to the Soviets. In time-honored Communist fashion, the Khalq leaders, Taraki and Amin, wasted little time in purging their rivals in the more moderate Parcham faction; the Parcham leader, Babrak Karmal, was dispatched to effective exile in Czechoslovakia. A representative of the Soviet Central Committee visited Kabul to request moderation from the Khalq. Taraki and Amin responded respectfully but did nothing to comply, and before long were in Moscow requesting substantial amounts of Soviet aid.

The problem with the Khalq, from Moscow's perspective, was not so much that they were using violence against their opponents (though that was discomforting, when the opponents in question were fellow Marxists whose policies were more to the Soviet taste) but that their strong-arm tactics were conspicuously failing to bring Afghan society under control. In March 1979, an uprising in Herat marked the arrival in Afghan politics of militarized Islamism. In the short term, Taraki used the unrest as an opportunity to secure more aid from Moscow, but the Kremlin's displeasure was now palpable. KGB representatives in Kabul put pressure on Taraki to arrest his politically dangerous fellow leader Amin, but Taraki hesitated, and eventually, after a failed assassination attempt on Amin, was himself executed in captivity on Amin's orders in October 1979. Now Amin was left as the sole leader, and one justifiably mistrustful of the Soviets, who in turn were now suspecting that he was preparing to defect to the American camp. All the while, armed Islamists were continuing to destabilize Afghanistan.

It was in this context that the Soviet leadership went back on what they had said to Taraki on his visit to Moscow in March – that direct Soviet intervention was out of the question. At the start of December, KGB commandos started to infiltrate Afghanistan, and on 27 December several hundred of them attacked Amin's presidential palace and summarily executed Amin and several of his relatives and closest aides.[39]

The Soviets had underestimated the international indignation that this intervention would provoke. The consequences ranged from the acceleration of the arms race to the American boycott of the 1980 Moscow Olympics. Even more importantly, the USSR had intervened to prop up a regime that could not possibly have existed on its own. The result was a bloody and prolonged conflict that would kill more than a million people (the vast majority of them Afghans). The Soviet regime had also done its bit to unleash the forces of global Islamism that would manifest themselves with full destructiveness two decades later. The Afghan War gave Osama bin Laden his formative experience of fighting infidels. Together with the Iranian revolution of 1979, it heralded a global order that was no longer bipolar: for bin Laden, as for Khomeini, the Soviets and the Americans were as bad as each other.

The Soviet failure to diagnose this new condition in world politics was hardly in itself reprehensible; after all, the Americans did no better. Where the Soviets were found wanting, however, was in applying a now obsolete Marxist-Leninist framework to political movements around the globe that differed wildly in their goals and their chances of success. A small number of successes – Vietnam, Angola – led Soviet ideologists to conclude that Third World "revolutionaries," if given their head, could quickly steer their portions of humanity onto the "progressive" path of international socialism. In a sense, the Brezhnev regime, inheritors of the Russian revolution, were encouraging Third World vanguard parties to perform the same role as the Bolsheviks had done in 1917 when they had forced a backward agrarian country to jump several stages on the historical time line laid out by Marx. But Ethiopia in 1977 or Afghanistan in 1979 were rather different cases from the Russian empire, even at its lowest ebb. And historical parallels of this kind smoothed over the unpalatable fact that Bolshevik Russia had undergone three decades of state terror, mass repression, and annihilationist total war before it had arrived at the Brezhnevite socialism that was purportedly the gold standard of progressive humanity in the late 1970s. Would the USSR be able to stand idly by as client states in Africa and Asia tore themselves apart for a few decades? More to the point, would it be prepared to bankroll them as they did so?

The Gorbachev era finally delivered a decisive negative at least to the second of those questions. Even before the advent of perestroika and glasnost, influential figures in Soviet policy-making were drawing the conclusion that colonialism Soviet-style was a singularly unrewarding activity for the patron. And, in a seminal ideological move, they would soon extend that conclusion from the Third World to the Soviet Union's post-1945 backyard.

———————————— The Retreat from Empire ————————————

An account of the long decline of the Soviet empire should start with its high-water mark: Czechoslovakia 1968, the most notorious (if hardly the most egregious) case of Soviet intervention in the affairs of another state. This was a situation quite unlike Hungary in 1956, where a reformist Marxist leadership had attempted to ride the wave of popular discontent with disturbing consequences for public order. The Czechoslovaks, quite unlike the Hungarians, were known for their tranquility and willingness to play by Soviet rules. Here there was no national-liberationist rhetoric and no demonstrating on the streets. Rather, Moscow intervened to squash gradualist reformism and liberalization originating in a socialist party that never claimed to be anything other than loyal to Moscow. In 1968 and 1969, the KGB surpassed even itself in ruthlessness as it imposed "normalization" on Czechoslovak politics and society.[40]

In the 1970s, the Soviet leadership continued to discipline its eastern European satellites from time to time – the Hungarians, for example, were made to shelve market-orientated economic reforms – but it also witnessed problems that it was powerless to forestall or to fix. The most difficult case was Poland, which shared a long and crucial border with the Soviet Union yet was more estranged, politically and culturally, than any other state in the bloc. The Poles also reacted strongly to the austerity measures forced on their leaders by growing energy costs, aid to the Third World, and economic stagnation. A price rise of more than a third for staple foods in December 1970 provoked strikes and riots all over the country; dozens of people were killed. Another big price hike in 1976 sparked more protest. Discussions of free trade unionism gathered momentum in the late 1970s.

Culturally, moreover, Poland had at least one foot in the West. In 1979, Polish TV showed 583 films from capitalist countries and only 395 from socialist.[41] More importantly, Poles had a powerful reference point outside the Eastern bloc: the Catholic Church, which from 1978 was headed by a native Pole. The new Pope visited Poland in June 1979 to an ecstatic reception; all the while the KGB fretted about the spread of Catholic activism to the western parts of the USSR.

The Poles' economic grievances and religious and cultural affiliations were complemented neatly by the hatred and distrust that many of them felt toward the Soviet Union. In March 1979, Soviet representatives in Poland edgily monitored preparations by independent organizations to mark the fortieth anniversary of the Katyn massacre (which Moscow, in defiance of world opinion, continued to insist had been perpetrated by the Germans).

When yet another price hike on 1 July 1980 provoked yet another wave of strikes, the ensuing political crisis was hugely overdetermined. Worker demands quickly turned more political, and by autumn the Polish Communist leadership found itself in fraught negotiations with an independent trade union, Solidarity, that had already gained a mass membership. The regime conducted these negotiations, moreover, under the unforgiving eye of its superpower patron. Over the next few months, the Polish leaders would play for time, desperate to avoid Soviet military intervention but also keen to avoid using coercion against their own people. In December 1981, in the face of massive Soviet intimidation, the head of the Polish party-state, General Jaruzelski, introduced martial law.

The Polish leaders would have been superhuman not to have been intimidated, given the Soviet history of interventions in the bloc. But Soviet threats, as archival evidence has now shown, were a bluff. Although plans were drawn up in 1980 for the introduction of troops into Poland from the western borderlands of the Soviet Union, by early 1981 the balance of opinion in the Soviet ruling elite had begun to shift against the idea. In June 1981, the Soviet General Staff was almost unanimous in advising against Soviet involvement in a Polish conflict, and the Politburo took the same view. It was not that Poland had broken the resolve of Soviet Communism; the fact was rather that, by 1981, that resolve was not what it once had been. When faced with the option of another expensive and open-ended entanglement that would be certain to bring down international condemnation on the USSR, the Soviet leaders impolitely declined.[42]

The shift in outlook had a powerful short-term cause: the Soviet intervention in Afghanistan, which was already widely perceived by the Soviet elite as a grave error. But broader ideological changes were also in train. In the early 1980s, the USSR was far more likely than in the previous decade to see its relations with satellites and clients in cost-benefit terms. In 1983–4, Mikhail Gorbachev, a recent addition to the Politburo, started receiving reports on the state of Soviet trade with eastern Europe: since 1976, the latter had enjoyed a trade surplus that ran to billions of rubles (8.5 billion rubles, or about 14 percent of trade between these partners, in 1981–2 alone).[43] In the first half of the 1980s, the USSR was supplying 36 countries with arms, a third of these going to the Third World. But this was now a business far more than a means of geopolitical expansion: Iraq alone paid $13 billion for Soviet arms during the 1980s.[44]

Economic hard-headedness was accompanied by doctrinal revisions. Soviet research institutes in the late 1970s and early 1980s saw a further wave of Marxist debate on the character of Third World revolutions. Some of the regimes that the Soviets had previously favored – such as Mengistu's in Ethiopia – were now reclassified as nonprogressive. In the mid-1980s, the KGB was supplying Gorbachev amply with information on the moral and political failings of various Soviet clients in the Third World. By 1987, the Soviet leadership had drawn in its horns and was turning down requests for aid (not least in view of the fact that the USSR, a country undergoing a severe economic crisis of its own, was owed not far short of 100 billion rubles by the Third World at the end of the 1980s). Soviet global geopolitics had finally become substantially de-ideologized.[45]

But the principal benefits of this retreat from ideology were felt in Europe. In the late 1980s, the key eastern European satellites once again hit trouble. Yet another sudden price rise in Poland provoked yet more popular unrest, which took hard political form far more quickly than in 1956 or 1980–1. Within months the government made unofficial overtures to Lech Wałęsa, the leader of Solidarity, and official negotiations began in February 1989. The elections that followed in June delivered a crushing defeat for the Communists. In Hungary, from mid-1988 onward, the Communists themselves took steps to reform and renew the system, thus preparing the way for pluralism. The GDR faced yet another refugee crisis when the Hungarians opened their border with the West to Austria; the Honecker regime was soon brought down by the most genuinely "popular" revolution of 1989. In Czechoslovakia, too, Communism was toppled rather than merely stepping aside: mass popular protest in central Prague in November 1989 brought a terminal crisis in the regime's legitimacy and will to rule.

All of these outcomes were in keeping with the histories and political cultures of the particular countries. What was different, of course, was the obvious refusal of the USSR to intervene. How exactly should we account for this demonstrative Soviet withdrawal from a region of such acute geopolitical preoccupation over the previous forty years? One reason was that, as noted above with respect to the Third World, the Gorbachev leadership was aware that the USSR had entered a phase of imperial overstretch. In the 1940s and 1950s, when the Soviets had plundered eastern Europe for reparations, resources and human capital, it had done rather well out of the bloc, but the cost-benefit analysis of the 1980s was pointing in the opposite direction.[46] Economic calculations alone, however, cannot explain the softening of Soviet attitudes. The new generation of Soviet leaders figureheaded by Gorbachev were reform Communists of the kind that had been brutally suppressed in Prague in 1968. Their instincts were increasingly social-democratic. For them, coercion was not the way to achieve the desirable medium-term outcome of harmonious and constructive relations between the USSR and a broadly social democratic Europe.

Even these broad ideological shifts, however, were a necessary rather than a sufficient condition for the sudden collapse of Communism in eastern Europe. Gorbachev himself would have been horrified, even as late as 1987, if he had been told what the international consequences of his "new thinking" would be. As in other areas of policy, his opaque rhetoric dulled the fears of the army and the KGB – and his own sense of danger. Gorbachev confidently expected, until it was much too late, that Soviet influence on eastern Europe would usher in an era of civilized social democracy in central and eastern Europe on Soviet terms: imperial domination, with all its human and economic costs, would thus be converted to a more humane and economically efficient hegemony. This, however, was fundamentally to overestimate the sticking power of socialism in eastern Europe once Soviet military force was withdrawn. The drift of the "new thinking" led Gorbachev, often unwittingly, to hand over the Soviet Union's hard-earned trump cards. In the GDR, moreover, the withdrawal of Soviet backing implied not only the end of authoritarian socialism but also the creation of an entirely new state. In October 1989, just a month before the Berlin Wall was opened, Gorbachev visited Berlin and seems to have underestimated the likelihood that, with the GDR leadership weakened, German national unification would gain decisive momentum.[47]

Mikhail Gorbachev was a true believer in the friendship of peoples – not a Hollywood version of the same. As a result he was able to gain the moral high ground in his negotiations with the West, which at times put Ronald Reagan and Margaret Thatcher on the back foot but also offered them geopolitical gifts that they learned not to look in the mouth. The "Second Cold War" of the first Reagan administration in the early 1980s had certainly increased the economic pressure on the USSR, but there is absolutely no reason why a different Soviet regime could not have defied sanctions and, through a combination of coercion and austerity measures, kept the Cold War in the deep freeze for longer. No one but Gorbachev could have brought the Soviet empire to collapse so quickly and so peacefully. Yet, in showing himself to be the world's greatest internationalist, he inadvertently dealt the great power status of the USSR a blow that many of its people would find impossible to forgive him.

Post-Soviet Eurasianism?

Geopolitics was a painful business for Russian statesmen in the early 1990s. This recent superpower had been brought low by the political and economic crises provoked by Gorbachev's policies. Not only had the Soviet Union relinquished its eastern European bloc, it also had to give up large parts of its own country. The main successor state, the Russian Federation, now had a host of problematic new neighbors that previously would have been handled under the auspices of Soviet nationality policy: the Baltic states, the Caucasus, Moldova, Ukraine. Worse still, the military and economic foundations on which great power status rested had subsided: Russia was poor and debt-ridden, its army was demoralized, and its political structures were in flux. Given the levels of corruption and the extent of special interests, Russian foreign policy risked becoming not two-track (as at various points in the Soviet era) but entirely fragmented.[48] This lack of cohesion was all the more regrettable in the face of triumphalist Western powers who were convinced they had "won" the Cold War.

An observer of the new Russia in the early period of its existence might have sketched out two geopolitical scenarios, both of them undesirable but neither at all implausible. First, Russia might remain for the foreseeable future a weak state incapable of presenting anything even approaching its old Cold War threat to the liberal West. Given the residual size of its arsenal and its sensitive geopolitical position, however, this would imply substantial and – unlike the Cold War – unpredictable consequences for the rest of the world. In the second scenario, Russia might snap back from its humiliation, drink from the wells of revanchist nationalism, and readopt Soviet habits of geopolitical thinking, treating its ex-Soviet neighbors and Eastern bloc satellites as vassals and once again throwing its considerable weight around in the UN and in its bilateral relations with a range of NATO countries.

Another way of conceptualizing these alternatives – one that became increasingly common in the late 1990s and early 2000s – was to ask the eternal question "Whither Russia?" and to propose the equally eternal alternative answers "West" and "East." Either Russia would throw in its lot with Western liberal democracy and work responsibly toward inclusion in the G-7 club or it would seek to turn itself into a hegemon in the Eurasian land mass, in the process doing business with a number of politically illiberal but economically resurgent states (notably China).

Which theory has proved correct as of the late 2000s? The first point to note is that post-Soviet Russia, for all its foreign policy demarches, such as the dispatching of 200 troops to Pristina in 1999 or the gas disputes with Ukraine from 2005 onward, did not prove to be an entirely loose cannon. Russian diplomats, like any responsible and effective statesmen, tried to have their cake and eat it – and, much of the time, with the aid of a little good fortune, they succeeded. Over the first 15 years of postcommunism, as Russian great power ideology was shorn of its Communist connotations, political leaders (notably Vladimir Putin) drew benefit from striking anti-Western poses and talking tough with the European Union and its individual members. They additionally cultivated ties with the Far East, most publicly through the Shanghai Cooperation Organization. But they also retained the benefits of a close working relationship with the West. In 1997, despite Russian economic weakness, the G-7 became the G-8.[49] The Western orientation of Russia (which is fully compatible with regular anti-Western rhetoric) was not overridden even by the most challenging issue to face its relationship with the West in the post-Soviet era: the enlargement of NATO to the east and the meddling of America and its allies in parts of the former Soviet Union where Russia considers it should have a great power monopoly.

There is no doubt, as many Western diplomats and statesmen can surely attest, that the post-Soviet Russians can be infuriating to deal with. Especially in the Putin era, when the state was flush with oil revenues, Russian foreign policy sometimes had an arrogance and an insensitivity that were both breathtaking and counterproductive. The clearest example is Russia's propensity to apply blackmail to economic partners over oil and gas deliveries: this practice may hurt Russia's crucial trade with the EU more than it assists Russia to maximize its revenues and achieve politically desirable outcomes in nearby states such as Ukraine and Georgia.

Many Western commentators over the last ten or fifteen years have drawn from rebarbative Russian diplomacy the conclusion that Russia is taking a radical anti-Western course, and that we are on course for a "new cold war" over political and economic issues in what Russia regards as its sphere of influence.[50] They draw more evidence for this hypothesis from Russia's illiberal government, its close contacts with China, and its bullying relationship to many parts of its "near abroad." The 2008 war with Georgia over South Ossetia, followed by the anti-Ukrainian rhetoric of President Medvedev in the buildup to the 2010 Ukrainian presidential elections, might seem to clinch the argument.

Many Russians, of course, would answer these charges by saying that it suited the West all too well to have an economically and politically enfeebled Russia, and that Putin and Medvedev have done no more, and no less, than any responsible statesmen would do: exploit the leverage and self-sufficiency that economic recovery and energy resources afford them to assert Russia's national interests. This does not mean that Russia is turning its back on the West; if anything, quite the opposite. For all the fashionable talk of Eurasianism and the relative cordiality of Sino–Russian relations, the Russians are more comfortable dealing with the Germans, the British, and even the Americans. The problem is not only that the Chinese and the Russians have a Cold War history in many ways even more fraught than that of the Soviet–American confrontation, or even that the Chinese are still regarded by Moscow as a demographic threat to the Russian Far East. More important is that the Chinese pay less for oil and gas, have less extensive pipeline infrastructure, and are not stable trade partners of several decades' standing. The Sino–Russian rapprochement has been called an "anti-relationship" conceived more as a counterweight to the West than as a positive statement of long-term commitment.[51]

The reassertion of Russian influence is profoundly disappointing to the many Western observers because it gives the lie to a vision of the world of which they had grown very fond during the 1990s: the notion that all the world's problems could be solved by a parliament of like-minded nations, that the developed and liberal West could draw into its orbit more and more of the East, that shared economic and cultural interests ("globalization") would allow nations to overcome their political particularism. Old-fashioned geopolitics is back with us (if it ever went away). The bipolarity of the Cold War has given way to a much-attested "multipolarity," which sounds benign and egalitarian but in fact is hard to distinguish from the idea of the domination of the world by a number (more than two) of large powers.

Yet it would be absurd on this basis to draw close parallels between, say, the early twenty-first century and the run-up to one or other of the world wars. In our present age, thankfully, the pursuit of economic and political goals by major powers is not especially likely to take the form of military conflict. To be sure, the USA is not a stranger to the war-making reflex but, given the colossal imbalance between its forces and those of any other state, it might be expected to succumb to it even more frequently; it is after all a liberal democracy, and any militarist lobby faces domestic constraints that are lacking in a state like Russia. The other major global powers of the early-to-mid twenty-first century (China, India and, some way further down, Russia) have very little incentive, at least for the medium term, to rattle sabers. They are doing well enough out of the world order as it currently exists.

At the same time, any configuration of major powers produces its own structures and interrelationships. Russia's structural position, to take up a hoary cliché, will lie between East and West. But the cliché generally seeks to explain Russia's cultural "otherness" – its "Asiatic" qualities – in the European context. In the geopolitical arena of the twenty-first century, it seems, Russia's intermediate position will need to be understood a little less airily and metaphorically. For the first time in two centuries or more, "the East" will be not a myth or a cultural "other" but a hard geopolitical reality. Russia, accordingly, may have new opportunities to exploit its location at a gigantic global crossroads to further its national interests. Its position, most likely, will be analogous to that of Gaullist France during the Cold War: it will be an obstreperous and disagreeable member of the community to which it formally belongs and from which it derives great benefit (the West) while building pragmatic ties with the other side.

Conclusion

It is time now to put aside the crystal ball and return to the stated purpose of this book: history. The key question, in this chapter as in all the others, is the following: if we take the period 1941 to c. 2009 as a whole, what shape can we give the story that escapes our view if we take different chronological perspectives? In particular, what happens if we abandon habit and shift the Cold War confrontation from the center of our account of geopolitics in the last 60 years or so? If, as Vojtech Mastny has suggested, the "long peace" of the Cold War was less order than disorder in disguise, what other factors might we consider in search of a geopolitical framework for this period?[52]

When Andrei Amalrik asked in a world-famous *samizdat* essay whether the Soviet Union would survive until 1984, his main reason for believing that it would not was not any of the reasons that may plausibly be adduced for the Soviet Union's actual collapse (ill-judged Communist reformism, economic crisis, imperial overstretch). He was most worried about the rise of China.[53]

It turns out that Amalrik was wrong to suppose that China would pose a direct military threat (even though, with his recent memories of Sino–Soviet armed clashes in 1969, this was an entirely reasonable supposition). Even in the early twenty-first century, as argued above, it seems unlikely that China will turn expansionist aggressor any time soon. But China's self-assertion under Mao and Deng Xiaoping was only the most extreme example of a paradoxical phenomenon of the Cold War era: as the world's military hardware became ever more concentrated in the hands of the two superpowers and their close allies, the nonaligned rest of the world became ever more autonomous and ambitious.

Just as the traditional imperial powers had regarded much of the non-European world as an appendage to their own domain, so the superpowers sought to manipulate the Third World to their ends. With superpower support or connivance, dozens of wars were fought, millions of people were killed, and a large handful of countries were left in ruins. Between 1964 and 1982, Soviet armed forces took part in almost 30 military conflicts around the world (Latin America, Africa, Near and Far East, Southeast Asia and Europe), while the Americans intervened, in one way or another, in around 30 countries in the post-1945 era.[54] In neither case did the superpowers do much to further their professed goals – anticolonial liberation, socialism, liberal democracy – and they did a great deal to undermine them.

But, without downplaying the usually hideous moral costs of American and Soviet involvement around the globe, it is reasonable to argue that both superpowers greatly overestimated their ability to affect outcomes in the non-European world and found themselves drawn into conflicts by forces larger than purely economic calculations. One of those forces was the simple fear that they would be bested by the other side in the Cold War. Another was ideology: the sense that geopolitical decisions had to follow a grand logic conforming to the presumed historical mission of the American or Soviet nation. The Soviets, given their own historical experience and their Marxist-Leninist theoretical heritage, could not help believing that the Third World – as a poor, oppressed, politically unstable, rapidly modernizing zone of the globe – "belonged" to them. But if they had imperial designs on the Third World, this was empire in a different sense of the word from any familiar before 1914: the USSR was not involving itself in global affairs primarily for motives of economic exploitation or military strategy. To a large extent, it valued control – as measured by the adoption in far-flung parts of the world of "Marxism" – for its own sake.

Third World interventionism, then, is the first great innovation in Russian geopolitical thinking in the second half of the twentieth century. And, for all that it might now seem inevitable, it was by no means reached easily. Soviet leaders were all ideological animals, but they were also, within certain limits set by ideology, flexible and pragmatic. They did not want to test their strength against the West if they could avoid it, and they did not want to take over the globe (or even Europe) in the sense of military conquest – though on a few occasions (Berlin 1948, Korea 1950–53, Cuba 1962, Afghanistan 1979) they behaved in ways that seemed to the other superpower to imply an aggressive global agenda, strangely failing to anticipate that their actions would be seen in that light. Stalin's policies in the late 1940s and early 1950s were characterized by old-fashioned – if sometimes spiteful and ill-considered – Realpolitik. It was not until the mid-1950s that a Soviet cottage industry of theorizing the nonaligned movement started to take policy in new directions. Between the 1950s and the early 1980s, Soviet foreign policy never entirely shed pragmatism, but it was consistently vulnerable to the blandishments of demanding Third World clients, and especially discomfited by the biggest and most unruly ex-client of all – China.

In the second half of the 1980s Soviet policy on the wider world underwent revolutionary changes. Not only did the Kremlin withdraw from its burdensome commitments in the Third World, it also allowed an area of undoubted geopolitical importance to the USSR – eastern Europe – to go its own way. While there was an enormous amount for even Russians to be thankful for in the largely nonviolent collapse of Communist eastern Europe, it did not come about as a result of fundamental ideological change in the Soviet elite. Rather, it was the result of Mikhail Gorbachev's charm, ingenuity, and naivety.

There was a price to be paid, of course, for this unprecedented peaceful retreat from domination, and Russian statesmen (not to mention Russian society) paid it for most of the 1990s in the form of national humiliation. Nonetheless, Russia's diplomatic performance and geopolitical weight remained respectable out of all proportion to the disastrous weakness of the Russian state and economy at that time. Russia's elites retained a great power mentality in the absence of a great power state, sometimes acting as if they had forgotten 1989 and 1991 had ever happened. And, when Russia began to recover at the turn of the century, weakness and humiliation could be replaced by an understandable, if sometimes obnoxious, sense of robustness.

9

From Isolationism to Globalization

As is well known, Russia's relationship to "the West" has been a vexed question for the past three centuries. In the wake of the Great Patriotic War, however, it entered a radically new phase. In the 1920s and 1930s, the Russian population was poorly informed about the wider world. Very few Soviet people had reliable knowledge, let alone direct experience, of life beyond socialism. In the mid-1940s, however, millions of them marched into Germany, while mass population displacement permitted exchange of information across state borders on an enormous scale. Stalin's response to the consequent danger of ideological infection from the bourgeois world was characteristically heavy-handed: to cast into the Gulag former POWs and other Soviet citizens who had spent suspiciously long periods abroad or in contact with foreigners. Yet the problem of Western influence did not go away over the following decades, and it increasingly took forms that were not amenable to coercive solutions. The defiant isolationism of Stalin's USSR was compromised by the global rise of audiovisual mass culture and the opening of the Soviet Union to an unprecedented amount of diplomatic and cultural contact with the nonsocialist world. The Soviets had their own cultural resources in the mass media age, and patriotism was bolstered by an extensive and generally popular socialist mass culture. But this culture still received careful protection from foreign influence, whether in the form of direct censorship or in the deeply internalized edificatory ethos of writers, journalists, broadcasters, and filmmakers. When practically all cultural barriers were lifted in the early 1990s, Russia faced in acute form the prospect so often decried in parts of non-Anglophone western Europe: the dilution of authentic national culture in an ocean of American trash. Yet, as this chapter will end by suggesting, the prophecies of cultural doom have proved to be greatly exaggerated: by the early twenty-first century, Russia had a nonsocialist mass culture that was recognizably its own.

——————— Xenophobia and Trophy Westernization ———————

The late Stalin period was the high-water mark of Soviet xenophobia. Even before the Cold War had set in, the authorities were concerned to set firm limits on the influence of their recent allies. In November 1945, Stalin sent a telegram from his residence in Sochi to point out the political error of publishing a speech by Churchill in *Pravda*. In what would soon become a mantra of Soviet ideology, he observed that "we must conduct a fierce struggle against servility toward foreigners." In due course, the weekly magazine *Britanskii soiuznik* (*The British Ally*), which had existed for four years with a circulation of 50,000, was deemed politically harmful. Abakumov, the head of state security, made objections to the magazine's excessively favorable coverage of the Beveridge Report, the achievements of British science and scholarship, the English quality of life, and British foreign policy in Greece, Indonesia, Israel, and Egypt. In May 1947, the All-Union Society for Cultural Relations with Foreign Countries (VOKS) was revealed to have accepted films from foreign embassies without the necessary permission. The British embassy had provided 14 films in 1946 and 11 in 1947; *Brief Encounter* had been shown a total of 15 times. In perhaps the most invasive anti-Western measure of the early Cold War era, Soviet citizens were forbidden by a decree of 15 February 1947 from marrying foreigners. Ernest Bevin asked Stalin to allow Russian women who had married Englishmen during the war to leave the country (a mere 17 women), but Stalin declined the request.[1]

Censorship was accompanied by crude efforts to assert Russian supremacy in all worthwhile fields of endeavor. In October 1947, the head of Agitprop spent time organizing a campaign to show that Aleksandr Popov was the inventor of radio (following a radio technology congress in Rome which had just given the nod to Marconi). By January 1948, the authorities had decided that the Nobel Prize committee was so biased against Soviet writers and scientists that a rival Lenin Prize was to be established instead.[2] The contortions of wartime propaganda, which had had to shelve blanket condemnation of the "bourgeois" world, could now be forgotten. It seems safe to assume that the Russian-infused Soviet patriotism of the late Stalin era played well with many citizens. Members of the listening audience wrote in to the central radio administration to query the large number of foreign operas played on air, insisting that Russian folksongs and other popular material be given precedence.[3]

But the bombast came with a good deal of ambiguity in Soviet attitudes to the outside world. Assertions of Soviet supremacy concealed anxiety and insecurity. This was especially evident in the population at large, which was gripped by a fear of war with the former allies. The *New York Times* correspondent Harrison

Salisbury wrote in May 1949 that ordinary Muscovites were "almost pathetic in their pleasure" on hearing the news that the Berlin blockade had been lifted.[4] The main problem for the Soviet regime, however, was that its population was far less ignorant of and indifferent to the contemporary bourgeois world than it would have liked. In September 1947 even Andrei Zhdanov, the Soviet ideology chief, admitted when briefing a new colleague that Agitprop faced serious difficulties: Soviet people wanted to live better, and many of them had recently seen the outside world.[5] On their long wartime march westward, Soviet people had discovered shocking contrasts between their own immiseration and the relative prosperity of even the poorer parts of central Europe. The induction into "Western" affluence had begun as early as autumn 1939 with the invasion of Eastern Poland. Red Army soldiers were primed to say "We have everything" in conversations with locals, but this affected indifference was belied by their spending sprees in the shops and markets of the occupied territory. Eastern Poland was a consumer paradise for these ordinary Soviet men.[6] The further the Red Army went west, the more eye-opening the revelations. One Soviet soldier was astonished to be shown the shoe and clothes collection of a war widow in Czechoslovakia in 1945, who then apologized for what she considered the poverty of her household in the wake of German plunder.[7]

In 1946, the prominent writer and budding functionary Konstantin Simonov was sent as the head of a delegation to the United States with a propaganda mission: to assure the Americans of the USSR's peaceful intentions. On the same trip he also spent time in Canada and France. Like millions of his compatriots, he felt the "moral and psychological blow" of coming face to face with the shocking contrast between living standards in the victorious USSR and less obviously victorious "Europe," although Soviet patriotism, in the wake of victory, offered some means of overcoming the jarring sense of injustice and deprivation.[8] Even elite Soviets might feel like poor relations on their travels. In a letter to the foreign minister Viacheslav Molotov in 1946, a journalist complained that the Western press mocked Soviet visitors for being dressed identically and tastelessly (in blue coat, black suit, hat, brown shoes, socks, and tie) as compared to the far more elegantly clad Westerners, and he accused *Spetstorg*, a special closed shop of the NKVD, of sabotaging the country's cultural image in the West by failing to supply the people who were going abroad with "nice," "stylish" clothes of a good variety.[9] Vera Dunham, in her study of late Stalinist fiction, nicely captured the liminal position of the Soviet elite in this period:

> The bourgeois West, with its artifacts and mores, has in fact become the measure of Soviet achievements. Both the leadership and the run-of-the-mill engineer sent abroad to supervise deliveries of capitalist gadgetry engage in comparisons

obsessively. While he eats steak or buys purses or underwear that his wife has asked him to bring back, the emissary's facial muscles betray invidious admiration for American goods and food, shifting instantly to a mandatory kind of put-down ... Like strange peeping Toms, Soviet officials look in on their own world from the outside.[10]

But officialdom did not have a monopoly on such feelings. In the postwar period, hundreds of thousands of armed forces personnel would continue their direct everyday exposure to the non-Soviet world in the Soviet-occupied parts of central Europe. Germany was renowned in the mid-1940s as a good place to buy up desirable goods such as cigarettes, alcohol, and sausages. Army discipline suffered in the face of temptations to steal and extort from the local population. Efforts in the later 1940s to tighten supervision made serving in Germany less attractive but did not diminish the incongruous abundance to be found in a devastated and defeated "Western" country.[11]

No one, least of all the army's top brass, was immune to the siren call of Western riches. A search of Zhukov's dacha in January 1948 revealed a cornucopia of valuables plundered from central Europe: more than 4,000 meters of fabric, 323 furs, 44 carpets and tapestries, 55 paintings, and so on. As a secret police memo to Stalin concluded, "When you go into this house, it is hard to imagine that you are just outside Moscow and not in Germany." Zhukov was by no means the only case in the military elite of excessive acquisition of "trophy" items. In February, General-Major A. M. Sidnev, who had been in charge of the MVD in Berlin between 1945 and 1947, confessed to looting and theft in Germany – his luggage on the trip home had included 40 suitcases and crates crammed with clothing, household goods, and valuables – and pointed to a wider culture of corruption in the security forces.[12] Many Soviet officers were able to gain ownership – semilegally or illegally – of "trophy" cars from Germany. It has been estimated that, in 1950, almost one-third of all cars in Moscow were of foreign provenance.[13]

It would appear that all Soviet citizens took advantage of whatever opportunities they had to acquire coveted Western goods. In an interrogation of February 1948, E. S. Khruleva-Gorelik admitted to having acquired goods on a trip to Czechoslovakia in 1946–7 and then selling them at "speculative" prices.[14] As it happened, the interrogators were much more interested in her reported anti-Soviet utterances and undesirable acquaintances. But the extent of uncontrolled contact between Soviet citizens and the people and material culture of the West was bound to concern the postwar Soviet authorities, and it often served as the gateway to further-reaching political accusations.[15] Even POWs in the USSR might be seen as a bridgehead of Western influence. In the camps of the northern region of Vologda, in which 60,000 enemy soldiers and officers spent time between

1939 and 1949, "camp marriages" were a recognized – if deplored – phenomenon. Nurses were disciplined and fired for "intimate relations" with prisoners; such cases continued even after marriages between Soviet citizens and foreigners were banned in the law of 15 February 1947. Some German POWs, for their part, tried to resist repatriation at the end of the 1940s – perhaps because they had become attached to Soviet women.[16]

In other domains, however, the Soviet regime tolerated manifestations of Western culture that would have been extraordinary in the 1930s. The depleted and politically constrained Soviet film industry was not giving audiences much to enjoy, and the "trophy films" confiscated from Germany were allowed to step into the breach. Within a week of the Nazi surrender, an official from the Soviet Ministry of Cinematography was combing the Reich's main film archive at Babelsberg. Among his selections were hundreds of light entertainment movies of American and western European provenance. Even if films were edited or accompanied by edifying commentary when shown back home, and even if they did not necessarily get shown in the largest cinemas, they still made a huge impact. At least 35 feature films from Nazi Germany were shown in the Soviet Union between 1947 and 1949, while the most successful movie of the immediate postwar period was a German musical called *A Girl of My Dreams*. In 1951, only one-quarter of films in distribution were Soviet, and in 1952 Johnny Weismuller's Tarzan was all the rage in Moscow cinemas.[17]

Another cultural legacy of the war was the existence in Moscow of restaurants and bars with an American flavor. One of the most prestigious was a "Cocktail Hall" on Moscow's main drag, Gorky Street. Spread over two floors, it had elaborate drinks and an American-style bar with revolving chairs. All in all, postwar Moscow had around thirty establishments where patrons could hear Western-style dance music. In 1951, Salisbury commented enthusiastically on the jazz band at the Hotel Astoria restaurant whose repertoire was 80 percent American.[18]

Such glimpses of American popular culture brought inspiration to the most eye-catching subculture of late Stalinist Russia. The *stiliagi* ("stylish ones") constructed a world of their own from dance styles and fashions in dress. They avidly copied the jargon and body language they associated with the West in their efforts to live a colorful "good life" in postwar Russia. They attached great importance to fashionable dress, in particular wide ties and "Tarzan haircuts." In almost all cases, their outfits had to be homemade, which underlines the extent to which this was a Soviet "imagined West" rather than a faithful reproduction. Those with greater pretensions to cultural authenticity called themselves *shtatniki* and claimed to imitate more faithfully current American fashions. Further channels of Western cultural influence included "music on bones" (black market jazz recordings that were manufactured on used X-ray plates) and foreign broadcasts, which in the late 1940s were accessible to a few hundred thousand people, mainly in urban centers (though soon enough they had to contend with Soviet jamming).[19]

The *stiliagi* were a tiny minority of urban youth. But they were hardly unique in taking an interest in the non-Soviet world. The available evidence on popular mentalities – much of it from the dismal source of files on prosecutions for anti-Soviet behavior – suggests that ideological campaigns in the late Stalin era were not particularly effective, and that the Soviet population was better informed and more curious as a result of the war. Soviet ingenuity fed off the scraps of material that evaded the censorship. The Cold War enemy was keen to communicate with ordinary people, but until the 1950s it had only two established ways of doing so. The first was the journal *Amerika*, which first appeared in 1944 and was subject to the same kind of restrictions as *Britanskii soiuznik*. On its first publication the journal's circulation was limited to 10,000 copies, a figure that was increased to 50,000 as of June 1946. But the Soviet authorities made every effort to ensure that copies would reach the right kind of people: only 14,000 copies actually went on sale (10,000 of those in Moscow), while the rest went to subscribers and institutions. In 1949, representatives of the Soviet book and periodical trade reported to Agitprop that the journal was not selling well. While this claim is hardly credible, it was symptomatic of growing restrictions that in 1952 caused the Americans to cancel publication in frustration.[20]

This left them with the Voice of America, which started Russian-language broadcasts in February 1947, initially for two hours a day. In due course the station expanded its operations to broadcast in nine languages of the USSR. By 1950 the Americans claimed a substantial regular audience based on a figure of 3–4 million suitably equipped radio sets in the USSR. The authorities fought back through jamming and political repression: in this era Soviet people might face prosecution under the notorious legislation on anti-Soviet activity (article 58-10 of the criminal code) for listening to foreign radio. Face-to-face contact with Westerners was extraordinarily limited. According to material from the VOKS, only nineteen American delegations (comprising a total of 57 people) visited between 1947 and 1951, and most of these were high-profile fellow travelers.[21]

To all appearances, the USSR was on the defensive from the start of its cultural war with the United States. The Soviet ideological apparatus was experienced at imposing controls and restrictions but less adept at projecting an appealing message to the West. In 1946–7, officials of VOKS in America contacted Moscow to ask for resources in order to carry out more effective propaganda campaigns, but their efforts were mostly unsuccessful. When VOKS attempted to launch a propaganda counteroffensive at the American Cultural and Scientific Conference for World Peace in March 1949, its delegation was forced home early; there would be no other such Soviet delegation to the US until 1953.[22]

—— After Stalin: The Soviet Union Re-engages the World ——

In the mid-1950s, de-Stalinization – which combined ideological revision and slight domestic liberalization with a more proactive and optimistic strategy in the Cold War – brought a substantial increase in cultural traffic between the USSR and the rest of the world. It was symptomatic that the writer who coined the term "Thaw" (in 1954) was the most "European" of all Soviet literary intellectuals. Ilya Ehrenburg had spent his formative years as a writer in Paris. His four-volume memoirs, published in the early 1960s, offered readers a smooth introduction to European culture of the first half of the twentieth century. In this era the Soviet educated public was permitted to take a more informed interest in the history, culture, and languages of western Europe. Such people were likely to be among the 20 million or so with radio sets capable of picking up Western broadcasts. If they could evade Soviet jamming, they had plenty of programming to enjoy: Voice of America was by now broadcasting for more than 16 hours per day.[23] As early as 1957, almost two-thirds of students in higher education were learning English, and the early 1960s saw the establishment of a system of prestigious secondary schools specializing in foreign languages.[24]

There was also sharp increase in the human traffic between the Soviet Union and the West. The intrepid Khrushchev took the lead. After a two-month trip in 1955 to court the Third World in India, Burma and Afghanistan, he encountered Western leaders in person at the Geneva summit of July 1955, poking Nelson Rockefeller in the ribs and taking the opportunity to order self-winding watches for his family and a Swiss Army knife for himself. In April 1956 the Soviet leadership made a landmark official visit to England: the first such high-level Soviet visit to a Western country. Khrushchev had wanted to arrive on an impressive four-engine Tu-104, but the plane was not yet trusted by Soviet engineers; he took the boat instead. Khrushchev's anxiety over points of protocol indicated the importance of the event. All the same, the visit was considered a success, and Queen Elizabeth struck Khrushchev as "the sort of young woman you'd be likely to meet walking along Gorky Street on a balmy Sunday afternoon." His only antagonistic meeting was with representatives of the opposition Labor Party.[25]

In September 1959 came Khrushchev's visit to America. Overcoming his apprehension that Camp David might be a kind of quarantine station, Khrushchev wasted no time in handing over to Eisenhower a replica of the Soviet rocket to the moon. Throughout his stay, he combined poorly concealed wide-eyed curiosity with crude boasting. His experiences ranged from a visit to the set of *Can-Can* to a reception at Averell Harriman's house in New York where Khrushchev found that the guests "looked like typical capitalists, right out of the posters painted during our Civil War – only they didn't have the pigs' snouts our artists always gave them."[26]

The Soviet leader's lack of sophistication was emblematic of a society emerging from isolation but it was not necessarily typical of the lucky few Soviet people who had the opportunity to see America. The slight thawing of superpower relations in the second half of the 1950s brought a number of cultural agreements that allowed budding members of the Soviet elite to spend extended periods of study abroad. A graduate exchange program sent a few dozen Soviet students to major American universities. These Soviet graduates were mature thirty-somethings. They were selected not by open competition but by recommendation of the appropriate agencies. Nevertheless, they were far from being ideological automata. Aleksandr Yakovlev, later an architect of Gorbachev's cultural and political reforms, went to Columbia University in the fall of 1958; even if he remained dutifully anti-American in his public statements, the experience left its mark. Oleg Kalugin, another member of Columbia class of '58 who later spent a decade as a KGB officer in New York and Washington, recalled spending hours traveling around on public transport; his recreations included seeing more than a hundred films and visiting a strip club.[27]

Less exalted travelers were also making their way westward, though not as far as Manhattan. In 1956, according to official figures, a total of 560,000 Soviet citizens went abroad, and a further 1.5 million followed over the following two years. By the early 1960s, tens of thousands of Soviet people were traveling to socialist eastern Europe – not a large number, but an enormous increase over the Stalin era. The capitalist world, by contrast, was reserved for the well-connected few. In 1961, a mere 228 Soviet citizens went on "tourist" visits to the USA, more than two-thirds of them Party members.[28]

A respectable educated Soviet citizen might now expect to have numerous encounters with foreign culture over the course of a lifetime. One woman (b. 1949) from the middle Volga city of Saratov, a lecturer for many years at the local polytechnic, attended the World Youth Festival of 1957 as a child, learned English to a high level (though from outdated textbooks), listened to the Beatles, and happened to be in Czechoslovakia on the tenth anniversary of the 1968 invasion. She also recalled a general nonpolitical enthusiasm for President Kennedy, who was thought to look like a Russian. Her experiences were not untypical of her cohort at Saratov's School No. 42, the subject of a recent interview project.[29]

The increased scope for contact with the West did not, of course, reduce the Soviet regime's commitment to control the terms on which that contact occurred. Potential tourists were carefully vetted by Party organizations. Tour groups were subject to close surveillance: by their group leader, perhaps by a trade union representative attached to the tour group, and of course by KGB agents.[30] Nor

FIGURE 9.1 *Krokodil* cartoon, "What People Find Most Striking" (1961). This crude contrast between the tourist experience in the USA and the USSR shows that state-sponsored xenophobia remained strong even after several years of "Thaw".
Source: UCL School of Slavonic and East European Studies Library.

should we imagine that Soviet travelers were always eager to be impressed. Evgeniia Gutnova, an eminent historian specializing in medieval English history, describes her feelings of apprehension before a visit to Britain in 1965: she was worried about flying and also about making herself understood to English colleagues at an enormous academic conference. She also – at least before this first trip to the West began to broaden her horizons – had rather little critical distance from the Soviet ideological mainstream. Even this highly educated member of

Soviet society remembered feeling at the time that Pasternak's publication of *Doctor Zhivago* abroad in 1958 was an "unpatriotic act."[31]

Few Soviet travelers, however, were left indifferent by the consumer abundance they found even not very far west of the USSR. A respectable and ideologically correct middle-aged Soviet functionary, on a trip to Karlovy Vary in 1960, could not help but make comparisons between Czechoslovakia and the Soviet Union. The Czechs were tastefully but not extravagantly dressed, hard-working and honest. They were distinguished by a well-developed property instinct largely lacking in Soviet people:

> Our current generation has been brought up in the socialist spirit, to recognize common social property rather than personal, so we spend our savings mainly on personal things: clothing, toiletries, organizing leisure and medical treatment. Their current generation … has passed through a different school, the school of property, and without question they are unable to renounce property-owning tendencies that manifest themselves in the acquisition of things like cars, motorcycles, and so on.

Translated from Sovietspeak, this meant that the Czechoslovak standard of living was far higher – and the housing situation was far more favorable, given the relative lack of wartime destruction and the postwar mass expulsion of the German population.[32] One Soviet painter who visited Norway in December 1965 recorded in his diary his amazement at the neon advertising and Christmas decorations: "I was flabbergasted … but we didn't show that we felt emotional inside." Not all Soviet travelers were as self-controlled. A certain Denisov, chairman of the Russian Consumer Union, was arrested in London for shoplifting cardigans in Marks and Spencer; only strenuous efforts by the Soviet consulate brought his release.[33]

Some shortage-plagued Soviet citizens were discovering that there was even more to foreign travel than shopping. The trips undertaken by one Leningrad radio journalist might serve as a parable of the deepening Soviet encounter with the bourgeois world. In 1964, Lev Markhasev was part of a delegation to Czechoslovakia. For him, as for his colleagues on the trip, "abroad was heaven," even if it was preceded by an inquisition at the district Party committee. Despite the patronizing and downright anti-Soviet attitudes adopted by the Czech guides, he was impressed by everything he saw: "the bright colors, the cold cleanliness, the petty bourgeois neatness." In 1970, on a trip to Norway and Sweden, Markhasev was struck by the Scandinavian sexual revolution but even more by the Norwegian quality of life: here he, like many other well-informed Soviets, found what he could identify as really-existing socialism. The arc of Markhasev's learning curve was completed on a visit to London in 1974, where he was obliged to pay his respects to Marx's grave in Highgate Cemetery (whose statue had been left head-

FIGURE 9.2   An African visitor to the World Youth Festival, Moscow 1957.
Source: © Eugeny Khaldei / PhotoSoyuz.

less by some vandal), but also found time for *Last Tango in Paris* on Leicester Square.[34]

Tourist traffic was also coming in the opposite direction. From 1956 onward the USSR received about half a million foreign tourists annually. By 1973, the figure was close to 3 million, which did not compare well with the nearly 7 million visitors to Poland but still represented a sizable increase on earlier Soviet history.[35] The economic function of foreign tourism was at least as important as its propaganda value. In the immediate postwar period, the authorities had mooted the idea that tourism could help to fix the Soviet balance of payments. The early Cold War era turned out not to be a propitious moment, but the scheme picked up momentum again in the late 1950s. By the mid-1960s, the Soviet economic system was taking serious measures to boost the profitability of Western tourists. The first *berezka* (foreign currency store) was opened in Moscow in January 1962, and the Kosygin administration stepped up the production of souvenirs ranging from shot glasses to dolls in national dress. New bars were to stock ice and introduce

Western cocktails. In practice, the lack of knowledge of the Western consumer placed severe limits on how responsive the Soviet tourist industry could be, and the commercial aims of the Inturist organization were in lasting tension with the function of conveying a suitable impression of socialism.[36]

All the same, it was clear that there was more than profit calculations to the liberalization of Soviet policy on foreign contacts. The Khrushchev regime was counting on less tangible benefits such as international prestige. A landmark case of Soviet exposure to the West came in 1957, when Moscow hosted the World Youth Festival with the intention of demonstrating "peaceful coexistence" in action and showcasing Soviet postwar recovery. This attempt at an international propaganda coup presented unfamiliar challenges to the authorities. The capital threw its arms open to an unprecedented number of foreign visitors (34,000 young people and almost 1,000 foreign correspondents). Strenuous efforts were made to ensure that public order and decorum would be maintained. Raids were carried against the *stiliagi* in the preceding months, and law enforcement professionals were supplemented by 20,000 Komsomol members for the duration of the festival. Strenuous efforts were made to monitor interaction between foreigners and Soviet citizens: the police dutifully reported to the KGB cases of foreigners visiting Soviet people at home, young people were arrested for black market trading with foreigners, and 107 women were detained for "promiscuous" behavior. Rumors abounded that Komsomol patrols were going around shaving the heads of "loose" Soviet girls, but also that their efforts were largely unsuccessful: urban folklore alleged the existence of a distinct cohort of "festival children" born of mixed capitalist/socialist liaisons. In reality, the demographic effects of the festival were not nearly so drastic, but its cultural impact was considerable. The official media inadvertently did much to incite a spirit of "festival romance" and sexual liberation by speaking freely of the friendship – and even "love" – which the festival was designed to bring into being. Many young Soviets took these words more literally than they were intended.[37]

The Youth Festival was followed by a number of events where the superpowers could display their own achievements and compete for pre-eminence. At the Brussels World Fair of 1958, the Americans presented an IBM computer that answered questions in ten languages, voting machines, and a 360-degree motion picture tour of the US. As a nod to democratic self-criticism, they also put on an "Unfinished Work" exhibition that contained a section on the "American Negro" (it was closed after ten weeks). The Soviet pavilion offered machine tools, model hydroelectric dams, and statistics on industrial growth.

Then, under the terms of a 1958 US–Soviet cultural agreement, came a notable exchange of exhibits: in the summer of 1959, the Soviets were granted an Exhibition of Science, Technology, and Culture at the New York Coliseum, while the Americans put on a National Exhibition at Sokol'niki Park in Moscow.

FIGURE 9.3 Khrushchev and Nixon give a press conference at the American National Exhibition, Moscow 1959.
Source: © Eugeny Umnov / PhotoSoyuz.

Negotiations in advance were protracted. The Soviets tried to limit the distribution of souvenirs, and the Americans were forbidden from handing out free cosmetics to women. The Moscow hosts also insisted on editorial control over the newspaper headlines on display inside the American pavilion. Precautions were taken on the American side too: Eisenhower summoned the four black members of the exhibition team to ask them how they came to learn Russian and to confirm their political reliability.[38]

The exhibition was a major event. Soviet people flocked to see it: the official figure was 2.7 million visitors over the six weeks, while daily attendance averaged in excess of 60,000. Although the American guides were heckled by Soviet agitators, they fielded a vast number of questions and felt they had gone down well with their audiences. The curiosity of ordinary Soviet visitors related above all to standard of living. The twenty most asked questions included: "How much do American cigarettes cost?" and "What is meant by the American dream?" Visitors showed much admiration for American know-how (even if they could not quite appreciate the purpose of orange juice squeezers and toasters). They took advantage of free samples of Pepsi-cola; even Khrushchev approved of this drink and authorized its distribution in the USSR afterward.

The American National Exhibition was also the scene of one of the most famous of Cold War showdowns, when Richard Nixon and Nikita Khrushchev confronted each other in the "kitchen sink debate." As Zdeněk Mlynář, a prominent member of the Prague 1968 generation, later observed, Stalin would never have permitted himself such detailed comparisons with the West: for him, Communism required a different yardstick entirely.[39] But Khrushchev could not help himself. In May 1957, for example, he promised that the USSR would surpass American meat output by 1960. Such statements were not just bombast but also an effort to spur Soviet people to work better. Khrushchev's genuine admiration for aspects of American know-how was most notoriously exemplified by his espousal of American large-scale farming of maize following a visit made to the USSR by Iowa agricultural guru Roswell Garst in autumn 1955. The Soviets promptly ordered 5,000 tons of American hybrid seeds, and Khrushchev opined that maize should be grown not only in fertile Ukraine but also in the remote fastness of Yakutia and Chukotka.[40]

All the same, we should not assume that Khrushchev's noisy competitiveness with respect to the West, or individual Soviet encounters with the nonsocialist world, left Soviet people crushed by a sense of their own inferiority. The American National Exhibition of 1959 is easy to interpret in the vein of Western triumphalism: as a Trojan horse of modern consumerism allowed into the citadel of socialism. Soviet visitors were certainly impressed by many of the consumer technologies and (especially) by the cars. But surveillance reports and comment books suggest that the Soviet response was not always as the American hosts imagined. At least some viewers seem to have reacted skeptically to what was presented as typical of the American way of life, partly because this was the Soviet propaganda line, but presumably also because they were so used to being lied to by their own government. Some Soviet visitors took exception to what they saw as the exhibition's excessive focus on consumerism and entertainment, leaving disappointed that they were not given more detail on American achievements in technology. While this may have something to do with the large proportion of young males observed among the visitors, it also reflected a broader Soviet focus on scientific and technical achievement and a commitment to catch up the Americans (if necessary by ripping them off). Visitors to the exhibition could also take refuge in long-standing Soviet prejudices about American vulgarity and "lack of culture."[41]

The converse of vulgarity was the rarefied world of modern art. As at earlier moments in Soviet history, "formalism" was a bogey term that connoted bourgeois decadence. Khrushchev again led the way. In November 1962, the Soviet leader attended the exhibition "Thirty Years of Moscow Art" and gave the artists present a notorious harangue laced with profanities. It is clear that a large proportion of the Soviet population shared Khrushchev's tastes, even if they did not express them so bluntly. Notions of the decline of the West were well developed among members of the Soviet public, who found in modern art ample evidence of civilizational decay. In this light, the once revolutionary Soviet Union was the guardian of the true culture of the Old Masters and the Renaissance.[42] As in many other societies, the willingness to take a generous view of foreign culture correlated quite closely with class and education. For a section of the intelligentsia population, Sergei Obraztsov's account of visits to London in 1953 and 1954, a landmark close-up portrayal of a nonsocialist society, was analogous to Proust's madeleine as a means of recovering lost memory: it was an opportunity to reestablish contact with a broader European culture from which Soviet people had been separated three decades earlier.[43] For many other Soviet citizens, patriotism and prejudice continued to place limits on their curiosity toward the outside world.

The outside world, however, lay not only to the west of the USSR. In the 1950s, as cordial relations were established with Nehru's India, the Soviet Union began regular imports of Indian films. Between 1954 and 1991, more than 200 were shown in the USSR, the vast majority of them mass-appeal productions from the Bombay film industry. By the 1960s, Soviet critics had woken up to the fact that edification in such movies took a distant second place to entertainment. But public strictures worried viewers very little. Bollywood brought the Soviet audience color, optimism, romance, and an emotionally satisfying treatment of everyday problems that were handled in less heartwarming fashion by most home-produced films. Over the three and a half decades of their Soviet life, 50 Indian films drew audiences of more than 20 million, which made Indian cinema the best performer among mass cultural imports. While India's debt to Hollywood was distressingly clear to the critics, Bollywood remained the acceptable face of global mass culture for the Soviet Union: it alleviated the drabness of Soviet life, but at the same time managed to remain chaste and nonmaterialistic, all the while giving voice to a sentimentality born of suffering. The Indians, like the Slavs, had a "soul" that lay beyond the comprehension of rationalistic Westerners.[44]

In the post-Stalin era, the Soviet population also had less ethereal reasons to feel no worse than the West. The case for Soviet superiority was stated by an Italian Communist journalist posted to Moscow in the late 1950s. According to Giuseppe Boffa, "by a series of historical circumstances the Soviet standard of living is temporarily inferior to that of leading capitalist nations." But this was no reason to succumb to "the facile demagogy of capitalist apologists": the point of reference should be not the contemporary West but rather the upward trend of the USSR in the 1950s. Over his five years in the USSR, Boffa observed definite improvements: "from year to year people ate better, dressed better, had more fun." In his view the Soviet diet was better than that of an Italian, and the Soviet level of education was higher than anywhere else. He took seriously the Soviet ambition to achieve the highest standard of living in the world within fifteen years or so.[45]

Nor was Boffa the only foreign traveler who found Soviet society to be stable and self-respecting. Even in the late Stalin era, the Soviet Union was in patches acquiring a modern urban civilization that left few traces of the squalid 1930s. One postwar visitor was impressed by Moscow's broad streets, bright lighting, and courteous service (at least in hotels for foreigners).[46] Admittedly, closer inspection was not so forgiving of Soviet life. John Brown, a lapsed Marxist who visited in the Khrushchev era, noticed "a great deal of social competition in Russia about wearing clothes from abroad that are of better materials and better cut than those from the state factories" and formed the general impression that Russians labored under "a feeling of inferiority about things from the west."[47] John Gunther's *Inside Russia Today*, a best-selling account of a visit made late in 1956, noted improvements in standard of living since the author's previous visit in 1939, but Soviet people – Muscovites, even – were still "wretchedly, appallingly dressed" and as a result "acutely conscious of the clothes foreigners wear, particularly their shoes."[48] All the same, Russians were hardly in awe of their Western visitors. Brown found them ready to hold forth on the defects of capitalism in casual conversations.[49] Two decades later, according to the keen observations of the *New York Times* correspondent Hedrick Smith, not much had changed: a sense of inferiority to the West on certain counts was combined with a sincere conviction that "ours is best."[50]

The post-Stalin USSR was engaged in direct competition with the West (and especially America) on a wide range of economic and cultural fronts: genetics, philosophy, literature, ballet, art, chess – not to mention sport.[51] Whether the key criterion was Olympic medals or piano competitions, Soviet performance was nothing to be ashamed of. In certain fields the Soviets could boast the status of world leaders. Science and technology was a reliable source of patriotic self-assurance. *Sputnik* in 1957 radically changed not just the technology race but also the symbolic politics of the superpower competition. John Gunther observed in 1957 that the relationship between the Soviet Union and the West could never be the same again after this awesome achievement.[52] Four years later, Soviet socialism acquired a winning international icon when Iurii Gagarin made his 80-minute flight. The resulting publicity drive quickly generated a new cult of personality. Gagarin, a peasant boy made good from Smolensk province, was the embodiment of the Soviet dream. His officially approved memoir of the flight delivered the obvious geopolitical message: "as I crossed the Western hemisphere, I thought of

Columbus, of how he, overcoming pain and suffering, discovered the New World, but it was called America after Amerigo Vespucci."[53] At least he did not claim Columbus as a Russian.

Gagarin was a notably charming face for the Soviet Union to present to the wider world. When he parachuted back onto Soviet soil several hundred miles away from the planned landing site, the villagers who first came upon him took him for a foreigner – because he smiled.[54] The Soviet Union remained a society characterized by fear and suspicion of contact with all outsiders, and especially foreigners. Defense of the Soviet borders from contamination from abroad was still, as in the 1930s, a sacred cause. In the first annual report he submitted as head of the KGB, Iurii Andropov informed Brezhnev that in 1967 more than 114,000 letters and packages had been confiscated in the international post for containing anti-Soviet material. Soviet border guards needed to keep up their vigilance. Altogether, 7.8 million people crossed the Soviet border in 1967, almost half of them foreigners; a little more than 2,000 "violators of state borders" had been detained.[55]

As the subsequent émigré Vladimir Shlapentokh recalled, in 1959 he was asked by a train conductor to move to another carriage simply because Frenchmen were sitting next to him.[56] Most Soviet people had deeply internalized the belief that contact with foreigners would get you into trouble. Almost every foreign correspondent in Moscow had as a rite of passage a cordial or convivial encounter with ordinary Soviet people that failed to turn into firmer social contact as the new acquaintances evasively declined an invitation or deliberately gave a false telephone number. Even the Soviet people most opposed to the existing political order – the dissenters famous to British and American broadsheet audiences – were by no means guaranteed to be wholehearted admirers of the West, or to respond warmly to interest from foreigners. They formed a largely inward-looking group and might on occasion look askance at privileged Western journalists whose experiences and prospects were so different from their own.[57]

The ambiguities of Soviet response to the wider world are further evident in higher education, the milieu with the highest concentration of foreigners. By the end of the Stalin era, there were around 10,000 undergraduates and graduates from European and Asian "people's democracies" studying in more than 200 institutions across the USSR. Many of these foreigners were shocked by low Soviet living standards and met a xenophobic reaction in the USSR. They were unusually vulnerable to robbery, as the possessions of East Germans or Czechoslovaks were a magnet to Soviet thieves, while any close – especially sexual – relationships foreign men conducted with local women might lay them open to condemnation or violent confrontation. In the Khrushchev era, foreign students were a constant concern for the guardians of Soviet morality and ideology. A further challenge to Soviet notions of decorum came from the influx of African students in the early

Liquid Tchaikovsky.

Stolichnaya
is real <u>Russian</u> Vodka. In fact, it's
the <u>only</u> real Russian Vodka you can buy in this country.
The Russians drink Stolichnaya chilled and neat.
They don't believe in mixing about with the taste.
A poet once described the taste as "liquid Tchaikovsky."
Mix it if you must (may the Tsars forgive you!), but please
taste it neat first.   Stolichnaya
Tsar of all the Vodkas.

FIGURE 9.4   Advertisement for Stolichnaya vodka, 1978. Under a 1972 trade agreement, the Soviet government allowed the Western marketing of this most recognizable of Russian brands. In exchange, it received the right to import and market Pepsi-Cola in the USSR.

1960s. Students from sub-Saharan Africa numbered only a few dozen in 1959–60 but around 4,000 by the end of the 1960s. Their perceived presence was still greater than their actual numbers, and mixed-race relationships were quick to elicit disapproving or even violent responses. Fair-skinned American Ph.D. students, by contrast, got a warm reception from their peers in Moscow State University, even if they too might on occasion be robbed.[58]

Nor was the famously autarchic Soviet economy impervious to foreign influence. By the 1970s, the Soviet regime was, around the margins, prepared to acquiesce in the spread of Western consumer culture. In 1973 came the launch of the first Soviet jeans, of which nearly 17 million pairs had been produced by 1975. In the late 1970s, the authorities entered negotiations with American firms for the production of authentic foreign denims. The Soviet women's magazine, *Rabotnitsa*, regularly printed photographs of Western fashions, which it borrowed especially from the West German *Burda Moden*. In 1983, the magazine went so far as to publish a "dictionary of fashion" which glossed terms such as *bleizer*, *anorak* and *banany* (the Soviet equivalent of hammer pants). Its readers, we may safely presume, scarcely needed this assistance.[59]

In this era the Soviet government also returned to a policy of trade and technology transfer with the West. In 1966, after a few years of careful brokering and negotiation, it finalized a $900 deal with Fiat for an Italian-style car factory. Production started in the appropriately named Tol'iatti (formerly Stavropol'-on-Volga) in 1970, and by 1974 the plant was producing 2,200 cars per day.[60] Here was the Magnitogorsk of the 1960s: a large and innovative industrial project backed up by substantial Western know-how. But it was hard to escape the feeling that the differences between the two cases were significant: cars were a rather different matter from iron ore, and workers could now expect to be housed in individual flats in prefabricated concrete blocks rather than in barracks or mud huts.

Toward the end of the Brezhnev era, the ability of the Soviet Union to withstand a close-quarters encounter with the nonsocialist world received another test with the Moscow Olympics. This event was an autumnal fruit of détente. Richard Nixon helped to bring the Games to the USSR at his meeting with Brezhnev in 1974, a time when the immediate precedents were unpromising: the World Student Games held in Moscow the previous year had been marred by poor facilities and open anti-Israeli sentiment. By the time the Moscow Olympics actually took place, the temperature of the Cold War had dropped several degrees – largely because of the Soviet invasion of Afghanistan – and the Americans decided to boycott the event. They drew the obvious parallel with the Berlin Olympics of 1936: another sporting event designed as a propaganda coup for an authoritarian country.

Undaunted, the Soviet authorities went to enormous lengths to stage-manage the affair. Special supplies were delivered to shops in central Moscow in order to create an impression of socialist abundance (though the enormous queues that formed rather belied this impression). The USSR Research Institute of Hydrometeorological Information successfully chased away the clouds from the opening ceremony. The ceremony itself was, in the word of the *Daily Mail* correspondent Christopher Booker, a "mesmerizing" one-hour display. In a symbolic gesture, 22 goose-stepping soldier gymnasts released doves to fly to the West (though one "dissident" bird headed in the opposite direction and settled on the stadium roof). An astonishing array of soldiers manned the road between stadium and metro station, and Moscow's international airport was closed all afternoon to foreign traffic except that from "friendly" countries. All told, more than 200,000 troops and militia men were deployed around the capital.[61]

Yet, even within the limits set by Soviet policing, Booker found plenty of evidence to undermine the propaganda image. On a trip to a nondescript residential area, he was dismayed by housing estates that presented "a scene of desolation." Even the Olympic Village failed to impress: "Anything less like a village and more like a bleak housing estate on the outskirts of Glasgow, it would have been hard to imagine." Booker was able to confirm the well-attested Soviet fascination with Western consumer culture: even a plastic carrier bag from Marks and Spencer had a black market retail value (Booker was offered two rubles). He was moved to observe that "the people of this country suffer from a colossal national inferiority complex," and signs of economic crisis were manifold. They were certainly picked up by the small army of Western journalists, who were hitting the bottle and feeling homesick within days of the opening ceremony.[62]

Booker was unusual in his willingness to explore beyond the press center and Olympic venues and to venture forthright assessments of the health of the Soviet system. But even he acknowledged that the socialist world had something the capitalist West lacked. On his return home, he found London "strangely small-scale and scruffy" compared to the "wide open, litter-free spaces of Moscow." Life in Russia, he felt, was less trivial than in the West. It was austere in the way of Britain in the late 1940s, and the political system put severe limits on individual and civil freedom, but that made Soviet people less distracted by the meretricious aspects of the modern world – from plastic consumer goods to plastic presidential candidates.[63] Even for an intelligent and highly skeptical observer, it was hard to imagine Soviet people being able to adopt modern Western civilization rather than merely drooling at it.

─────────── The Challenge of Mass Culture ───────────

Moscow's aura of otherness was, however, a touch misleading. Knowledge about the wider world was coming not primarily through face-to-face contact but through the all-powerful instrument of mass culture. Admittedly, this culture reached a Soviet audience in somewhat attenuated forms, but eager readers and (especially) listeners were able to make the best of what they had.

The Western frontiers of the Soviet Union were especially permeable to foreign influence. Channels of communication between Lithuania and Poland remained open despite the wartime conflict between the two countries: individuals traveled back and forth, bringing Polish clothes, consumer goods, and bibles. By 1968, two-thirds of the Lithuanian population could watch Polish television, which was significantly more appealing than Soviet offerings. In Estonia, Finland served as the conduit for Western culture. In 1970, for example, about 1,700 Estonians were able to visit their linguistically cognate northern neighbor. Partly as a result of such Western contacts, Estonia was widely regarded as the Soviet Union's cultural cutting edge. Besides a lively "serious" theater scene, the republic could boast the first Soviet production of *West Side Story* (in 1965); Moscow and Leningrad audiences had seen only the rather tamer *My Fair Lady* the previous year.[64]

As for the Soviet heartland, the population of the capital was of course considerably better informed than average about the wider world. In 1975, the Moscow authorities found in an unpublished survey that well over half of working people in their city were listening to Western radio stations, and among students the number was an impressive 80 percent.[65] While access to foreign radio did not necessarily turn Soviet youngsters into liberal free-thinkers (or, still less, into critics of the Soviet system), it did make them more inclined to make comparisons between their own country and a glamorous Western world that was assumed to live better than they did. One Moscow informant (b. 1942) was sentenced as a social "parasite" after getting drunk with a foreigner. This experience did not make him a dissident, though it did mean that he never had any chance of being permitted to travel abroad. Instead, he was probably typical of his milieu in constructing in his own head a "virtual West assembled partly from books and partly from Western films."[66]

Virtual contact with the West was possible not only through semilicit reading and film-viewing; it was also made a theme of legitimate Soviet mass culture. In the film *Holiday at Your Own Expense* (1981), a naive provincial girl heads to Moscow to look up a chance acquaintance armed with just his name (which is Iura Pavlov, roughly equivalent to "Robert Jones"). After tracking down her man, she enters a smart milieu that includes a foreigner – the Hungarian visitor László. When she learns that Iura is leaving on a trip to Budapest, she seeks out a deputy minister in her desperate (but ultimately successful) attempts to make the trip "at her own expense." The Hungarian half of the narrative turns into a typical "ugly duckling" narrative, as the heroine throws off her gaucheness to win the first prize at a costume ball – which is to take a role in a Hungarian film director's version of Turgenev's *A Month in the Country*. When Iura changes his feelings, Katia is no longer interested; at the end of the film she heads back to the Urals, to be followed by the now devoted László. The film presents Hungary as an exotic and enticing central European Other, which provides an often humorous counterpoint to the Soviet version of Communism and the Russian national character.

Hungary, of course, was the "near West." Its deviations from the Soviet standard could be presented as lovable manifestations of a warm-blooded indigenous culture. Cinematic depictions of the "far West" were a rather different matter. The villain of *An Office Romance* (1977), a heartless and cowardly charmer, has just returned from Switzerland and wastes few opportunities to show off his suavity and Western consumer goods. Other films offered close-up depictions of the capitalist world. An early example was the wildly popular film *Amphibian Man* (1962), an adaptation of a 1920s' science fiction novella by Aleksandr Beliaev, which caused a sensation with Soviet audiences for its underwater photography and its fetching leading couple. The novella's dystopian backdrop was rendered as a decadent cross between a banana republic and Las Vegas. A few years later, the protagonists of Leonid Gaidai's cult comedy *The Diamond Arm* (1968) are on a cruise when precious jewels find their way into a plaster cast on the hapless hero's arm. Here again, the "West" is hot and sweaty and full of unsavory types.

But these were humorous caricatures rather than swingeing indictments, and it seems they would have done little to stifle Soviet people's fascination with the outside world. Cult foreign films such as *The Umbrellas of Cherbourg* (1964) permitted Soviet viewers to indulge their fantasies of a more cheerful Western existence. With its bright pinks and blues, this film is quite literally colorful and communicates a petty bourgeois gentility that makes more of an impression than the downturn in the rainwear market of northern France. From the 1960s onward, the Soviet culture industry found that many imports were far too lucrative to be passed over on ideological grounds. Brigitte Bardot, Marilyn Monroe, and the stars of Bollywood were guaranteed to be good box office material. Domestic produce was much less of a banker. Although Soviet filmmakers did produce blockbusters that sold 50 million tickets or more, in general ticket sales did not cover the considerable costs of producing a film in the overbureaucratized system of Soviet cultural production.[67]

Yet, when the Soviet screen itself switched to color and on-location filming, contemporary depictions of the West could hardly fail to beguile the viewer. *Teheran-43*, a rambling two-part film centered on a plot to assassinate Stalin at the first of the "Big Three" summits during World War II, offered lingering shots of 1970s London and Paris that were surely the principal focus of interest for some of its Soviet viewers. One of the cult TV phenomena of the late Brezhnev era was a dramatization of Conan Doyle's Sherlock Holmes stories, where Riga stood in for London.[68] The classic document of late Soviet ambivalent fascination toward the West was the twelve-part TV series *Seventeen Moments of Spring*, which appeared in the late summer of 1973. On one level, this adaptation of a spy novel by the popular author Iulian Semenov was an entirely orthodox piece of Cold War culture. The central character, Stirlitz (known in his former life as Maksim Isaev), is a Soviet agent embedded in the Nazi leadership who corresponds to the socialist realist model of the ascetic "positive hero." His mission is to foil a plan hatched by Himmler to conclude a separate peace with the USA through proxy negotiations with Allen Dulles in Bern. Yet *Seventeen Moments* also offered the viewer a beguiling view of the "imagined West" – complete with personal car ownership, Brazilian coffee, and limitless quantities of cognac. It managed to be both patriotic and alienating.

In the realm of mass audiovisual culture, the Soviet regime was trapped by the unintended consequences of its drive to create a modern civilization. Production of wireless radio sets increased in the postwar period to the extent that they became routine items in the Soviet household, thereby challenging the pre-eminence of the wired relay point that had been a fixture in the barracks and communal flats of the Stalin era. While this allowed the more rapid spread of Soviet culture to the benighted rural "periphery" and allowed the government to proclaim full "radiofication" by 1960, it put short-wave receivers at the disposal of millions of Soviet people at just the moment Western radio stations were stepping up their Russian-language broadcasts. The Soviets' automatic response was to jam, but this was inefficient and vastly expensive. By the mid-1950s, senior functionaries were concluding that the game was not worth the candle, and in the mid-1960s jamming was discontinued. The alternative to repression was emulation. From the early 1960s onward, Western pop music found its way on to Soviet radio schedules, and in 1964 Moscow launched a radio station, Maiak (literally Beacon), which adopted a snappy round-the-clock blend of light music and short news bulletins. The debt to Western broadcasting models was only too clear, even if Maiak was hamstrung by the impossibility of "instant news" under the Soviet censorship regime and by the enduring animus, of authorities and cultural producers alike, toward Western-style mass culture.[69]

Whether they drew their information from Maiak, from the BBC or from bootlegged recordings, young people were imagining and acting out the West on an unprecedented scale. Soviet metropolitan youth now had an Americanized slang more extravagant than that of the *stiliagi*; desirable accessories in the 1970s included *shoozy*, a *voch*, a *beg*, even a *stripovyi dzhamper*. Soviet pop groups – formed in institutions such as clubs, factories, and institutes – at this time numbered around 5,000 in Moscow alone.[70] Even Soviet soldiers in Afghanistan wanted to practice their English and find out about Paul McCartney.[71] Westernization, from a KGB viewpoint, was acting as a conduit not just for the time-honored "petty bourgeois values" (*meshchanstvo*) but also for other patterns of behavior and belief that Soviet ideology regarded as deviant. In the major Eastern Ukrainian city of Dnepropetrovsk, for example, the popular music of the 1960s helped to foster a religious revival among the young. This was not the religion of strict church ritual: Christian groups were drawing in young people by using the latest musical styles and technologies (radio, record players, and especially tape recorders). If beat music was largely the preserve of the city's social elite in the 1960s, by the mid-1970s it had spread much more widely.[72]

In interpreting these developments, it is worth holding back from Cold War triumphalism. To partake voraciously of Western mass culture was not the same as to become hostile to the Soviet order. As the example from Dnepropetrovsk indicates, Western pop might make young people Christian collectivists rather than political opponents or slaves of modern commercialism. The greater access to globalized mass culture may in some ways have bolstered Soviet society – by providing urban educated people with gratifying evidence that they were becoming men and women of the world (however vicariously) while retaining the kudos of superpower status. For a Soviet consumer or viewer, moreover, the wider world did not automatically mean the West: Soviet culture had to some extent "gone global" via the developing world, thanks notably to the wildly popular Bollywood productions that were a fixture on the Soviet big screen from the mid-1950s to the very end. Nevertheless, the mass culture of the post-Stalin decades was becoming less narrowly socialist, and the resulting diversification of styles of behavior and ways of thinking surely undermined Soviet society's capacity to mobilize in defense of its Cold War prerogatives when these came under threat in the late 1980s.

------------------ Americanization and After ------------------

The descent down the slippery slope of Westernization gathered life-threatening speed on the watch of the last Soviet leader. Mikhail Gorbachev's own encounters with the nonsocialist world had steadily gained intensity since his days as a regional Party boss. Gorbachev made his first trips to the Eastern bloc – to the GDR, Bulgaria, and Czechoslovakia – in the late 1960s. In the 1970s, besides further travel to this socialist "near abroad," he visited Italy, France, Belgium, and West Germany. As early as 1971, he had the opportunity to see Rome's Coliseum and Capitol, to appreciate the qualities of Italian red wine, to find out how much ordinary Italians paid for shoes, and even to encounter some hippies in Sicily. He also discovered that a Soviet person did not encounter hostility when he left his own country – with the notable exception of his experience of Czechoslovakia in 1969. The comparison between the West and the USSR was not always in favor of the former: Gorbachev continued to believe in the superiority of Soviet education and healthcare provision. But his commitment to the prevailing socialist interpretation of democracy was shaken by what he saw of western European political systems, and there was absolutely no escaping the fact that people abroad lived far better than their Soviet counterparts.[73]

Gorbachev was unprecedented among Soviet leaders in the extent of his willingness to find things of value in Western societies, cultures, and polities. But, like most other people, he found on his travels what he was looking for; his West was an "imagined West" that had more to do with civility, industriousness, and social democracy than with the brasher kinds of commercialism that provided Soviet ideologues with their traditional bugbear. Here, as in so many other areas, his experiences and outlook made for a striking contrast with those of his successor. In September 1989, Boris Yeltsin took a break from the political struggle in the Soviet parliament and made a lightning trip to America. He saw the sights of New York, spoke in locations from Manhattan to Dallas, and was even granted a brief unofficial conversation with President Bush. Among his strongest impressions were the scenes of consumer abundance he found on an impromptu visit to a supermarket outside Houston. As a relatively unworldly apparatchik, Yeltsin was only now having the standard Damascene moment of a late Soviet functionary: he was suddenly presented with vivid and incontrovertible evidence of the falsehood of Soviet propaganda claims regarding the crisis of capitalism. More importantly, as a proud populist, he felt viscerally the failure of the Soviet system to provide a decent quality of life for its people.[74]

Yeltsin's simple instincts were more to the point than Gorbachev's cerebral quest for convergence between Communism and Western social democracy. In the early 1990s, Westernization was more narrowly conceived by the population than at less liberal moments such as the 1950s and the 1970s: it primarily meant goods, and the goods in question were mostly American. Given the manifold inadequacies of the Soviet consumer and culture industries, foreign mass production had a huge and profitable gap to fill when the Soviet economy collapsed. Newspaper stands and bookshops filled up with glossy magazines and cheap novels from abroad. American TV serials and advertising became fixtures on Russian TV schedules. America was also feeding Russia – for a price. As Russian meat production fell, the market for American hotdogs rose from $122,000 in 1992 to over $70 million in 1996. American chicken producers were even more successful on the Russian market, taking advantage of the local preference for dark meat (legs and thighs) as opposed to the white meat beloved of American consumers. As Western tobacco companies found their activities circumscribed at home, the former Soviet Union offered them a vast land of opportunity. As early as 1990, the Soviet government placed an order with Philip Morris and RJR Nabisco for 34 billion cigarettes.[75]

A little later in the 1990s, however, the Russian market reacted against the perceived invasion by foreign producers and took a turn toward commercial nationalism. Russian consumers from the very beginning of the post-Soviet era had an ambivalent relationship to foreign goods, which were highly desirable but also somehow inauthentic.[76] In due course they were expressing a preference for home produce. Foreign chocolates made up 80 percent of the market in 1992, but by the end of 1997 their share had fallen to about one-third. One entrepreneur, Vladimir Dovgan', made his fortune by proclaiming – not always accurately – the

Russian origins of his food and vodka.[77] In the first half of the 1990s, the Russian media were swamped by Western companies advertising products that bore only an approximate relation to real consumer needs. In due course, however, advertisers discovered that appeals to Russian national pride could be just as effective as the glamour of slick Western products. The shift to Russian themes was helped by the 1998 financial crisis, which made TV advertising more affordable for Russian producers and Russian goods more affordable for the Russian consumer. The late 1990s and early 2000s accordingly saw an exponential rise in advertising *à la russe*, a trend best illustrated by the booming beer market. Gestures to the national past ranged from the faux-medieval brew Three Heroes (*Tri bogatyria*), which drew on a well-known theme from Russian folklore, to the pseudo-tsarist Siberian Crown (*Sibirskaia korona*), which exploited all the usual imagery of prerevolutionary pomp and ceremony.[78]

Such examples suggest that Westernization (i.e., the slavish reliance of a backward Russia on the cultural know-how of the Other) had faded into globalization (the versatile use of an international cultural idiom). Globalization's central paradox is that it is not incompatible with strong particular identities – whether they be local, religious, national, or state-patriotic. In Russia's case, nationalism fed off familiar bones of contention: NATO expansion, the perceived unwillingness of Western leaders to assuage Russian feelings of humiliation, the failure of the West (starting in the Baltic states) to make proper acknowledgment of the Russian war experience, the fact that the West was seen to have sold Russia damaged ideological goods in the form of "shock therapy." Resentment of the West and consciousness of past suffering were so pervasive as to make Russian patriotic discourse stand out from its counterparts elsewhere in Europe. Typologically, however, cultural and ideological developments in post-Soviet Russia were of a piece with other nationalisms in the postindustrial and postideological age. Russian nationalism required the artful projection in the very latest mass media of a common past: the Soviet Union, understood not only as superpower but also as heritage. Russian mass culture was accordingly gripped by fond retrospection. The end of 1995 brought the first in a series of New Year musical retrospectives, "Old Songs about the Most Important Things," which involved well-known contemporary performers dressing up and delivering stylized versions of songs from successive decades of Soviet culture. The family resemblance to analogous Western music compilations for successive generations of music lovers is only too clear. Russia had decidedly entered the era of postmodern nostalgia.

Even the Soviet Union's own fraught encounters with Western culture could be dusted off and adopted as part of the new national heritage. In 2008, the director Valerii Todorovskii brought out a film on the *stiliagi*, those postwar pioneers of Soviet Westernness. Set in the mid-1950s, the film offers a playful and entertaining account of this subculture and its interactions with mainstream Soviet life. The hero is called Mels, which is short for Marx-Engels-Lenin-Stalin, though in his *stiliaga* identity he drops the last letter to become known as the quasi-American "Mel." Characters break into slickly choreographed dance routines in locations from a communal flat to a Komsomol meeting. In the penultimate scene Mel(s) learns a painful truth from a well-traveled friend, an apparatchik in the making who has renounced the *stiliagi* to secure a prestigious diplomatic placement in the USA: in America, the friend tells him, there are no *stiliagi*, and outlandish ties would simply be laughed at on the real Broadway. But the force of this observation is parried by a fairytale final scene where Mel enters the twenty-first century, walking down Tverskaia Street, Moscow's main drag, with a collection of the subcultural youth of post-Soviet Russia. The implication is that Russia is now properly liberal and can take up global trends without dangerously compromising its Russianness.[79]

A complementary, and perhaps more convincing, comment on Russia's mass-cultural relationship to the wider world came the following year with the broadcast of *Seventeen Moments of Spring*, that urtext of late Soviet civilization, in a brand-new color version.[80] While some viewers quite legitimately objected for aesthetic reasons, and the Communist Party protested on patriotic grounds, this high-profile restoration project showed that Stirlitz was still capable of bridging – or fudging – the divide between "us" and "them," between state patriotism and vicarious cosmopolitanism. Swastikas might not look good in color, but everything else in the Soviet version of Berlin still did.

10

Conclusion

The Second Russian Revolution?

This book started by exploring the significance of World War II in Russia's recent history. It seems inescapable that it should end by considering the other great chronological marker of the post-1941 era: the collapse of the Soviet Union. Historians will no doubt argue a good deal more about the causes of this event, debating in particular the balance to be struck between structural factors and contingency, but the consequences of the Soviet collapse by now form a more intriguing subject for reflection. Enough time has passed for us to pose the question: what exactly changed in 1991?[1]

In the immediate aftermath of the collapse, it was only natural that most observers, whether far or near, believed that the transformation had been nothing short of revolutionary. After all, a mighty militarized superpower had fallen apart. Fifteen new nation-states had been created. A centralized economic system had disintegrated, leaving much of Russian society in desperate straits. The assets of the Communist Party had been seized, and a new class of property owners seemed to be emerging. Russia-watchers differed enormously in their assessments of the political and economic prospects of the former Soviet Union, but the magnitude of events was unquestionable.

Nearly twenty years on, perspectives have changed somewhat. Russia's era of "transition" is widely recognized as having come to an end, bringing the country to a destination at some remove from liberal democracy. Political stability has returned, but democratic accountability of office-holders has not arrived. Russia's attempts to coerce some of its neighbors in the post-Soviet "near abroad" have provoked much talk of a new Cold War. Even among specialists, it is becoming almost conventional to stress the continuities with Soviet rule. Russia can easily be seen as remaining mired in "petro-authoritarianism." Economics is permeated by politics, which is in turn permeated by the military and security elites. The

ruling class is Soviet, whether in background or in mindset (or both). The dominant political figure of the early twenty-first century, after all, is a KGB man: what
more proof is needed?[2]

What we find here is a reprise of the oldest debate in the Russianist book:
whither Russia? Is this sprawling country becoming more like us, more
"Western," "modern," liberal, and enlightened? Or is it stuck in "traditional,"
patrimonial patterns of rule, beset by a "resource curse," full of resentment and
suspicion toward the outside world? In the last few years, scholars taking the
second of these positions have quite often appeared to be having the better of the
argument. My own account in this book has identified a number of continuities
across the 1991 divide. The centrality of natural resources to Russia's economy
and political system is all too palpable, as is the cross-contamination of political,
military, and economic elites. Russia is now a far more illiberal country than it
seemed to many to be becoming in the mid-1990s. It is not a transparently governed and equitable nation-state. The disparities between regions and social
groups are enormous. In more than one place I have had recourse to the metaphor
of "archipelago" to characterize the unevenness of Russia as a society and as a
territory. Continuities are also ideological: the Soviet victory in World War II and
the USSR's subsequent superpower history underpin Russian patriotism in the
early twenty-first century.

But tracing social institutions and patterns of rule back to the Soviet era is not
the same as finding the roots of Russian political culture somewhere in the age of
Ivan III, as some historians still do.[3] A great many things in British society and
politics could presumably be tracked back to Cromwell or the Norman Conquest,
if one were so minded, but somehow the idea of a millennium-long Sonderweg
has always had more purchase when applied to Russia.

Although the political and economic order of present-day Russia has many
flaws, it is unsatisfactory to dismiss it as abnormal, pathological, and conforming
to age-old Russian type. This view relies on a perhaps overconfident notion of
what is in fact "normal" in the world we currently inhabit. Flawed, partial democracies are more common than stable, well-functioning liberal democracies.
Moreover, even the world's greatest liberal democracy, the United States, has
shown itself capable of acting illiberally in defense of what it regards as its vital
interests.

The other main reason why *longue durée* explanations of Russian history leave
this author cold is that they have little time for the specific challenges that Russia
has faced in the relatively recent past. The history of Russia – whether written in
Russia or elsewhere – has too often been dominated by exceptionalism: the notion
that Russia belongs in a category entirely of its own. The exceptionalist tendency
in Western scholarship was, of course, only accentuated by the fact that Western
academic study of Russia was launched in earnest during the Cold War, when the

Soviet Union by definition belonged in a category of its own. Yet, while it would be obtuse to analyze Russia as a nation-state in the Anglo-French mould, historical analysis of Russia could do with a more strongly articulated comparative dimension. Otherwise, it is simply impossible to reach meaningful conclusions about the degree of Russia's exceptionality.

As the introduction to this book suggested, one of the most illuminating comparative frameworks to apply to twentieth-century Russia is that of empire and decolonization. Readers might object that this is an insight of dubious novelty: thanks to Ronald Reagan, we have known for a long time that the Soviet Union was an "evil empire." But the resounding moral judgment in this description has tended to make us forget the fundamental aptness of the second word of Reagan's sound bite. Yes, the Soviet Union was an empire (although its representatives furiously denied this right up to the moment of its collapse). By the mid-1950s, moreover, it was by far the largest empire in the world. One might even argue that it was the world's only meaningful empire: a very large power exercising political and military domination over a significant number of other territories.

It is very easy to see this development as the outcome of a Soviet plan for world domination. Yet it also had its ambiguities. The main ambiguity – and the reason that World War II is a crucial moment in Russian history even in a long-range Ivan-to-Putin perspective – is that the events of 1941–5 were simultaneously a war of national liberation and a war of imperial expansion. It was very hard, even for the most ruthless Soviet leaders, to disentangle the two: to work out whether the main rationale of policy was to increase the political stability and economic robustness of Soviet Russia or to seize territory and power for their own sake (and face the consequences). At times these two aims could be combined without too much trouble, but on occasion they were close to irreconcilable. The thorniest issue for Soviet Russia as it emerged from the wreckage of 1945, and one that caused even Stalin to miscalculate badly, was Germany. It would have been much better for the Soviet Union, as well as for the world as a whole, if Stalin had not committed the USSR to the defense and maintenance of an unviable East German state. But ideological mistrust of the West and old-fashioned imperialism led the Soviet leadership to bite off more of central Europe than it could digest.[4]

As a result of this and other decisions taken in the late Stalin era, the Soviet Union in the postwar decades had a split personality. On the one hand, as I argued in the introduction, it was taking steps toward internal decolonization – by treating its population less like slaves or imperial subjects and more like modern (if illiberal) citizens. On the other hand, it had become far more empire-like by virtue of its control of eastern Europe. By the early 1980s, the Soviet Union's imperial overstretch had been diagnosed not only by Western political scientists but also by Kremlin policymakers. It was a long way, however, from diagnosis to effective cure, and many Russians would later feel that Gorbachev, by letting the empire crumble so abjectly, had killed the patient.

The history of the postwar Soviet Union qua empire is, then, full of blunders as well as cynicism, deceit, and violence. At the risk of being mistaken for an apologist of Soviet imperial rule, I should point out how difficult it was both to be an empire and to divest oneself of empire in the twentieth century. The Turks were assisted (if that is the right word) by the collapse of the Ottoman state and then by a victorious war of national independence. The British had their problems, but for the most part managed to export them to former colonies that were a good distance from London. The Germans, between 1938 and 1944, acquired the largest and most powerful European empire in history, but it almost immediately collapsed under the strain of fighting the wars necessary for its existence and under the weight of its own contradictions. The postwar Soviet empire was made possible by the German devastation of a continent, but maintaining that empire required vast resources – economic, military, and ideological – that could far more gainfully have been expended elsewhere.

But, to return to the stated purpose of this conclusion, how does all this help us to analyze the effects of the Soviet collapse? For a start, it should make us less surprised by the illiberal turn in Russian politics. The evidence suggests that liberal democracy is imposed in the wake of imperial collapse only at gunpoint (as in postwar Germany and Japan). Humiliation and economic turmoil take their toll on a society's openness to tolerance and pluralism and on its capacity to resist oligarchic takeover of the political system. The political elite, for its part, finds it hard to shake off imperial reflexes. The 1990s crisis over Chechnya might well have been handled more calmly and rationally – as a specific secessionist claim rather than a fundamental threat to Russian statehood – at a less postimperial moment.

The Soviet collapse of 1991 was not driven by a quest for liberal democracy, and perhaps we should spend less time bemoaning the fact that such a democracy has failed to come about. Rather, 1991 was quite transparently about the creation of a viable, postimperial Russian nation-state, whether liberal, illiberal, or somewhere in between. If we keep this rather obvious fact in mind, the particular significance of the post-1941 era becomes much clearer. It has now been widely observed that Soviet nationalities policy over the long run was a maker more than a breaker of nations: as well as carrying out campaigns of ethnic violence, the Soviet state gave dozens of ethnic groups subpolitical forms of national life that they had lacked under the old Russian empire. What is less widely appreciated is that the Soviet experience also "made" the Russian nation.[5] Of course, the Russians in 1917 did not face the obstacles to nationhood of the Kalmyks or the Chechens or even the Ukrainians: they had a language and a high culture backed up by massive state resources, a well-established state religion, and a formidable territory and political power in their name. The Russian problem was quite the reverse: how could a coherent Russian nation be disentangled from the sprawling imperial power that Russia had been since the seventeenth century (the period covered by the three volumes of this Blackwell history)? This question was not so urgent while the European balance of power was favorable to Russia (as was the case until the middle of the nineteenth century), or while two-thirds of the population (Russian and non-Russian) could be kept down by serfdom or other forms of disempowerment. By 1917, however, these conditions had quite spectacularly ceased to obtain.

In the 1920s and 1930s, Soviet Russia sought to make good its geopolitical weakness by subjecting its population to exploitation more ruthless than anything that occurred under the tsars: by effectively turning back the clock to the pre-1861 age of serfdom while at the same time applying all the coercive powers of the modern state and all the production capacities of a modern industrial economy. After 1945, however, the USSR had to find a new way of being: because it was now international hegemon rather than pariah, and because under these changed circumstances Stalinist exploitation of the population was both inappropriate and ineffective (at least once the immediate reconstruction effort was over).

What emerged in the post-Stalin era was a discourse of participatory modern citizenship, a commitment to material well-being, and a modern patriotism based not only on past conquests and current superpower status but also on present and future achievements in realms such as culture (high and not-so-high), science and technology, and sport. It is tempting to be skeptical about this postwar Sovietness, since it did not prevent the Soviet Union collapsing ingloriously in 1989–91. But that would be to make unwarranted assumptions about the causes of the Soviet collapse and also to understate the degree to which Sovietness lived on in the mixed identities of the population of the former Soviet Union.

Nowhere, of course, were identities and feelings so mixed as in the new Russian Federation. Most often, this phenomenon is interpreted as Russian nostalgia for the Soviet Union or resentment at the loss of great power prerogatives. Russians are seen as remaining in the grip of an imperial identity that is their essence: in this light, "Soviet Union" was just a politically correct way of saying "Russia." Perhaps, however, it is more illuminating to turn this relationship between nation and empire on its head: in the post-1941 era, the USSR was not just a means of maintaining age-old Russian imperialism but also an incubator for a genuinely new kind of Russian state. Just as the Communist leaderships of the Ukrainian or the Georgian republics made possible in the post-Stalin era forms of national life – cultural revival, more indigenous and nationally minded elites – that stopped well short of sovereignty, so Russia's postwar leadership cohorts were doing something similar for the RSFSR. And, while these regional first secretaries, managers, and propagandists remained loyal Party men above all, when Gorbachev undermined the power of the central Party in 1987–89, they were ready to move their political capital into the currency of Russian separatism.

Yet, when Boris Yeltsin and his supporters achieved their aim of full independence at the end of 1991, they faced immense practical problems in creating a viable new Russia. How was the national to be detached from the imperial? What was to be done about the Russian minority populations outside the Russian Federation, and about the non-Russian populations within the country? How was such an enormous and diverse country, with a long history of imperial conquest but no experience of genuine federalism, to govern itself? Here Russia was facing challenges that were truly unique.

In seeking answers to these questions, Russia's post-1991 rulers have produced not especially coherent or consistent answers. At times – as with the 1991 citizenship law, or the negotiated federalism of the 1990s, or the guarantees of the public religious life of the Muslim population – they have seemed liberal. At many other times – the wars in Chechnya, the post-1999 intolerance of dissent and independent political activity, the government's marriages of convenience first with big business and then with the military and security elites – they have been anything but. The most recent Kremlin regime has encouraged notions that post-Soviet Russia is a modern, economically dynamic nation-state but has also done much to encourage Soviet nostalgia.

My point is not that the inconsistency is bad or (still less) that it is good but that it is hard to imagine how it could be otherwise. The attempt to build a viable Russian nation-state is unprecedented in history; a certain amount of fudge and studied ambiguity is the least that should be expected. And the most rousing source of ambiguity – to return to the principal theme of this book – is World War II, which is a symbol of the Soviet superpower era but also pre-eminently a Russian national symbol. No wonder that the current Russian regime does not feel that it can allow the memory of the war to be "falsified": this is an ideological requirement just as nonnegotiable as the insistence of the Turkish state that its citizens refrain from slander of Kemal. But we should not be misled by the imperialist overtones of much current Russian discourse. The history of Russia since 1941 is, in essence, a story of national self-discovery overlaid by an imperial history. It is, to use a Stalinist turn of phrase, Soviet in form, national in content. The story is not an especially pretty one, but it is highly significant. When the shadow of war lifts, in twenty or thirty years, maybe – just maybe – it will reveal a stable, peaceful, and democratic Russian nation-state.

Notes

---------------------------------- Chapter 1 ----------------------------------

1 Mark Harrison, *Accounting for War: Soviet Production, Employment, and the Defence Burden, 1940–1945* (Cambridge, 1996), pp. 159–61, 165; B. A. Anderson and B. D. Silver, "Demographic Consequences of World War II on the Non-Russian Nationalities of the USSR," in Susan J. Linz (ed.), *The Impact of World War II on the Soviet Union* (Totowa, 1985), p. 208.

2 Eric J. Duskin, *Stalinist Reconstruction and the Confirmation of a New Elite, 1945–1953* (Houndmills, 2001), p. 12; Susan J. Linz, "World War II and Soviet Economic Growth, 1940–1953" and Sheila Fitzpatrick, "Postwar Soviet Society: The 'Return to Normalcy', 1945–1953," both in Linz (ed.), *The Impact of World War II*, pp. 16, 137, 144; Nicholas Ganson, *The Soviet Famine of 1946–47 in Global and Historical Perspective* (New York, 2009), p. 154 n. 15.

3 Duskin, *Stalinist Reconstruction*, p. 16; M. N. Potemkina, "Evakonaselenie v ural'skom tylu: Opyt vyzhivaniia," *Otechestvennaia istoriia*, 2 (2005), pp. 86–7; Frederick Kagan, "The Evacuation of Soviet Industry in the Wake of 'Barbarossa': A Key to the Soviet Victory," *Journal of Slavic Military Studies*, 8 (1995), pp. 399, 401.

4 Fitzpatrick, "Postwar Soviet Society," p. 135; M. M. Zagorul'ko (ed.), *Voennoplennye v SSSR 1939–1956: Dokumenty i materialy* (Moscow, 2000), pp. 12, 54, 217.

5 Notable exceptions include Catherine Merridale, *Ivan's War: The Red Army 1939–1945* (London, 2005); Amir Weiner, *Making Sense of War: The Second World War and the Fate of the Bolshevik Revolution* (Princeton, 2001); and Mark Edele, *Soviet Veterans in World War II: A Popular Movement in an Authoritarian Society, 1941–1991* (Oxford, 2009).

6 This is the main argument of Weiner, *Making Sense of War*.

7 Figures on war losses from G. F. Krivosheev (ed.), *Rossiia i SSSR v voinakh XX veka: Statisticheskoe issledovanie* (Moscow, 2001), pp. 213, 250–1, 263.

8   Mark Edele and Michael Geyer, "States of Exception: The Nazi–Soviet War as a System of Violence, 1939–1945," in Michael Geyer and Sheila Fitzpatrick (eds.), *Beyond Totalitarianism: Stalinism and Nazism Compared* (Cambridge, 2009), p. 386.

9   Richard Overy, *Russia's War* (London, 1997), pp. 190–7.

10 Overy, *Russia's War*, pp. 127–8.

11 Amir Weiner, "Saving Private Ivan: From What, Why, and How?" *Kritika: Explorations in Russian and Eurasian History*, 1 (2000), p. 320.

12 See William McCagg, *Stalin Embattled, 1943–1948* (Detroit, 1978).

13 See John Barber, "The Image of Stalin in Soviet Propaganda and Public Opinion during World War 2," in John Garrard and Carol Garrard (eds.), *World War 2 and the Soviet People* (Houndmills, 1993), pp. 38–49.

14 I. V. Stalin, *Sochineniia*, vol. 2 (XV) (Stanford, 1967), pp. 203–4, 206.

15 See Mark Edele, "A 'Generation of Victors'? Soviet Second World War Veterans from Demobilization to Organization," Ph.D. dissertation (University of Chicago, 2004); a shorter version is Edele, "Soviet Veterans as an Entitlement Group, 1945–1955," *Slavic Review*, 65 (2006), pp. 111–37.

16 See Bertram D. Wolfe, *Khrushchev and Stalin's Ghost* (Westport, 1957), pp. 164–92.

17 See Denise J. Youngblood, *Russian War Films: On the Cinema Front, 1914–2005* (Lawrence, 2007), chaps. 6–7.

18 For Gorbachev's own account of these events, see M. S. Gorbachev, *Zhizn' i reformy*, vol. 1 (Moscow, 1995), pp. 38–42, 45–6.

19 Gorbachev, *Zhizn' i reformy*, pp. 157–8.

20 "Komissiia po protivodeistviiu popytkam fal'sifikatsii istorii v ushcherb interesam Rossii," at www.kremlin.ru/articles/216485.shtml (last checked 28 August 2009).

21 In recent years, the Holocaust on Soviet territory has come out of the shadows as a topic for specialist historical research. But in Russia it mostly takes the form of document collections rather than interpretation, and at least some of it is awkwardly intertwined with current political concerns – notably, the desire to demonstrate the extent of collaboration in the Baltic states. For a good recent summary, see David Shneer, "Probing the Limits of Documentation," *Kritika: Explorations in Russian and Eurasian History*, 10 (2009), pp. 121–33.

22 In June 1944, according to Harrison Salisbury, a portrait of Stalin with grey hair drew a huge crowd to an art shop in central Moscow: this was apparently the first time a representation of the Soviet leader had been permitted to show any signs of him ageing. The episode is recounted in Amir Weiner, "Robust Revolution to Retiring Revolution: The Life Cycle of the Soviet Revolution, 1945–1968," *Slavonic and East European Review*, 86 (2008), p. 208.

Chapter 2

1   Roger R. Reese, *Red Commanders: A Social History of the Soviet Army Officer Corps, 1918–1991* (Lawrence, 2005), chap. 4.

2   V. V. Cherepanov, *Vlast' i voina: Stalinskii mekhanizm gosudarstennogo upravleniia v Velikoi Otechestvennoi voine* (Moscow, 2006), p. 181.

3 In February 1942 Mikoian, Voznesensky, and Kaganovich were added to bring the membership to eight, and in November 1944 Voroshilov was replaced by Bulganin.

4 Iurii Gor'kov, *Gosudarstvennyi Komitet Oborony postanovliaet (1941–1945): Tsifry, dokumenty* (Moscow, 2002), p. 80.

5 Cherepanov, *Vlast' i voina*, pp. 211–13.

6 Sanford R. Lieberman, "The Evacuation of Industry in the Soviet Union during World War II," *Soviet Studies*, 35 (1983), pp. 90–102.

7 Yoram Gorlizki and Hans Mommsen, "The Political (Dis)Orders of Stalinism and National Socialism," in Michael Geyer and Sheila Fitzpatrick (eds.), *Beyond Totalitarianism: Stalinism and Nazism Compared* (Cambridge, 2009), p. 80. On the failures of Nazi administration, see Mark Mazower, *Hitler's Empire: Nazi Rule in Occupied Europe* (London, 2008), pp. 223–56.

8 Mark Harrison, "The USSR and Total War: Why Didn't the Soviet Economy Collapse in 1942?" in Roger Chickering, Stig Förster, and Bernd Greiner (eds.), *A World at Total War: Global Conflict and the Politics of Destruction, 1937–1945* (Cambridge, 2005); see table on p. 141.

9 Cherepanov, *Vlast' i voina*, pp. 53–5, 448–51, 350–1 respectively.

10 For prisoner numbers as reported by the Head of the Gulag, see O. V. Khlevniuk, *Istoriia stalinskogo Gulaga. Konets 1920-x – pervaia polovina 1950-kh godov: Sobranie dokumentov v 7-mi tomakh*, vol. 3 (Moscow, 2004), pp. 217–19. For a general discussion of prisoner numbers and figures on mortality, see Edwin Bacon, *The Gulag at War: Stalin's Forced Labour System in the Light of the Archives* (Houndmills, 1994), pp. 101–21, 148–9.

11 On coercive measures against Soviet troops, see Mark Edele and Michael Geyer, "States of Exception: The Nazi–Soviet War as a System of Violence, 1939–1945," in Geyer and Fitzpatrick, *Beyond Totalitarianism*, pp. 364, 385–7.

12 Cherepanov, *Vlast' i voina*, p. 69.

13 Edele and Geyer, "States of Exception," p. 362.

14 Gorlizki and Mommsen, "The Political (Dis)Orders," p. 81.

15 Cynthia S. Kaplan, "The Impact of World War II on the Party," in Susan J. Linz, *The Impact of World War II on the Soviet Union* (Totowa, 1985), p. 160; T. H. Rigby, *Communist Party Membership in the USSR, 1917–1967* (Princeton, 1968), p. 239.

16 Rigby, *Communist Party Membership*, pp. 25–1, 275–6.

17 Rigby, *Communist Party Membership*, pp. 280–1, 290.

18 William O. McCagg, *Stalin Embattled, 1943–1948* (Detroit, 1978), chap. 4.

19 Amy Knight, *Beria: Stalin's First Lieutenant* (Princeton, 1993), p. 126.

20 Knight, *Beria*, p. 118.

21 Knight, *Beria*, pp. 140–1.

22 V. N. Khaustov et al. (eds.), *Lubianka. Stalin i MGB SSSR. Mart 1946-mart 1953: Dokumenty vysshikh organov partiinoi i gosudarstvennoi vlasti* (Moscow, 2007), pp. 37–8, 41–2.

23 Juliane Fürst, "Prisoners of the Soviet Self? – Political Youth Opposition in Late Stalinism," *Europe–Asia Studies*, 54 (2002), p. 355.

24 Yoram Gorlizki, "Rules, Incentives and Soviet Campaign Justice after World War II," *Europe–Asia Studies*, 51 (1999), pp. 1245–65.

25 V. V. Denisov et al. (eds.), *TsK VKP(b) i regional'nye partiinye komitety 1945–1953* (Moscow, 2004), p. 6.

26 Moshe Lewin, "Rebuilding the Soviet Nomenklatura, 1945–1948," *Cahiers du monde russe*, 44 (2003), pp. 219–52.

27 Kaplan, "The Impact of World War II," pp. 168–9.

28 Amir Weiner, *Making Sense of War: The Second World War and the Fate of the Bolshevik Revolution* (Princeton, 2001), chap. 1.

29 James W. Heinzen, "Informers and the State under Late Stalinism: Informant Networks and Crimes against 'Socialist Property,' 1940–53," *Kritika: Explorations in Russian and Eurasian History*, 8 (2007), p. 803.

30 Cynthia V. Hooper, "Terror from Within: Participation and Coercion in Soviet Power, 1924–1964," Ph.D. dissertation (Princeton University, 2003), pp. 249–52.

31 See Denisov, *TsK VKP(b) i regional'nye partiinye komitety.*

32 My discussion of Kremlin politics in the late Stalin era draws mainly on Yoram Gorlizki and Oleg Khlevniuk, *Cold Peace: Stalin and the Soviet Ruling Circle, 1945–1953* (New York, 2004).

33 Yoram Gorlizki, "Party Revivalism and the Death of Stalin," *Slavic Review*, 54 (1995), pp. 1–22.

34 See Philip G. Roeder, *Red Sunset: The Failure of Soviet Politics* (Princeton, 1993), esp. chap. 4.

35 Iu. V. Aksiutin, *Khrushchevskaia 'ottepel'' i obshchestvennye nastroeniia v SSSR v 1953–1964 gg.* (Moscow, 2004), pp. 37–41.

36 Aksiutin, *Khrushchevskaia 'ottepel''*, pp. 42–3.

37 On Beria's fall, see William Taubman, *Khrushchev: The Man and His Era* (London, 2003), pp. 245–57.

38 On the struggle between Khrushchev and Malenkov, see Taubman, *Khrushchev*, pp. 258–66.

39 A good discussion of these issues is George W. Breslauer, *Khrushchev and Brezhnev as Leaders* (London, 1982), chaps. 2–4.

40 D. M. Fel'dman, *Terminologiia vlasti: Sovetskie politicheskie terminy v istoriko-kul'turnom kontekste* (Moscow, 2006), quotation on p. 41.

41 Fel'dman, *Terminologiia vlasti*, part 2.

42 A. Artizov et al. (eds.), *Reabilitatsiia: Kak eto bylo. Dokumenty Prezidiuma TsK KPSS i drugie materialy. Mart 1953 – fevral' 1956* (Moscow, 2000), pp. 103–4.

43 Artizov, *Reabilitatsiia*, pp. 129–30.

44 Artizov, *Reabilitatsiia*, pp. 158–60.

45 A. A. Fursenko (ed.), *Prezidium TsK KPSS. 1954–1964. Chernovye protokol'nye zapisi zasedanii. Stenogrammy. Postanovleniia* (Moscow, 2003), p. 56.

46 Fursenko, *Prezidium TsK KPSS*, pp. 96–7.

47 Artizov, *Reabilitatsiia*, p. 317.

48 Fursenko, *Prezidium TsK KPSS*, p. 99.

49 See Karl Eimermacher's introduction to his collection of documents on the Speech, *Doklad N. S. Khrushcheva o kul'te lichnosti Stalina na XX s''ezde KPSS: Dokumenty* (Moscow, 2002).

50 Eimermacher, *Doklad N. S. Khrushcheva*, p. 35.

51   Susanne Schattenberg, "'Democracy' or 'Despotism'? How the Secret Speech Was Translated into Everyday Life," in Polly Jones (ed.), *The Dilemmas of De-Stalinization: Negotiating Cultural and Social Change in the Khrushchev Era* (London, 2006), p. 65.

52   Aksiutin, *Khrushchevskaia 'ottepel'*, p. 171.

53   M. S. Gorbachev, *Zhizn' i reformy*, vol. 1 (Moscow, 1995), p. 84.

54   See Polly Jones, "From the Secret Speech to the Burial of Stalin: Real and Ideal Responses to De-Stalinization," in Jones (ed.), *The Dilemmas of De-Stalinization*, pp. 42–51, which has numerous examples.

55   Benjamin K. Tromly, "Re-Imagining the Soviet Intelligentsia: Student Politics and University Life, 1948–1964," Ph.D. dissertation (Harvard University, 2007), chap. 4.

56   A. Artizov et al. (eds.), *Reabilitatsiia: Kak eto bylo. Fevral' 1956 – nachalo 80-kh godov* (Moscow, 2003), pp. 7–8.

57   Jones, "From the Secret Speech to the Burial of Stalin," p. 50.

58   Schattenberg, "'Democracy' or 'Despotism'?"

59   Jones, "From the Secret Speech to the Burial of Stalin," pp. 51–8.

60   Gorlizki, "Party Revivalism."

61   Karen Petrone, *Life Has Become More Joyous, Comrades: Celebrations in the Time of Stalin* (Bloomington, 2000), chap. 7.

62   Examples in this paragraph from A. Pyzhikov, *Khrushchevskaia 'ottepel'* (Moscow, 2002), pp. 134–5, and Jerry F. Hough and Merle Fainsod, *How the Soviet Union Is Governed* (Cambridge, MA, 1979), pp. 300–1.

63   Schattenberg, "'Democracy' or 'Despotism'?", p. 67.

64   Rigby, *Communist Party Membership*, pp. 298–300, 302–5.

65   See Stephen V. Bittner, "Local Soviets, Public Order, and Welfare after Stalin: Appeals from Moscow's Kiev *Raion*," *Russian Review*, 62 (2003), pp. 281–93.

66   See Vladimir A. Kozlov, *Mass Uprisings in the USSR: Protest and Rebellion in the Post-Stalin Years* (Armonk, 2002).

67   Hough and Fainsod, *How the Soviet Union Is Governed*, p. 299.

68   Tromly, "Re-Imagining the Soviet Intelligentsia," p. 61.

69   See Ethan Pollock, *Stalin and the Soviet Science Wars* (Princeton, 2006).

70   Rigby, *Communist Party Membership*, p. 327.

71   Timothy J. Colton, *Moscow: Governing the Socialist Metropolis* (Cambridge, MA, 1995), p. 427.

72   Evan Mawdsley and Stephen White, *The Soviet Elite from Lenin to Gorbachev: The Central Committee and its Members, 1917–1991* (Oxford, 2000), pp. 102–4.

73   Jerry F. Hough, *The Soviet Prefects: The Local Party Organs in Industrial Decision-Making* (Cambridge, MA, 1969), p. 37.

74   Paul R. Josephson, "Atomic-Powered Communism: Nuclear Culture in the Postwar USSR," *Slavic Review*, 55 (1996), pp. 304–5.

75   Josephson, "Atomic-Powered Communism," pp. 307, 321. For a more whimsical account of the popularity of science in the 1960s, see Petr Vail' and Aleksandr Genis, *60-e: Mir sovetskogo cheloveka* (Moscow, 1996), pp. 100–6.

76   Amy W. Knight, *The KGB: Police and Politics in the Soviet Union* (Boston, 1988), pp. 54–9, 63.

77   Knight, *The KGB*, pp. 60–7, 185–6, 189–90, 199.

78 On Andropov's group of consultants in the Central Committee, see G. A. Arbatov, *Zatianuvsheesia vyzdorovlenie (1953–1985 gg.): Svidetel'stvo sovremennika* (Moscow, 1991), pp. 80–5. On the early 1970s, see I. E. Sinitsin, *Andropov vblizi: Vospominaniia o vremenakh 'ottepeli' i 'zastoia'* (Moscow, 2004), pp. 12–15.

79 R. Medvedev, *Neizvestnyi Andropov: Politicheskaia biografiia Iuriia Andropova* (Moscow, 1999), pp. 81, 120, 136.

80 Christopher Andrew and Vasili Mitrokhin, *The Mitrokhin Archive: The KGB in Europe and the West* (London, 1999), p. 711.

81 A. I. Kokurin and N. V. Petrov (eds.), *Lubianka: Organy VChK-OGPU-NKVD-NKGB-MGB-MVD-KGB. 1917–1991. Spravochnik* (Moscow, 2003), pp. 718–19.

82 Thane Gustafson, *Crisis Amid Plenty: The Politics of Soviet Energy under Brezhnev and Gorbachev* (Princeton, 1989).

83 Bruce Parrott, "Political Change and Civil–Military Relations," in Timothy J. Colton and Thane Gustafson (eds.), *Soldiers and the Soviet State: Civil–Military Relations from Brezhnev to Gorbachev* (Princeton, 1990), pp. 47, 49, 54.

84 Parrott, "Political Change," pp. 60–2.

85 William E. Odom, *The Collapse of the Soviet Military* (New Haven, 1998), pp. 39–41.

86 Simon Kordonskii, *Rynki vlasti: Administrativnye rynki SSSR i Rossii*, 2nd ed. (Moscow, 2006), p. 11.

87 Hedrick Smith, *The Russians* (London, 1976), p. 357.

88 Gustafson, *Crisis Amid Plenty*, p. 312.

89 R. G. Pikhoia, *Sovetskii Soiuz: Istoriia vlasti, 1945–1991* (Novesibirsk, 2000), pp. 6–7.

90 Colton, *Moscow*, p. 426.

91 John P. Willerton, *Patronage and Politics in the Brezhnev Era* (Cambridge, 1992), p. 13. For Brezhnev's close attention to cadre questions, see F. Burlatskii, *Glotok svobody* (Moscow, 1997), pp. 298–9.

92 Sinitsin, *Andropov vblizi*, pp. 85, 90.

93 Pyzhikov, *Khrushchevskaia 'ottepel'*, p. 130.

94 Il'ia Zemtsov, *Partiia ili mafiia: Razvorovannaia respublika* (Paris, 1976), p. 26.

95 Luc Duhamel, "Justice and Politics in Moscow 1983–1986: The Ambartsumyan Case," *Europe–Asia Studies*, 52 (2000), pp. 1307–29.

96 Knight, *The KGB*, p. 97.

97 William A. Clark, "Crime and Punishment in Soviet Officialdom, 1965–90," *Europe–Asia Studies*, 45 (1993), p. 275.

98 Jerry F. Hough, *Democratization and Revolution in the USSR, 1985–1991* (Washington, DC, 1997), pp. 63–4.

99 Pikhoia, *Sovetskii Soiuz*, p. 636.

100 Judith Devlin, *The Rise of the Russian Democrats: The Causes and Consequences of the Elite Revolution* (Aldershot, 1995), p. 54.

101 Hough, *Democratization and Revolution*, p. 139.

102 Gorbachev, *Zhizn' i reformy*, pp. 425–6, 442, 484.

103 Pikhoia, *Sovetskii Soiuz*, p. 634.

104 Hough, *Democratization and Revolution*, p. 283; Michael McFaul, *Russia's Unfinished Revolution: Political Change from Gorbachev to Putin* (Ithaca, 2001), p. 79.

105 On the shenanigans of politics in the post-Soviet era, see Andrew Wilson, *Virtual Politics: Faking Democracy in the Post-Soviet World* (New Haven, 2005).

106 George W. Breslauer, *Gorbachev and Yeltsin as Leaders* (Cambridge, 2002), p. 308.

107 For a trenchant analysis, see Allen C. Lynch, *How Russia Is Not Ruled: Reflections on Russian Political Development* (Cambridge, 2005).

108 A good summary is Richard Sakwa, *Putin: Russia's Choice* (London, 2004), chap. 1.

109 The arguments are reviewed in Bettina Renz, "Putin's Militocracy? An Alternative Interpretation of Siloviki in Contemporary Russian Politics," *Europe–Asia Studies,* 58 (2006), pp. 903–24.

110 Yevgenia Albats, *KGB: State Within a State* (London, 1995), p. 23.

111 See Zoltan Barany, *Democratic Breakdown and the Decline of the Russian Military* (Princeton, 2007).

112 Barany, *Democratic Breakdown*, p. 54.

113 For developments under Medvedev, see Roger McDermott, "Medvedev's Ambitious Military Reform Plans," *Eurasia Daily Monitor*, 5/211 (4 November 2008) and Pavel Felgenhauer, "Medvedev Publicly Supports Serdyukov," *Eurasia Daily Monitor*, 6/53 (19 March 2009). For a longer-term view, see Carolina Vendil Pallin, *Russian Military Reform: A Failed Exercise in Defence Decision Making* (London, 2009).

--- Chapter 3 ---

1 G. A. Kozlov (ed.), *Political Economy: Socialism* (Moscow, 1977), p. 14.

2 Paul R. Gregory, *The Political Economy of Stalinism: Evidence from the Soviet Secret Archives* (Cambridge, 2004), pp. 112, 118, 127, 269.

3 Stephen Whitefield, *Industrial Power and the Soviet State* (Oxford, 1993), p. 24.

4 James R. Millar, *The ABCs of Soviet Socialism* (Urbana and Chicago, 1981), p. 40; Mark Harrison, "The Soviet Union: The Defeated Victor," in Mark Harrison (ed.), *The Economics of World War II: Six Great Powers in International Comparison* (Cambridge, 1998), pp. 275–6; Eugene Zaleski, *Stalinist Planning for Economic Growth, 1933–1952* (Chapel Hill, 1980), pp. 309–11, 321.

5 Zaleski, *Stalinist Planning*, pp. 327–30.

6 Thanks to Don Filtzer for this calculation, which is derived from physical quantities given in William Moskoff, *The Bread of Affliction: The Food Supply in the USSR during World War II* (Cambridge, 1990), p. 139.

7 Zaleski, *Stalinist Planning*, pp. 332–40.

8 N. Voznesensky, War *Economy of the USSR in the Period of the Great Patriotic War* (Moscow, 1948), pp. 36, 41, 69. Later, less partisan accounts have borne out the successes of Soviet arms production. See especially Mark Harrison, "The USSR and Total War: Why Didn't the Soviet Economy Collapse in 1942?" in Roger Chickering, Stig Förster and Bernd Greiner (eds.), *A World at Total War: Global Conflict and the Politics of Destruction, 1937–1945* (Cambridge, 2005), pp. 137–56.

9 Mark Harrison, *Accounting for War: Soviet Production, Employment, and the Defence Burden, 1940–1945* (Cambridge, 1996), pp. 165–6.

10 Marshall I. Goldman, *Détente and Dollars: Doing Business with the Soviets* (New York, 1975), p. 21.

11 Zaleski, *Stalinist Planning*, pp. 375–6, 470, 474–6.

12 For a survey of peasant survival strategies in the postwar period, see Jean Lévesque, "'Into the Grey Zone': Sham Peasants and the Limits of the Kolkhoz Order in the Post-War Russian Village, 1945–1953," in Juliane Fürst (ed.), *Late Stalinist Russia: Society between Reconstruction and Reinvention* (London, 2006), pp. 103–19. For the 1950 survey, see V. P. Popov, *Rossiiskaia derevnia posle voiny (iiun' 1945–mart 1953): Sbornik dokumentov* (Moscow, 1993), p. 146.

13 Timothy Dunmore, *The Stalinist Command Economy: The Soviet State Apparatus and Economic Policy 1945–53* (London, 1980), pp. 6–22.

14 Philip Hanson, *The Rise and Fall of the Soviet Economy* (London, 2003), p. 241.

15 James R. Millar, *The Soviet Economic Experiment* (Urbana, 1990), p. 90.

16 Ethan Pollock, *Stalin and the Soviet Science Wars* (Princeton, 2006), chap. 7; Erik van Ree, *The Political Thought of Joseph Stalin: A Study in Twentieth-Century Revolutionary Patriotism* (London, 2002), chap. 8.

17 Note figures presented in Basile Kerblay, *Modern Soviet Society* (London, 1983), p. 96.

18 P. I. Kushner, *Selo Viriatino v proshlom i nastoiashchem: Opyt etnograficheskogo izucheniia russkoi kolkhoznoi derevni* (Moscow, 1958), p. 162.

19 Kushner, *Selo Viriatino*, pp. 170, 175.

20 Lazar Volin, *A Century of Russian Agriculture: From Alexander II to Khrushchev* (Cambridge, MA, 1970), pp. 302–3, 306–7; Neil J. Melvin, *Soviet Power and the Countryside: Policy Innovation and Institutional Decay* (Houndmills, 2003), pp. 38–9.

21 Roy A. Medvedev and Zhores A. Medvedev, *Khrushchev: The Years in Power* (London, 1977), pp. 32–3.

22 My account of the Khrushchev reforms in agriculture draws primarily on Zhores A. Medvedev, *Soviet Agriculture* (London, 1987), chap. 6.

23 Grigory Ioffe and Tatyana Nefedova, *Continuity and Change in Rural Russia: A Geographical Perspective* (Boulder, 1997), pp. 72–3; Tat'iana Nefedova and Dzhudit Pellot [Judith Pallot], *Neizvestnoe sel'skoe khoziaistvo, ili Zachem nuzhna korova?* (Moscow, 2006), p. 20.

24 Ioffe and Nefedova, *Continuity and Change*, p. 79.

25 Grigory Ioffe et al., *The End of Peasantry? The Disintegration of Rural Russia* (Pittsburgh, 2006), pp. 16, 26.

26 Ioffe and Nefedova, *Continuity and Change*, p. 75.

27 Millar, *The Soviet Economic Experiment*, p. 91; Paul R. Gregory and Robert C. Stuart, *Soviet Economic Structure and Performance* (New York, 1990), p. 311.

28 Medvedev, *Soviet Agriculture*, p. 238.

29 M. S. Gorbachev, *Zhizn' i reformy*, vol. 1 (Moscow, 1995), pp. 183–6.

30 Kerblay, *Modern Soviet Society*, p. 76; Ioffe et al., *The End of Peasantry?* pp. 80–1.

31 Kerblay, *Modern Soviet Society*, pp. 85, 87–8; Medvedev, *Soviet Agriculture*, p. 366; Ioffe et al., *The End of Peasantry?* p. 21.

32 Edward A. Hewett, *Reforming the Soviet Economy: Equality versus Efficiency* (Washington, DC, 1988), p. 115.

33   Hewett, *Reforming the Soviet Economy*, pp. 199–200.
34   Millar, *The ABCs of Soviet Socialism*, p. 69.
35   Hewett, *Reforming the Soviet Economy*, pp. 184–5, 189.
36   Hewett, *Reforming the Soviet Economy*, p. 168.
37   Hewett, *Reforming the Soviet Economy*, p. 172.
38   Harrison, *Accounting for War*, p. 168.
39   Hewett, *Reforming the Soviet Economy*, pp. 192, 194.
40   Hewett, *Reforming the Soviet Economy*, pp. 182, 210, 214.
41   Millar, *The ABCs of Soviet Socialism*, p. 76.
42   Moshe Lewin, *Political Undercurrents in Soviet Economic Debates: From Bukharin to the Modern Reformers* (London, 1975), chaps. 6–7.
43   Joseph S. Berliner, *Factory and Manager in the USSR* (Cambridge, MA, 1957), pp. 302, 306, 311.
44   Hewett, *Reforming the Soviet Economy*, pp. 231, 234; Gregory and Stuart, *Soviet Economic Structure and Performance*, pp. 147–9.
45   Note the analysis and examples in Peter Rutland, *The Politics of Economic Stagnation in the Soviet Union: The Role of Local Party Organs in Economic Management* (Cambridge, 1993).
46   William J. Conyngham, *The Modernization of Soviet Industrial Management: Socio-economic Development and the Search for Viability* (Cambridge, 1982), pp. 13–16.
47   Rutland, *The Politics of Economic Stagnation*, p. 75.
48   Stephen Whitefield, *Industrial Power and the Soviet State* (Oxford, 1993), p. 95.
49   Rutland, *The Politics of Economic Stagnation*, pp. 76, 78.
50   Hewett, *Reforming the Soviet Economy*, p. 174; Julian Cooper, "The Defense Industry and Civil–Military Relations," in Timothy J. Colton and Thane Gustafson (eds.), *Soldiers and the Soviet State: Civil–Military Relations from Brezhnev to Gorbachev* (Princeton, 1990), p. 181.
51   Rutland, *The Politics of Economic Stagnation*, p. 116.
52   Rutland, *The Politics of Economic Stagnation*, pp. 82, 84, 165.
53   Rutland, *The Politics of Economic Stagnation*, chap. 6; Thane Gustafson, *Crisis amid Plenty: The Politics of Soviet Energy under Brezhnev and Gorbachev* (Princeton, 1989).
54   Cooper, "The Defense Industry and Civil–Military Relations," pp. 165, 167.
55   Gregory and Stuart, *Soviet Economic Structure and Performance*, pp. 146–7.
56   Julie Hessler, *A Social History of Soviet Trade: Trade Policy, Retail Practices, and Consumption, 1917–1953* (Princeton, 2004), chap. 6 (household budget figure on p. 269); Iu. A. Poliakov, "Moskovskii Gosudarstvennyi Universitet v Sverdlovske (1942–1943 gg.)," *Otechestvennaia istoriia*, 2 (2005), p. 58.
57   Jeffrey W. Jones, "'People without a Definite Occupation': The Illegal Economy and 'Speculators' in Rostov-on-the-Don, 1943–48," in Donald J. Raleigh (ed.), *Provincial Landscapes: Local Dimensions of Soviet Power, 1917–1953* (Pittsburgh, 2001), pp. 236–54.
58   Gorbachev, *Zhizn' i reformy*, p. 78.
59   Cynthia Hooper, "A Darker 'Big Deal': Concealing Party Crimes in the Post-Second World War Era," and James Heinzen, "A 'Campaign Spasm': Graft and the Limits of the 'Campaign' against Bribery after the Great Patriotic War," both in Juliane

Fürst (ed.), *Late Stalinist Russia: Society between Reconstruction and Reinvention* (London, 2006), pp. 123–41, 142–63; James W. Heinzen, "Informers and the State under Late Stalinism: Informant Networks and Crimes against 'Socialist Property,' 1940–53," *Kritika: Explorations in Russian and Eurasian History*, 8 (2007), pp. 789–815.

60   Konstantin M. Simis, *USSR: Secrets of a Corrupt Society* (London, 1982), pp. 17–18.

61   A. Katsenelinboigen, "Coloured Markets in the Soviet Union," *Soviet Studies*, 29 (1977), pp. 62–85.

62   James R. Millar, "The Little Deal: Brezhnev's Contribution to Acquisitive Socialism," *Slavic Review*, 44 (1985), p. 697.

63   Goldman, *Détente and Dollars*, chap. 7; Gregory and Stuart, *Soviet Economic Structure and Performance*, pp. 332–3.

64   See Randall W. Stone, *Satellites and Commissars: Strategy and Conflict in the Politics of Soviet-Bloc Trade* (Princeton, 1996).

65   I. Birman, *Personal Consumption in the USSR and the USA* (London, 1989), p. 163.

66   Donald Filtzer, *Soviet Workers and De-Stalinization: The Consolidation of the Modern System of Soviet Production Relations, 1953–1964* (Cambridge, 1992), figures on pp. 49, 75–6; Kerblay, *Modern Soviet Society*, pp. 190–1.

67   "The Novosibirsk Report," in T. I. Zaslavskaia, *A Voice of Reform* (Armonk, 1989), pp. 158–83.

68   Michael Ellman and Vladimir Kontorovich, *The Disintegration of the Soviet Economic System* (London, 1992), pp. 14–15.

69   Hewett, *Reforming the Soviet Economy*, pp. 260–7.

70   See Daniel Tarsychs, "The Success of a Failure: Gorbachev's Alcohol Policy, 1985–88," *Europe–Asia Studies*, 45 (1993), pp. 7–25.

71   Ellman and Kontorovich, *The Disintegration of the Soviet Economic System*, pp. 20–1.

72   Anthony Jones and William Moskoff, *Ko-ops: The Rebirth of Entrepreneurship in the Soviet Union* (Bloomington, 1991), pp. 5, 15.

73   J. R. Blasi et al., *Kremlin Capitalism: The Privatization of the Russian Economy* (Ithaca, 1997), p. 25.

74   Blasi et al., *Kremlin Capitalism*, p. 28.

75   Ellman and Kontorovich, *The Disintegration of the Soviet Economic System*, p. 25; Donald Filtzer, *Soviet Workers and the Collapse of Perestroika: The Soviet Labour Process and Gorbachev's Reforms, 1985–1991* (Cambridge, 1994), chap. 2.

76   Filtzer, *Soviet Workers and the Collapse of Perestroika*, p. 219.

77   Andrew Barnes, *Owning Russia: The Struggle over Factories, Farms, and Power* (Ithaca, 2006), p. 75; Blasi et al., *Kremlin Capitalism*, p. 2.

78   Blasi et al., *Kremlin Capitalism*, pp. 54, 67, 72, 93.

79   Barnes, *Owning Russia*, pp. 84–5.

80   Blasi et al., *Kremlin Capitalism*, pp. 72, 98–100.

81   Barnes, *Owning Russia*, pp. 110–14.

82   Barnes, *Owning Russia*, pp. 115, 120–8.

83   Jerry F. Hough, *The Logic of Economic Reform in Russia* (Washington, DC, 2001), p. 89.

84   Whitefield, *Industrial Power and the Soviet State*, pp. 103–4.

85 Blasi et al., *Kremlin Capitalism*, p. 130.

86 Clifford G. Gaddy and Barry W. Ickes, *Russia's Virtual Economy* (Washington, DC, 2002), p. 27; Michael Burawoy et al., "Domestic Involution: How Women Organize Survival in a North Russian City," in Victoria E. Bonnell and George W. Breslauer (eds.), *Russia in the New Century: Stability or Disorder?* (Boulder, 2001), pp. 231–61.

87 Vadim Volkov, *Violent Entrepreneurs: The Use of Force in the Making of Russian Capitalism* (Ithaca, 2002), pp. 2, 24, 26, 34, 133.

88 Juliet Johnson, *A Fistful of Rubles: The Rise and Fall of the Russian Banking System* (Ithaca, 2000), chap. 2 (details of survey on p. 36).

89 Johnson, *A Fistful of Rubles*, chap. 3.

90 Johnson, *A Fistful of Rubles*, chap. 4.

91 Alya Guseva, *Into the Red: The Birth of the Credit Card Market in Postcommunist Russia* (Stanford, 2008), chaps. 4–5.

92 Ioffe et al., *The End of Peasantry?* p. 81.

93 Barnes, *Owning Russia*, pp. 87–97, 150.

94 Ioffe et al., *The End of Peasantry?* p. 28.

95 Barnes, *Owning Russia*, pp. 149–55.

96 Guseva, *Into the Red*, pp. 109, 116, 147–8.

97 Stephen Fortescue, *Russia's Oil Barons and Metal Magnates: Oligarchs and the State in Transition* (Houndmills, 2006), pp. 60–71.

98 For a good general account of economic policy under Putin, see Richard Sakwa, *Russian Politics and Society*, 4th ed. (London, 2008), pp. 299–308.

99 Barnes, *Owning Russia*, p. 170.

100 Barnes, *Owning Russia*, pp. 171–4, 209–17; Fortescue, *Russia's Oil Barons*, pp. 121–48.

101 Fortescue, *Russia's Oil Barons*, p. 146.

102 Barnes, *Owning Russia*, pp. 179–80, 217.

103 John D. Grace, *Russian Oil Supply: Performance and Prospects* (Oxford, 2005). My account of the post-Soviet oil industry relies on this work.

104 Simon Kordonskii, *Resursnoe gosudarstvo* (Moscow, 2007). On the redistributive aspect of Russian political economy, see O. E. Bessonova, *Razdatochnaia ekonomika Rossii: Evoliutsiia cherez transformatsii* (Moscow, 2006).

------------------------------ Chapter 4 ------------------------------

1 Moshe Lewin, *The Making of the Soviet System: Essays in the Social History of Interwar Russia* (New York, 1985), pp. 44, 221, 265.

2 Golfo Alexopoulos, "Amnesty 1945: The Revolving Door of Stalin's Gulag," *Slavic Review*, 64 (2005), figures on pp. 275, 279, 305–6.

3 Alexopoulos, "Amnesty 1945," pp. 298–302.

4 Donald Filtzer, *Soviet Workers and Late Stalinism: Labour and the Restoration of the Stalinist System after World War II* (Cambridge, 2002), pp. 28–9.

5 Filtzer, *Soviet Workers and Late Stalinism*, p. 23.

6 Filtzer, *Soviet Workers and Late Stalinism*, pp. 14–16, 23–4.

7 Filtzer, *Soviet Workers and Late Stalinism*, pp. 29–39.

8 Sheila Fitzpatrick, "Postwar Soviet Society: The 'Return to Normalcy,' 1945–1953," in Susan J. Linz (ed.), *The Impact of World War II on the Soviet Union* (Totowa, NJ, 1985), pp. 131, 136, 146, 148; V. F. Zima, *Golod v SSSR 1946–1947 godov: Proiskhozhdenie i posledstviia* (Moscow, 1996).

9 Amir Weiner, *Making Sense of War: The Second World War and the Fate of the Bolshevik Revolution* (Princeton, 2001), pp. 83, 88, 122.

10 Fitzpatrick, "Postwar Soviet Society," pp. 130, 135, 138, 140–1, 149.

11 Miriam Dobson, "'Show the Bandit-Enemies No Mercy!' Amnesty, Criminality and Public Response in 1953," in Polly Jones (ed.), *The Dilemmas of De-Stalinization: Negotiating Cultural and Social Change in the Khrushchev Era* (London, 2006), p. 22.

12 Dobson, "'Show the Bandit-Enemies No Mercy,'" pp. 23–6.

13 Nanci Adler, *The Gulag Survivor: Beyond the Soviet System* (New Brunswick, 2002), pp. 154, 190; Miriam Dobson, "POWs and Purge Victims: Attitudes Towards Party Rehabilitation, 1956–57," *Slavonic and East European Review*, 86 (2008), pp. 328–45.

14 See for example Caroline Humphrey, *Marx Went Away – But Karl Stayed Behind* (Ann Arbor, 1998), p. 133.

15 Mervyn Matthews, *The Passport Society: Controlling Movement in Russia and the USSR* (Boulder, 1993), p. 31.

16 Anatolii Vishnevskii, *Serp i rubl': Konservativnaia modernizatsiia v SSSR* (Moscow, 1998), p. 91; Basile Kerblay, *Modern Soviet Society* (London, 1983), pp. 14, 75–7.

17 Michaela Pohl, "The Virgin Lands between Memory and Forgetting: People and Transformation in the Soviet Union, 1954–1960," Ph.D. dissertation (Indiana University, 1999), pp. 157–8, 166, 245.

18 Vishnevskii, *Serp i rubl'*, p. 94.

19 T. H. Rigby, *Communist Party Membership in the USSR, 1917–1967* (Princeton, 1968), pp. 275–6, 281, 286–8.

20 Rigby, *Communist Party Membership*, pp. 298–300, 304.

21 Mervyn Matthews, *Education in the Soviet Union: Policies and Institutions since Stalin* (London, 1982), pp. 21, 27; Catriona Kelly, *Children's World: Growing Up in Russia, 1890–1991* (New Haven, 2008), p. 146.

22 Benjamin K. Tromly, "Re-Imagining the Soviet Intelligentsia: Student Politics and University Life, 1948–1964," Ph.D. dissertation (Harvard University, 2007), p. 61.

23 Tromly, "Re-Imagining the Soviet Intelligentsia," p. 76.

24 Kerblay, *Modern Soviet Society*, p. 156.

25 Tromly, "Re-Imagining the Soviet Intelligentsia," pp. 311, 344, 348.

26 Kerblay, *Modern Soviet Society*, p. 161.

27 Kelly, *Children's World*, pp. 147–8; Mervyn Matthews, *Class and Society in Soviet Russia* (London, 1972), p. 121.

28 The best general discussion of social stratification in Soviet education is Murray Yanowitch, *Social and Economic Inequality in the Soviet Union* (London, 1977), chap. 3. On the Ufa study, see Kerblay, *Modern Soviet Society*, p. 165.

29 Kerblay, *Modern Soviet Society*, pp. 234–5; Yanowitch, *Social and Economic Inequality*, chaps. 2–3.

30 Petr Vail' and Aleksandr Genis, *60-e: Mir sovetskogo cheloveka* (Moscow, 1996), pp. 248–9.

31 Matthews, *Class and Society in the Soviet Union*, pp. 145–6.

32 Catriona Kelly, *Refining Russia: Advice Literature, Polite Culture, and Gender from Catherine to Yeltsin* (Oxford, 2001), pp. 327–9, 334–7.

33 Irina Shilova, ... *I moe kino: Piatidesiatye. Shestidesiatye. Semidesiatye* (Moscow, 1993), p. 32.

34 Kerblay, *Modern Soviet Society*, p. 155.

35 Matthews, *Class and Society in Soviet Russia*, pp. 110, 116–17, 119; Yanowitch, *Social and Economic Inequality*, pp. 130–1.

36 V. Zaslavsky, *The Neo-Stalinist State: Class, Ethnicity, and Consensus in Soviet Society* (Armonk, 1982), p. 47. For a fuller account of the new labor market after Stalin, see Donald Filtzer, *Soviet Workers and De-Stalinization: The Consolidation of the Modern System of Soviet Production Relations, 1953–1964* (Cambridge, 1992), chaps. 2–3.

37 Stephen Whitefield, *Industrial Power and the Soviet State* (Oxford, 1993), pp. 146, 149.

38 Zaslavsky, *The Neo-Stalinist State*, p. 31; William E. Odom, *The Collapse of the Soviet Military* (New Haven, 1998), pp. 35–9; Herbert Goldhammer, *The Soviet Soldier: Soviet Military Management at the Troop Level* (New York, 1975); Ellen Jones, *Red Army and Society: A Sociology of the Soviet Military* (London, 1985), pp. 53–7.

39 Goldhammer, *The Soviet Soldier*, pp. 42–3.

40 Neil J. Melvin, *Soviet Power and the Countryside: Policy Innovation and Institutional Decay* (Houndmills, 2003), pp. 5, 42–3, 46; Kerblay, *Modern Soviet Society*, p. 96; Humphrey, *Marx Went Away*, p. 140.

41 Kerblay, *Modern Soviet Society*, p. 105.

42 Humphrey, *Marx Went Away*, p. 270.

43 Rigby, *Communist Party Membership*, p. 290.

44 Vishnevskii, *Serp i rubl'*, pp. 117–19. Figures on infant mortality courtesy of Don Filtzer, derived from document at GARF, f. A-374, op. 34, d. 1540.

45 Vishnevskii, *Serp i rubl'*, pp. 123–4.

46 Kelly, *Children's World*, pp. 396–7.

47 E. V. Gruzdeva and E. S. Chertikhina, "Soviet Women: Problems of Work and Daily Life," in Murray Yanowitch (ed.), *The Social Structure of the USSR: Recent Soviet Studies* (Armonk, 1986), p. 155.

48 Ethel Dunn, "Russian Rural Women," in D. Atkinson et al. (eds.), *Women in Russia* (Stanford, 1977), pp. 176, 178.

49 Norton T. Dodge, "Women in the Professions," in Atkinson, *Women in Russia*, p. 207.

50 Lynne Attwood, *The New Soviet Man and Woman: Sex-Role Socialization in the USSR* (Houndmills, 1990), pp. 4–6.

51 Joseph S. Berliner, "Foreword," in James R. Millar, *Politics, Work, and Daily Life in the USSR: A Survey of Former Soviet Citizens* (Cambridge, 1987), p. xi.

52 Natalya Chernyshova, "Shopping with Brezhnev: Soviet Urban Consumer Culture, 1964–1985," Ph.D. dissertation (King's College London, 2008), chap. 4.

53 Ellen Jones, "Social Change and Civil–Military Relations," in Timothy J. Colton and Thane Gustafson (eds.), *Soldiers and the Soviet State: Civil–Military Relations from Brezhnev to Gorbachev* (Princeton, 1990), p. 253.

54 Kelly, *Children's World*, pp. 555, 557.

55   A. Kassof, "Afflictions of the Youth League," *Problems of Communism*, 5 (1958), p. 18.

56   Steven L. Solnick, *Stealing the State: Control and Collapse in Soviet Institutions* (Cambridge, MA, 1998), pp. 74–5.

57   Rigby, *Communist Party Membership*, pp. 352–9.

58   Mark Edele, "Soviet Veterans as an Entitlement Group, 1945–1955," *Slavic Review*, 65 (2006), pp. 111–37.

59   Stephen Lovell, "Soviet Russia's Older Generations," in Lovell (ed.), *Generations in Twentieth-Century Europe* (Houndmills, 2007), pp. 205–26.

60   N. A. Zbarskaia, "Osnovnye tendentsii izmeneniia demograficheskoi i sotsial'noi struktury rossiiskogo obshchestva: Itogi vserossiiskoi perepisi naseleniia 2002 goda," *Voprosy statistiki*, 11 (2004), pp. 63–8.

61   Zbarskaia, "Osnovnye tendentsii", p. 63.

62   O. B. Oskolkova and O. V. Belokon, *Pozhiloe naselenie sovremennoi Rossii: situatsiia i perspektivy* (Moscow, 1997); A. V. Pisarev, *Blagosostoianie pozhilogo naseleniia v sovremennoi Rossii* (Moscow, 2001).

63   Bertram Silverman and Murray Yanowitch, *New Rich, New Poor, New Russia: Winners and Losers on the Russian Road to Capitalism*, 2nd ed. (Armonk, NY, 2000), p. 52.

64   Theodore P. Gerber, "Educational Stratification in Contemporary Russia: Stability and Change in the Face of Economic and Institutional Crisis," *Sociology of Education*, 73 (2000), p. 224.

65   Silverman and Yanowitch, *New Rich, New Poor, New Russia*, pp. 17–18, 156.

66   Vladimir Shlapentokh, "Social Inequality in Post-Communist Russia: The Attitudes of the Political Elite and the Masses (1991–1998)," *Europe–Asia Studies*, 51 (1999), p. 1172.

67   Donald Filtzer, *Soviet Workers and the Collapse of Perestroika: The Soviet Labour Process and Gorbachev's Reforms, 1985–1991* (Cambridge, 1994), chap. 3.

68   Vladimir Tikhomirov, "The Second Collapse of the Russian Economy: Myths and Realities of the Russian Reform," *Europe–Asia Studies*, 52 (2000), pp. 207–36.

69   Simon Clarke, *The Development of Capitalism in Russia* (London, 2007).

70   For a sophisticated and empirically grounded version of this analysis, see L. D. Gudkov and B. V. Dubin, *Intelligentsiia: Zametki o literaturno-politicheskikh illiuziiakh* (Moscow, 1995).

71   Anne White, "Internal Migration Trends in Soviet and Post-Soviet European Russia," *Europe–Asia Studies*, 59 (2007), p. 896.

72   Dietwald Claus, "Looking for Russia's Middle Class," *The Moscow News*, 6 November 2007.

73   Tat'iana Nefedova and Dzhudit Pellot [Judith Pallot], *Neizvestnoe sel'skoe khoziaistvo, ili Zachem nuzhna korova?* (Moscow, 2006), pp. 10–12.

74   Susanne Wengle and Michael Rasell, "The Monetisation of L'goty: Changing Patterns of Welfare Politics and Provision in Russia," *Europe–Asia Studies*, 60 (2008), pp. 739–56.

75   Zoltan Barany, *Democratic Breakdown and the Decline of the Russian Military* (Princeton, 2007), chap. 1 (for Kursk disaster), pp. 65, 117–18.

76   See Lisa McIntosh Sundstrom, "Soldiers' Rights Groups in Russia: Civil Society through Russian and Western Eyes," in Alfred B. Evans et al., *Russian Civil Society:*

A Critical Assessment (Armonk, 2006), p. 187 (for figure on troop numbers) and pp. 178–96 passim for general argument.

77 Kate Brown, "Gridded Lives: Why Kazakhstan and Montana Are Nearly the Same Place," *American Historical Review*, 106 (2001), pp. 17–48; Lewis H. Siegelbaum, *Cars for Comrades: The Life of the Soviet Automobile* (Ithaca, 2008), p. 124.

78 For a recent version of this argument, see Simon Kordonskii, *Soslovnaia struktura postsovetskoi Rossii* (Moscow, 2008).

79 Vishnevskii, *Serp i rubl'*.

<hr>
Chapter 5
<hr>

1 A point made strongly in Orlando Figes, *The Whisperers: Private Life in Stalin's Russia* (London, 2007); note for example the powerful individual story with which the book opens, pp. xxvii–xxix.

2 Ronald Hingley, *The Russian Mind* (London, 1978), pp. 81–8.

3 Svetlana Boym, *Common Places: Mythologies of Everyday Life in Russia* (Cambridge, MA, 1994), p. 73.

4 Oleg Kharkhordin, "Reveal and Dissimulate: A Genealogy of Private Life in Soviet Russia," in Jeff Weintraub and Krishan Kumar (eds.), *Public and Private in Thought and Practice: Perspectives on a Grand Dichotomy* (Chicago, 1997), p. 359.

5 Vladimir Shlapentokh, *An Autobiographical Narration of the Role of Fear and Friendship in the Soviet Union* (Lewiston, 2004), pp. 27–8, 50. The argument is writ large in the same author's *Public and Private Life of the Soviet People: Changing Values in Post-Stalin Russia* (New York, 1989).

6 Naomi Roslyn Galtz, "The Strength of Small Freedoms: A Response to Ionin, by Way of Stories Told at the Dacha," in Daniel Bertaux et al. (eds.), *On Living Through Soviet Russia* (London, 2004), p. 177.

7 Lewis H. Siegelbaum, "Introduction: Mapping Private Spheres in the Soviet Context," in idem (ed.), *Borders of Socialism: Private Spheres of Soviet Russia* (Houndmills, 2006), p. 3.

8 Caroline Humphrey, *Marx Went Away – But Karl Stayed Behind* (Ann Arbor, 1998), esp. chap. 4; Alexei Yurchak, *Everything Was Forever, Until It Was No More: The Last Soviet Generation* (Princeton, 2006).

9 For much evidence on the activism of the wartime intelligentsia, see T. M. Goriaeva et al. (eds.), *Muzy v shineliakh: Sovetskaia intelligentsiia v gody Velikoi Otechestvennoi voiny. Dokumenty, teksty, vospominaniia* (Moscow, 2006).

10 Tatiana A. Chumachenko, *Church and State in Soviet Russia: Russian Orthodoxy from World War II to the Khrushchev Years* (Armonk, 2002), p. 85.

11 On broadcasting, see James von Geldern, "Radio Moscow: The Voice from the Center," in Richard Stites (ed.), *Culture and Entertainment in Wartime Russia* (Bloomington, 1995), pp. 44–61. Interesting reflections on the fusion of personal and ideological in wartime letters can be found in Jochen Hellbeck, "'The Diaries of Fritzes and the Letters of Gretchens': Personal Writings from the German–Soviet

War and Their Readers," *Kritika: Explorations in Russian and Eurasian History*, 10 (2009), esp. p. 605.

12 For a brief discussion of the home-front genre, see Denise J. Youngblood, *Russian War Films: On the Cinema Front, 1914–2005* (Lawrence, 2007), pp. 69–71.

13 Lisa A. Kirschenbaum, "'Our City, Our Hearths, Our Families': Local Loyalties and Private Life in Soviet World War II Propaganda," *Slavic Review*, 59 (2000), pp. 825–47. On cinematic depictions of the "woman warrior," see Youngblood, *Russian War Films*, pp. 60–9.

14 Charles P. Hachten, "Property Relations and the Economic Organization of Soviet Russia, 1941–1948," Ph.D. dissertation (University of Chicago, 2005), chaps. 3–4.

15 A wide selection of petitioners, from partisans to soldiers' mothers and orphans, can be found in A. Ia Livshin and I. B. Orlov (eds.), *Sovetskaia povsednevnost' i massovoe soznanie, 1939–1945* (Moscow, 2003).

16 Hachten, "Property Relations", chaps. 5 and 7.

17 Vera S. Dunham, *In Stalin's Time: Middleclass Values in Soviet Fiction* (Durham, NC, 1990), quotation on p. 41.

18 Julie Hessler, *A Social History of Soviet Trade: Trade Policy, Retail Practices, and Consumption, 1917–1953* (Princeton, 2004), pp. 318–21.

19 Vera Tolz, "'Cultural Bosses' as Patrons and Clients: The Functioning of the Soviet Creative Unions in the Postwar Period," *Contemporary European History*, 11 (2002), pp. 96–7.

20 Donald Filtzer, "Standard of Living versus Quality of Life: Struggling with the Urban Environment in Russia during the Early Years of Post-War Reconstruction," in Juliane Fürst (ed.), *Late Stalinist Russia: Society between Reconstruction and Reinvention* (London, 2006), pp. 84–5.

21 For examples, see Rebecca Manley, "'Where Should We Resettle the Comrades Next?': The Adjudication of Housing Claims and the Construction of the Post-War Order," in Fürst, *Late Stalinist Russia*, pp. 234–46.

22 Mark B. Smith, "Individual Forms of Ownership in the Urban Housing Fund of the USSR, 1944–64," *Slavonic and East European Review*, 86 (2008), pp. 288–9.

23 Charles Hachten, "Separate Yet Governed: The Representation of Soviet Property Relations in Civil Law and Public Discourse," in Siegelbaum (ed.), *Borders of Socialism*, pp. 70–3.

24 Mie Nakachi, "Population, Politics and Reproduction: Late Stalinism and Its Legacy", in Fürst, *Late Stalinist Russia*, pp. 23–45.

25 E. Iu. Zubkova, *Poslevoennoe sovetskoe obshchestvo: Politika i povsednevnost', 1945–1953* (Moscow, 1999), p. 26.

26 For a good general account of the literary Thaw, see George Gibian, *Interval of Freedom: Soviet Literature during the Thaw, 1954–1957* (Minneapolis, 1960).

27 The best study of Soviet cinema in this period is Josephine Woll, *Real Images: Soviet Cinema and the Thaw* (London, 2000).

28 See Kristin Roth-Ey, "Finding a Home for Television in the USSR, 1950–1970," *Slavic Review*, 66 (2007), pp. 278–306.

29 Susan Costanzo, "Reclaiming the Stage: Amateur Theater-Studio Audiences in the Late Soviet Era," *Slavonic and East European Review*, 86 (2008), figures on p. 376.

30 G. S. Smith, *Songs to Seven Strings: Russian Guitar Poetry and Soviet "Mass Song"* (Bloomington, 1984), p. 95 (for figures on tape recorder production).

31 Steven E. Harris, "Moving to the Separate Apartment: Building, Distributing, Furnishing, and Living in Urban Housing in Soviet Russia, 1950s–60s", Ph.D. dissertation (University of Chicago, 2003), p. 1. This work is the fullest study of the organization and implementation of the housing campaign.

32 Smith, "Individual Forms of Ownership", pp. 296–7.

33 Smith, "Individual Forms of Ownership", pp. 299–302.

34 A. Vishnevskii, *Serp i rubl': Konservativnaia modernizatsiia v SSSR* (Moscow, 1988), p. 91.

35 James R. Millar, "History, Method, and the Problem of Bias", in idem (ed.), *Politics, Work, and Daily Life in the USSR: A Survey of Former Soviet Citizens* (Cambridge, 1987), p. 25.

36 C. Varga-Harris, "Forging Citizenship on the Home Front: Reviving the Socialist Contract and constructing Soviet Identity during the Thaw", in Polly Jones (ed.), *The Dilemmas of De-Stalinization: Negotiating Cultural and Social Change in the Khrushchev Era* (London, 2006), pp. 101–16.

37 Stephen V. Bittner, "Local Soviets, Public Order, and Welfare after Stalin: Appeals from Moscow's Kiev *Raion*," *Russian Review*, 62 (2003), p. 283.

38 Stephen V. Bittner, "Exploring Reform: De-Stalinization in Moscow's Arbat District, 1953–68," Ph.D. dissertation (University of Chicago, 2000), p. 106.

39 Bittner, "Exploring Reform," p. 108.

40 Susan E. Reid, "Khrushchev Modern: Agency and Modernization in the Soviet Home," *Cahiers du monde russe*, 47 (2006), pp. 227–68.

41 See Vladimir A. Kozlov, *Mass Uprisings in the USSR: Protest and Rebellion in the Post-Stalin Years* (Armonk, 2002), chap. 8.

42 B. N. Ponomareva, *Konstitutsiia SSSR: Politiko-pravovoi kommentarii* (Moscow, 1982).

43 Stephen Lovell, *Summerfolk: A History of the Dacha, 1710–2000* (Ithaca, 2003), chap. 6.

44 Catriona Kelly, *Refining Russia: Advice Literature, Polite Culture, and Gender from Catherine to Yeltsin* (Oxford, 2001), pp. 314–16.

45 Oleg Kharkhordin, *The Collective and the Individual in Russia: A Study of Practices* (Berkeley, 1999), pp. 283, 286, 299.

46 Theodore H. Friedgut, *Political Participation in the USSR* (Princeton, 1979), pp. 239, 249, 253.

47 See the careful analysis of the campaign's origins and conduct in Chumachenko, *Church and State in Soviet Russia*, chap. 3 and Nathaniel Davies, *A Long Walk to Church: A Contemporary History of Russian Orthodoxy* (Boulder, 1995), pp. 34–45. The antireligious campaign had short-term political triggers, but its virulence cannot be adequately explained without reference to ideology.

48 Friedgut, *Political Participation*, p. 91.

49 Friedgut, *Political Participation*, pp. 109–10.

50 Deborah A. Field, "Irreconcilable Differences: Divorce and Conceptions of Private Life in the Khrushchev Era," *Russian Review*, 57 (1998), pp. 599–613.

51 Yoram Gorlizki, "Delegalization in Russia: Soviet Comrades' Courts in Retrospect," *American Journal of Comparative Law*, 46 (1998), pp. 403–25.

52 Eleonory Gilburd, "Picasso in Thaw Culture," *Cahiers du monde russe*, 47 (2006), pp. 74–5.

53 Juliane Fürst, "Friends in Private, Friends in Public: The Phenomenon of the Kompaniia among Soviet Youth in the 1950s and 1960s," in Siegelbaum (ed.), *Borders of Socialism*, p. 244.

54 Benjamin K. Tromly, "Re-Imagining the Soviet Intelligentsia: Student Politics and University Life, 1948–1964," Ph.D. dissertation (Harvard University, 2007), chaps. 2 and 4.

55 James R. Millar and Elizabeth Clayton, "Quality of Life: Subjective Measures of Relative Satisfaction," in Millar (ed.), *Politics, Work, and Daily Life in the USSR*, pp. 33 and 45.

56 B. A. Grushin, *Chetyre zhizni Rossii v zerkale oprosov obshchestvennogo mneniia. Zhizn' 2-ia. Epokha Brezhneva (chast' 1-ia)* (Moscow, 2003), p. 158.

57 Basile Kerblay, *Modern Soviet Society* (London, 1983), p. 142.

58 Anne E. Gorsuch, "Time Travelers: Soviet Tourists to Eastern Europe," in Anne E. Gorsuch and Diane P. Koenker (eds.), *Turizm: The Russian and East European Tourist under Capitalism and Socialism* (Ithaca, 2006), p. 206.

59 Christian Noack, "Coping with the Tourist: Planned and 'Wild' Tourism on the Soviet Black Sea Coast," in Gorsuch and Koenker, *Turizm*, p. 281.

60 Lewis H. Siegelbaum, "Cars, Cars, and More Cars: The Faustian Bargain of the Brezhnev Era," in Siegelbaum (ed.), *Borders of Socialism*, pp. 85, 88–9.

61 William Moskoff, *Labour and Leisure in the Soviet Union: The Conflict between Public and Private Decision-Making in a Planned Economy* (London, 1984), pp. 7–8, 13; Kerblay, *Modern Soviet Society*, p. 140.

62 I. Birman, *Personal Consumption in the USSR and the USA* (London, 1989), pp. 87–9, 106, 163.

63 Kerblay, *Modern Soviet Society*, pp. 132–3.

64 Kerblay, *Modern Soviet Society*, p. 132.

65 P. I. Kushner, *Selo Viriatino v proshlom i nastoiashchem: Opyt etnograficheskogo izucheniia russkoi kolkhoznoi derevni* (Moscow, 1958), pp. 196–7, 202, 220.

66 Millar, "History, Method, and the Problem of Bias," p. 33.

67 Examples from Natalya Chernyshova, "Shopping with Brezhnev: Soviet Urban Consumer Culture, 1964–1985", Ph.D. dissertation (King's College London, 2008), chap. 4.

68 Chernyshova, "Shopping with Brezhnev", chaps. 4–5.

69 Humphrey, *Marx Went Away*, p. 284.

70 Kushner, *Selo Viriatino*, pp. 189, 191–3.

71 Chernyshova, "Shopping with Brezhnev," chap. 6.

72 Kerblay, *Modern Soviet Society*, p. 115.

73 Catriona Kelly, *Children's World: Growing Up in Russia, 1890–1991* (New Haven, 2008), pp. 271–2, 336, 422–3, 557.

74 Kerblay, *Modern Soviet Society*, pp. 115, 119–20.

75 Kerblay, *Modern Soviet Society*, pp. 117, 122.

76 Vishnevskii, *Serp i rubl'*, pp. 126–9; Christopher Williams, "Abortion and Women's Health in Russia and the Soviet Successor States," in Rosalind Marsh (ed.), *Women in Russia and Ukraine* (Cambridge, 1996), pp. 133, 136.

77 S. I. Golod, *Chto bylo porokami, stalo nravami: Lektsii po sotsiologii seksual'nosti* (Moscow, 2005), pp. 73–6, 79–97; Vishnevskii, *Serp i rubl'*, p. 149 (citing Golod).

78 Vishnevskii, *Serp i rubl'*, p. 153.

79 Kerblay, *Modern Soviet Society*, pp. 123–4; Vishnevskii, *Serp i rubl'*, p. 151; Lynne Attwood, *The New Soviet Man and Woman: Sex-Role Socialization in the USSR* (Houndmills, 1990), pp. 191–2, 200.

80 Kerblay, *Modern Soviet Society*, pp. 138–9.

81 For a guide to Soviet informal practices, see Alena V. Ledeneva, *Russia's Economy of Favours: Blat, Networking and Informal Exchange* (Cambridge, 1998).

82 Kelly, *Refining Russia*, pp. 368–89.

83 Catharine Theimer Nepomnyashchy, "Markets, Mirrors, and Mayhem: Aleksandra Marinina and the Rise of the New Russian *Detektiv*," in Adele Marie Barker (ed.), *Consuming Russia: Popular Culture, Sex, and Society since Gorbachev* (Durham, NC, 1999), pp. 161–91.

84 For a full interpretation, see Eliot Borenstein, "Public Offerings: MMM and the Marketing of Melodrama," in Barker, *Consuming Russia*, pp. 49–75.

85 Olga Shevchenko, "'Between the Holes': Emerging Identities and Hybrid Patterns of Consumption in Post-socialist Russia," *Europe–Asia Studies*, 54 (2002), pp. 841–66.

86 Ledeneva, *Russia's Economy of Favours*, chap. 6.

87 Louis Skyner, "Rehousing and Refinancing Russia: Creating Access to Affordable Mortgaging," *Europe–Asia Studies*, 57 (2005), pp. 561–81.

88 Emma Kiselyova and Manuel Castells, "Russia in the Information Age," in Victoria E. Bonnell and George W. Breslauer (eds.), *Russia in the New Century: Stability or Disorder?* (Boulder, 2001), pp. 132–3, 153.

89 Floriana Fossato and John Lloyd with Alexander Verkhovsky, *The Web That Failed: How Opposition Politics and Independent Initiatives are Failing on the Internet in Russia* (Oxford: Reuters Institute for the Study of Journalism, 2008), p. 11.

90 Finn Sievert Nielsen, "The Eye of the Whirlwind: Russian Identity and Soviet Nation-Building. Quests for Meaning in a Soviet Metropolis," available online at www.anthrobase.com/Txt/N/Nielsen_F_S_03.htm (last accessed 8 July 2009).

───────────────────── Chapter 6 ─────────────────────

1 James von Geldern, "The Centre and the Periphery: Cultural and Social Geography in the Mass Culture of the 1930s," in Stephen White (ed.), *New Directions in Soviet History* (Cambridge, 1992), p. 65.

2 Petr Vail' and Aleksandr Genis, *60-e: Mir sovetskogo cheloveka* (Moscow, 1996), p. 81.

3 Hedrick Smith, *The Russians* (London, 1976), pp. 306–7.

4 An argument that is prominent in Lynne Viola, *The Unknown Gulag: The Lost World of Stalin's Special Settlements* (New York, 2007).

5   See Gerald Easter, *Reconstructing the State: Personal Networks and Elite Identity in Soviet Russia* (Cambridge, 2000).

6   Easter, *Reconstructing the State*, pp. 76, 78.

7   For the eloquent case of Karelia, a sensitive border region where the local preference for balanced economic development was overridden by Stalinist colonization, see Nick Baron, *Soviet Karelia: Politics, Planning and Terror in Stalin's Russia, 1920–1939* (London, 2007).

8   See James R. Harris, *The Great Urals: Regionalism and the Evolution of the Soviet System* (Ithaca, 1999).

9   Stephen Kotkin, *Magnetic Mountain: Stalinism as a Civilization* (Berkeley, 1995), pp. 78–9; John McCannon, *Red Arctic: Polar Exploration and the Myth of the North in the Soviet Union, 1932–1939* (New York, 1998).

10 Thanks to Julian Graffy for this information.

11 Kotkin, *Magnetic Mountain*, chap. 2.

12 Kate Brown, "Out of Solitary Confinement: The History of the Gulag," *Kritika: Explorations in Russian and Eurasian History*, 8 (2007), p. 84. I also owe my analysis of the Soviet Union's spatial structure to this article.

13 Pavel Polian, *Ne po svoei vole ... Istoriia i geografiia prinuditel'nykh migratsii v SSSR* (Moscow, 2001), p. 113.

14 V. K. Vinogradov et al. (eds.), *Lubianka v dni bitvy za Moskvu* (Moscow, 2002), pp. 38–9, 42–4, 49–50, 74–5.

15 Nataliia Gromova, *Evakuatsiia idet ... 1941–1944* (Moscow, 2008), pp. 10–11; V. I. Fomin, *Kino na voine: Dokumenty i svidetel'stva* (Moscow, 2005), pp. 115, 230–1.

16 V. N. Khaustov et al. (eds.), *Lubianka. Stalin i NKVD-NKGB-GUKP "Smersh", 1939–mart 1946* (Moscow, 2006), pp. 325–6.

17 M. N. Potemkina, "Evakonaselenie v ural'skom tylu: Opyt vyzhivaniia," *Otechestvennaia istoriia*, 2 (2005), pp. 86–98.

18 Potemkina, "Evakonaselenie," pp. 87–9, 94.

19 Gromova, *Evakuatsiia*, pp. 24–5.

20 A. V. Zakharchenko, "Sotsial'no-bytovoi aspekt zhizni rabochikh aviatsionnykh zavodov povolzh'ia v gody Velikoi Otechestvennoi Voiny," *Otechestvennaia istoriia*, 2 (2005), pp. 81–6.

21 Potemkina, "Evakonaselenie," pp. 90, 95–6. For a case study of Leningrad evacuees, see A. Z. Vakser, *Leningrad poslevoennyi: 1945–1982 gody* (St. Petersburg, 2005), pp. 7–9.

22 Numbers taken from Pavel Polian, *Zhertvy dvukh diktatur: Zhizn', trud, unizheniia i smert' sovetskikh voennoplennykh i ostarbaiterov na chuzhbine i na rodine*, 2nd ed. (Moscow, 2002), pp. 135–6. On the postwar reception of returnees, see also Vanessa Voisin, "Retribute or Reintegrate? The Ambiguity of Soviet Policies Towards Repatriates: The Case of Kalinin Province, 1943–1950," *Jahrbücher für Geschichte Osteuropas*, 55 (2007), pp. 34–55.

23 Timothy Dunmore, *The Stalinist Command Economy: The Soviet State Apparatus and Economic Policy 1945–53* (London, 1980), p. 37 and elsewhere in chap. 3.

24 Dunmore, *The Stalinist Command Economy*, pp. 64–5.

25 V. V. Denisov et al. (eds.), *TsK VKP(b) i regional'nye partiinye komitety 1945–1953* (Moscow, 2004), p. 8.

26 Timothy J. Colton, *Moscow: Governing the Socialist Metropolis* (Cambridge, MA, 1995), p. 328.

27 I. V. Stalin, "Privetstvie Moskve," in idem, *Sochineniia*, vol. 3 (XVI) (Stanford, 1967), pp. 93–6.

28 Vladimir Paperny, *Architecture in the Age of Stalin: Culture Two*, trans. John Hill and Roann Barris (Cambridge, 2002), pp. 87–90, 98.

29 Colton, *Moscow*, pp. 353–4, 365–6, 372.

30 My account of Vorkuta draws on Alan Barenberg's Ph.D. dissertation, "From Prison Camp to Mining Town: The Gulag and Its Legacy in Vorkuta, 1938–65" (University of Chicago, 2007).

31 John J. Stephan, *The Russian Far East: A History* (Stanford, 1994), pp. 256–7.

32 Judith Pallot, "Forced Labour for Forestry: The Twentieth Century History of Colonisation and Settlement in the North of Perm' Oblast," *Europe–Asia Studies*, 54 (2002), pp. 1061, 1069.

33 Pallot, "Forced Labour for Forestry," p. 1069.

34 Barenberg, "From Prison Camp to Mining Town," chap. 6.

35 Niobe Thompson, *Settlers on the Edge: Identity and Modernization on Russia's Arctic Frontier* (Vancouver, 2008), chaps. 2–3.

36 Steven L. Solnick, *Stealing the State: Control and Collapse in Soviet Institutions* (Cambridge, MA, 1998), chap. 5.

37 See Paul R. Josephson, *New Atlantis Revisited: Akademgorodok, the Siberian City of Science* (Princeton, 1997).

38 Tat'iana Voronina, "Pamiat' o BAMe. Tematicheskie dominanty v biograficheskikh interv'iu s byvshimi stroiteliami," *Neprikosnovennyi zapas*, 2/64 (2009), pp. 76–95.

39 On Russian roadlessness and inconclusive Soviet attempts to overcome it, see Lewis H. Siegelbaum, *Cars for Comrades: The Life of the Soviet Automobile* (Ithaca, 2008), pp. 125–72.

40 Hugh MacDonald, *Aeroflot: Soviet Air Transport since 1923* (London, 1975), pp. 247–50.

41 Benjamin K. Tromly, "Re-Imagining the Soviet Intelligentsia: Student Politics and University Life, 1948–1964," Ph.D. dissertation (Harvard University, 2007), pp. 81–2.

42 Blaine Ball and George J. Demko, "Internal Migration in the Soviet Union," *Economic Geography*, 54 (1978), pp. 96–8, 112.

43 A. I. Kokurin and N. V. Petrov, *Lubianka: Organy VChK-OGPU-NKVD-NKGB-MGB-MVD-KGB. 1917–1991. Spravochnik* (Moscow, 2003), p. 703.

44 V. Zaslavsky, *The Neo-Stalinist State: Class, Ethnicity, and Consensus in Soviet Society* (Armonk, 1982), chap. 6; Cynthia Buckley, "The Myth of Managed Migration: Migration Control and Market in the Soviet Period," *Slavic Review*, 54 (1995), pp. 896–916.

45 Colton, *Moscow*, pp. 459–80.

46 O. V. Khlevniuk, "Regional'naia vlast' v SSSR v 1953 – kontse 1950-kh godov: Ustoichivost' i konflikty," *Otechestvennaia istoriia*, 3 (2007), p. 31.

47 Jerry F. Hough and Merle Fainsod, *How the Soviet Union Is Governed* (Cambridge, MA, 1979), p. 232.

48 Jerry Hough, *The Soviet Prefects: The Local Party Organs in Industrial Decision-making* (Cambridge, MA, 1969), chap. 2.

49 Harris, *The Great Urals*, pp. 201–2.

50 Thane Gustafson, *Crisis Amid Plenty: The Politics of Soviet Energy under Brezhnev and Gorbachev* (Princeton, 1989), p. 105. A more systematic investigation of center–periphery relations in the postwar period is underway at the University of Manchester in the project "Networks and Hierarchies in the Soviet Provinces, 1945–1970": see www.socialsciences.manchester.ac.uk/disciplines/politics/research/sovietprovinces/

51 Peter Rutland, *The Politics of Economic Stagnation in the Soviet Union: The Role of Local Party Organs in Economic Management* (Cambridge, 1993), chap. 4.

52 On which see Vakser, *Leningrad poslevoennyi*, pp. 269–77.

53 Lisa A. Kirschenbaum, *The Legacy of the Siege of Leningrad, 1941–1995: Myth, Memories, and Monuments* (Cambridge, 2006), pp. 161–8, 187–200.

54 Karl D. Qualls, "Local–Outsider Negotiations in Postwar Sevastopol's Reconstruction, 1944–53," in Donald J. Raleigh (ed.), *Provincial Landscapes: Local Dimensions of Soviet Power, 1917–1953* (Pittsburgh, 2001), pp. 277, 281–2.

55 K. Kelli [Catriona Kelly], "'Ispravliat'' li istoriiu? Spory ob okhrane pamiatnikov v Leningrade 1960–1970-kh godov," *Neprikosnovennyi zapas*, 2/64 (2009), pp. 117–39.

56 Geoffrey Hosking, *Beyond Socialist Realism: Soviet Fiction since Ivan Denisovich* (London, 1980), pp. 50–83; Kathleen F. Parthé, *Russian Village Prose: The Radiant Past* (Princeton, 1992).

57 Douglas R. Weiner, *A Little Corner of Freedom: Russian Nature Protection from Stalin to Gorbachev* (Berkeley, 1999), pp. 357–73, 444.

58 Weiner, *A Little Corner of Freedom*, pp. 372–3.

59 Timothy J. Colton, *Yeltsin: A Life* (New York, 2008), pp. 98–9.

60 Richard Sakwa, *Russian Politics and Society*, 4th ed. (London, 2008), pp. 240–2.

61 For the contrast between Tatarstan and Sakha, and a discussion of post-Soviet regional politics in general, see Mary McAuley, *Russia's Politics of Uncertainty* (Cambridge, 1997), chaps. 2–3.

62 K. Stoner-Weiss, "The Russian Central State in Crisis: Center and Periphery in the Post-Soviet Era," in Z. Barany and R. G. Moser (eds.), *Russian Politics: Challenges of Democratization* (Cambridge, 2001), p. 112.

63 G. V. Golosov, *Political Parties in the Regions of Russia: Democracy Unclaimed* (Boulder, 2004), pp. 64–5; Sakwa, *Russian Politics and Society*, pp. 257–9.

64 Stoner-Weiss, "*The Russian Central State* in Crisis," p. 125.

65 Grigory Ioffe et al., "Russia's Fragmented Space," in Blair A. Ruble et al. (eds.), *Fragmented Space in the Russian Federation* (Washington, DC, 2001), pp. 33–4, 38, 69.

66 Cynthia Buckley and Regina Smyth, "The Ties That Bind: The Importance of Region in the Construction of Social and Political Citizenship," in Ruble, *Fragmented Space*, pp. 81–122.

67 Stoner-Weiss, "The Russian Central State in Crisis," p. 121.

68 McAuley, *Russia's Politics of Uncertainty*, p. 315.

69   Vladimir Gel'man, "Leviathan's Return: The Policy of Recentralization in Contemporary Russia," in Cameron Ross and Adrian Campbell (eds.), *Federalism and Local Politics in Russia* (London, 2009), p. 16.

70   Sakwa, *Russian Politics and Society*, pp. 271–3; Susanne Wengle and Michael Rasell, "The Monetisation of L'goty: Changing Patterns of Welfare Politics and Provision in Russia," *Europe–Asia Studies*, 60 (2008), pp. 739–56.

71   J. Paul Goode, "The Puzzle of Putin's Gubernatorial Appointments," *Europe–Asia Studies*, 59 (2007), p. 371.

72   Elena Chebankova, "Putin's Struggle for Federalism: Structures, Operation, and the Commitment Problem," *Europe–Asia Studies*, 59 (2007), pp. 279–302.

73   Joel C. Moses, "Who Has Led Russia? Russian Regional Political Elites, 1954–2006," *Europe–Asia Studies*, 60 (2008), pp. 1–24.

74   For reports that trade in the Russian Far East may be benefiting China, Japan, and South Korea more than Russia, see Yuri Zarakhovich, "Moscow Tightens its Grip on the Regions as Wealth Declines," *Eurasia Daily Monitor*, 6/85 (4 May 2009).

75   Judith Thornton and Charles E. Ziegler, "The Russian Far East in Perspective," in Thornton and Ziegler (eds.), *Russia's Far East: A Region at Risk* (Seattle and London, 2002), p. 4.

76   Pallot, "Forced Labour for Forestry," pp. 1056–7. On the latter case, see John Round, "Marginalised for a Lifetime: The Everyday Experiences of Gulag Survivors in Post-Soviet Magadan," *Geografiska Annaler: B*, 87 (2006), pp. 15–34.

77   For a nuanced analysis, which strikes a tone of qualified optimism with regard to the adaptive potential of the Russian periphery, see Viacheslav Glazychev, *Glubinnaia Rossiia: 2000–2002*, 2nd ed. (Moscow, 2005). On the plight of the small town intelligentsia, see Anne White, *Small-Town Russia: Postcommunist Livelihoods and Identities: A Portrait of the Intelligentsia in Achit, Bednodemyanovsk and Zubtsov, 1999–2000* (London, 2004).

78   Anne White, "Internal Migration Trends in Soviet and Post-Soviet European Russia," *Europe–Asia Studies*, 59 (2007), pp. 887–911.

79   Natalia Rulyova, "Domesticating the Western Format on Russian TV: Subversive Glocalisation in the Game Show Pole Chudes (The Field of Miracles)," *Europe–Asia Studies*, 59 (2007), pp. 1367–86.

80   Valerii Sirozhenko, "2005 god: sbyvshiesia i nesbyvshiesia prognozy," *Knizhnoe obozrenie pro*, 224 (2006).

Chapter 7

1   Two contrasting but complementary accounts of these matters are Terry Martin, *The Affirmative Action Empire: Nations and Nationalism in the Soviet Union, 1923–1939* (Ithaca, 2001) and Francine Hirsch, *Empire of Nations: Ethnographic Knowledge and the Making of the Soviet Union* (Ithaca, 2005).

2   Jeffrey Brooks, *Thank You, Comrade Stalin! Soviet Public Culture from Revolution to Cold War* (Princeton, 2000), pp. 159, 287 n. 1.

3　David Brandenberger, *National Bolshevism: Stalinist Mass Culture and the Formation of Modern Russian National Identity, 1931–1956* (Cambridge, MA, 2002), pp. 116, 121.

4　D. G. Nadzhafov and Z. S. Belousova (eds.), *Stalin i kosmopolitizm: Dokumenty Agitpropa TsK KPSS 1945–1953* (Moscow, 2005), pp. 23–4.

5　Gerhard Simon, *Nationalism and Policy Toward the Nationalities in the Soviet Union: From Totalitarian Dictatorship to Post-Stalinist Society* (Boulder, 1991), pp. 184–6.

6　Nathaniel Davis, *A Long Walk to Church: A Contemporary History of Russian Orthodoxy* (Boulder, 1995), pp. 16–19.

7　Davis, *A Long Walk to Church*, pp. 21–4.

8　Tatiana A. Chumachenko, *Church and State in Soviet Russia: Russian Orthodoxy from World War II to the Khrushchev Years* (Armonk, 2002), pp. 42–6, 58, 66.

9　Pavel Polian, *Ne po svoei vole … : Istoriia i geografiia prinuditel'nykh migratsii v SSSR* (Moscow, 2001), pp. 95–6, 98.

10　Polian, *Ne po svoei vole*, pp. 99–102.

11　On Lithuania, see Timothy Snyder, *The Reconstruction of Nations: Poland, Ukraine, Lithuania, Belarus, 1569–1999* (New Haven, 2003), esp. pp. 80–4.

12　Simon, *Nationalism*, pp. 173, 195, 200; Polian, *Ne po svoei vole*, p. 113.

13　Simon, *Nationalism*, p. 198.

14　Katrin Boeckh, *Stalinismus in der Ukraine: Die Rekonstruktion des sowjetischen Systems nach dem Zweiten Weltkrieg* (Wiesbaden, 2007), p. 296.

15　See Snyder, *The Reconstruction of Nations*, chap. 8.

16　Polian, *Ne po svoei vole*, pp. 103–4.

17　Simon, *Nationalism*, p. 202.

18　Snyder, *The Reconstruction of Nations*, pp. 187, 194.

19　Simon, *Nationalism*, pp. 203, 216; Anatol Lieven, *The Baltic Revolution: Estonia, Latvia, Lithuania and the Path to Independence* (New Haven, 1993), p. 90.

20　E. Iu. Zubkova, *Pribaltika i Kreml'. 1940–1953* (Moscow, 2008), pp. 180–1; Polian, *Ne po svoei vole*, pp. 139–40. These numbers are derived from internal Soviet reports; other historians, using more indirect methods, have estimated a substantially higher figure.

21　Polian, *Ne po svoei vole*, pp. 147–50.

22　Zubkova, *Pribaltika i Kreml'*, pp. 156–7.

23　Brandenberger, *National Bolshevism*, pp. 185, 187, 222.

24　For a full account, see Joshua Rubenstein and Vladimir P. Naumov (eds.), *Stalin's Secret Pogrom: The Postwar Inquisition of the Jewish Anti-Fascist Committee* (New Haven, 2001).

25　Harrison E. Salisbury, *Moscow Journal: The End of Stalin* (Chicago, 1961), p. 104.

26　Nikolai Mitrokhin, *Russkaia partiia: Dvizhenie russkikh natsionalistov v SSSR. 1953–1985 gody* (Moscow, 2003), pp. 44–5.

27　Yuri Slezkine, *The Jewish Century* (Princeton, 2004), pp. 294–7.

28　Polian, *Ne po svoei vole*, pp. 146–7, 156–62.

29　Amir Weiner, "The Empires Pay a Visit: Gulag Returnees, East European Rebellions, and Soviet Frontier Politics," *Journal of Modern History*, 78 (2006), pp. 338–9.

30 Simon, *Nationalism*, pp. 228–9, 239.
31 On the case of the Baltic republics, see Jeremy Smith, "Republican Authority and Khrushchev's Education Reform in Estonia and Latvia, 1958–1959," in Olaf Mertelsmann (ed.), *The Sovietization of the Baltic States, 1940–1956* (Tartu, 2003).
32 On the likely motives for the 1954 handover, see Gwendolyn Sasse, *The Crimea Question: Identity, Transition, and Conflict* (Cambridge, MA, 2007), pp. 107–26.
33 For the situation in the Virgin Lands, the most volatile melting pot of the Khrushchev era, see Michaela Pohl, "The Virgin Lands between Memory and Forgetting: People and Transformation in the Soviet Union, 1954–1960," Ph.D. dissertation (Indiana University, 1999), chap. 6.
34 Razmik Panossian, *The Armenians: From Kings and Priests to Merchants and Commissars* (New York, 2006), p. 349; Ronald Grigor Suny, *Looking toward Ararat: Armenia in Modern History* (Bloomington, 1993), p. 186.
35 A. Pyzhikov, *Khrushchevskaia 'ottepel'* (Moscow, 2002), pp. 201–2.
36 Lowell Tillett, *The Great Friendship: Soviet Historians on the Non-Russian Nationalities* (Chapel Hill, 1969), chap. 10.
37 Romuald Misiunas and Rein Taagepera, *The Baltic States: Years of Dependence, 1940–1990* (Berkeley, 1993), pp. 133, 136, 139–40, 177–8.
38 Pyzhikov, *Khrushchevskaia 'ottepel'*, p. 194.
39 Misiunas and Taagepera, *The Baltic States*, pp. 140–6; Smith, "Republican Authority and Khrushchev's Education Reform."
40 Philip Roeder, "Soviet Federalism and Ethnic Mobilization," *World Politics*, 43 (1991), pp. 203–4.
41 Rasma Karklins, *Ethnic Relations in the USSR: The Perspective from Below* (London, 1986), pp. 32, 45 n. 16.
42 Robert J. Kaiser, *The Geography of Nationalism in Russia and the USSR* (Princeton, 1994), pp. 152, 199–204.
43 Kaiser, *The Geography of Nationalism*, p. 209.
44 Ronald Grigor Suny, *The Making of the Georgian Nation* (Bloomington, 1994), p. 299; Suny, *Looking toward Ararat*, pp. 184–5.
45 Kaiser, *The Geography of Nationalism*, p. 226; Roeder, "Soviet Federalism," p. 217.
46 Basile Kerblay, *Modern Soviet Society* (London, 1983), p. 111; Roeder, "Soviet Federalism," pp. 204–5, 207–8; Kaiser, *The Geography of Nationalism*, p. 238.
47 Karklins, *Ethnic Relations in the USSR*, pp. 52, 57, 68; Mitrokhin, *Russkaia partiia*, p. 65.
48 Georgi M. Derluguian, *Bourdieu's Secret Admirer in the Caucasus: A World-System Biography* (Chicago, 2005), p. 58.
49 Kaiser, *The Geography of Nationalism*, p. 169; Lieven, *The Baltic Revolution*, pp. 183–4; P. Kolstoe, *Russians in the Former Soviet Republics* (London, 1995), pp. 47–8.
50 Kaiser, *The Geography of Nationalism*, pp. 248–50, 255–7.
51 Kaiser, *The Geography of Nationalism*, p. 344; Roeder, "Soviet Federalism," p. 223.
52 Karklins, *Ethnic Relations in the USSR*, pp. 105, 108.
53 Kaiser, *The Geography of Nationalism*, pp. 258, 260.
54 Kaiser, *The Geography of Nationalism*, p. 178.

55 V. Zaslavsky, *The Neo-Stalinist State: Class, Ethnicity, and Consensus in Soviet Society* (Armonk, 1982), p. 94.

56 Kaiser, *The Geography of Nationalism*, pp. 262, 265.

57 Suny, *Looking toward Ararat*, pp. 187–8.

58 V. Stanley Vardys and Judith B. Sedaitis, *Lithuania: The Rebel Nation* (Boulder, 1997), pp. 84–92.

59 Andrew Wilson, *The Ukrainians: Unexpected Nation* (New Haven, 2002), pp. 153–5.

60 Yaroslav Bilinsky, "Mykola Skrypnyk and Petro Shelest: An Essay on the Persistence and Limits of Ukrainian National Communism," in Jeremy R. Azrael (ed.), *Soviet Nationality Policies and Practices* (New York, 1978), pp. 119–28.

61 Roeder, "Soviet Federalism," p. 224; Suny, *Looking toward Ararat*, p. 182.

62 Estimate from R. W. Davies and Stephen G. Wheatcroft, *The Years of Hunger: Soviet Agriculture, 1931–1933* (Houndmills, 2004), p. 409.

63 Galina M. Yemelianova, *Russia and Islam: A Historical Survey* (Houndmills, 2002), p. 124.

64 Edward Allworth, *Central Asia, 130 Years of Russian Dominance: A Historical Overview* (Durham, NC, 1994), pp. 540–1; Alexandre Bennigsen and Marie Broxup, *The Islamic Threat to the Soviet State* (London, 1983), p. 125.

65 Allworth, *Central Asia*, pp. 542, 547–8.

66 Allworth, *Central Asia*, p. 551.

67 Michael Rwykin, *Moscow's Muslim Challenge* (Armonk, 1982), pp. 54–5, 57.

68 Yaacov Ro'i, *Islam in the Soviet Union: From the Second World War to Gorbachev* (London, 2000), introduction.

69 Ro'i, *Islam in the Soviet Union*, chap. 1.

70 Ro'i, *Islam in the Soviet Union*, pp. 86–7, 291, 299, 304; Yemelianova, *Russia and Islam*, p. 128.

71 Ro'i, *Islam in the Soviet Union*, pp. 74, 97.

72 *Memoirs of Nikita Khrushchev*, ed. Sergei Khrushchev, vol. 2 (University Park, 2006), pp. 3–17.

73 On what this meant in practice – on the combination of repression and social integration employed by the postwar state in Ukraine – see Boeckh, *Stalinismus in der Ukraine*, esp. chap. 5.

74 Weiner, "The Empires Pay a Visit."

75 Colin Thubron, *In Siberia* (London, 1999), p. 132.

76 Anna Kushkova, "V tsentre stola: Zenit i zakat salata 'Oliv'e,'" *Novoe literaturnoe obozrenie*, 76 (2005), pp. 278–313.

77 Jeff Sahadeo, "Druzhba Narodov or Second-Class Citizenship? Soviet Asian Migrants in a Post-Colonial World," *Central Asian Survey*, 26 (2007), pp. 559–79.

78 Mitrokhin, *Russkaia partiia*, pp. 69, 93.

79 Catriona Kelly, "'A European City in Russia': Living with Transnational History in St. Petersburg." Paper presented at conference "National Identity in Eurasia: Identities and Traditions," Oxford, March 2009.

80 Emil A. Draitser, *Taking Penguins to the Movies: Ethnic Humor in Russia* (Detroit, 1998).

81 Steven L. Burg, "Nationality Elites and Political Change in the Soviet Union," in Lubomyr Hajda and Mark Beissinger (eds.), *The Nationalities Factor in Soviet Politics and Society* (Boulder, 1990), pp. 25–7; Derluguian, *Bourdieu's Secret Admirer*, p. 170; Kathleen Collins, *Clan Politics and Regime Transition in Central Asia* (Cambridge, 2006), pp. 112–15.

82 Sasse, *The Crimea Question*, pp. 170–4.

83 Lieven, *The Baltic Revolution*, pp. 194–7, 219–22.

84 Lieven, *The Baltic Revolution*, pp. 239–46.

85 Paul S. Pirie, "National Identity and Politics in Southern and Eastern Ukraine," *Europe–Asia Studies*, 48 (1996), p. 1090.

86 A fine brief analysis of Ukraine's slide to independence is Wilson, *The Ukrainians*, pp. 156–71.

87 See Charles King, *The Moldovans: Romania, Russia, and the Politics of Culture* (Stanford, 2000).

88 Irakly Areshidze, *Democracy and Autocracy in Eurasia: Georgia in Transition* (East Lansing, 2007), chap. 1.

89 See Thomas de Waal, *Black Garden: Armenia and Azerbaijan through Peace and War* (New York, 2003).

90 For full details on Shanib's career and its context, see Derluguian, *Bourdieu's Secret Admirer*.

91 For a good recent account, see James Hughes, *Chechnya: From Nationalism to Jihad* (Philadelphia, 2007).

92 Collins, *Clan Politics*, chap. 4.

93 Gregory Gleason, "Uzbekistan: From Statehood to Nationhood?" in Ian Bremmer and Ray Taras (eds.), *Nation and Politics in the Soviet Successor States* (Cambridge, 1993), pp. 341, 348.

94 David Nissman, "Turkmenistan: Searching for a National Identity," in Bremmer and Taras, *Nation and Politics*, p. 387.

95 See Nazarbaev's own account of his views in his memoir *My Life, My Times and the Future* ... (Northamptonshire, 1998), p. 76.

96 Collins, *Clan Politics*, pp. 117–19; Gene Huskey, "Kyrgyzstan: The Politics of Demographic and Economic Frustration," in Bremmer and Taras, *Nation and Politics*, pp. 404–6.

97 De Waal, *Black Garden*, p. 3.

98 Lieven, *The Baltic Revolution*, pp. 194–5.

99 On the underlying realities of Russia's relations with its near abroad, see Bertil Nygren, *The Rebuilding of Greater Russia: Putin's Foreign Policy towards the CIS Countries* (London, 2008).

100 Tom Everett-Heath, "Instability and Identity in a Post-Soviet World: Kazakhstan and Uzbekistan," in Everett-Heath (ed.), *Central Asia: Aspects of Transition* (London, 2003), pp. 181–204; Sally N. Cummings, *Kazakhstan: Power and the Elite* (London, 2005).

101 See Pauline Jones Luong, *Institutional Change and Political Continuity in Post-Soviet Central Asia: Power, Perceptions, and Pacts* (Cambridge, 2002).

102 Alisher Ilkhamov, "Neopatrimonialism, Interest Groups and Patronage Networks: The Impasses of the Governance System in Uzbekistan," *Central Asian Survey*, 26 (2007), pp. 65–84.

103 Derluguian, *Bourdieu's Secret Admirer*, p. 171; estimate of war losses in Martha Brill Olcott, *Central Asia's Second Chance* (Washington, DC, 2005), p. 45.

104 Natalia Leshchenko, "The National Ideology and the Basis of the Lukashenka Regime in Belarus," *Europe–Asia Studies*, 60 (2008), pp. 1419–33.

105 Pirie, "National Identity," p. 1087.

106 This, more or less, is the conclusion of Sasse, *The Crimea Question*.

107 See the excellent immediate account in Andrew Wilson, *Ukraine's Orange Revolution* (New Haven, 2005).

108 The number itself is a controversial and politicized question: see Hilary Pilkington, "Introduction," in Pilkington and Galina Yemelianova (eds.), *Islam in Post-Soviet Russia: Public and Private Faces* (London, 2003), p. 2.

109 Vera Tolz, *Russia: Inventing the Nation* (London, 2001), pp. 252–3.

110 Yemelianova, *Russia and Islam*, p. 138.

111 As concluded, for example, in Hughes, *Chechnya*.

112 John Garrard and Carol Garrard, *Russian Orthodoxy Resurgent: Faith and Power in the New Russia* (Princeton, 2008), p. 245.

—————————— Chapter 8 ——————————

1 Geoffrey Hosking, *Russia and the Russians: A History from Rus to the Russian Federation* (London, 2001), p. 1.

2 Christopher Andrew and Vasili Mitrokhin, *The Mitrokhin Archive II: The KGB and the World* (London, 2006), p. 64. For a broader account, see Ilya Prizel, *Latin America through Soviet Eyes: The Evolution of Soviet Perceptions during the Brezhnev Era, 1964–1982* (Cambridge, 1990).

3 Caroline Kennedy-Pipe, *Russia and the World, 1917–1991* (London, 1998), pp. 88–9.

4 Norman M. Naimark, *The Russians in Germany: A History of the Soviet Zone of Occupation, 1945–1949* (Cambridge, MA, 1995), p. 17.

5 The Soviet–American parallels are nicely explored in Odd Arne Westad, *The Global Cold War: Third World Interventions and the Making of Our Times* (Cambridge, 2005), chaps. 1–2.

6 The defensive Soviet mindset, and Stalin's enduring suspicion of the British, are given their due in Gabriel Gorodetsky, *Grand Delusion: Stalin and the German Invasion of Russia* (New Haven, 1999).

7 Jan T. Gross, *Revolution from Abroad: The Soviet Conquest of Poland's Western Ukraine and Western Belorussia*, expanded edition (Princeton, 2002).

8 The possible reasons for the error – which does seem overwhelmingly to have been Stalin's rather than a more general misreading of the situation by the Soviet establishment – are reviewed in David E. Murphy, *What Stalin Knew: The Enigma of Barbarossa* (New Haven, 2005).

9   An insight that underpins Mark Mazower, *Hitler's Empire: Nazi Rule in Occupied Europe* (London, 2008).

10 F. Chuev, *Sto sorok besed s Molotovym* (Moscow, 1991), p. 90. Very insightful on Stalin's mindset at the end of the war is V. Zubok and C. Pleshakov, *Inside the Kremlin's Cold War: From Stalin to Khrushchev* (Cambridge, MA, 1996), a work that substantially informs the following discussion.

11 See Jamil Hasanli, *At the Dawn of the Cold War: The Soviet–American Crisis over Iranian Azerbaijan, 1941–1946* (Lanham, 2006).

12 On the postwar turmoil in eastern and central Europe, see Mark Mazower, *Dark Continent: Europe's Twentieth Century* (London, 1998), chap. 7.

13 Krystyna Kersten, *The Establishment of Communist Rule in Poland, 1943–1948* (Berkeley, 1991), p. 166.

14 For good general accounts of the imposition of Communist rule across the region, see Joseph Rothschild, *Return to Diversity: A Political History of East Central Europe since World War II*, 2nd ed. (Oxford, 1993), chap. 3, and R. J. Crampton, *Eastern Europe in the Twentieth Century – and After*, 2nd ed. (London, 1997), chap. 13.

15 See Hannes Adomeit, *Imperial Overstretch: Germany in Soviet Policy from Stalin to Gorbachev: An Analysis Based on New Archival Evidence, Memoirs, and Interviews* (Baden-Baden, 1998), chap. 2.

16 David Holloway, *Stalin and the Bomb: The Soviet Union and Atomic Energy, 1939–1956* (New Haven, 1994), pp. 271–2.

17 My account of this phase in Sino–Soviet relations draws mainly on Sergei N. Goncharov, John W. Lewis and Xue Litai, *Uncertain Partners: Stalin, Mao, and the Korean War* (Stanford, 1993).

18 See Kathryn Weathersby, "Soviet Aims in Korea and the Origins of the Korean War, 1945–1950: New Evidence from the Russian Archives," *Cold War International History Project*, working paper no. 8 (Washington, 1993).

19 Ilya V. Gaiduk, *Confronting Vietnam: Soviet Policy toward the Indochina Conflict, 1954–1963* (Washington DC, 2003).

20 Westad, *The Global Cold War*, pp. 89–90.

21 Andrew and Mitrokhin, *The Mitrokhin Archive II*, pp. 8–9.

22 See R. Allison, *The Soviet Union and the Strategy of Non-Alignment in the Third World* (Cambridge, 1988).

23 A fine recent account of the breakdown of the Sino–Soviet relationship puts ideological differences to the fore: see Lorenz M. Lüthi, *The Sino–Soviet Split: Cold War in the Communist World* (Princeton, 2008).

24 Aleksandr Fursenko and Timothy Naftali, *Khrushchev's Cold War: The Inside Story of an American Adversary* (New York, 2006), pp. 132–7.

25 An excellent account of the Cuban missile crisis and its background is Fursenko and Naftali, *Khrushchev's Cold War*, pp. 426–92.

26 My account draws on Charles Gati, *Failed Illusions: Moscow, Washington, Budapest, and the 1956 Hungarian Revolt* (Washington DC, 2006); and Johanna C. Granville, *The First Domino: International Decision Making during the Hungarian Crisis of 1956* (College Station, 2004).

27   Michael J. Sodaro, *Moscow, Germany, and the West from Khrushchev to Gorbachev* (London, 1991), p. 10.

28   Hope M. Harrison, *Driving the Soviets Up the Wall: Soviet–East German Relations, 1953–1961* (Princeton, 2003), pp. 99–100.

29   Robert H. Donaldson, *Soviet Policy toward India: Ideology and Strategy* (Cambridge, MA, 1974).

30   My account relies on Ilya V. Gaiduk, *The Soviet Union and the Vietnam War* (Chicago, 1996).

31   Vladislav M. Zubok, *A Failed Empire: The Soviet Union in the Cold War from Stalin to Gorbachev* (Chapel Hill, 2007), pp. 192–226.

32   Galia Golan, *Soviet Policies in the Middle East from World War Two to Gorbachev* (Cambridge, 1990), chap. 3.

33   Kennedy-Pipe, *Russia and the World*, p. 135.

34   Westad, *The Global Cold War*, pp. 198–9.

35   Golan, *Soviet Policies in the Middle East*, chap. 5.

36   Oles M. Smolansky with Bettie M. Smolansky, *The USSR and Iraq: The Soviet Quest for Influence* (Durham and London, 1991).

37   Westad, *The Global Cold War*, chap. 6.

38   My account draws on Robert G. Patman, *The Soviet Union in the Horn of Africa: The Diplomacy of Intervention and Disengagement* (Cambridge, 1990); and Westad, *The Global Cold War*, chap. 7.

39   On the Soviet intervention in Afghanistan, see Westad, *The Global Cold War*, chap. 8; and A. V. Shubin, *Ot 'zastoia' k reformam: SSSR v 1917–1985 gg.* (Moscow, 2001), chap. 1.

40   Christopher Andrew and Vasili Mitrokin, *The Mitrokhin Archive: The KGB in Europe and the West* (London, 1999), pp. 322–41.

41   Shubin, *Ot 'zastoia' k reformam*, p. 42.

42   The best recent account of the Polish crisis is Matthew J. Ouimet, *The Rise and Fall of the Brezhnev Doctrine in Soviet Foreign Policy* (Chapel Hill, 2003), chaps. 4–7.

43   Ouimet, *The Rise and Fall of the Brezhnev Doctrine*, p. 253.

44   Shubin, *Ot 'zastoia' k reformam*, p. 19.

45   Westad, *The Global Cold War*, pp. 380–4.

46   On the generally unfavorable terms of Soviet trade with the Eastern bloc, see Randall W. Stone, *Satellites and Commissars: Strategy and Conflict in the Politics of Soviet-Bloc Trade* (Princeton, 1996).

47   On the role of Gorbachev and unintended consequences in the collapse of the Soviet empire, see Jacques Lévesque, *The Enigma of 1989: The USSR and the Liberation of Eastern Europe* (Berkeley, 1997); Zubok, *A Failed Empire*, chaps. 9–10; Adomeit, *Imperial Overstretch*, chap. 4.

48   For an acute assessment of Russia's erratic and "sectionalized" foreign policy in the Yeltsin years, see Bobo Lo, *Russian Foreign Policy in the Post-Soviet Era: Reality, Illusion and Mythmaking* (Houndmills, 2002).

49   For this relatively upbeat assessment, see Allen C. Lynch, "The Realism of Russia's Foreign Policy," *Europe–Asia Studies*, 53 (2001), pp. 53–71.

50 For a best-selling recent example, see Edward Lucas, *The New Cold War: How the Kremlin Menaces Both Russia and the West* (London, 2008).

51 Bobo Lo, *Axis of Convenience: Moscow, Beijing, and the New Geopolitics* (London, 2008).

52 Vojtech Mastny, *The Cold War and Soviet Insecurity: The Stalin Years* (New York, 1996), p. 4.

53 Andrei Amalrik, *Will the Soviet Union Survive until 1984?* (London, 1970), pp. 42–52.

54 R. Medvedev, *Neizvestnyi Andropov: Politicheskaia biografiia Iuriia Andropova* (Moscow, 1999), p. 3; Westad, *The Global Cold War*, p. 404.

--------------------------------- Chapter 9 ---------------------------------

1 D. G. Nadzhafov and Z. S. Belousova (eds.), *Stalin i kosmopolitizm: Dokumenty Agitpropa TsK KPSS 1945–1953* (Moscow, 2005), pp. 31, 93–4, 107–8, 116–17; Oleg Troianovskii, *Cherez gody i rasstoianiia: Istoriia odnoi sem'i* (Moscow, 1997), p. 150.

2 Nadzhafov and Belousova, *Stalin i kosmopolitizm*, pp. 145–7, 151–3.

3 David Brandenberger, *National Bolshevism: Stalinist Mass Culture and the Formation of Modern Russian National Identity, 1931–1956* (Cambridge, MA, 2002), p. 220.

4 Harrison E. Salisbury, *Moscow Journal: The End of Stalin* (Chicago, 1961), p. 28.

5 Dmitrii Shepilov, *Neprimknuvshii* (Moscow, 2001), pp. 87–8.

6 Jan T. Gross, *Revolution from Abroad: The Soviet Conquest of Poland's Western Ukraine and Western Belorussia*, 2nd ed. (Princeton, 2002), p. 28.

7 Natal'ia Kozlova, *Sovetskie liudi: Stseny iz istorii* (Moscow, 2005), p. 102. For a broader account, see Oleg Budnitskii, "The Intelligentsia Meets the Enemy: Educated Soviet Officers in Defeated Germany," *Kritika: Explorations in Russian and Eurasian History*, 10 (2009), esp. pp. 673–9.

8 K. Simonov, *Glazami cheloveka moego pokoleniia: Razmyshleniia o I. V. Staline* (Moscow, 1990), pp. 91–2.

9 E. Iu. Zubkova et al. (eds.), *Sovetskaia zhizn', 1945–1953* (Moscow, 2003), pp. 79–80.

10 Vera S. Dunham, *In Stalin's Time: Middleclass Values in Soviet Fiction*, 2nd ed. (Durham, NC, 1990), p. 246.

11 Norman Naimark, *The Russians in Germany: A History of the Soviet Zone of Occupation, 1945–1949* (Cambridge, MA, 1995), pp. 29–36.

12 V. N. Khaustov, V. P. Naumov and N. S. Plotnikova (eds.), *Lubianka. Stalin i MGB SSSR. Mart 1946 – mart 1953: Dokumenty vysshikh organov partiinoi i gosudarstvennoi vlasti* (Moscow, 2007), pp. 135–6, 140–8.

13 Lewis H. Siegelbaum, *Cars for Comrades: The Life of the Soviet Automobile* (Ithaca, 2008), pp. 216–17.

14 Khaustov et al., *Lubianka*, pp. 156–7.

15 For a case of arrest in the "anti-cosmopolitanism" campaign that seems to have been triggered by envy of trophy items, see Donald J. Raleigh (ed.), *Russia's*

Sputnik Generation: Soviet Baby Boomers Talk about Their Lives (Bloomington, 2006), p. 165.

16 A. L. Kuz'minykh, "Inostrannye voennoplennye i sovetskie zhenshchiny," *Otechestvennaia istoriia*, 2 (2008), pp. 114–19.

17 Kristin Roth-Ey, *Soviet Culture in the Media Age* (forthcoming, 2010), chap. 1; Mark Edele, "Strange Young Men in Stalin's Moscow: The Birth and Life of the Stiliagi, 1945–1953," *Jahrbücher für Geschichte Osteuropas*, 50 (2002), pp. 55–6; Salisbury, *Moscow Journal*, p. 244.

18 Edele, "Strange Young Men," pp. 46–7; Salisbury, *Moscow Journal*, p. 182.

19 Edele, "Strange Young Men".

20 Rósa Magnúsdóttir, "Keeping Up Appearances: How the Soviet State Failed to Control Popular Attitudes to the United States of America, 1945–1959," Ph.D. dissertation (University of North Carolina, Chapel Hill, 2006), pp. 65–6, 109–16.

21 Magnúsdóttir, "Keeping Up Appearances," pp. 117–22, 134.

22 Magnúsdóttir, "Keeping Up Appearances," pp. 125, 138.

23 A. Pyzhikov, *Khrushchevsaia 'ottepel'* (Moscow, 2002), p. 141.

24 Robert D. English, *Russia and the Idea of the West: Gorbachev, Intellectuals, and the End of the Cold War* (New York, 2000), p. 61.

25 William Taubman, *Khrushchev: The Man and His Era* (London, 2003), pp. 349–53, 355–8; Troianovskii, *Cherez gody i rasstoianiia*, pp. 194–6.

26 Taubman, *Khrushchev*, p. 428.

27 Yale Richmond, *Cultural Exchange and the Cold War: Raising the Iron Curtain* (University Park, 2003), pp. 27–35.

28 Pyzhikov, *Khrushchevskaia 'ottepel'*, p. 141; Anne E. Gorsuch, "Time Travelers: Soviet Tourists to Eastern Europe," in Anne E. Gorsuch and Diane P. Koenker (eds.), *Turizm: The Russian and East European Tourist under Capitalism and Socialism* (Ithaca, 2006), pp. 206, 210.

29 Raleigh, *Russia's Sputnik Generation*, pp. 56, 64–8, 76.

30 Gorsuch, "Time Travelers," pp. 208–9.

31 E. V. Gutnova, *Perezhitoe* (Moscow, 2001), pp. 316–17, 340.

32 Ivan Ivanovich Belonosov, quoted in Kozlova, *Sovetskie liudi*, pp. 136–7. More generally on shopping opportunities for Soviet tourists in Eastern Europe, see Gorsuch, "Time Travelers," pp. 217–19.

33 Examples from Natalya Chernyshova, "Shopping with Brezhnev: Soviet Urban Consumer Culture, 1964–1985," Ph.D. dissertation (King's College London, 2008), chap. 4.

34 Lev Markhasev, *Sled v efire: Vospominaniia i zametki* (St. Petersburg, 2004), pp. 238–40, 242, 285, 290.

35 Pyzhikov, *Khrushchevskaia "ottepel,"* p. 141; *Sovetskoe zazerkal'e. Inostrannyi turizm v SSSR v 1930–1980-e gody* (Moscow, 2007), p. 92.

36 Shawn Salmon, "Marketing Socialism: Inturist in the Late 1950s and Early 1960s," in Gorsuch and Koenker, *Turizm*, pp. 190–8.

37 Pia Koivunen, "The 1957 Moscow Youth Festival: Propagating a New, Peaceful Image of the Soviet Union," in Melanie Ilic and Jeremy Smith (eds.), *Soviet State and*

Society under Nikita Khrushchev (London, 2009), pp. 45–65; Magnúsdóttir, "Keeping Up Appearances," pp. 207–9; Kristin Roth-Ey, "'Loose Girls' on the Loose? Sex, Propaganda and the 1957 Youth Festival," in M. Ilic, S. Reid and L. Attwood (eds.), *Women in the Khrushchev Era* (Basingstoke, 2004), pp. 75–95.

38 A good account from an American perspective is Walter L. Hixson, *Parting the Curtain: Propaganda, Culture, and the Cold War, 1945–1961* (London, 1997), pp. 161–213.

39 Mikhail Gorbachev and Zdeněk Mlynář, *Conversations with Gorbachev: On Perestroika, the Prague Spring, and the Crossroads of Socialism* (New York, 2002), p. 36.

40 Taubman, *Khrushchev*, pp. 305, 374.

41 See Susan E. Reid, "Who Will Beat Whom? Soviet Popular Reception of the American Exhibition in Moscow, 1959," *Kritika: Explorations in Russian and Eurasian History*, 9 (2008), pp. 855–904.

42 Eleonory Gilburd, "Picasso in Thaw Culture," *Cahiers du monde russe*, 47 (2006), pp. 78–83.

43 Eleonory Gilburd, "Books and Borders: Sergei Obraztsov and Soviet Travels to London in the 1950s," in Gorsuch and Koenker, *Turizm*, p. 245.

44 See Sudha Rajagopalan, *Leave Disco Dancer Alone! Indian Cinema and Soviet Movie-Going after Stalin* (New Delhi, 2008). For discussion of soul, see pp. 58–61.

45 Giuseppe Boffa, *Inside the Khrushchev Era* (London, 1959), pp. 170–1, 181.

46 Michel Gordey, *Visa to Moscow* (London, 1952), pp. 12–15.

47 John Brown, *Russia Explored* (London, 1959), pp. 31, 40.

48 John Gunther, *Inside Russia Today* (London, 1957), pp. 51, 64–5.

49 Brown, *Russia Explored*, pp. 37–8.

50 Hedrick Smith, *The Russians* (London, 1976), p. 381.

51 For a compendious study, see David Caute, *The Dancer Defects: The Struggle for Cultural Supremacy during the Cold War* (Oxford, 2003).

52 Gunther, *Inside Russia Today*, pp. 21–2.

53 Iurii Gagarin, *Doroga v kosmos: Zapiski letchika-kosmonavta SSSR* (Moscow, 1961), p. 164.

54 Andrew Jenks, "The Cosmonaut Who Couldn't Stop Smiling: Yuri Gagarin and the Many Faces of Modern Russia," paper presented at conference "National Identity in Eurasia: Identities and Traditions," New College, Oxford, March 2009. The Gagarin myth will be explored at greater length in a forthcoming monograph by Jenks.

55 A. I. Kokurin and N. V. Petrov (eds.), *Lubianka: Organy VChK-OGPU-NKVD-NKGB-MGB-MVD-KGB. 1917–1991. Spravochnik* (Moscow, 2003), pp. 718–20.

56 Vladimir Shlapentokh, *An Autobiographical Narration of the Role of Fear and Friendship in the Soviet Union* (Lewiston, 2004), p. 57.

57 Barbara Walker, "Moscow Human Rights Defenders Look West: Attitudes toward U.S. Journalists in the 1960s and 1970s," *Kritika: Explorations in Russian and Eurasian History*, 9 (2008), pp. 905–27.

58 Benjamin K. Tromly, "Re-Imagining the Soviet Intelligentsia: Student Politics and University Life, 1948–1964," Ph.D. dissertation (Harvard University, 2007),

pp. 262–77; Julie Hessler, "Death of an African Student in Moscow: Race, Politics, and the Cold War," *Cahiers du monde russe*, 47 (2006), pp. 35–9; Loren R. Graham, *Moscow Stories* (Bloomington, 2006), pp. 40–3.

59 Examples in this paragraph from Michael Binyon, *Life in Russia* (London, 1983), p. 176, and Chernyshova, "Shopping with Brezhnev," chap. 5.

60 Siegelbaum, *Cars for Comrades*, pp. 88–92, 98–9.

61 Christopher Booker, *The Games War: A Moscow Journal* (London, 1981), pp. 77, 79, 83.

62 Booker, *The Games War*, pp. 70–1, 98, 111, 143.

63 Booker, *The Games War*, pp. 208–9.

64 Romuald Misiunas and Rein Taagepera, *The Baltic States: Years of Dependence, 1940–1990* (London, 1993), pp. 180–1, 242, 244; thanks to Anne Gorsuch for information on musicals.

65 Timothy J. Colton, *Moscow: Governing the Socialist Metropolis* (Cambridge, MA, 1995), p. 422.

66 Mariia Dubnova and Arkadii Dubnov, *Tanki v Prage, Dzhokonda v Moskve: Azart i styd semidesiatykh* (Moscow, 2007), pp. 24–5, 28.

67 Roth-Ey, *Soviet Culture in the Media Age*, chap. 1.

68 For a good analysis, see Elena Prokhorova, "Fragmented Mythologies: Soviet TV Mini-Series of the 1970s," Ph.D. dissertation (University of Pittsburgh, 2003), chap. 4.

69 Roth-Ey, *Soviet Culture in the Media Age*, chap. 3.

70 Binyon, *Life in Russia*, pp. 177, 185.

71 See the account of a checkpoint encounter in Robert Fisk, *The Great War for Civilisation: The Conquest of the Middle East* (London, 2006), pp. 76–7.

72 Sergei I. Zhuk, "Religion, 'Westernization,' and Youth in the 'Closed City' of Soviet Ukraine, 1964–84," *Russian Review*, 67 (2008), pp. 661–79.

73 M. S. Gorbachev, *Zhizn' i reformy*, vol. 1 (Moscow, 1995), pp. 161–3, 169.

74 Accounts of the trip can be found in Leon Aron, *Yeltsin: A Revolutionary Life* (London, 2000), pp. 321–44, and Timothy J. Colton, *Yeltsin: A Life* (New York, 2008), pp. 171–3.

75 Alan M. Ball, *Imagining America: Influence and Images in Twentieth-Century Russia* (Lanham, 2003), pp. 226–7.

76 Olga Shevchenko, "'Between the Holes': Emerging Identities and Hybrid Patterns of Consumption in Post-socialist Russia," *Europe–Asia Studies*, 54 (2002), pp. 846, 852–4.

77 Ball, *Imagining America*, p. 238.

78 Jeremy Morris, "Drinking to the Nation: Russian Television Advertising and Cultural Differentiation," *Europe–Asia Studies*, 59 (2007), pp. 1387–1403.

79 I am indebted to Birgit Beumers for introducing me to this film in her paper "Nostalgia for a Soviet Past? National Memory in Post-Soviet Cinema," at the conference titled "National Identity in Eurasia: Identities and Traditions," New College, Oxford, March 2009.

80 As reported by Vesti on 4 May 2009: see www.vesti.ru/doc.html?id=282491 (last checked 18 May 2009). Thanks to Andrei Rogatchevski for this reference.

Chapter 10

1   For those readers interested in the debate on causes, a very good place to start is Stephen F. Cohen, "Was the Soviet System Reformable?" *Slavic Review*, 63 (2004), pp. 459–88, and the debate that surrounded this article in *Slavic Review*. A stimulating recent contribution is Nikolay Mitrokhin, "'Strange People' in the Politburo: Institutional Problems and the Human Factor in the Economic Collapse of the Soviet Empire," *Kritika: Explorations in Russian and Eurasian History*, 10 (2009), pp. 869–96.

2   Cogent versions of this argument can be found in Allen C. Lynch, *How Russia Is Not Ruled: Reflections on Russian Political Development* (Cambridge, 2005); and Steven Rosefielde, *Russia in the 21st Century: The Prodigal Superpower* (Cambridge, 2005).

3   See for example Steven Rosefielde and Stefan Hedlund, *Russia since 1980: Wrestling with Westernization* (Cambridge, 2009), pp. 9–19.

4   An argument that is expertly made in Hannes Adomeit, *Imperial Overstretch: Germany in Soviet Policy from Stalin to Gorbachev* (Baden-Baden, 1998).

5   For a dedicated account of this process, see Geoffrey Hosking, *Rulers and Victims: The Russians in the Soviet Union* (Cambridge, MA, 2006).

Guide to Further Reading

This is a selection of English-language works (primarily monographs) that should help the interested reader to explore the themes of this book in greater depth. For a fuller range of sources, consult the endnotes to each chapter.

 General

Existing accounts of Soviet history tend to be weighted toward the revolutionary and interwar periods, but the better survey texts are still well worth reading for the student of postwar history. Note especially Geoffrey Hosking, *A History of the Soviet Union* (3rd edn., 1992); Robert Service, *A History of Twentieth-Century Russia* (1997); and Ronald Suny, *The Soviet Experiment: Russia, the USSR, and the Successor States* (1998). An illuminating and interactive website is "Seventeen Moments in Soviet History" (www.soviethistory.org).* The work that most closely matches the chronological parameters of this book is John Keep's fine *A History of the Soviet Union, 1945–1991* (2nd edn., 2002), while an excellent and richly annotated document collection is Edward Acton and Tom Stableford, *The Soviet Union: A Documentary History*, vol. 2: 1939–1991 (2005). The most engaging introduction to later Soviet and post-Soviet history is Stephen Kotkin, *Armageddon Averted: The Soviet Collapse, 1970–2000* (2nd edn., 2008). Of the longer accounts of the postcommunist period, see especially Richard Sakwa, *Russian Politics and Society* (4th edn., 2008).

---

* All cited websites live at time of going to press.

--------------------------------- The War ---------------------------------

Richard Overy, *Russia's War* (1998), is still the best place to start reading about the war from the Soviet perspective. Evan Mawdsley, *Thunder in the East: The Nazi–Soviet War, 1941–1945* (2005), is an up-to-date account of the military aspects, while Catherine Merridale, *Ivan's War: The Red Army, 1939–45* (2005) is an excellent social history. The crucial economic dimension is presented in Mark Harrison, *Accounting for War: Soviet Production, Employment, and the Defence Burden, 1940–1945* (1996). Useful collections are John Garrard and Carol Garrard (eds.), *World War 2 and the Soviet People* (1993), and Robert W. Thurston and Bernd Bonwetsch, *The People's War: Responses to World War II in the Soviet Union* (2000). The classics are Alexander Werth, *Russia at War, 1941–1945* (1964), and John Erickson, *The Road to Stalingrad: Stalin's War with Germany* (1975). On the social and political legacy of the war, see Susan J. Linz (ed.), *The Impact of World War II on the Soviet Union* (1985); Amir Weiner, *Making Sense of War: The Second World War and the Fate of the Bolshevik Revolution* (2001); and Mark Edele, *Soviet Veterans of the Second World War: A Popular Movement in an Authoritarian Society, 1941–1991* (2008). For stimulating historiographical reflections, see Amir Weiner, "Saving Private Ivan: From What, Why, and How?," *Kritika: Explorations in Russian and Eurasian History*, 1 (2000). On the memory of the war, see Nina Tumarkin, *The Living and the Dead: The Rise and Fall of the Cult of World War II in Russia* (1995), and Denise Youngblood, *Russian War Films: On the Cinema Front, 1914–2005* (2007).

------------------- Soviet and Post-Soviet Politics -------------------

Sovietology now has a dubious reputation, but it produced many fine analyses of the Soviet system. For the postwar period, a sample might include: Werner G. Hahn, *Postwar Soviet Politics: The Fall of Zhdanov and the Defeat of Moderation, 1946–53* (1982); Michel Tatu, *Power in the Kremlin: From Khrushchev's Decline to Collective Leadership* (1969); George W. Breslauer, *Khrushchev and Brezhnev as Leaders* (1982); Seweryn Bialer, *Stalin's Successors: Leadership, Stability, and Change in the Soviet Union* (1980); Jerry F. Hough and Merle Fainsod, *How the Soviet Union Is Governed* (1979). The best recent additions to the literature include Timothy J. Colton, *Moscow: Governing the Socialist Metropolis* (1995); William Taubman, *Khrushchev: A Life* (2003); and Yoram Gorlizki and Oleg Khlevniuk, *Cold Peace: Stalin and the Soviet Ruling Circle, 1945–1953* (2004). Fine studies of the Soviet Union's key institutions are: T. H. Rigby, *Communist Party Membership in the USSR, 1917–1967* (1968); Evan Mawdsley and Stephen White, *The Soviet*

Elite from Lenin to Gorbachev: The Central Committee and its Members, 1917–1991 (2000); Amy W. Knight, *The KGB: Police and Politics in the Soviet Union* (1988); Timothy J. Colton and Thane Gustafson (eds.), *Soldiers and the Soviet State: Civil–Military Relations from Brezhnev to Gorbachev* (1990). Important perspectives on the unraveling of the Soviet political order are to be found in Philip G. Roeder, *Red Sunset: The Failure of Soviet Politics* (1993); Archie Brown, *The Gorbachev Factor* (1997); William E. Odom, *The Collapse of the Soviet Military* (1998); Steven L. Solnick, *Stealing the State: Control and Collapse in Soviet Institutions* (1998). A good way into the enormous literature on postcommunism is Archie Brown (ed.), *Contemporary Russian Politics: A Reader* (2001). The dominant political figure of the 1990s has now been the subject of two fine – and contrasting – biographies: Leon Aron, *Yeltsin: A Revolutionary Life* (2000); and Timothy J. Colton, *Yeltsin: A Life* (2008). A good way to approach the dominant figure of the early twenty-first century is by reading Richard Sakwa, *Putin: Russia's Choice* (2004).

─────────────── Economics ───────────────

Fine general accounts of the Soviet system include: Philip Hanson, *The Rise and Fall of the Soviet Economy* (2003); James R. Millar, *The ABCs of Soviet Socialism* (1981); Alec Nove, *The Soviet Economic System* (3rd edn., 1986). János Kornai, *The Socialist System: The Political Economy of Communism* (1992), is a now-classic work in a comparative and theoretical vein. The economic outcomes of the war are variously illuminated in Eugene Zaleski, *Stalinist Planning for Economic Growth, 1933–1952* (1980); Timothy Dunmore, *The Stalinist Command Economy: The Soviet State Apparatus and Economic Policy 1945–53* (1980); and Julie Hessler, *A Social History of Soviet Trade: Trade Policy, Retail Practices, and Consumption, 1917–1953* (2004). The everyday economy of mature socialism is illuminated in two seminal articles: Aron Katsenelinboigen, "Coloured Markets in the Soviet Union," *Soviet Studies*, 29 (1977), and James R. Millar, "The Little Deal: Brezhnev's Contribution to Acquisitive Socialism," *Slavic Review*, 44 (1985). On rural issues, an excellent place to start is Zhores A. Medvedev, *Soviet Agriculture* (1987), while Thane Gustafson, *Crisis Amid Plenty: The Politics of Soviet Energy under Brezhnev and Gorbachev* (1989), is a rich analysis of the nexus of power and resources in one especially important sphere of the Soviet economy. On late Soviet economic reform and its failures, see Edward A. Hewett, *Reforming the Soviet Economy: Equality versus Efficiency* (1988); and Michael Ellman and Vladimir Kontorovich (eds.), *The Disintegration of the Soviet Economic System* (1992). On post-Soviet struggles over financial institutions, see Juliet Johnson, *A Fistful of Rubles: The*

Rise and Fall of the Russian Banking System (2000), and Alya Guseva, *Into the Red: The Birth of the Credit Card Market in Postcommunist Russia* (2008). Judicious analysis of recent developments in the relationship between business and the state can be found in Andrew Barnes, *Owning Russia: The Struggle over Factories, Farms, and Power* (2006), and Stephen Fortescue, *Russia's Oil Barons and Metal Magnates: Oligarchs and the State in Transition* (2006).

Soviet and Russian Society

Mervyn Matthews, *Class and Society in Soviet Russia* (1972), and Basile Kerblay, *Modern Soviet Society* (1983), are fine general studies. Also very useful is Murray Yanowitch, *Social and Economic Inequality in the Soviet Union* (1977), as well as the same author's selection of work by Soviet sociologists, *The Social Structure of the USSR: Recent Soviet Studies* (1986). On the immediate postwar period, Vera Dunham, *In Stalin's Time: Middleclass Values in Soviet Fiction* (2nd edn., 1990), is a classic of sociological intuition by a literary scholar, while Juliane Fürst (ed.), *Late Stalinist Russia: Society between Reconstruction and Reinvention* (2006), offers a good selection of the latest archivally based research. On the Khrushchev era, Polly Jones (ed.), *The Dilemmas of De-Stalinization: Negotiating Cultural and Social Change in the Khrushchev Era* (2006), is another useful collection, while Miriam Dobson, *Khrushchev's Cold Summer: Gulag Returnees, Crime, and the Fate of Reform after Stalin* (2009), is a stimulating new monograph. On state–society relations, two contrasting but complementary works are Vladimir A. Kozlov, *Mass Uprisings in the USSR: Protest and Rebellion in the Post-Stalin Years* (2002), and Victor Zaslavsky, *The Neo-Stalinist State: Class, Ethnicity, and Consensus in Soviet Society* (1982). The ethnographic perspective is best represented by Caroline Humphrey, *Marx Went Away – But Karl Stayed Behind* (1998), and Finn Sivert Nielsen, "The Eye of the Whirlwind: Russian Identity and Soviet Nation-Building. Quests for Meaning in a Soviet Metropolis," available at http://www.anthrobase.com/Txt/N/Nielsen_F_S_03.htm. Donald Filtzer's series of books on the Soviet working class is essential reading for any serious student of Soviet history: *Soviet Workers and De-Stalinization: The Consolidation of the Modern System of Soviet Production Relations, 1953–1964* (1992); *Soviet Workers and the Collapse of Perestroika: The Soviet Labour Process and Gorbachev's Reforms, 1985–1991* (1994); and *Soviet Workers and Late Stalinism: Labour and the Restoration of the Stalinist System after World War II* (2002). Vladislav M. Zubok, *Zhivago's Children: The Last Soviet Intelligentsia* (2009), is a fine recent work on the Soviet educated elite of the postwar decades. Grigory Ioffe and Tatyana Nefedova, *Continuity and Change in Rural Russia: A Geographical Perspective* (1997), is full of insights on rural Russia. Nathaniel Davis, *A Long Walk to Church:*

A Contemporary History of Russian Orthodoxy (1995), is a good account of Russian religious life. Ellen Jones, *Red Army and Society: A Sociology of the Soviet Military* (1985), considers the military as a social institution. On family life and the *longue durée* of social change in twentieth-century Russia, Catriona Kelly, *Children's World: Growing up in Russia, 1890–1991* (2008), is in a class of its own. A pioneering discussion of private life in the later Soviet Union is Vladimir Shlapentokh, *Public and Private Life of the Soviet People: Changing Values in Post-Stalin Russia* (1989); an important recent contribution is Lewis H. Siegelbaum (ed.), *Borders of Socialism: Private Spheres of Soviet Russia* (2006).

―――――――――――― International Affairs ――――――――――――

The best general accounts of the Cold War from the Soviet perspective are Vladislav M. Zubok, *A Failed Empire: The Soviet Union in the Cold War from Stalin to Gorbachev* (2007), and Odd Arne Westad, *The Global Cold War: Third World Interventions and the Making of Our Times* (2005). A useful textbook is Caroline Kennedy-Pipe, *Russia and the World, 1917–1991* (1998). For the KGB perspective, see Christopher Andrew and Vasili Mitrokhin, *The Mitrokhin Archive: The KGB in Europe and the West* (1999), and *The Mitrokhin Archive II: The KGB and the World* (2006); for further important context, see Craig Nation, *Black Earth, Red Star: A History of Soviet Security Policy, 1917–1991* (1992). Several key moments of Cold War confrontation have been subject to re-evaluation in the post-Soviet era. See for example: Sergei N. Goncharov, John W. Lewis and Xue Litai, *Uncertain Partners: Stalin, Mao, and the Korean War* (1993); Ilya V. Gaiduk, *The Soviet Union and the Vietnam War* (1996), and the same author's *Confronting Vietnam: Soviet Policy toward the Indochina Conflict, 1954–1963* (2003); Lorenz M. Lüthi, *The Sino–Soviet Split: Cold War in the Communist World* (2008); Charles Gati, *Failed Illusions: Moscow, Washington, Budapest, and the 1956 Hungarian Revolt* (2006); Hope M. Harrison, *Driving the Soviets Up the Wall: Soviet–East German Relations, 1953–1961* (2003). An invaluable online resource is the Cold War International History Project (available through www.wilsoncenter.org). A key work on the all-important German question is Hannes Adomeit, *Imperial Overstretch: Germany in Soviet Policy from Stalin to Gorbachev* (1998). The end of the Cold War, and in particular its elements of contingency, is well described in Jean Lévesque, *The Enigma of 1989: The USSR and the Liberation of Eastern Europe* (1997), and Mary Elise Sarotte, *1989: The Struggle to Create Post-Cold War Europe* (2009). For more recent developments, Bobo Lo, *Russian Foreign Policy in the Post-Soviet Era: Reality, Illusion and Mythmaking* (2002), is a good place to start.

———————————— Nationalism ————————————

The single best survey of postwar Soviet nationalities policy is Gerhard Simon, *Nationalism and Policy Toward the Nationalities in the Soviet Union: From Totalitarian Dictatorship to Post-Stalinist Society* (1991), while Robert J. Kaiser, *The Geography of Nationalism in Russia and the USSR* (1994), is an invaluable work of reference. On wartime and postwar Soviet patriotism, see David Brandenberger, *National Bolshevism: Stalinist Mass Culture and the Formation of Modern Russian National Identity, 1931–1956* (2002). The crucial Russian question is the theme of Geoffrey Hosking, *Rulers or Victims? The Russians in the Soviet Union* (2006). For developments in the Baltic republics up to and including the collapse of the Soviet Union, see Romuald Misiunas and Rein Taagepera, *The Baltic States: Years of Dependence, 1940–1990* (1993), and Anatol Lieven, *The Baltic Revolution: Estonia, Latvia, Lithuania and the Path to Independence* (1993). For matters Ukrainian right up to the present day, see Andrew Wilson, *The Ukrainians: Unexpected Nation* (3rd edn., 2009), and *Ukraine's Orange Revolution* (2005). Gwendolyn Sasse, *The Crimea Question: Identity, Transition, and Conflict* (2007), is an unusually eloquent case study of a region within Ukraine. Charles King, *The Moldovans: Romania, Russia, and the Politics of Culture* (2000), discusses one of the less well-known Soviet republics, but sheds much light on nationality in the Soviet Union more generally. Islam, both in Russia and in the other Soviet republics, is well covered in Yaacov Ro'i, *Islam in the Soviet Union: From the Second World War to Gorbachev* (2000), and Adeeb Khalid, *Islam after Communism: Religion and Politics in Central Asia* (2007). On the South Caucasus, see Ronald Suny, *Looking toward Ararat: Armenia in Modern History* (1993), and *The Making of the Georgian Nation* (1994), and Thomas de Waal, *Black Garden: Armenia and Azerbaijan through Peace and War* (2003). There are now quite a few good books on Chechnya, but a useful recent contribution is James Hughes, *Chechnya: From Nationalism to Jihad* (2007). Note also the insightful Georgi M. Derluguian, *Bourdieu's Secret Admirer in the Caucasus: A World-System Biography* (2005), which illuminates recent conflicts in the North Caucasus and much else besides. A useful way into post-Soviet developments in the former Soviet Union is Ian Bremmer and Ray Taras (eds.), *Nations and Politics in the Soviet Successor States* (1993).

Index

CPSIA information can be obtained
at www.ICGtesting.com
Printed in the USA
LVHW012050230821
695924LV00002B/145